The Kinneavy Papers

James L. Kinneavy

The Kinneavy Papers

Theory and the Study of Discourse

Edited by

Lynn Worsham
Sidney I. Dobrin
Gary A. Olson

State University of New York Press
and the
Association of Teachers of Advanced Composition

Published by
State University of New York Press, Albany and by
the Association of Teachers of Advanced Composition

Cover Art: "Cosmic Drama, Revolution" by Denis Sargent, 1999, collection of the artist.

This book was made possible in part by a grant from the University of South Florida Publications Council

Printed in the United States of America
Designed and typeset by Gary A. Olson

For information, address State University of New York Press, State University Plaza, Albany, N.Y., 12246

Production by Diane Ganeles. Marketing by Fran Keneston.

Library of Congress Cataloging-in-Publication Data

The Kinneavy papers: theory and the study of discourse / edited by Lynn Worsham, Sidney I. Dobrin, and Gary A. Olson.
p. cm.
Includes bibliographical references and index.
ISBN 0-7914-4691-3 (acid free)—
ISBN 0-7914-4692-1 (pbk: acid free)
1. Rhetoric. I. Worsham, Lynn, date. II. Dobrin, Sidney I., 1967- III. Olson, Gary A., date.

P301.K48 2000
808—dc21 99-056704
CIP

10 9 8 7 6 5 4 3 2 1

For Jim Kinneavy,
who helped create the discipline of Rhetoric
and Composition through his dedication to
rigorous scholarship

Contents

Part 3: Cultural Studies and Composition

Part 4: Special Issues in Composition

Acknowledgments

We would like to acknowledge the support and friendship of Steve Rubin and Sara Deats, both of whom have taken a personal interest in the success of scholarship in rhetoric and composition. We would like to thank Diane Ganeles for her eagle-eyed attention to detail, and Fran Keneston for her marketing expertise. We are particularly grateful to Priscilla Ross, whose editorial vision has contributed substantially to the development of rhetoric and composition as an intellectual discipline. Finally, we are especially indebted to the artist Denis Sargent, who generously gave us permission to use "Cosmic Drama, Revolution" on the cover of this book.

Foreword

Lester Faigley

Students who enter rhetoric and composition today find it difficult to imagine that the discipline barely existed in the 1960s. Writing was taught extensively in colleges and universities during those years, but few saw rhetoric and composition as a scholarly field. With a handful of prominent exceptions, what passed as theory was a hodgepodge lifted from other disciplines, and what was called research during those years was concerned with relatively unproblematic pedagogical issues: what "works" to produce "good" writing. At the beginning of *A Theory of Discourse*, first published in 1971, Jim Kinneavy writes about the state of the field:

> The present anarchy of the discipline of what is commonly catergorized as "composition," both in high schools and colleges, is so evident as scarcely to require proof.
>
> Composition is so clearly the stepchild of the English department that it is not a legitimate area of concern in graduate studies, is not even recognized as a subdivision of the discipline of English in a recent manifesto put out by the major professional organization (MLA) of college English teachers, in some universities is not a valid area of scholarship for advancement in rank, and is generally the teaching province of graduate students or fringe members of the department.
>
> The present chaotic subsistence of freshman and upper-division courses in composition underscores their precarious claim to existence. The agenda of freshman composition vary from nothing to everything. (1)

He concludes this section by noting that "there is even the uneasy suspicion that there is nothing more to composition *as* composition than could and should be covered in an adequate high school course." Then he announces his manifesto: "On the contrary, it is the thesis of this work that the field of composition—or discourse, as it will presently be termed—is a rich and fertile discipline with a worthy past which should be consulted before being consigned to oblivion, an exciting present, and a future that seems as limitless as either linguistics or literature." To a great extent, Jim's prophecy has come true. Theory in rhetoric and composition has flourished over the past thirty years and especially in the past decade, as evidenced by the richness of the chapters in this volume, aptly titled *The Kinneavy Papers*.

Jim Kinneavy was but one of a brilliant generation who brought theory to the study and teaching of writing. Anne Berthoff, Wayne Booth, Francis Christensen, Ed Corbett, Janet Emig, Janice Lauer, Richard Ohmann, Ross Winterowd, Richard Young, and others all made important contributions. Nonetheless, the landmark work of that era is *A Theory of Discourse*, a work that remains unsurpassed today in its scholarly depth and breadth. His work alone displayed a scope as limitless as either linguistics or literature and set a high standard for the field as a whole. John Warnock told me that reading *A Theory of Discourse* for the first time was like the sun coming up. Suddenly a field was possible. I would compare my experience of reading *A Theory of Discourse* for the first time in 1977 to Balboa's first view of the Pacific. Like everyone else in those years, I had come to rhetoric through a back door (mine was linguistics) and had no sense of its expanse or how it might be informed by philosophy. A large ocean was before me that I didn't know existed. I was fortunate to have a guide on that broad ocean when I joined the English department at Texas in 1979. Jim was then building one of the first doctoral concentrations in rhetoric and composition in the country. He accepted me as a student as he did all who came to him. He often took Steve Witte and me to lunch, where he patiently filled in some of the larger voids in our education while we grabbed napkins to take notes.

The range of his reading was always amazing. During the years he was a Christian Brother, he taught almost everything—physics, chemistry, mathematics, philosophy, theology, music, French, and typing, along with English literature and composition—and he moved with ease across disciplines throughout his career. To say he kept up with new developments in theory is an understatement. When Gayatri Spivak was a member of the faculty at Texas, she found Jim was the only member of the department who had also read the untranslated work of Derrida. Indeed, many of his former students and those who attended his lectures can recall occasions when some bright young upstart, wanting to impress, announced some new book he had just read to learn shortly that Jim had not only read the book but had taught it. And his own ideas found their way to many places. Greg Myers writes of seeing Jim's *Greek Rhetorical Origins of Christian Faith* on the desk of a postmodern theologian at Oxford. The Penn State football coach, Joe Paterno, was among the many who heard Jim lecture on this subject.

Theory was not an abstract pursuit for Jim Kinneavy but always part of his broader goal of making rhetoric the focus of moral and ethical education. Jim's main project during his last years was an attempt to identify universally recognized human rights, which might provide a broad basis for implementing such an education. I am sorry that this important book remains unfinished, but with Jim there would always be an important book left unfinished because his mind was still as sharp and active as ever. Few scholars have influenced as much good work from their students as Jim, and I know of none more generous in intellectual spirit. His own synoptic vision of discourse was matched with an ability to see the rhetorical implications in the work of others and to encourage them to pursue those implications. Jim Kinneavy's intellectual energy and commitment to the civic and ethical concerns of rhetoric remain a guiding beacon to the field. The essays in this book are a testament to his legacy.

Introduction

The Kinneavy Papers: Theory and the Study of Discourse presents the most outstanding scholarly articles published in ***JAC*** over the last decade: the winners of the James L. Kinneavy Award. Yet, the papers collected here also document an era of dramatic change and growth in the sophistication of scholarship in rhetoric and composition studies. No longer restricted to the narrow confines of a field circumscribed by empirical method or by naive expressivism, composition scholars have developed a theoretical discourse that has truly revolutionized how we view the field, its scholarship, and the teaching of writing. The James L. Kinneavy Award and ***JAC*** have been instrumental in this change. Over the last two decades, the journal has made a place for rigorous intellectual work in composition studies by publishing scholarship that finds in contemporary theory the language to ask new questions, to reframe existing problems, and to move beyond current impasses in thought and action. As the journal in the discipline of rhetoric and composition most often associated with "theory," ***JAC*** has promoted intellectual inquiry that crosses disciplinary boundaries in ways that are productive and useful to composition. The journal has attempted to expand the borders of rhetoric and composition by encouraging scholars to explore intersections of composition theory with theoretical work in other disciplines and fields of study. The result of such encouragement both by ***JAC*** and by other forums and individuals is that composition scholars now have the opportunity to engage regularly in important intellectual dialogues that take them across many disciplinary borders. The essays in this collection document the kinds of attempts made over the last decade to shift the direction of composition research and to broaden its significance through productive cross-disciplinary dialogue.

Not only does this book recognize the kinds of sophisticated scholarship published over the last decade, it also pays tribute to Jim Kinneavy, who endowed the James L. Kinneavy Award precisely as a way to encourage substantive theoretical scholarship. Jim was always an ardent supporter of ***JAC*** and of the movement to establish rhetoric and composition as an intellectual discipline. He understood that establishing an award for exemplary scholarship is more than a token recognition of individual scholarly labors; such an award is also a material way to give presence and prestige to a field and its constituents. Jim's endowment of this award has been a gift to all of us. It is unimpeachable evidence of a spirit of generosity that defined his own scholarship and his devotion to the intellectual enterprise of rhetoric and composition studies. Jim presented the first award to Reed Way Dasenbrock in 1989, and until his death in 1999 he never missed the award ceremony held each year at the annual ATAC meeting at the CCCC Convention. Jim was writing the Foreword to this book when he became ill and passed away on August 10, 1999. *The Kinneavy Papers* not only marks the tenth anniversary of the James L. Kinneavy Award; it also celebrates its founder as one of the discipline's most learned and beloved scholars.

Through the example of his scholarship and teaching, Jim left us more capable of "doing theory," of understanding that the meaning of literacy includes a metalinguistic understanding of the structure and function of discourse—an understanding, in short, that "doing theory" is ultimately a part of "being literate." We, the editors of ***JAC*** during the now eleven years of the Kinneavy Award's existence, believe therefore that the present moment in the history of the discipline invites this collection of the eleven principal award winners and the six essays that merited honorable mention. The last years of the millennium have been increasingly tough times for theorists, especially in composition studies where a backlash against theory has taken many forms—for example, a reassertion of expressivism and creative writing as the antidote to the difficulties wrought by too much theorizing, and an equally vigorous reassertion of teaching over and against scholarship as the true "mission" of rhetoric and composition studies. We have therefore elected to move against the effort to turn back the clock by opening with the essays in Part One, **Pedagogical Theory**, which investigates ways to theorize the teaching of writing. Richard Miller examines the ways in which a "pedagogy of obedience" has been institutionalized as a dominant form of educational practice. Jasper Neel employs two competing conceptions of writingcommon in ancient Greece as a framework for juxtaposing the kind of writing done by a technical writer and that done by a literary critic. Patricia Sullivan calls for a reconceptualization of the graduate curriculum in English in which each and every course is seen as "a scene of writing as well as a scene of reading," *not* as separate intellectual activities. Drawing on her experience at the Nebraska Literacy Project, Nancy Welch illustrates how participants created the "voices of critique" that they needed to address both their classrooms and their institutions.

The four essays in Part Two, **Philosophical Issues**, provide a powerful, though implicit, argument for bringing together philosophy and composition theory in significant and consequential ways. Joseph Petraglia provides a thoughtful critique of the central premises of social construction, while Reed Way Dasenbrock draws on Jacques Derrida's "critique of presence" to demonstrate that by overemphasizing the similarities between writing and speaking, compositionists have not always made wise pedagogical choices. David Smit analyzes the scholarly literature on collaborative learning, concluding that it fails to provide a convincing rationale for using collaborative practices in writing classes. Finally, George Pullman attempts to level the hierarchy between writing and interpretation by showing that because invention is part of the way interpretations are performed, literary studies is "epistemologically connected" to rhetorical theory.

In Part Three, **Cultural Studies and Composition**, Michael Murphy argues that composition is not an effective radical discourse because it subscribes to modernist strategies of resistance; his solution is to transform composition into a thoroughly *post*modern discipline focused especially on cultural studies. Bruce McComiskey proposes a "more complete" social-process approach to composition by presenting a conception of rhetorical inquiry based on "the complete cycle of cultural production, contextual distribution, and critical consumption." For John Trimbur, composition studies has paid too little attention to its own "narrativity," and he analyzes Mike Rose's *Lives on the Boundary* as an example of how to gain critical insight into the conjunctures of discourses and practices in composition narratives. Arguing that the liberatory potential of hypertext is limited by the lack of adequate theorizing of the ethical and political issues of identity, Pamela Gilbert considers what kind of reader and reading practices hypertext requires.

The final section, **Special Issues in Composition**, presents five articles on the kinds of social, cultural, and political issues that have been central to the contribution that ***JAC*** has made to the theoretical enterprise of composition studies. Drawing on students' journals and their comments in a class she observed, Joy Ritchie traces students' exploration of the "contradictory and conflicting social-sexual identities" that members of the class presented during the semester. While David Bleich questions whether compositionists should continue to teach expository prose, the basic skill that underlies academic discourse, Susan Jarratt addresses the problem of speaking for others by looking at how "others" speak. Richard Coe analyzes Kenneth Burke's revision (first published in ***JAC***) of his famous definition of *humanity*—human beings are "wordlings" or "bodies that learn language"—and he shows how this revision provides critical insights for composition instruction. Finally, William Covino discusses how scholarship in the history of rhetoric can help compositionists reconceptualize "advanced" writing pedagogy.

Together these seventeen essays represent the finest interventions in composition theory published over the last decade. Engaging with the critical discourses of philosophers, feminists, literary theorists, postcolonial critics, cultural theorists, and others, these scholars have enriched the discourse of the field with new terms and concepts, broadened our conceptions of the multiple roles and functions of discourse in unanticipated ways, and opened up a seemingly infinite number of questions and new possibilities for composition theory and pedagogy. Jim Kinneavy was proud to support the kind of work represented here, and he was pleased to see the discipline move steadily toward the recognition and respect it deserves. This collection will forever remain a tribute to his desire for a theoretical discourse adequate to the work of wordlings.

Lynn Worsham
Sidney I. Dobrin
Gary A. Olson

Part 1

Pedagogical Theory

What Does It Mean to Learn? William Bennett, the Educational Testing Service, and a Praxis of the Sublime

Richard E. Miller

I must admit that, despite my best intentions, my mind wandered as I read William Bennett's latest contribution to the debate about family values, *The Index of Leading Cultural Indicators*. It's not that *The Index* lacks a certain drama; indeed, the endless stream of statistics, bar and pie charts, quotes and quips from Plato to Hillary Clinton are run together in such a way that they tell and re-tell a troubling story about a once-great-nation fallen into decline. And yet, despite the barrage of depressing information about violence (up), teenage sex (up), television use (up), divorce (up), I found myself thinking not about the collapse of cultural standards, but about that other family man and teacher, Thomas Gradgrind, intoning, "Fact, fact, fact" before the blank faces of the schoolchildren in Dickens' *Hard Times*. Like Dickens' schoolmaster, Bennett has a profound faith in the power of facts to order the souls of the populace: one could even say that *The Index* itself assumes a form of Gradgrindian pedagogy by presenting its "facts and figures on the state of American society" without anything so distracting or overtly interpretive as authorial commentary. Within the world of this text, it seems, facts are understood to speak for themselves, and one would no more argue with them than one would argue with the actuarial tables in blue books that line Gradgrind's study.

This granted, I'd like to sidestep for the moment Bennett's assertion that his data show our government's misguided effort to be "more than an auxiliary in the development of a free people's moral disposition and character" (12), in order to consider the limitations of the mode of presentation on which Bennett relies—a mode I call, for the sake of convenience, a "pedagogy of obedience." Within this pedagogy as it is practiced in *The Index*, the social world, with all its lived complexities, incoherences, gaps, and contradictions, is flattened out and translated into a series of discrete, measurable events: rates on teenage pregnancies, juvenile violence, drug use, time in front of the television, etc. Since the text provides no overt commentary about this information, the reader's job is to remain fixed on *what* has happened, as detailed in the facts and figures, and to put aside questions about *how* the statistics were collected, *which* statistics have been presented, and *what* other statistics or interpretations might have been called on. With these lines of inquiry shut off, the ideal reader of *The Index* finds in Bennett's statistical display objective proof that schools, families, churches, neighborhoods, and other social and civic organizations have all failed to teach the nation's children to demonstrate "civility and respect for legitimate authority" (12). In this way, the argument and the pedagogy of Bennett's text work hand in hand: while the book presents statistics that track the moral decay of our social infrastructure, it responds to this problem with a pedagogical approach that teaches its readers to bow to the cited authorities.

We see this, for example, in Bennett's section on "Education," where he cites Albert Shanker's assertion that "ninety-five percent of the kids who go to college in the United States would not be admitted to college anywhere else in the world" (89). Within the constellation of Bennett's statistics on the state of education, Shanker's statement is presented as a factual assessment of a decline in academic standards that has apparently racked our nation. But why would an average reader accept the implication that our schools have failed, when he or she has nothing more to go on here than the information that Shanker is president of the American Federation of Teachers and a footnote placing the quote in an article entitled, "Schools 'Really Bad' Says AFT Leader"? Why couldn't this statistic be seen as proof of an ongoing, relatively successful effort to democratize access to higher education in the United States? Is the reader really meant to admire other educational systems where colleges and universities are restricted to a small fraction of the total populace? Rather than pursue this line of inquiry, which might serve to alleviate the sense that our educational system has failed because it has become more accessible, the reader is invited to recognize that the speaker in question is a person of higher authority, an elected official, an expert whose insights warrant not so much thoughtful consideration as unquestioned respect. That the statistic itself seems to have been pulled out of thin air is presumably of little moment at a time when our most pressing business is getting out the news about this latest version of our educational crisis.

What it means to learn within this system, then, is to accept what has been handed down by one's superiors, to repeat their findings, to grant the assumptions behind their facts and figures, to chant their conclusions.

"Rush is Right," as the bumper stickers say, so let it be known: SAT scores are down, spending on education is up. Aside from spreading this news, though, it's hard to see exactly what one is meant to do with such information, particularly since Bennett's charts of SAT scores versus state expenditures reveal that "there is no systematic correlation between spending on education and student achievement" (83). While Bennett is content to move on to disciplinary problems in the schools after this pronouncement, the reader is left to wonder what to make of the data about scores and spending. Should one demand less spending, since it doesn't seem to matter anyway? Or perhaps less test taking, since it's clearly a waste of money?

If Bennett's text offers no detailed solutions to the problems it has charted, it does dramatize in a particularly straightforward way the dynamic interplay that exists between systems of examination, dominant definitions of learning, and active pedagogical practice. Within Bennett's text, this relationship gets worked out in the following way: a decline in test scores marks an undeniable decline in "learning," which manifests itself most pressingly as a decline in obedience, which is shown in turn by a rise in both the number and the severity of disciplinary problems in the schools. The solution, implicit in this formulation, is this: reduce government spending and increase discipline, which should produce greater obedience and higher test scores. This is a familiar argument, and its reign as a certain form of common sense is unlikely to be disturbed by a counter-argument attacking its assumptions about what passes for learning within such a system.

Since such interchanges do little to alter how higher education goes about its business, I would like to deviate from this familiar path of argument and focus, instead, on the ways in which the "pedagogy of obedience" has been institutionalized as a dominant form and concern of our educational practice. With this in mind, I will begin by detailing one set of institutional mechanisms that has been designed to define and measure what it means to learn in school, in general, and to regulate what constitutes acceptable acts of reading and writing, in particular. From there, I will then explore another way to respond to the question posed by my title, "What does it mean to learn?" Thus, although I've begun with a consideration of how Bennett's text constructs and educates its ideally obedient reader, I would like to turn now to more material examples of how learning to read and write has been linked to a pedagogy of obedience. And this requires that we revisit that particular object of critique in Dickens' *Hard Times*—the monitorial method of instruction, which dominated popular education in Great Britain during the first half of the nineteenth century.

Institutionalizing the Pedagogy of Obedience: From Joseph Lancaster's Borough Road School to the ETS

At the turn of the nineteenth century, the British government had yet to become formally involved in the business of educating either the poor or members of the lower middle class. This task was taken up, instead, by two separate private societies: The British and Foreign School Society, established in 1808, which offered nondenominational education, and the National Society, founded in 1811, which was allied with the Church of England and proffered both general and religious instruction. Both societies relied on the "monitorial" method of instruction to fulfill their philanthropic missions. The method was reputedly imported from India to England by Dr. Andrew Bell, who described seeing in the colonies "a youth of eleven years of age, with his little assistants under him, teaching upwards of fifty boys" (Hyndman 17). Bell's reasons for promoting this system, where a single teacher watched as his assistants monitored the responses of his students, were economic rather than pedagogic: in a flight of fancy, Bell dreamed of the day when "a single master, who, if able and diligent, could, without difficulty, conduct ten contiguous schools, each consisting of a thousand scholars" (Godsen 2). What the single master at the hub of this ideal institution would do "without difficulty" with his ten thousand students was issue instructions. The student monitors would see to it that the master's orders were carried out as they swept through the ordered rows of students. It's the bureaucrat's ultimate fantasy, where all is order and obedience, hierarchy and control.

Although Joseph Lancaster was never able to achieve the ratio between teachers and students that Bell envisioned, he did realize a respectably cost-effective relationship of one teacher to five hundred students at his famous Borough Road School during the first decades of the nineteenth century. His favored method of instruction is singled out by Michel Foucault in *Discipline and Punish* as a vivid example of panopticism at work in the school system. Foucault describes Lancaster's pedagogy as follows:

> First the oldest pupils were entrusted with tasks involving simple supervision, then of checking work, then of teaching; in the end, all the time of all the pupils was occupied either with teaching or with being taught. The school became a machine for learning, in which each pupil, each level and

> each moment, if correctly combined, were permanently utilized in the general process of teaching. (165)

The figure that accompanies Foucault's discussion nicely illustrates this arrangement where the single master sits at the front of and slightly above a large number of boys, arranged according to height, dutifully seated in rows facing him. Behind the master and visible to the students is the clock, which controls all movements and activities in the classroom. To the master's right is a row of young boys seated in an area reserved for newcomers, "dunces," and the chronically inattentive—those students, in other words, in need of especially close and multiple surveillances. Monitors circulate through the room inspecting the work the other students have done, performing an almost identical gesture in unison. One student, as if to illustrate the inherent unruliness of this mass, looks away from his lesson and directly at the viewer, in an action unseen by the monitors but one that nevertheless falls safely under the gaze of the schoolmaster. To be a student within this system is to be seen, and the only way to be seen without fear of censure is to have successfully learned to stay within the bounds of the modelled behavior.

Whether or not Lancaster actually believed that the ability to read could be readily translated into an ability to teach any subject, his reliance on the monitorial method was necessitated by an overarching problem that impeded the expansion of public education in Great Britain during this period—namely, mutually reinforcing critical shortages of both trained instructors to staff new classrooms and adequate funding to build new schools. As long as the societies that educated Britain's poorest citizens had to rely exclusively on donations to fund their schools and to pay their instructors, they had no choice but to employ a system of instruction that delivered its educational product to the most students at the lowest cost. Or, to put it another way, so long as the British government declined to fund this sector of public education (as it did until the 1830s), the monitorial method was ensured its place as the dominant teaching practice used to educate the nation's poor. And within such a system, what its students were taught was that learning principally involved the replication of modelled activities and that the reward for being able to reproduce the modelled activities was steady advancement through a hierarchy structured by multiple and reciprocal monitorings. In short, without outside intervention from either the government or some competing pedagogical approach—the very kind of interventions that Foucault would argue signal the further expansion of disciplinary power and that Bennett, no doubt, would decry as overstepping government's auxiliary role—Britain's poorest students were sentenced to work within an educational organization whose very structure was designed with *only* disciplinary and economic concerns in mind.

It's a ghastly system, but one that, for my purposes, provides a provocative example of how, in the past, an interest in educating the masses was readily transformed into a comprehensive pedagogical apparatus for fostering obedience. But I also recognize that it is also a fairly easy target, for who is likely to come forward to defend such a method of instruction? It's a relic of the past, an historical curiosity worthy of a stall in the Museum of Pedagogical Practices, perhaps, but nothing more. This, at least, was my own reaction to my historical research, until I learned that this "machine for learning" is not out of commission but rather continues to operate, providing a general pedagogical blueprint for the nation's largest organized effort to train teachers in the assessment of student writing—the Educational Testing Service. What brought me to the Educational Testing Service's summer grading marathon of Advance Placement exams was my abiding interest in the questions I've raised here: where do the statistics that bolster the perpetual sense of educational crisis come from? How is learning transformed within systems of education into a product that can be measured and evaluated? And how do these institutional mechanisms of assessment, in turn, influence pedagogical practice, in general, and the teaching of reading and writing, specifically? Grading the AP English exams for ETS enabled me to see how the answer to these questions has been translated into an institutionalized system for assessing student writing that is, as the AP literature everywhere proclaims, both "consistent and reliable."[1]

In order to assure that each of the exams is graded according to the same standard, ETS disrupts many of the conventions that govern assessment in the classroom today. At ETS, the act of responding to a student text is reduced to the solitary assignation of a number between one and nine; the grader's assessment is entirely public and subject to both peer and superior review; and, finally, the contextual nature of the interchange between the student text and the teacher's response is shorn off, leaving only the raw act of having the grader place the student text on a pre-established grid. Everything in the process has been streamlined to ensure that the most essays are graded in the least amount of time with, to be sure, the greatest level of "accuracy." This is accomplished by establishing a hierarchy of linked monitorings strikingly similar to those used in the schools of Bell and Lancaster: all the readers for an individual question are placed in the same room, where they are divided up into small groups and assigned to Table Leaders. Each group stays with its Table Leader for the entire grading session, with the "acorns" (as first-time readers are called in reference to the College Board's logo) generally placed on either side of their leader. The Question Leader sits at the head of the room underneath a clock, monitoring the progress of the individual tables and announcing lunch and stretching breaks. The Question Leader and the Table Leaders are periodically called from the room to meet with the Chief Faculty Consultant, who provides an ongoing statistical breakdown of how each individual reader in the room is doing—the number of essays read, the range and frequency of scores assigned, comparisons of scores assigned to the same student across the three exam questions, etc. At this time, erratic readers and readers who are not assigning the full range of scores are identified and strategies for addressing broader, room-wide trends are planned out.[2]

From a certain perspective, this system is a marvel both to watch and to participate in. There's something peaceful and reassuring about the way it hums along, churning year after year through undifferentiated masses of student essays and producing, in the end, a tidy, organized whole, with each essay in its "proper" place. And yet, it's worth observing that the same appearance of order could be achieved by assigning scores to the essays at random, respecting only the distributional demands of the bell curve. Introducing this element of chance into the process would, of course, spell disaster for ETS, which is in the business of producing assessments that *reliably* measure the ability of individual students to place out of entry-level instruction in college. Thus, the hierarchical monitoring is only half of the ETS equation; while it ensures steady progress through the mass of papers and allows for critical interventions when grading glitches occur, it is further linked to a program of instruction that guides all readers to use the *same* system of evaluation in the same way throughout the entire grading process. To this end, the first day of grading is spent "norming" the readers, a process whereby model student responses are read and their affixed grades explained. Working from sheets that describe the differences between each score in relation to the essay question, the readers then begin to assess practice essays, determining their scores and comparing their results with the other readers at their table. While there is a good bit of discussion this first day about how to read and evaluate the essays, the primary function of this work is to get the readers to accept the scores previously assigned to the practice essays by the Table Leaders. This goal is realized when the readers have internalized the system of assessment developed by the Chief Faculty Consultant, the Question Leader, and the Table Leaders. All discussion is carried out to this end: questions, which are rare, tend to be informational, "Why is this a 4 and not a 6?" What is never interrogated is the logic that underwrites the system of assessment or the essay assignment itself; discussion of these matters, which surfaces occasionally throughout the week in the cafeteria and in the hallways, is seen, quite rightly, to slow things down in the grading room.

In moving from the use of the monitorial method in the early nineteenth century as a "machine for learning" to the application of that same method at ETS today as a "machine for assessing," I may seem to have strayed some distance from the question posed by my title, "What does it mean to learn?" Indeed, in the language of ETS my essay, at this point, may have wandered so far afield that it is now "off topic" and worthy of only the lowest possible score, the non-registering dash. While one of my overriding concerns in this essay is to illustrate the virtues of pursuing thoughts down serpentine paths and the pleasures learning can afford when understood not simply as a project of reproduction but as a process of unexpected juxtapositions as well, I am also interested in tracing out what it might mean to learn within the ETS system of assessment. With this in mind, following Bennett's lead, we can start with some facts and figures that suggest the exam's power to both shape and reflect the learning experience of high school students across the nation. In 1993, 170,000 students sat for ETS' English Language and English Literature exams. According to the *Advanced Placement Course Description: English*, AP courses "are offered in more than 10,000 high schools in every state in the United States, every province and territory in Canada, and 63 other countries. They are recognized by nearly 2,900 U.S. and foreign colleges and universities, which grant credit, appropriate placement, or both to students who have performed satisfactorily on AP examinations" (i). Aside from the cultural capital that students and teachers gain from being involved in AP courses, there are financial incentives from both above and below to encourage students to take these exams: for roughly seventy dollars, the student has a chance to save the cost of up to six credits' tuition by placing out of first-year composition and entry-level literature courses. And, as a number of high school teachers explained to me at the assessment site, in some states individual schools have their budgets increased on the basis of how many AP classes they offer, since such courses are seen to provide a clear indication of a given school's commitment to "excellence."

It is, of course, in the best interest of all involved parties that students do well in these courses and on their exams, which is one important reason why so many dedicated high school teachers give up a piece of their summers to grade for ETS. In exchange for a nominal honorarium, the teachers learn the shape of the exams, the types of questions asked, and, most importantly, what, in the eyes of the examiners, distinguishes a good response from a bad one. Teachers may further avail themselves of the annual booklets put out by ETS that analyze the previous year's questions and provide samples of exemplary essays and extended commentary explaining the rationale behind the system of assessment. They may also draw on the AP's *Teacher's Guide to Advanced Placement Course in English Language and Composition*, which offers tips on how to design AP courses and sample course outlines. Armed with all this information, the teachers can then return to their classrooms and prepare their students to write the kinds of responses that are mostly likely to receive high marks from the examiners.[3]

Measuring the effect that this examination system has on actual classroom practice is beyond the scope of this study, but it is safe to say that the ETS trumpets its statistics on the number of high schools and colleges involved with the program to advertize the extent of the AP exam's influence. For our purposes, though, what is most significant to note here is the way in which a method for evaluating response becomes, itself, a system for generating response. The examiners model responses for the teachers who, in turn, model responses for their students, in a reproductive chain that is meant to define what constitutes "good writing" at the national level. All of this is fine, I suppose, as long as you agree with the system of assessment and think that the examination itself prompts the kind of writing that is or should be required of students in first-year composition and literature courses. As I sat there in San Antonio, however, working my way through essay after essay that sought to analyze how a three paragraph excerpt from Joan Didion conveyed the author's view about the Santa Ana winds, I couldn't help but feel that there was almost no relationship between the disembodied, mechanized results of the examinees' hastily dashed off studies in style and the kind of writing I seek to have my students produce in my courses. Specifically, in this testing situation, the students stuck doggedly to the instructions that they "*might* consider such stylistic elements as diction, imagery, syntax, structure, tone, and selection of detail" in formulating their responses (*English Language and Composition*; emphasis added). As a result of these instructions, none of the essays I read opted to use Didion's essay to explore what it would mean to accept the "deeply mechanistic view of human behavior" that she writes of, for instance, nor did they risk going off topic by having Didion serve as a springboard to other issues (much the way Didion herself uses Raymond Chandler in the selected passage). Instead, the students, knowing their place, praised the organizational brilliance of the three paragraph excerpt; they shuddered dramatically at Didion's descriptions of the wind's powers; they sighed in disappointment along with her at science's unsatisfactory explanation of how the winds work their evil magic. As the last link in this hierarchy of obedience, the students fulfilled their assigned task, struggling to say what was expected of them, while making sure to leave their doubts and questions about the work unrecorded.

The relevance of the monitorial method of instruction to a consideration of what it means to learn, then, is that it vividly illustrates the consequences of relying on a pedagogy that defines reading and writing primarily in terms of obedience. In a system where teachers either do not or are not allowed to question the criteria used to define good writing, students learn to leave those questions unasked themselves: their job, instead, is to read the model essay placed before them and to replicate the modelled commentary on that essay. Not too surprisingly, the test rewards those students most highly who most know their place: those who have set pieces to offer for the exam's "open" question and those who can articulate appropriately pious attitudes about the writing samples. High scores go to those essays that speak convincingly of writing's power to move us to a consideration of the eternal verities or that compellingly detail the author's effective use of language in evoking a powerful emotional response: high scores, in other words, for writing that participates in the dog and pony show of literary appreciation.

With this in mind, it is worth noting that, of the twelve hundred essays I assessed during my time in San Antonio, not one student argued against Didion's views about nature or criticized her stylistic choices as inappropriate, ineffective, or unworthy of study. Nor did a single student essay go beyond the questioner's concern with style to consider, for instance, the possible cultural and political significance of the fact that Didion's piece about an evil wind blowing through L.A. was written in 1968. Nor, finally, did a single response I read suggest that the exam itself might be flawed in some fundamental way. Nothing even close to this occurred. Indeed, of the sixty exams I graded that were either blank or consisted of no more than two or three sentences, not one of these writers elected to throw off the collar for a moment and, if nothing else, release some steam about how the exam positioned the students as mere admirers of their superiors. Thus, when I picture the student who sat for this three hour exam, opened the test booklet to the first page, and wrote only the words, "Why am I so fucking stupid?" I see evidence not of resistance, but of the consequences of internalizing the rationale of this approach. In this case, the test has served its purpose of confirming a larger, more general institutional assessment of the student's mental abilities. Consequently, even in this apparently defiant act, we find the writer bowed in obedience; the student has learned his or her place in the system, and that place is to accept the designation that he or she is a failure.

Students like this one don't disappear, of course. They join the rest of those who either didn't take the exam or didn't ace it and end up being placed in first year composition courses around the country. They bring with them not only this internalized system of shame, but the whole set of assumptions this system is based on as well, including the sense that the primary function of student writing is to reproduce admiration of a professional writer's text. There are other ways to read and write than those imagined by the AP exam and other ways to learn than by obedience and repetition, of course. Before turning to these alternatives, however, I hope at this point to have teased to the surface the recursive relationship that exists between systems of assessment and the production of student writing. In this instance, the answer to the question, "what does it mean to learn," is, perhaps solipsistically, to acquire the ability to anticipate and respond to the demands, codes, and conventions of the dominant examination system. If tests always simultaneously solicit and monitor responses, transforming the results into a hierarchical pattern and distributing rewards accordingly, the very obviousness of this observation has as yet served to conceal its significance, which lies in the suggestion that there are always at least two teachers in the classroom: the ostensible instructor and the dominant system of examination. Within the pedagogy of obedience, these two teachers collapse in on one another and become indistinguishable: as the AP guide says in its section on "Setting and Maintaining Standards for the Reading," "to prevent the exercise of personal or whimsical judgments, all the teachers who score the essays subscribe to a set of common standards and conform consistently to a prescribed regimen" (24). In this modernist utopia, then, the impersonal is elevated to the heavens, the teacher and the examination become identical, and all interested parties treat each other with the appropriate level of respect and civility.

Acknowledged and Overstepped Boundaries: Imagining a Pedagogy of Exploration

If it is undeniably true that any act of assessment requires obedience both from the examiner and the examinee, then to speak of an institutionalized alternative to the "pedagogy of obedience" may seem nothing more than a fanciful indulgence. After all, let's consider the facts. It is an inescapable fact that all courses at accredited institutions, regardless of the pedagogical practices used by individual instructors, terminate in some formal evaluation of each student's performance. Assessment, whether through multiple choice exams, short essays, or portfolio review, is here to stay. Yet, it's also a fact that teachers of literature and composition have commitments besides getting students to notice the skillful deployment of rhetorical strategies in the texts of admired writers. And it is a related fact that working conditions in the teaching profession tend to provide a level of autonomy that allow for the possibility of teaching students to attend to more in their reading than the author's style and to aim for more in their writing than the production of seamlessly persuasive essays. Fact, fact, fact. Simply stating the facts that suggest we have some room to move pedagogically is no more likely to produce change in the ways literature and composition are taught than is the publication of a haphazard series of pie and bar charts about education in the U.S.

Near the end of *Hard Times*, Thomas Gradgrind himself comes to realize that his utilitarian pedagogy, with its moral calculus of pleasures and pains, can neither help him to understand his children's actions nor can it assist him in protecting them from the potentially dire consequences of their deeds. To learn how to do these things, Gradgrind must turn to Sissy Jupe, the circus girl who is humiliated in the opening scene of *Hard Times* because her experientially based ways of knowing the world are invisible to her examiners. What Gradgrind comes to learn from Sissy is that facts have no utility unless they can be manipulated to suggest a realm of possibility beyond themselves. It is, after all, not the schoolmaster's blue books of statistics that allow young Tom Gradgrind to escape from the law and his sister Louisa to elude certain disgrace; it is, rather, Sissy's ability to imagine alternative solutions to these seemingly foregone conclusions. The alternative to a pedagogy of obedience, Dickens suggests, lies in the use of the imagination or the fancy, a faculty whose very nature is to elude both assessment and a strictly regimented system of instruction grounded in immediately verifiable data.

Of course, one could say that, by the end of *Hard Times*, Dickens has stacked the deck so heavily against Gradgrindian pedagogy that he's made it impossible for anyone to speak of its possible virtues. And, similarly, it could be claimed, with some accuracy, that I've done the same thing by naming the approach I've discussed here the "pedagogy of obedience." At times, it seems that this problem is endemic to the topic of teaching, as evidenced by the alternatives that populate the landscape, where we find, for example, Berthoff's "pedagogy of knowing" versus the "pedagogy of exhortation," Giroux's "pedagogy of possibility" versus an implied alternative that I like to call "the pedagogy of despair," and, of course, Freire's "pedagogy of liberation" versus the discipline's favorite whipping boy, "the banking concept of education." And yet, as Donna Dunbar-Odom has recently argued, the "liberatory" pedagogies associated with these terms have tended to devolve into their own regimes of truth—their own, if you will, "pedagogies of obedience"—with certain writerly acts qualifying, for instance, as the right kind of resistance and others registering only as a failure to engage in the common struggle against oppression. And so we find ourselves once again in this bind: if it is inescapable that all pedagogical practice demands a level of cooperation from its students, and it surely is, then the very suggestion of an alternative to the pedagogy of obedience, whatever its appellation, may seem not only paradoxical, but impracticable within an institutional setting.

The only way out of this impasse is to recognize that there is no pure alternative within the academy to the pedagogy of obedience: whatever model one comes up with will always, inevitably, be partly captured by the overriding need to regulate, organize, and evaluate the responses students produce. In other words, every "liberatory" pedagogy necessarily has moments of practice which are indistinguishable from "banking-concept" pedagogies. Thus, rather than try to escape this dialectical bind, in what follows I would like to consider a project with a more modest goal—namely, I would like to consider what it might mean to imagine reading and writing as less readily examinable activities. In pursuing this project, I prefer to rely on the image of "exploration" partly because of the fact that, in the wake of postcolonial criticism, the term no longer connotes only a positive sense of pure adventure and discovery, but rather summons, as well, images of contamination, including visions of crossed boundaries and of possible transgressions, both known and unknown, into forbidden territories. Thus, the questions I'm interested in pursuing at this point are these: what happens when, in place of carefully regulated and examinable interchanges between reader and text, one admits the possibility that individual acts of reading and writing are the result of chance encounters, personal initiatives, private projects? And how and why might one go about promoting not only this view of reading and writing as interrelated acts in the unruly process of exploration, but also encouraging open engagement in such acts? It goes without saying that a pedagogy that solicits students to "explore" connections between texts may itself be construed as an implicit form of examination, a kind of quest where the reader is sent off to discover the intellectual baubles planted in advance by omniscient authors or crafty instructors. Understood in this way, "to learn is to explore" quickly reveals itself to be part of that deadly hermeneutic, "to learn is to find hidden meanings." As I hope to illustrate in what follows, however, there is another way to understand learning as exploration, a way that can be used to undermine the sense that what lies ahead for the reader is merely an arduous exercise in uncovering what the author (or the teacher) knew all along.

Reading Misreadings: Chance and the Sublime in Freud, Kant, and Longinus

I've always been drawn to oversights, mistakes, errors, misreadings. Plagued by forgetfulness, I've learned to take pleasure in looking again at what I missed the first time. Within the pedagogy of obedience, this activity is of little more than editorial interest, however: it is work to be crossed off and completed as quickly as possible. And it is precisely for this reason that "misreading" suggests itself to me as the best place to commence a discussion of what a "pedagogy of exploration" might entail. Although the drift of the preceding discussion might seem to suggest a move in a more predictable direction—to an example, say, culled from a student paper written in one of my courses—I have decided, instead, to turn to Freud's *Leonardo da Vinci and a Memory of His Childhood* for reasons that will become apparent shortly.[4] Freud was, of course, interested in examinations and errors, art and perfection, as I have been throughout this essay. In *Leonardo*, Freud relies on his work with the artist's notebooks and paintings, as well as some fragmentary biographical information, to argue that Leonardo "succeeded in sublimating the greater part of his libido into an urge for research" (30). Specifically, Leonardo's childhood memory of being visited in his crib by a vulture who opened the artist's mouth and struck his lips many times with its tail reveals, in Freud's analysis, Leonardo's strong attachment to his mother (the vulture), his repression of this love for her, and his subsequent efforts to put himself in her place, with the end result that he "has become a homosexual" (43, 55). The meticulous records Leonardo later kept of the money he spent on his pupils are seen to provide further evidence of the "psychical development" of the artist's homosexuality. Indeed, when Leonardo's childhood memory and the diary entries are placed alongside one another, they make it possible to decipher the meaning of Leonardo's remembrance of the dream about the vulture: "It was through this erotic relation with my mother that I became a homosexual" (62-63). As always with Freud, little is left to chance, so that the available fragments of a life necessarily fall into place to compose a seamless narrative of the subject's etiology.

Though Freud toys with the idea that one can only reach the sublime heights of artistic creativity through the sublimation of libidinal desires, he ultimately concludes that, within his psychoanalytic system, Leonardo is better understood as an obsessional neurotic, with a "stunted adult sexual life" that "manifested itself in ideal love for boys" (93-94). In other words, Leonardo's sublimation of his libidinal desires brought him not to the sublime, but rather into the realm of "constitutional inferiority," a psychic space characterized by, among other things, "obsessional brooding," "the avoidance of every crudely sensual activity," and a life of abstinence that left the impression that he was an "asexual human being" (93-94). In this way, Freud's treatment of Leonardo reveals something about systems of examination not disclosed in our earlier exploration of the subject: had everything gone according to plan, had Leonardo made "the correct decision in his choice of object" during the onset of puberty (52), he never would have had artistic and scientific achievements that Freud himself calls "sublime" (82). At the same time, Freud provides an example of a way of reading that focusses, for the moment at least, not on "the norm," but on deviations from the norm, seeing in those deviations failures, to be sure, but also invitations to explore further.

But what does it mean, ultimately, to assess Leonardo's work as "sublime"? While Freud is less than precise about what the term might mean, Kant's famous definition in the *Critique of Judgment* rules out its application to objects or actions, works of art or artistic performances. For Kant, the sublime, as opposed to the beautiful, "is not to be sought in the things of nature, but only in our ideas" (88). Specifically, this occurs when the mind "finds the whole power of the imagination inadequate to its ideas" (95), a failure that "forces us, subjectively, to *think* nature itself in its totality as a presentation of something supersensible, without being able *objectively* to arrive at this presentation" (108). While experiencing this failure is painful, it is not wholly unpleasant, for the mind finds purpose and what Kant calls the "negative pleasure" of "respect and admiration" in the fact that "every standard of sensibility [is] inadequate to the ideas of understanding" (83, 97). Within Kant's well ordered system, then, one could not properly speak of sublime achievements, unless one meant achievements that, when contemplated, generated an experience of both the mind's and the imagination's inability to present an image adequate to the achievement.

Freud, himself, appears to have had just such an experience when he tried to conclude Leonardo's psychic history. In the final chapter of *Leonardo*, Freud starts out both establishing and defending the integrity of psychoanalysis as an independent scientific field, arguing that by working with the known circumstances of a subject's life and the subject's recorded responses, one can "disclose the original motive forces of his mind, as well as their later transformations and developments" (97). If any problems arise in the analysis, it is not the fault of the method, but must rather be understood to have been produced by "the uncertainty and fragmentary nature of the material" available for study (97). Midway through this argument, though, Freud is forced to concede that the very application of his psychoanalytic method creates the appearance of inevitability where chance was actually at play all along: Leonardo's response to his illegitimate birth and his attachment to his mother need not have occurred in the ways that they did. Indeed, Freud admits, "in someone else [the repressive response] might perhaps not have taken place or might have assumed much less extensive proportions" (98). By acknowledging this—perhaps lamentable—state of affairs, where the events of one's life only assume an order when looked at through the lens of psychoanalysis, Freud is brought, it seems, to the verge of the sublime: we must admit, he says, "that in fact everything to do with our life is chance, from our origin out of the meeting of spermatozoon and ovum onwards—chance which nevertheless has a share in the law and necessity of nature, and which merely lacks any connection with our wishes and illusions" (100). Although Freud is incapable of producing an image that can account for the "countless causes" at work in nature, a fact that would appear to undermine the argument for psychoanalysis' status as a science, this same fact seems to give him pleasure. Thus, when he reflects on the role chance plays in our lives, he is forced to conclude that "we all still show too little *respect* for Nature," invoking the very kind of negative pleasure Kant asserts is called for in response to apprehending the sublime (100; emphasis added).

If Freud is, indeed, transported to the sublime as a result of contemplating the ultimate inability of his system to account for the totality of human development, where does that leave us? That is, if it is true that "*everything* to do with our life is chance," then the possibility of developing a meaningful system for evaluating, measuring, or interpreting acts of reading and writing, on the one hand, or psychic events, on the other, seems lost. And, of course, Freud's *Leonardo* dramatically illustrates the consequences of forgetting for a moment that chance constantly threatens to bring entire interpretive enterprises crashing to the ground. Despite Freud's closing observations about the role chance plays in one's life, he stands by his results, where "it seems at any rate as if only a man who had had Leonardo's childhood experiences could have painted the Mona Lisa and the St. Anne, . . . as if the key to all [Leonardo's] achievements and misfortunes lay hidden in the childhood phantasm of the vulture" (90). So much depends, it seems, on the metaphoric and allusive powers of that vulture: it is "the key" that unlocks the mysteries of Leonardo's life and the source of his creative powers. It is the self-sufficient bird that opens its vagina mid-flight to be impregnated by the wind (41); it represents "the mother" in Egyptian hieroglyphics (39); and its head rests atop the Egyptian Mother Goddess *Mut* whose name so closely resembles the German word for "mother" that Freud is compelled to ask if this could "be merely a coincidence?" (39).

And yet, as it turns out, it isn't even a coincidence, since that "vulture" is no vulture at all, but a kite, and all the remarkable connections between Leonardo and his mother show themselves to be nothing but a phantasm of Freud's system. The problem, it seems, is that Freud relied on a version of Leonardo's work that mistranslated the key word in Leonardo's childhood memory. Although Freud announces in *Leonardo* that his goal is "*to translate* the phantasy from its own special language into words that are generally understood" (36) and although he "translates" the phantasy a number of times,[5] he seems to place the actual act of translating the phantasy itself from Italian into German as something outside the limits of the psychoanalyst's concern. While this self-imposed limit makes it possible for Freud to pursue the vulture to Egypt, discovering there cultural artifacts that simultaneously produce and reinforce his explanation of the enabling conditions that led Leonardo to paint the Mona Lisa, his "translations" no longer hold when this limit is challenged and the "mistranslation" is discovered.[6] In light of such a discovery, it seems safe to say that Freud has failed dramatically in *Leonardo*.

Or is it? Could it be that Freud's failures are, in fact, not entirely his own, but also partly his readers'? While it may seem well warranted to assess Freud's efforts in *Leonardo* to limit the intrusion of a chance error into the domain of language a "failure," it is possible to argue that this very failure makes his work sublime in a way not discussed in the *Critique of Judgment*. Longinus offers just such an alternate definition in his treatise, *On the Sublime*. Responding to Caecilius' assertion that Lysias was altogether superior to Plato because he made fewer faults in his speeches, Longinus asserts: "For my part, I am well aware that lofty genius is far removed from flawlessness; for invariably accuracy incurs the risk of pettiness, and in the sublime, as in great fortunes, *there must be something which is overlooked*" (99; emphasis added). Obviously, errors alone don't constitute sublime writing for Longinus. His point, rather, is that error-free writing is more often the product of petty rather than sublime aspirations. With this in mind, it becomes possible to argue that the magnitude of Freud's error is perhaps evidence of the sublime quality of his writing: only by trying to accomplish a project so grand as accounting for the formation of the self and the source of artistic achievement could he have overlooked something so fundamental to his argument as the correct translation of the central term in his analysis.

Whatever the merits of such an understanding of the sublime, Longinus's definition does serve to explain the odd conclusion to *Leonardo*, where Freud seems to undermine the scientific status of psychoanalysis with each passing sentence. Longinus argues that the effect of sublime speech "is not persuasion but transport" (80), and that this "genuine passion," in the right place, "bursts out in a wild gust of mad enthusiasm and as it were fills the speaker's words with frenzy" (84). What Roberts translates here as "transport" is the Greek word *ekstasis* which has as its first meaning a displacement, and thus, by extension, entrancement and astonishment (Liddell and Scott 244). To read *Leonardo* in this way is to credit the writing with producing exactly the opposite effect one would expect from a case study of an artist whose "powerful instinctual passions . . . express[ed] themselves in so remarkably subdued a manner" (97). Freud's aim is not to provide a rational argument that persuades the reader of the reasonableness of the self-imposed limits of psychoanalysis but, rather, to transport the reader, through his ecstatic prose, to accept, perhaps even to join in, the activities of psychoanalytic interpretation. And, in this regard at least, however much one might wish for another outcome, it seems safe to say that the ecstatic effect of Freud's prose has been unparalleled in modern times.

To put Freud aside for the moment, though, it is no doubt curious that Kant's definition of the sublime involves a conflict between reason and the imagination, while Longinus' definition elevates madness to the highest form of expression. This definitional tension recalls the central debate in the *Phaedrus* over the effects of love. Longinus, himself, is drawn to this dialogue when he discusses what Plato has to teach us about sublime writing:

> [Plato] shows us, if only we were willing to pay him heed, that another way . . . leads to the sublime. . . . It is the imitation and emulation of previous great poets and writers. . . . Was Herodotus alone a devoted imitator of Homer? No, Stesichorus even before his time, and Archilochus, and above all Plato, who from the great Homeric source drew to himself innumerable tributary streams. (89)

Here, Longinus not only makes the claim that Plato's ultimate source of inspiration was literary rather than philosophical, he also maintains that the Homeric influences on Plato's work are "innumerable," uncountable, unmeasurable. With so many doors leading from Plato's dialogues to Homer's poems, how does one know which one to go through? While Longinus would have us believe that Stesichorus gained access to the sublime by imitating Homer, in the *Phaedrus* Socrates maintains that Stesichorus was actually rewarded with blindness for his mimetic act (490). Indeed, as Socrates tells the story, it was only when Stesichorus stopped imitating Homer and wrote a recantation of his poem about Helen that the Gods returned to him his ability to see.

Does the sublime lead to reason or madness? Does it produce clarity of vision or blindness? Does it involve imitation or invention? If we return again to the *Phaedrus*, we see that after Socrates offers his reading of Stesichorus' plight and repeats word for word the poet's recantation, he then produces what Longinus might well have thought of as sublime speech: a speech "flashing forth at the right moment scatter[ing] everything before it like a thunderbolt" (Longinus 80), a speech less concerned with persuasion than transport, a speech celebrating a certain kind of madness over reason, a speech, finally, that Socrates himself attributes to Stesichorus. Socrates imitates Stesichorus imitating Homer. A sublime chain. There are, of course, other alternatives, other explanations, other explorations for what is going on in this dialogue. It would be possible to maintain, along with reader-response theorists, that in this case it is not the text at all which is sublime, but the reading process itself, where answers shimmer evanescently, and the discussion of ideas, great and small, roils on, not toward a conclusion but rather toward periods of suspension, reflection, exhaustion, cessation.

The Hairpin Turn

I turned to this bundle of concerns about chance and the sublime in order to pursue a way of reading and writing not so readily amenable to examination—an alternative to the notion that "to learn is to obey," an approach that explores and exploits ambiguity rather than seeking to conceal and contain it. The journey through, to continue the metaphor, has lead me far from whatever might be called my field of expertise, and I've no doubt muddled some of the finer points in making my way between the texts. In spite of or perhaps because of this fact, this process has suggested to me that to learn is, perhaps, to sublime, if "to sublime" may be made to mean "to displace one's expectations." Thus, to the long list of viable answers I've discussed in this essay to the question, "What does it mean to learn?" I would like to add, "to learn is to displace, both oneself and the object of study." This, surely, is what it means to "explore." And yet, at the same time, I have seen as well that to learn is also to displace the sublime, to constantly seek to control and contain the mad enthusiasm of the text, trading transport for persuasion in hopes of regulating chance. Exploration inevitably gives way to discovery, as chance gives way to determination. Oscillating between these two treatments of the sublime, it is clear that there would be nothing left to say if this containment could ever be successfully completed.

Such exploratory opportunities exist in all texts, of course. They are as present in Bennett's *Index* as they are in the works by Freud, Kant, Longinus, and Plato. In order to invite students to pass through these "intertextual" doorways and to embark on such projects of exploration, where they are encouraged to engage with language as a realm of possible meanings and to see reading and writing as inextricably related acts of discovery, it is necessary that one develop a pedagogical practice that values unruly acts of reading and writing and to solicit responses that are, at times, ponderous and confused. This may seem counter-intuitive: after all, it's one thing to endorse exploration; it's quite another to promote the production of writing that is circuitous, fanciful, or lost and to reward essays that go "off topic," make odd or unexpected juxtapositions, and establish connections on the tightest of hairpin turns. And yet, if writing is understood as a dialogical act, where the writer simultaneously makes and reports meaning, drawing on internal resources and responding to external pressures, then the educational process and its systems of examination might serve a more heuristic purpose if they assisted students in exploring a range of hermeneutic processes, rather than having students focus exclusively on issues of style, summary, and personal response. This means, I believe, acknowledging that the writing process is not simply the means by which a writer's prose is moved to a point of greater and greater clarity—but that it can also be a recursive system whereby the developing ideas in an unfolding text become increasingly complex, contingent, muddied, stalled, even abandoned.

When students are presented with the idea that successful mastery of the writing process produces a smooth voyage to clarity, they come to understand that anything that stands in the way of clarity must be expunged: ambiguity, obscure references, contradictions, paradoxes, tangential thoughts—the fundamental material, one might say, of lived experience and of one's mental life. "Making one's point" then becomes the highest value. The essays I read at ETS may be construed as a consequence of such a pedagogy: the students, fearful of being wrong or unclear, stuck as close to the text as possible (e.g., "Didion doesn't like this wind"). While it's easy enough to go on and fault (or assess) writing of this kind on the basis of its organization or diction—to engage, in other words, in the stock in trade of teacher commentary—the real problem, I would maintain, is that such writing is not messy enough. The drive to be clear evolves into a concern with being safe and the safest place to be is to reiterate the author's or the teacher's position with admiration, respect, civility.

While such writing has its place (indeed, I tend to think that it has nothing else but its place), the alternative that I've argued for here is to pursue literary explorations as one way of releasing the student writer from the enervating experience of the solitary encounter with the solitary text, where all the work that remains is to re-speak the author's words. What this means in practice is providing students with the opportunity to read and write about something other than a single text in isolation and to focus, instead, on getting students to establish relationships between texts—juxtaposing terms and ideas, pursuing connections, exploring hunches, making a run for the sublime. In establishing "dialogues" among different texts in this way, students find that they must constantly negotiate between the desire to take the discussion anywhere they please and the opposing desire to follow the leads suggested by or inferred from the texts. As they work between these two poles of freedom and regulation, open exploration and directed travel, they often produce questions they can't answer, offer hypotheses they can't support, and make arguments that don't hold together. There is an immense value to such writing: it is the very stuff of preliminary research, the bone and marrow of intellectual life. As Socrates says at the conclusion of the

Phaedrus, "Every great art must be supplemented by leisurely discussion, by stargazing, if you will, about the nature of things" (60). Developing a pedagogical practice that allows such "stargazing" to occur, where students can explore different hermeneutic practices as they speculate on questions as vast as "the nature of things," is, I believe, a project of central importance to teachers of literature and composition. It is also, needless to say, a project whose very success will always be necessarily difficult to assess.

Notes

1. It should be clear that my critique of the system is not aimed at the people who participate in it: indeed, during the six days I spent in San Antonio as a member of this grading marathon in June 1994, I found my fellow assessors and the Table Leaders to be a remarkably kind and generous lot. Everyone I spoke with took the work seriously and labored to keep each others' spirits up, even as the task of grading over forty thousand essays responding to the same question threatened to rob all of us of our sanity.

2. It was just such a review of the output sheets that revealed that our room as a whole was not giving out enough scores at the top end of the scale. Consequently, appropriate steps were taken to remind us of what an excellent response to our question looked like. The hope, apparently, was that the graders would recognize that their own standards were unreasonably elevated and begin to distribute more scores at the high end of the spectrum.

3. The rewards for knowing this system are not simply pedagogical and cultural, however. The examination system itself actually produces a whole side industry of test-taking experts: two of the other graders at my table "moonlighted" back in their home states as consultants to local high schools, providing teacher-training workshops on how to maximize student performance on the exam.

4. I didn't just come across Freud's *Leonardo* while in the midst of these thoughts about the tension between systems of examination and chance. Rather, it was reading Derrida's essay, "My Chances/*Mes Chances*: A Rendezvous with Some Epicurean Stereophonies" that first suggested to me the possible relevance of Freud's work on Leonardo to my argument.

5. Freud recommends, for instance, that the phantasy might be "translated: 'My mother pressed innumerable passionate kisses on my mouth'" (*Leonardo* 64).

6. Freud's own silence on the broader subject of mistranslations is evident in *The Psychopathology of Everyday Life*. Although he provides many examples of slips of the pen and problems with foreign words, he has nothing to say about a reader who, though devoted to the study of parapraxis in himself and in others, is blind to the possibility of parapraxis occurring in a text he is reading.

Works Cited

Advanced Placement Course Description: English. College Entrance Examination Board. May 1995.

The 1991 Advanced Placement Examination in English Language and Composition and Its Grading. College Entrance Examination Board. 1993.

Aronowitz, Stanley, and Henry A. Giroux. *Education Under Siege.* South Hadley, MA: Bergin, 1985.

Bennett, William J. *The Index of Leading Cultural Indicators: Facts and Figures on the State of American Society.* New York: Simon, 1994.

Berthoff, Ann E. "Is Teaching Still Possible? Writing, Meaning, and Higher Order Reasoning," *College English.* 46 (1984): 743-55.

Derrida, Jacques. "My Chances/*Mes Chances*: A Rendezvous with Some Epicurean Stereophonies." *Taking Chances: Derrida, Psychoanalysis, and Literature.* Ed. Joseph J. Smith and William Kerrigan. Baltimore: Johns Hopkins UP, 1984. 1-32.

Dickens, Charles. *Hard Times.* 1854. London: J.M. Dent and Sons, 1974.

Dunbar-Odom, Donna. "'Where Do I Stand?': New Teachers in the 'Problem-Posing' Classroom." Penn State Conference on Rhetoric. July 1994.

English Language and Composition, Section II, Question Three. Educational Testing Service. 1994

Foucault, Michel. *Discipline and Punish.* Trans. Alan Sheridan. New York: Random House, 1979.

Freire, Paulo. *The Pedagogy of the Oppressed.* Trans. Myra Bergman Ramos. New York: Continuum, 1989.

Freud, Sigmund. *Leonardo da Vinci and a Memory of His Childhood.* Trans. Alan Tyson. New York: Norton, 1989.

—. *The Psychopathology of Everyday Life.* Trans. Alan Tyson. New York: Norton, 1960.

Gadda, George, Ejner Jensen, Finlay McQuade, and Harriet Wilson. *Teacher's Guide to Advanced Placement Courses in English Language and Compostion.* College Entrance Examination Board. 1985.

Godsen, P.H. *How They Were Taught: An Anthology of Contemporary Accounts of Learning and Teaching in England 1800-1950*. Oxford: Blackwell, 1969.

Hyndman, Michael. *Schools and Schooling in England and Wales: A Documentary History*. London: Harper, 1978.

Kant, Immanuel. *The Critique of Judgment*. Trans. J.H. Bernard. New York: Hafner, 1951.

Liddel, Henry George, and Robert Scott. *An Intermediate Greek-English Lexicon*. 1889. London: Oxford UP, 1975.

Longinus. "On the Sublime." *The Critical Tradition: Classic Texts and Contemporary Trends*. Ed. David Richter. New York: St. Martin's, 1989. 78-106.

Plato. *Phaedrus*. Trans. W.C. Helmbold and W.G. Rabinowitz. New York: Macmillan, 1956.

Dichotomy, Consubstantiality, Technical Writing, Literary Theory: The Double Orthodox Curse

Jasper Neel

Imagine this scene. A technical writer employed by a large computer manufacturer must update the documentation for a redesigned fluid-mechanics process control system. No new hardware has been developed, but the software, which each end user must reinstall and reconfigure, has changed considerably. The writer has one month in which to delete all the outdated material, write approximately seventy-five screens of new material, and ensure that the new documentation seems both uniform and univocal. The revised documentation, which will exist only on-line and will offer hypertext navigational features, will require about two-hundred screens. The statistical process control (SPC) oversight program will require an additional twenty screens.

Imagine a second scene. An associate professor of literature who specializes in reader-response criticism must publish a book in order to be promoted. The professor must take into account all that has already been written about reader response and must be careful to demonstrate how the new book corrects and expands prior books. Since this professor has tenure, there is no particular deadline, but writing the book is a daunting task: first because the professor must find a university press interested in publishing yet another theory book in the area of reader response, and second because the professor must write a book that will please at least two unknown and anonymous referees. Though the literature professor must use MLA documentation style and generate a text that other professors will recognize as "a book," no particular rules about length, style, or delivery system constrain the writing process.

For now, let these scenes form a split-screen backdrop as I try to articulate two different conceptions of writing that come to us from ancient Greece. My purpose in articulating these conceptions is to use them as a field in which to compare the above writing scenes. I want to know whether the two scenes are the same, merely similar, or absolutely different. More importantly, I want to know whether the two scenes imply similar, different, or mutually exclusive pedagogies. I recognize that the reader-response school does not encompass all literary theory, just as software documentation does not encompass all technical writing. I use reader response and software documentation merely as extreme examples. I want to work at the extremes to see what, if anything, they show about the middle, if any such place exists.

An Ancient Dichotomy

Writing, as Plato would have it, is at best an innocuous pastime; at worst, it is a dangerous distraction capable of generating the illusion of false wisdom and incapable of communicating true knowledge. "It shows great folly," Plato's Socrates says near the end of *Phaedrus*, "to suppose that one can transmit or acquire clear and certain knowledge of an art through the medium of writing, or that written words can do more than remind the reader of what he already knows on any given subject" (275c). According to Plato, when it comes to writing, one must believe "that nothing worth serious attention has ever been written in prose or verse" (279e). "Any serious student of serious realities," Plato says in the "Seventh Letter,"

> will shrink from making truth the helpless object of men's ill-will by committing it to writing. . . . When one sees a written composition, whether it be on law by a legislator or on any other subject, one can be sure, if the writer is a serious man, that his book does not represent his most serious thoughts; they remain stored up in the noblest region of his personality. (344b-c; see also 343b)

Aristotle does not deal quite so harshly with writing as does Plato, but he carefully places it two removes from its "content." "Spoken words," he says in the second paragraph of *De Interpretatione*, "are the symbols of mental experience and written words are the symbols of spoken words." While Aristotle admits that all people do not have the same writing or the same speech, "the mental experiences, which these directly symbolize," he argues, "are the same for all, as also are those things of which our experiences are the images" (16a5-10). I take this last clause to imply that some reality exists outside mental experience and is the universal of which mental experience is the image. I take the whole passage to imply that mental experience, the "content" that language must carry, is the same for everyone and that it exists both prior to and outside of any sort of language, whether spoken or written. In *De Anima* Aristotle repeats this quadripartite division into reality-experience-expression-inscription (431a1-10).

One can with some certainty describe the epistemological and ontological assumptions that Plato and Aristotle make about writing. Both exclude it entirely from the process of knowing, thereby separating it from invention. After this first move, however, an apparent disagreement occurs. Aristotle seems willing to allow writing to serve authorial intent. Although he does not allow writing a role in the *episteme*, neither does he condemn it utterly. Plato, of course, goes much further by separating writing absolutely from the best of a person's thought and self.

These notions of writing have widespread support. Nearly everyone who bothers to consider the matter at all agrees that writing represents speech, which in turn represents thought. Provoked to go beyond this initial notion, a few would agree with Plato, but most would agree with Aristotle. Even such trendy theorists as Richard Rorty and Jacques Derrida, when pressed to discuss the matter at all, seem to regard the teaching of writing as a classical, traditional undertaking (Olson, "Social" 6-9 and "Derrida" 4-7).

Outside university humanities departments, the Platonic and Aristotelian notions of writing predominate. Carolyn Miller has shown how the Aristotelian "windowpane" notion, expounded most forcefully in this century by A.J. Ayer, has dominated technical writing since it first appeared in the 1940s in the aerospace and electronics industries. Building on her essay, David Dobrin has explored the tradition of Cartesian rationalism that comes to us through Bacon, Locke, Burke, Spencer, and the early Wittgenstein.

There is, of course, an alternative notion of writing. But one must work a little harder to find its ancient roots. One can begin with Heraclitus, who seems to have considered all existence as a dance of opposites, with no entity able to exclude its opposite. "In writing," according to one of his few extant fragments, "the course taken, straight and crooked, is one and the same." Were one to set up a Heraclitean thought-writing duality, one would have a forever self-re-creating, transmogrifying dance of opposition, resulting in a Janus-faced notion (Stokes 478). While one can argue, as many classical scholars do, that Heraclitus built his philosophy on a unified logos, the Heraclitean "unity" is a unity of opposition resembling Saussurean "difference" if not Derridean "différance." In the *Refutatio Heresiorum*, Hippolytus quotes Heraclitus as saying, "They do not understand how that which differs with itself is in agreement: harmony consists of opposing tension, like that of the bow and the lyre." Plutarch renders the most famous Heraclitean dictum: "It is not possible to step twice into the same river. (It is impossible to touch the same mortal substance twice, but through the rapidity of change. . . . The combination and separation are simultaneous) . . ." (McLean and Aspell 35).

When one claims to see Heraclitean notions of writing in the works of Protagoras and Gorgias, one must argue inferentially because history has left us so few texts. Even so, the few scraps that remain imply notions rather different from those of Plato and Aristotle. Protagoras taught that all arguments carry within themselves their opposites; Gorgias, using a rhetorical strategy sometimes labeled "apogogic," assumed a plurality of voices for any possible argument (Barrett 9-18; see also Guthrie, Kerferd, and Sprague). Protagoras has been roundly condemned for millennia for his radical humanism ("man is the measure of all things") and his agnosticism. Gorgias has been condemned with equal vigor for his relativism: "Nothing exists," he wrote, "and if anything did exist humans could not know it, and if they could know it, they would have no means to communicate what they knew" (Freeman 125-39; Romeyer-Dherbey 7-52).

Just as one can summarize Plato and Aristotle, one can also summarize Heraclitus, Protagoras, and Gorgias. From their perspective, there is no prior place where thinking and meaning can prepare themselves for transportation in writing. If, as Heraclitus would have it, one cannot step twice into the same stream, then one cannot describe that stream as anything other than a brief, now lost, historical moment that was in the process of change even during the moment described. If, as Gorgias would have it, nothing exists, then the quadripartite Aristotelian notion of reality-experience-expression-inscription is nothing more than anthropocentric ego glorification. If, as Protagoras would have it, humankind is the measure of all things and if humans have no way to know about the existence of the gods, then Plato's divine Forms fade into triviality, if not willful self-delusion. As a result of all this, writing no longer plays a tertiary role. Rather, the unfinished and unfinishable process of writing permeates every aspect of whatever would like to present itself as outside of and prior to writing.

For the sake of convenience, I will call the Platonic-Aristotelian notion of writing classical; the Heraclitean-Protagorean-Gorgian notion sophistic.

A Modern Dichotomy

In spite of powerful theoretical work by Bazerman (6-17, 318-32), who tries to show the "situated, purposeful, strategic, symbolic activity" that makes all technical writing "rhetorical"; in spite of studies by Michael

Halloran, Greg Myers, and Jone Rymer that show the rhetorical processes of scientific writing; in spite of important pedagogical efforts by Paul Anderson to bring a kind of reader response to technical writing; in spite of the work by Dobrin and Miller mentioned above; in spite of Merrill Whitburn's entire career; the classical notion dominates both theory and praxis in the field of technical writing. One can attend an STC convention or local chapter meeting or read through the dozens of technical writing texts published each year without ever suspecting all this theory exists. For example, in explaining how to write what they call "functional documents" (a phrase that would make a theorist's imagination race), Flower, Hayes, and Swarts articulate the "'scenario principle,' which states that functional prose should be structured around a human agent performing actions in a particularized situation" (42). Readability in technical writing, according to Jack Selzer, "is simply the efficiency with which a text can be comprehended by a reader, as measured by reading time, amount recalled, questions answered, or some other quantifiable measure of a reader's ability to process a text" (73). In her Herculean effort to make "document design" into a legitimate professional specialization, Karen Schriver makes clear that technical "writers need to find ways to design text that anticipate a quick, probably passive reading." Her method is to begin with "empirical findings about users' needs" and then specify "ways to design text that meets those needs" (319-20).

The textbooks are even more forthright. "Technical writing," argue Kelley and Masse, "is writing about a subject in the pure sciences or the applied sciences in which the writer informs the reader through an objective presentation of facts" (6). "The primary . . . characteristic of technical and scientific writing," Britton contends, "lies in the effort of the author to convey one meaning and only one meaning in what he says" (11). "Because readers use a technical document," Lannon explains, "it must be based on facts, and it must have one single meaning. Poetry and fiction, then, would not be forms of technical writing because they are largely based on intuition, feelings, and imagination" (4). "Technical writing is meant to get a job done," says Markel. "Everything else is secondary" (5). "Our readers are busy people who are interested only in facts," Blicq urges. "Information they do not need irks them. For these people we must keep strictly to the point" (41). "Technical writing is ideally characterized by the maintenance of an attitude or impartiality and objectivity, by extreme care to convey information accurately and concisely, and by the absence of any attempt to arouse emotion" (Mills and Walter 5). And so on.

Look what a difference one finds when one moves to the sophistical notion of writing. Louise Phelps describes writing in that world as "marked by themes of loss, illusion, instability, marginality, decentering, and finitude" (5). Foucault and Derrida (however bitter their own disputes may have been and however much each would resent being called a sophist) articulate and exemplify the notion of writing I am describing. At the end of the Introduction to *The Archaeology of Knowledge*, after having foregrounded a notion of history as discontinuous and put the notion of "self" radically in question, Foucault turns to a sort of apologia for his *oeuvre* where he describes the sort of writing he does and approves. He concludes the description by shifting abruptly to the form of a hostile question followed by a canny answer. "Aren't you sure of what you're saying?" his made-up questioner demands,

> Are you going to change yet again, shift your position according to the questions that are put to you, and say that the objections are not really directed at the place from which you are speaking? Are you going to declare yet again that you have never been what you have been reproached with being? Are you already preparing the way out that will enable you in your next book to spring up somewhere else and declare as you're now doing: no, no I'm not where you are lying in wait for me, but over here, laughing at you?

"What," comes the canny reply,

> do you imagine that I would take so much trouble and so much pleasure in writing, do you think that I would keep so persistently to my task, if I were not preparing—with a rather shaky hand—a labyrinth into which I can venture, in which I can move my discourse, opening up underground passages, forcing it to go far from itself, finding overhangs that reduce and deform its itinerary, in which I can lose myself and appear at last to eyes that I will never have to meet again. I am no doubt not the only one who writes in order to have no face. Do not ask who I am and do not ask me to remain the same: leave it to our bureaucrats and our police to see that our papers are in order. At least spare us their morality when we write. (17)

Technical writers need no particular ingenuity to discover themselves as the "bureaucrats" and "police" who keep society's papers (machines, social services, marketing structures) "in order" so that the Foucauldian project can play itself out secure in the certainty that electricity will flow to the word processor, food will be in the market, criminals will not attack in the night.

At the end of "Plato's Pharmacy," having reduced the writer of *Phaedrus* to a state of ear-stopping confusion and uncertainty, Derrida writes and describes the play of writing: "The walled-in voice" that is written into *Phaedrus*,

> strikes against the rafters, the words come apart, bits and pieces of sentences are separated, disarticulated parts begin to circulate through the corridors, become fixed for a round or two, translate each other, become rejoined, bounce off each other, contradict each other, make trouble, tell on each other, come back like answers, organize their exchanges, protect each other, institute an internal commerce, take themselves for a dialogue. Full of meaning. A whole story. An entire history. (169-71)

The kinds of dichotomies I am making are obvious: between ancient Greek and modern Euro-American theory, between sophistical and Platonic notions of epistemology, between theory and praxis, between technical writing and literary theory, and so on. I want to keep those dichotomies as clear as possible for a while longer, working constantly to stay at the extremes.

A Practical Dichotomy

The technical writer in the scene I have described writes in a densely structured, highly determined environment. The process control and its computerization have already been invented. The system already works. While the writer must make frequent decisions about order and emphasis as well as about what the reader already knows, "topic" and "focus" are rigidly controlled. Company guidelines, which are embedded in a host publishing system that includes a required seven-level markup language, largely determine what the final document will look like. The task analysis and usability testing stages in the company's standard documentation procedure give the writer both a rigidly determined mandate and a clear evaluation of the text's successes and failures. Because much of the former documentation survives and the writer has insufficient time to rewrite it, the syntactic style has already been set, leaving little room for significant modification. A company editor will read the final text to ensure that it looks and sounds like other company publications.

These straightening factors are, however, mitigated by the comfort zone in which the writer writes. The writer remains comfortable because there is no question about the documents's value. Without documentation, the computerization remains largely useless. Although no end user is likely to read the entire text, nearly every end user will read parts of it, and no customer would even consider buying the equipment without documentation. Both the value of the writer's work and the certainty of the reader's motive remain beyond question.

Which of the two conceptions of writing informs this technical writer's situation? Almost certainly the classical. The most comfortable fit in that model occurs with Aristotle. The technical writer knows that the computer-controlled process constitutes the "reality" to be described. It exists without the documentation. Thus, the writer must learn how the computerized equipment controls the process and how to install both hardware and software. Then the writer must explain this knowledge in a CD-ROM text, conduct usability testing to ensure the effectiveness of the documentation, and revise the text in light of what the usability testing shows. Company guidelines dictate a three-part structure: first an overview explaining what the system does and protecting the manufacturer from liability suits; then an installation procedure; and finally a reference guide. Depending on what the task analysis shows, the writer may or may not include a tutorial. Someone in manufacturing will write an SPC monitoring program to ensure that the flow rate, temperature, pressure, and a host of other variables remain within defined parameters. Installing and assuring the reliability of the SPC program will be treated as a separate and particularly important part of the documentation package. Because the hypertextual function will operate across the boundaries separating the different parts of the text, at the level of hypertext the document becomes one large Aristotelian "field."

Elements of Plato do occur in this scene, even though they may remain hidden. Most, if not all, technical writers would accept Plato's dicta against the writing they do on the job. They would readily agree that their most serious thoughts do not appear in their texts. While they would hope that these texts tell the "truth" about technical processes and in fact communicate information about such processes, they would also agree that this sort of "truth" is not the most interesting sort. Process control documentation, in Plato's words, does not deal with "serious realities," merely with a technical process. Pirsig remains the paradigmatic figure here: the technical writer supporting himself as a servant of industry while seeking "Quality" on his own time.

The sophistical model plays no significant role here. Heraclitus may be right about the ontology of streams, but he is wrong about process controls. Considerable difference exists between a straight and a crooked description of the process. When, for example, some aspect of the process begins to operate outside the SPC parameters, the program will tell the operator to shut down the system. This command has no meaningful opposite. All operators will be drilled *ad nauseam* on how and why to stop the process when the program tells them to do so. Perhaps more to the point, a genuine reality test exists: either the process control update works or it does not work. Gorgias is plain wrong. The process to be controlled and the system for control both exist. The writer can learn about both and communicate the appropriate knowledge to the reader. Indeed, the technical writer's company stands legally liable if the documentation is incorrect or if the product does not do what the documentation claims.

In sum, the technical writer writes in a quite orthodox, classical world. In this world, writing (which may include all types of graphics) functions best when it functions as a conduit for verifiable, technical information. At the same time, the writing has nothing to do with, or at least operates many removes from, the writer's soul, where the best parts of the writer remain stored up to be employed and deployed for more important matters. Yes, the writer must decide on the 250 linkages for the hypertext function, linkages whose labels and chaining sequences depend on the writer's experience and intuition. Yes, many technical writers now control the product interface by participating in product design from the beginning. Nevertheless, writing in the technical writer's world fits almost perfectly into the classical conception.

Making one's way in the world as a reader-response critic, on the other hand, is rather different. To begin with, one must make obeisance to the Bleich-Fish-Holland triumvirate. And if one chooses to focus at length on describing readers, one must also take into account a trinity of hallowed theorists (Booth, Gibson, and Ong) who have already described the "implied reader," the "mock reader," and the "fictionalized audience." Since the triumvirate has already made the outrageous normal, one cannot succeed by being outrageous, which merely seems normal, and one runs the risk of vanishing entirely if one presents oneself as merely normal. Worse yet, the trinity has already staked out the simple and elegant modes of describing the reader. As a result, one must find some way of appearing normally outrageous while at the same time showing how to complicate the simple, elegant trinitarian notions.

Whereas reality for the technical writer exists in the form of hardware and software that, correctly installed and configured, moves vast quantities of viscid liquid through a pipe; reality for the reader-response critic exists in the form of a reader's responses to (canonized?) literature.

Whatever mode of validation one chooses (by appealing to a discourse community as Fish does, to subjective experience as Bleich does, to some sort of psychological modeling process as Holland does, or, as Peter Rabinowitz has recently done, by describing a multilayered reader whose roles range from actual reader and narrative reader to authorial reader and critical reader), the reality available for the reader-response critic differs markedly from that for the technical writer. No tangible, physical substance moves from the literary text to the reader's intellect. No absolutely reliable verification procedure to evaluate the reading process exists. In other words, one cannot easily imagine writing an SPC monitoring program to record violations of the reading specifications and stop the process if the reader makes too many parameter violations.

Which of the two conceptions of writing informs the literary critic's situation? Almost certainly not the classical. The critic utterly reverses Plato's notion of writing by assuming that writing is the most significant act a person can undertake. One can also infer that Aristotle's quadripartite notion gets reversed. Writing, or the ability to write, generates experience and teaches both writer and reader how to "criticize" anything that attempts to present itself as "reality." The "close reading" of literary texts coupled with the writing that grows from that reading is, to the critic, the single most important undertaking available for human beings. Whether one reads the triumvirate, the trinity, or such recent players as Rabinowitz, one cannot help noticing the absolute value placed on the writing that grows out of the reading of literature.

If Pirsig is the technical writer's model, Kafka and Hartman are the literary theorist's models. For Kafka, in an utter reversal of Plato's denunciations, writing replaced all forms of oral communication and became the only way he could think: "I hate everything that does not relate to literature," he wrote in his diary. "Conversations bore me (even if they relate to literature), to visit people bores me, the sorrows and joys of my relatives bore me to my soul. Conversation takes the importance, the seriousness, the truth, out of everything I think" (292). Hartman (as does his colleague Harold Bloom) gives this same seriousness to the writing of literary criticism, arguing that "we have entered an era that can challenge even the priority of literary to literary-critical texts." Hartman sees Longinus' criticism as being equal to the texts it treats, Derrida's as equal to the texts he (dis)interprets (17).

The sophistical seems to be the conception of writing that informs the critic's text. Almost every aspect of reader-response criticism exists as a Heraclitean opposition. To begin with, such criticism knows itself through its opposition to any of the criticisms that imply a closed, complete, accurate reading. Any particular modification of reader response (Rabinowitz's recent book being a good example) knows itself by differing from the triumvirate on one hand and from the trinity on the other. Notions about canon reformation that usually grow out of reader response exist by opposing the traditional, Anglo-male canon of the past. Just as one cannot step into the same stream twice, one cannot open the same book twice. Humanity, with all its inconsistencies, truly is the measure of everything. And nothing exists if by "existence" one means the articulation of a definitive reading of a given text. In short, writing—the never-finished processes of restatement, replacement, revaluation, and repetition—serves no greater end. The unending process of (re)writing is itself the end.

Note the differences between the undertakings of the theorist and the technical writer. Theorists neither expect nor desire that their books be the last on critical theory. They recognize at all points that their books can be unwritten. Indeed, they hope that their books will be unwritten because attempts to unwrite their books imply that those books have become so important that future theorists must account for them or get rid of them before offering their own interpretations. In other words nothing about a reader-response critic's book claims to be "correct." The joy of the book is that the new theorist can enter an old field, one presumably tilled to exhaustion, and raise a new, bountiful crop. The metaphor is apt because Plato uses it to distinguish the long, slow dialectical process toward truth from the short, easy process of using writing for trivial pastimes (*Phaedrus* 276c).

In contrast to the critic, the technical writer must fix anything in the documentation that is wrong. If, after the equipment is shipped, errors or ambiguities turn up, the writer must correct the documentation, bringing it in line with the reality of the process control. As long as the equipment remains the same, the documentation remains the same.

A Political Dichotomy

Now I can return to the questions with which I began. Are the technical writer and the theorist the same, merely similar, or utterly different? Are the pedagogical situations in literary criticism and technical writing the same, similar, or different?

Aristotle contends that arguing both sides of a question has the salutary effect of teaching the correct position because proofs are always easier to generate for the "right" side of any issue (*Rhetoric* 1355a).

Although one can certainly imagine how to argue that reader-response criticism and process control software documentation are alike, one can (perhaps with more ease) imagine how to argue that they differ profoundly. The differences are obvious. Whereas the technical writer documents a computer-controlled mechanical process, a process that must be activated and maintained following the instructions, the theorist offers nothing of the sort. People had read literature for millennia before the appearance in 1938 of Louise Rosenblatt's *Literature as Exploration*, the text usually considered to be the first attempt at reader-response theory. No one having trouble reading will ever refer back to Rosenblatt or Fish or even Booth to discover what has been configured or installed improperly or where the error in the system of reading lies. An act of reader-response criticism includes no product liability disclaimer because no critic has ever worried that someone might sue if the reading procedure described fails to work (whatever "work" might mean in such a scenario). The "knowledge" that emerges from hallowed texts such as *The Rhetoric of Fiction* or *Is There a Text in This Class?* is not technical; one cannot know it in the way one can know how to operate a process control system.

What of pedagogy? Does training in one form of writing support teaching in the other? All technical writing teachers know what literature faculty would say. The notion of an experienced technical writer offering a long list of successful technical manuals as justification for teaching literature courses would be regarded as perversely evil by every literature faculty. Of course, literature faculty do not object to literature professors teaching technical writing. As we all know, most professors of technical writing were trained in literature, and a shockingly high percentage (certainly more than 75 percent) of them have never written a technical manual of any sort. Worse yet, most of them, in Schriver's words, work as "untenured instructors or part-time adjunct faculty" because their literature colleagues regard their world as "atheoretical, anti-humanistic, smacking too much of the material world, and uninteresting" (323).

Do the pedagogies differ as profoundly as the acts of writing? Obviously I think they do, and I will end by trying to contrast the two pedagogies. One pedagogy values ambiguation and the increase of complexity. Tracing the increasing complexity of trinitarian notions of reader response shows this. Walker Gibson's 1950 essay describing the "mock reader" consists of five pages. Wayne Booth's 1961 book includes about thirty pages on the "implied reader." Walter Ong's 1977 book includes about sixty-five pages describing the "fictionalized audience." Peter Rabinowitz's 1987 book contains more than 150 pages on the roles of and rules for being a reader.

Looking from the perspective of the triumvirate, anyone can see how much more complex notions of the reader are now than they were in 1968 when Norman Holland published *The Dynamics of Literary Response*. This book, which had been preceded in 1938 by Rosenblatt's, was followed in 1972 by Wolfgang Iser's *The Implied Reader*, in 1975 by Holland's *5 Readers Reading*, in 1978 by Iser's *The Act of Reading* and David Bleich's *Subjective Criticism*, and then in 1980 by Stanley Fish's *Is There a Text in This Class?* and Jane Tompkins' collection of essays *Reader-Response Criticism*. After 1980, reader response expanded across North America developing into a full-fledged methodology as widespread and dominant as the New Criticism ever was. Each successive reader-response text makes the notion of reading more complicated, more fraught with layers, uncertainties, and difficulties. With the appearance in 1989 of Fish's *Doing What Comes Naturally*, the notion of "naturalness" in the reading process had taken on a kind of complexity comparable to that in quantum theory.

In contrast, the technical writer works constantly to make the documentation less complicated, briefer, less necessary. The currently impossible (but not unthinkable!) ideal would be a computerized process control system that installs, configures, and operates itself. In short, one pedagogy calls for an increasingly plurisignificant, increasingly expansive notion of writing, while the other calls for an increasingly univocal, increasingly reductive notion. More literary interpretation is better than less; there cannot possibly be enough. Less computer documentation is better than more; any at all is too much.

Professors of literary interpretation will go to almost any length to avoid telling students what to do in their papers. The single most annoying question posed to such professors goes like this: "If you'll just tell me what you want, I'll try to do it." Professors have to bite their tongues to avoid replying, "You reveal your naivete about intellectual matters by asking me to turn you into a trained technician." After all, specific directions about what to do defeat the purpose and limit the student's creativity. The notion of a rigidly standard essay format with codified rules for organization, structure, authorial voice, evidence, syntax, and interpretation violates the point of literary interpretation. Students must work their own way through their assignments just as Rabinowitz, as a relative latecomer in 1987, had to create his own way to participate in the exceedingly crowded field of reader response. Every honest professor of literary interpretation would admit that a paper that gets "A" from one professor might very well get "D" from another and vice versa. New insight, surprise, idiosyncrasy—these are the qualities that please the theorist.

In a technical writing class, however, it would be quite ordinary for students to write in a hierarchical markup language rigidly controlled both by the host publishing system and by the standard format for the particular task at hand. It would be quite ordinary for technical writing professors to articulate the rules of format, appearance, content, organization, structure, authorial voice, syntax, and evidence (if such a notion as "evidence" obtains). In extreme cases, students might be asked to document software. The "grading" procedure for their documents would consist of having a representative member of the target audience try to run the program. If the documentation works with no glitches or bugs, "A"; with just a few, "B"; with several but not enough to halt the program, "C"; with enough to threaten the program's execution, "D"; if the program fails, "F." Professors merely watch their linked terminals as users try to implement documentation. Everyone starts at "A." As bugs, glitches, and failures multiply, the grade drops. While different professors might draw slightly different lines between "A" and "B," no student whose documentation runs smoothly would get a grade below "B," and no student whose documentation fails to run the program would get a grade above "F." Most important of all, however, the technical writing professor will (or certainly should) build usability testing into the documentation process. Thus, only students who do not follow the assignment through its proper steps could ever reach the point of having their documentation fail. In other words, a properly run software documentation class leaves no room for failure. The whole point is the elimination of chance, guesswork, surprise and idiosyncrasy. Each writing task has a specific technical function to enable. Close collaboration among students as well as between students and professor ensures that, by the end of the term, everyone has an operational text, a text that has already been tried and found successful in the usability testing stage. Perhaps this is why the mere existence of a course entitled "Technical Documentation" both mystifies and horrifies most literature faculty.

And so we have these extremes. When they are drawn this way, technical writing suffers a sort of double orthodox curse. Literary theorists cannot help holding technical writers in contempt; the theoretical assumptions of literary theory demand it. Sophistical theory would not even allow technical documentation to present itself to the world as writing. It would be like trying to run a DOS program on an Apple with no interface software. To the theorist working from a sophistical base (and obviously I do not believe a theorist can operate from any other base), technical documentation simply is not interesting. Bruffee, for example, may claim social constructionism for writing in general, and Edward Barrett may apply that notion to the virtual environment of a hypertextual situation, but mentioning "social construction" to the theorist whose work supposedly enabled it produces nothing but a snort of condescension, as both the Rorty interview (Bruffee's response notwithstanding) and the repeated sneers of Stanley Fish clearly show. Barrett can claim that through the ideology of social construction, hypertext "escapes from the collapsed inner world of the machine and enters history" (xiv), but you can bet no theorists are reading his arguments, or even know where to look for them.

At the other extreme the technical writer does have a classical base, but this classical base reduces technical writing either to trivial pastime or to slavery. Worse yet, the literary theorist can (and usually does!) leap into the classical world and claim to be on a Platonic, dialectical journey toward Truth, a journey that never ends, a journey in which writing does in fact function as a pastime record of lovers' dialectical discussions in the office and the classroom.

How do we begin some sort of Rogerian argument? Technical writing teachers can initiate such a discussion in two ways. First, they can show that the extreme case of software documentation for an SPC-monitored process control system does not encompass all of technical writing. They can explain the complexities of proposals, of reports, and of technical writing assignments that involve the writer in a ground-up way so that the writer has input from the beginning. Second, technical writing teachers can study critical theory so as to understand what it shows not only about canonized literature but also about technical writing. They can bring poststructural analysis to bear on almost any technical writing situation, showing its full complexity and trying to avoid the tendency toward oversimplification. Certainly they can use poststructural analysis to debunk plain language notions or simplified English programs.

But Rogerian argument does require an interlocutor. If technical writing teachers attempt some sort of rapprochement (Rogerian or otherwise), will there be anyone to talk with? In submitting this essay to ***JAC*** I rest quite confident that no subscriber will have difficulty with it.

Even though it relies on Foucault, Derrida, reader-response theory, classical rhetoric, contemporary theories of argument, and the jargon of both composition studies and software documentation, all readers of ***JAC*** will understand my jargon with no trouble whatsoever. To what degree is that true of literature professors? How many of them would know what Rogerian argument is? How many would imagine that they could learn about teaching literature by reading *Technical Communication* or listening to a talk by Karen Schriver?

As long as we inhabit a political structure where one can qualify to teach technical writing by studying literature but not the reverse, is a conversation possible? Or are we forced to operate at the extremes I have described? In other words, can the middle become a hospitable neighborhood only through the good will and effort of the people who operate at what the other people regard not as an opposite extreme but as an intellectual vacuum?

Where are the departments that are truly strong at both extremes, yet have a Rogerian discussion of the differences going on? The sort of department I mean would offer work in technical and professional writing comparable to that at Rensselaer or Carnegie Mellon and literary theory comparable to that at Duke or Berkeley. Am I wrong in assuming that technical writers can and do move all the way from one extreme to the other, while literature professors do not see themselves either at an extreme or as part of any sort of continuum that would, if followed far enough, reach to the writing of software documentation for a process control?

Works Cited

Anderson, Paul V. *Technical Writing: A Reader-Centered Approach.* New York: Harcourt, 1987.

Aristotle. *De Anima (On the Soul). Aristotle: On the Soul, Parva Naturalia, On Breath.* Trans. W.S. Hett. Cambridge: Harvard UP, 1936. 2-203.

—. *De Interpretatione.* Trans. E.M. Edghill. *The Works of Aristotle.* Ed. W.D. Ross. London: Oxford, 1928. 16a-23b.

—. *Rhetoric and Poetics.* Trans. W. Rhys Roberts and Ingram Bywater. New York: Modern Library, 1954.

Barrett, Edward. "Introduction." *Society of Text: Hypertext, Hypermedia, and the Social Construction of Information.* Ed. Edward Barrett. Cambridge: MIT P, 1989. xi-xviii.

Barrett, Harold. *The Sophists: Rhetoric, Democracy, and Plato's Idea of Sophistry.* Navato, CA: Chandler, 1987.

Bazerman, Charles. *Shaping Written Knowledge: The Genre and Activity of the Experimental Article in Science.* Madison: U of Wisconsin P, 1988.

Bleich, David. *Subjective Criticism.* Baltimore: Johns Hopkins UP, 1978.

Blicq, Ron S. *Technically—Write! Communications in a Technological Era.* 3rd ed. Englewood Cliffs, NJ: Prentice, 1986.

Bloom, Harold. *The Anxiety of Influence: A Theory of Poetry.* New York: Oxford UP, 1973.

Booth, Wayne C. *The Rhetoric of Fiction.* Chicago: U of Chicago P, 1961.

Britton, Earl. "What is Technical Writing? A Redefinition." *The Teaching of Technical Writing.* Ed. D.H. Cunningham and H.A. Estrin. Urbana: NCTE, 1975. 23-33.

Bruffee, Kenneth A. "Response to the ***JAC*** Interview with Richard Rorty." *Journal of Advanced Composition* 10 (1990): 145-46.

—. "Social Construction, Language, and the Authority of Knowledge: A Bibliographical Essay." *College English* 48 (1986): 773-90.

Derrida, Jacques. "Différance." *Margins of Philosophy.* Trans. Alan Bass. Chicago: U of Chicago P, 1982. 1-27.

—. *Dissemination.* Trans. Barbara Johnson. Chicago: U of Chicago P, 1981.

Dobrin, David. "What's Technical About Technical Writing?" *New Essays in Technical and Scientific Communication: Research, Theory, Practice.* Ed. Paul V. Anderson, R. John Brockman, and Carolyn Miller. Farmingdale, NY: Baywood, 1983. 227-50.

Fish, Stanley. *Doing What Comes Naturally.* Durham: Duke UP, 1989.

—. *Is There a Text in This Class?* Cambridge: Harvard UP, 1980.

Flower, Linda, John R. Hayes, and Heidi Swarts. "Revising Functional Documents: The Scenario Principle." *New Essays in Technical and Scientific Communication.* Ed. Paul V. Anderson, R. John Brockman, and Carolyn Miller. Farmingdale, NY: Baywood, 1983. 41-58.

Foucault, Michel. *The Archaeology of Knowledge and The Discourse on Language.* Trans. A.M. Sheridan Smith. New York: Pantheon, 1972.

Freeman, Kathleen. *Ancilla to the Pre-Socratic Philosophers.* Cambridge: Harvard UP, 1966.

Gibson, Walker. "Authors, Speakers, Readers, and Mock Readers." *College English* 11 (1950): 265-69.

Guthrie, W.K.C. *A History of Greek Philosophy*, Vol 1. Cambridge: Cambridge UP, 1967.

Halloran, S. Michael. "The Birth of Molecular Biology: An Essay in the Rhetorical Criticism of Scientific Discourse." *Rhetoric Review* 3 (1984): 70-83.

Hartman, Geoffrey. *Saving the Text: Literature, Derrida, Philosophy.* Baltimore: Johns Hopkins UP, 1981.

Holland, Norman. *The Dynamics of Literary Response.* New York: Oxford UP, 1968.

—. *5 Readers Reading.* New Haven: Yale UP, 1975.

Iser, Wolfgang. *The Act of Reading.* Baltimore: Johns Hopkins UP, 1976.

—. *The Implied Reader.* Baltimore: Johns Hopkins UP, 1972.

Kafka, Franz. *The Diaries of Franz Kafka.* Ed. Max Brod. Trans. Joseph Kresh. 2 vols. New York: Schocken, 1948.

Kelley, Patrick, and Roger Masse. "A Definition of Technical Writing." *The Technical Writing Teacher* 4 (1977): 94-97.

Kerferd, G.B. *The Sophistic Movement.* Cambridge: Cambridge UP, 1981.

Lannon, John M. *Technical Writing.* 3rd ed. Boston: Little, 1985.

Markel, Michael H. *Technical Writing: Situations and Strategies.* 2nd ed. New York: St. Martin's, 1987.

McLean, George F., and Patrick J. Aspell, eds. *Readings in Ancient Western Philosophy.* New York: Appleton, 1970.

Miller, Carolyn R. "A Humanistic Rationale for Technical Writing." *College Writing* 40 (1979): 610-17.

Mills, Gordon H., and John A. Walter. *Technical Writing.* 5th ed. New York: Holt, 1986.

Myers, Greg. "The Social Construction of Two Biologists' Proposals." *Written Communication* 2 (1985): 219-45.

Olson, Gary A. "Jacques Derrida on Rhetoric and Composition: A Conversation." *Journal of Advanced Composition* 10 (1990): 1-21.

—. "Social Construction and Composition Theory: A Conversation with Richard Rorty." *Journal of Advanced Composition* 9 (1989): 1-9.

Ong, Walter. *Interfaces of the Word: Studies in the Evolution of Consciousness and Culture.* Ithaca, NY: Cornell UP, 1977.

Phelps, Louise Wetherbee. *Composition as a Human Science: Contributions to the Self-Understanding of a Discipline.* New York: Oxford UP, 1988.

Pirsig, Robert. *Zen and the Art of Motorcycle Maintenance.* New York: Bantam, 1974.

Plato. *Phaedrus and the Seventh and Eighth Letters.* Trans. Walter Hamilton. New York: Penguin, 1973.

Rabinowitz, Peter J. *Beyond Reading: Narrative Conventions and the Politics of Interpretation.* Ithaca, NY: Cornell UP, 1987.

Romeyer-Dherbey, Gilbert. *Les Sophists.* Paris: Presses Universitaires de France, 1985.

Rosenblatt, Louise. *Literature as Exploration.* 1938. New York: Barnes, 1976.

Rymer, Jone. "Scientific Composing Processes: How Eminent Scientists Write Journal Articles." *Writing in Academic Disciplines.* Ed. David Joliffe. Norwood: Ablex, 1988.

Saussure, Ferdinand de. *Course in General Linguistics.* Trans. Wade Baskin. 1959. New York: McGraw, 1966.

Schriver, Karen A. "Document Design from 1980-1989: Challenges That Remain." *Technical Communication* 36 (1989): 316-31.

Selzer, Jack. "What Constitutes a 'Readable' Technical Style." *Essays in Technical and Scientific Communication: Research, Theory, Practice.* Ed. Paul V. Anderson, R. John Brockman, and Carolyn Miller. Farmingdale, NY: Baywood, 1983. 71-89.

Sprague, Rosamond K., ed. *The Older Sophists.* Columbia: South Carolina UP, 1972.

Stokes, Michael C. "Heraclitus of Ephesus." *The Encyclopedia of Philosophy.* Ed. Paul Edwards, et al. Vol. 3. New York: Macmillan, 1967. 477-81. 4 vols.

Tompkins, Jane. *Reader-Response Criticism: From Formalism to Post-Structuralism.* Baltimore: Johns Hopkins UP, 1980.

Writing in the Graduate Curriculum: Literary Criticism as Composition

Patricia A. Sullivan

In 1900, the Pedagogical Section of the Modern Language Association sent a questionnaire to its members asking their opinion as to whether rhetoric was a proper subject for graduate work in English, and, if they felt that it was not, what they regarded as "their strongest reasons for excluding it from the list of graduate studies" (Mead xx). In reporting the results of the survey, W.E. Mead acknowledged that "owing to the prevalent vagueness of conception as to what Rhetoric really is and should cover, the various reports read a little like debates on a question in which the meaning of leading terms has not been agreed upon" (xx). Nonetheless, he was able to conclude that those professors who viewed rhetoric as a "science" generally felt that it had a legitimate place in the graduate curriculum, while those who construed rhetoric to mean "the arts of discourse" or "composition" felt that it was not a proper subject for graduate work. Those in the latter group shared what we would now call a "current-traditional" view of composition, as the following excerpts from Mead's report attest:

> Regarding Rhetoric as the art of speaking and writing correctly, I am of the opinion that it is an unsuitable subject for graduate study.
>
> Rhetoric should be mastered in its practical aspects before the student completes his undergraduate study; but as a science I believe it is eminently suited for graduate work.
>
> A graduate student should, of course, be able to present in appropriate literary form the results of labor in his chosen field; but he should have done preparatory work to that end before he became a graduate student.
>
> Mere theme-writing, however sublimated or raised even to the *n*th power, ought never to be a part of the credits for a higher degree.
>
> The object of teaching Rhetoric is not theoretical but practical, as

> propadeutic to composition and literature, and the undergraduate course should suffice for this. The graduate course should be literature itself, which has no limit. (xxii-xxx)

Equated with "speaking and writing correctly," "theme-writing," and presenting "results" in "appropriate literary form," writing was perceived as a set of skills that a student "mastered" before undertaking the graduate study of "literature itself." Such skills were presumably manifest in the papers the student composed, so that flaws in form could be taken as signs of intellectual deficiency, perhaps even an inherent unsuitability to the demands of literary study, as one of the more surly responses to Scott's questionnaire suggests: "When a man has obtained his A.B. degree, he ought to be able to write his language with sufficient correctness to be responsible in the future for his own style. If he has not thus learned to write reasonably well he probably never will learn" (xxii).

In the decades that have passed since the MLA conducted its survey, developments in literary theory and composition have radically altered the nature of English studies. Literary theory has come to concentrate on the activity of reading, the processes by which readers reconstruct texts. Contemporary theories of reading revise the relationship between texts and readers, displacing the authority and autonomy of texts by recognizing the constitutive powers of language and readers' creative capacities as language users. Accordingly, to read and interpret a literary work is to shape or modify or reconstitute the work "itself" (or what was formerly viewed as a static, autonomous object) so that the text that was formerly accorded an independent status is now viewed as a function of our scholarly and critical discourse. In a similar vein, composition theory has shifted its emphasis from the formal product to the activity of composing—the complex interplay of linguistic, cognitive, rhetorical, social, and cultural processes by which texts come into being. From the generative rhetorics and expressivist pedagogies of the 1960s to more recently articulated social and cultural theories of writing, composition has steadily moved in the direction of a constitutive theory of discourse, one which emphasizes both the agency of the writer and the importance of context in the production of meaning. Literary studies and composition, then, would now seem to share a common theoretical basis and not merely a common home in English departments. Indeed, as Jay Robinson has pointed out, "Theories linking reading and writing are becoming the dominant ones among those who study either reading or composition—theories that reconceive reading as the active construction of texts and their meanings; theories that reconceive writing as an act of perpetual making, perpetual revision, with publication or submission for a grade an arbitrary stopping point" (492).

In his introduction to *The Social Mission of English Criticism*, Chris Baldick addresses the pedagogical implications of contemporary theories of criticism and observes that "the real content of the school and college subject which goes under the name 'English literature' is not literature in the primary sense but criticism"; the student "is required to compose, not tragic dramas, but essays in criticism" (4-5). Significantly, Baldick not only identifies the "real content" of literary studies as criticism but also reminds us that criticism must be composed, that a student's work in literary studies—whether it goes by the name of interpretation, criticism, or analysis—entails acts of writing as well as reading. In limiting this insight to a school and college subject, however, Baldick, like many other scholars and educators today, implicitly reinforces the notion that composition properly belongs in the undergraduate curriculum, a notion which still allows us to represent literature and composition as separate intellectual activities in graduate courses. While graduate programs now admit rhetoric as an area of concentration or specialization for the Ph.D., it is rhetoric conceived as a "science," a method of analyzing the art of discourse rather than the practice of this "art" in its own right. Most graduate faculty assume that graduate students, by definition, "already know how to write," and thus writing assumes a secondary and often marginal role in graduate education. The written product, but not the writing process, compels the attention of graduate faculty. In this respect, graduate courses today still bear a remarkable resemblance to the tacit curriculum which Mead uncovered in the MLA survey ninety years ago. Despite development of theories which emphasize the processes and contexts of interpretation, we are still tied to current-traditional modes of writing instruction, for while we have allowed contemporary critical theories to inform our teaching of literature, we have not investigated the ways such theories problematize our assumptions about writing. In the remainder of this essay, I will explore the disjuncture between theory and practice to argue for a reconceptualization of the nature and role of writing in the graduate curriculum.

Writing in Graduate Literature Courses

To discern whether developments in critical theory and composition research were having a discernible impact on the pedagogical practices of graduate faculty and on the writing practices of graduate students in literary studies, I conducted a two-part study of graduate-student writing. First, I surveyed graduate students in English at six universities to learn what kinds of writing they had been assigned in their courses that term and the rhetorical frameworks in which these assignments had been cast.[1] I followed the survey with case studies of two master's and two doctoral students enrolled in four different literature seminars (Twentieth-Century American Literature, Studies in Hawthorne, Studies in Shakespeare, and Restoration Drama) at one of the universities I surveyed.[2] For each case study, I observed courses, interviewed the student before, during, and after the course, collected drafts and revisions of the writing he or she did in response to course assignments, and interviewed the professor of the course at the end of the term. My intent in presenting this study is not so much to offer the results of data-driven research as to highlight and illustrate, through the actual experiences of graduate-student writers, the broader theoretical issues underlying this essay.

From the survey, I learned that a great deal of writing is assigned in graduate courses in English, but writing is seldom taught as a process integral to the study of literature. The most common writing assignment reported by the one hundred graduate students who completed the survey was a term paper of fifteen pages or more. Seventy percent of the graduate students reported that they were assigned term papers of at least fifteen pages in their courses (with creative writing workshops and teaching practica excepted) during the term that the survey was conducted. Somewhat less frequently assigned were short (three to five page) and medium length (six to fifteen page) papers; forty-five and fifty-one students, respectively, reported they were assigned at least one paper of those lengths. Journals, essay exams, one-to-two-page "response" or "position" papers, and bibliographies comprised the other types of writing assigned. Of ninety-five students who responded that they had written or were writing at least one paper of medium length or longer, less than twenty percent reported that their professors had assigned or suggested paper topics or had discussed in class how to formulate arguments, conduct research, or develop ideas. Less than ten percent reported that their professors had asked to see or respond to drafts before the final version was evaluated, had asked the students to share their written work with other students in the class, or had specified an audience or suggested a forum other than the professors themselves.

In many respects, the four case studies confirmed the findings of the survey. In three of the four courses I observed, lengthy term papers were assigned and were due at the end of the term; little discussion occurred with regard to the papers in terms of their purpose, method of development, audience, or forum. In one of these courses (American Literature), the term paper was preceded by a short, analytical essay which was due at midterm; in another course (Shakespeare), a series of two-page "position" papers preceded the term paper; and in the third (Hawthorne), the term paper was the sole writing assignment. In the fourth course I observed (Restoration Drama), students were asked to keep a journal, which was collected and graded both at midterm and at the term's end but which was read only by the professor. Each of the four students who participated in the study reported that a term paper was the most commonly assigned writing task in their graduate experience, and none could recall receiving explicit instructions about content, purpose, or audience. Finally, with the exception of the student enrolled in the Shakespeare seminar, none of the students read or responded to another graduate student's paper in the courses I observed, and only one student said that he had done so in a previous graduate course.

The results of my survey and case studies suggest that under the current pedagogical model, the completed assignment is privileged over its production, the written product over the writing process. A pedagogical distinction is drawn, in other words, between course content and course assignments, between subject matter and what the student writes. Writing is separated from the study of a subject (an author or period) and relegated to the bottom tier of a tacit hierarchy of discursive practices—of reading, speaking, and writing. The most important "object" of three of the seminars I observed, both in terms of their subject matter and their *raison d'etre*, was the set of literary texts studied. (In none of these courses was secondary sources—scholarly or critical articles—made part of the required reading that the class discussed as a group.) The most important activity of these courses was reading. That is, students read the assigned set of literary texts to cover or to "know" the material and to critique, interpret, or otherwise analyze the texts themselves. Such "readings" were shared either through class discussion or through an oral report that was the responsibility of an individual student. Since students were expected to give formal evidence of their reading of literary texts and their awareness of critical issues, they were asked to write. But unlike the literary texts themselves and class discussion of those texts, the student's writing was not valued for what it contributed to the course and to other students' understanding of the issues. Rather, it was valued primarily for its evaluative properties as an academic exercise, as the basis for a grade.

I should point out that contemporary theories of criticism were mentioned and in some instances discussed at length in all but one course (Studies in Hawthorne, which was tacitly informed by the tenets and close-reading methodology of New Criticism.) In Restoration Drama, for example, the professor took pains to show how Dryden presaged poststructuralist, reader-response, and dialogic theories in his "Essay on Dramatic Poesy." Class discussion in Studies in Shakespeare frequently turned to feminist critiques of character, scene, and plot; and the professor incorporated such critiques in the list of topics he periodically distributed to the class for written analysis in their position papers and for in-class discussion. And in Twentieth-Century American Literature, the professor transformed his frequently acknowledged ambivalence toward contemporary critical theory into an ongoing, reflexive commentary upon the current state of literary studies, invoking its central pragmatic problem—"what you're to do as a critic"—to defend his own belief that "one should look closely at the text." In none of these courses, however, did awareness of theory translate into a comparable theory or pedagogy of writing. That is, each course reflected a text-based, product-centered approach to composition. Students were expected to produce critical essays, term papers, and a journal; but in each case, it was up to the student to discover a significant topic or issue, determine lines of reasoning that would resolve the issue, construct the audience to whom the discourse would be addressed, and devise a purpose for communicating. In some courses, professors acknowledged that a particular critical approach would make a difference in the way students read a particular text or set of texts, but no suggestion was made that such an approach might similarly influence the students' writing—the shape, voice, argument, or style of their discourse.

Although many of us wish to claim in theory that a distinction between literature and its interpretations is no longer tenable, our practices continue to emphasize the substance, not the act, of interpretation, for we continue to attend only to the ends, and not the means, of written production. The contexts for writing in many graduate literature courses are, in this sense, arhetorical, for writing does not take place within, or as a fundamental part of, the courses themselves. Writing is nearly always a matter of individual performance, a solitary act rather than a social or collaborative experience. This act most often occurs at the conclusion of course work, in the form of a term paper, so that a student's critical or scholarly discourse is removed from the course itself as a context for inquiry and learning. And the student's work is most often read by a single reader, the professor; students do not write for one another. Thus, acts of writing are both marginalized and privatized in the graduate classroom; literary texts are given precedence over the texts that the students themselves compose, and even in courses where theory is made part of the interpretive context, such theories are not translated into a comparable theory or pedagogy of writing.

Implicit in this pedagogical model, as I noted earlier, is the assumption that graduate students "already know how to write" by virtue of their higher educational status. This assumption is, I believe, the cognitive corollary of a current-traditional theory of writing and a product-oriented pedagogy: writing itself is conceived as a set of skills that a student "masters" at some point in his or her educational life. The point at which an individual makes the transformation from "novice" to "expert" may vary from student to student, but it is presumed to occur before the student attains a bachelor's degree so that the teaching of writing to graduate students is held to be redundant or superfluous.[3] If writing problems manifest themselves in a text a graduate student composes, such problems can be attributed to personal deficiency, not institutional *praxis*.

Recent composition scholarship, particularly that which takes a social view of the writing process, has shown "mastery" to be an exceedingly arbitrary concept; writing well is as much a function of context—the particular task at hand and the situation or situatedness of the writer—as of personal experience. The writer, regardless of ability, is subject to the conventions and constraints that inform his or her particular rhetorical situation. But for graduate students in literary studies, the arts of rhetoric are still equated with "speaking and writing correctly" and "presenting results in appropriate literary form"—in short, with the set of skills the student presumably mastered before undertaking graduate study. And so graduate students are simply asked to set these basic skills in motion and bring their professors the finished product, which is then evaluated according to how well it approximates an ideal, but apparently unteachable, text.

The assumption that writing is an automatic process is so deeply embedded in the collective unconscious (indeed, I would argue, in the political unconscious) of English departments that the term "composition" has come to serve, as James Slevin points out, as a synecdoche for "all the activities that are in fact undertaken within composition" (547). Most often the term designates a specific course—usually first-year English—so that composition is construed as an activity that only undergraduates engage in. The labels "First-Year English" or even

"Advanced Composition" serve the institutional function of putting composition in its proper place, but they also allow us to suppress and evade the rhetoricity of our own discipline: the ways complex interrelations of topic, audience, voice, genre, gender, culture, convention, disciplinary context, and self become folded into our own and our students' construction or reconstruction of texts. The institutionalized suppression and evasion of writing, moreover, leads us to reenact modes of instruction at the graduate level—such as assigning papers that will be read only when the course is over—that mirror an earlier world, a world or *Weltanschauung* that has been superseded by constitutive theories of reading and writing. The problem with such traditional modes, as David Punter argues, is that they "do almost nothing to help students to understand what literary *work* might be; . . . an enormous weight [is] placed on written production, and at the same time this production is required to fit into pre-established molds" (220). As a result, Punter says, "an alienated self, formed according to the imagined desires of the institution, attempts to speak to another alienated self, caught between subjectivity and convention . . ." (221). Punter's representation of the student writer as a self caught between subjectivity and convention is particularly apt of the graduate-student writer, whose discourse emanates from the dual (and oftentimes conflicting) ethos of both "graduate" and "student." Elsewhere I have discussed the conflicts this dual ethos or double perspective engenders for graduate students' perceptions of audience as they write essays on literature ("Writers'"). Here I wish to focus on two additional problems that graduate students encounter in the act of writing as a result of the current disjuncture between theory and pedagogical practice: problems of invention (the processes by which they formulate issues to write about) and argumentation (the manner of discourse in which these issues are explored and resolved.)

Invention, Tradition, and Individual Talent

In "The University and the Prevention of Culture," Gerald Graff writes, "A literary education that operationally boils down to a series of blunt confrontations with texts 'in themselves' will leave students at a loss as to what they are to say about literature. For the problem is that literary texts in themselves go only so far in telling us what we are supposed to say about them" (78). As a critical theorist, Graff identifies the problem of "what to say" about literary texts as a problem of reading, a problem whose solution depends on students' training in critical approaches that counter New Criticism's emphasis on the text itself. Graff nominates "speech act theory, pragmatism, and various forms of reader-response criticism" as possible contenders to the New Critical throne because each takes into account the linguistic codes and cultural values that exist, not in the text, but in the interaction between text and reader. While I share Graff's misgivings about text-oriented theories of reading which ignore the agency of the reader and contingencies of context, I wish to reconstrue the problem of what to say about literature as a problem of writing—more specifically, as part of a problematic of writing that both presumes and subsumes what Graff has posed as a problem of reading. The student who is assigned a piece of writing must have something to say, and if that writer is a graduate student, he or she must often say it for fifteen pages or more. While other disciplines routinely assign topics for research projects and papers at the graduate level, English studies nearly always leaves finding a topic part of the writing task, a task, moreover, that is completed as an addendum to rather than integral part of the course which forms the occasion for inquiry. While graduate students talk about literary texts in class, thereby having the benefit of a communal exchange of ideas, they most often write papers as individual, autonomous "subjects," isolated from the "interpretive community" which provided a forum for their ideas as members of a class.

The experiences of the two doctoral students who participated in my study, Karen and John, cast into relief what Graff has posed as a problem of reading and what I have posed as a problem of writing: both students found themselves at a loss of "what to say" at some moment of their writing processes as they endeavored to compose critical discourse to meet their respective writing assignments. At the outset of her seminar on Hawthorne, Karen confided that she wished professors would propose topics more often because, she noted, "there's always more to be said, but it isn't always obvious." Karen's course focused exclusively on the Hawthorne canon—the author's novels, tales, and sketches—which the class read closely and analyzed, in Karen's words, "mainly to cover the material." As Karen read the assigned texts in the course, she became intrigued by Hawthorne's use of a particular narrative technique in his fiction. As she put it, "There's a storyteller telling a story about a story, and I see it over and over again, and that's intriguing to me, and I want to sit down and analyze when and where he does it and why he does it." She hoped to explore Hawthorne's use of storytellers in her term paper. By the end of the course, however, Karen felt she could not begin to answer the question of why Hawthorne used that particular technique without knowing more about the narrative tradition in which Hawthorne was writing, and the seminar's emphasis on coverage and close reading of Hawthorne's works themselves left her with no time to conduct inquiry into outside sources. She felt she lacked the "right context" to explore her topic further, so she went to see her professor with that specific problem in mind: "I told him what I was interested in but that the more I thought about it the more I felt, 'There's just no topic here.' I asked, 'What am I going to write about once I get past the first paragraph?'"

In essence, Karen posed a question about writing; she could say, in her first paragraph, what she had observed about Hawthorne's use of a storyteller, and she could point out when and where he used this device; but she could not say why. Karen's professor, however, deferred to her judgment that she had no topic and suggested she think of something else to write about. If she could not see what directions her topic might lead her given her close readings of the Hawthorne canon and whatever criticism she might read in the allotted time, he told her, she should probably choose a different topic.

John identified himself in our initial interview as "a historical scholar," interested in "historical accuracy rather than aesthetic evaluation," but he noted (in a remark similar to Karen's wish that professors would suggest topics more often) that he was becoming "somewhat disillusioned with scholarship" because he has "this finite sense that all that can be written has." Nonetheless, John discovered a topic to write about during his seminar on Restoration Drama. Midway through the seminar, John became taken with Dryden's *All for Love* and wanted to explore his "intuitive feeling" that Dryden's version of the Antony and Cleopatra story was the "superior work." He began reading and meticulously summarizing other versions of the play and some works of secondary criticism on *All for Love* in his journal to gauge critical responses to the plays, and this activity consumed much of his time for the remainder of the course. He then went to speak to a former professor and mentor about issues that remained to be resolved with respect to the Antony and Cleopatra plot beyond the critical responses he had catalogued; however, he was told, in effect, that there was virtually nothing left to be done. In essence, the professor confirmed the fear John had expressed weeks earlier: his "finite sense that all that can be written has."

Karen's experience speaks to the immediate problem a student encounters when a literature course is primarily devoted, in Graff's words, to a blunt confrontation with texts themselves: the close reading model in the Hawthorne seminar left Karen without a coherent theoretical context for framing, developing, and evaluating her ideas, and so she was left wondering what to say in her term paper "beyond the first paragraph." Karen's difficulty in developing her topic, in other words, can be traced to constraints inherent in the course itself. John's experience, on the other hand, reveals a potential dilemma for graduate students that transcends the immediate course as the context for writing—what work there is left to do, what the student can contribute to an ongoing conversation or to what Adena Rosmarin calls the "interpretive history of a work" that hasn't already been said. Unlike the constraints that Karen encountered, John had ample time to read outside sources and to read intertextually, and his professor's assignment of a journal afforded him multiple opportunities to probe and refine his topic. Nonetheless, he too reached a point at which he wondered what to say, what work was left to be done.

Although specific features of each student's discourse situation were different, the problems Karen and John experienced in writing and the strategies by which they set out to resolve these problems were similar in some significant and revealing ways. First, both students found themselves trying to invent an *issue* for writing; that is, while each had a specific topic in mind, even a general theoretical approach (narrative and reception theory, respectively), these topics and theoretical approaches were not enough in and of themselves to propel the students into writing sustained, formal discourse. It was not in the act of reading or interpretation or analysis of works themselves that Karen and John found themselves at a loss as to what to say, but in what each as a writer had to bring to those texts, to the topics they had discovered through their transactions with the texts. Second, both students sought out their professors to help them formulate an issue and conceive a way of exploring or resolving it. That is, preparatory to actually writing or drafting their texts, Karen and John sought to construct themselves as writers by constructing a rhetorical situation for their work; they engaged in dialogue with an actual interlocutor (a professor) who represented the authorial audience of their prospective texts—that is, "Hawthorne critics" or "Dryden scholars." And third, both were told that they had chosen unfruitful topics of inquiry, that writing along the lines of the topic they had already conceived was pointless. By engaging their actual reader in the invention stage of their work, both students cast their professor (or in John's case, a previous mentor) in the role of co-writer or collaborator—a role both professors resisted, deferring the problem of what to say back to the student.

Karen and John both recognized what we too often forget in our assumption that writing is an "automatic process": graduate students in literary studies encounter a vast tradition of literary texts and scholarship in their courses, but they must read against this tradition in order to have something to say in their own texts. To write, in other words, they must have the sense that the subject or topic of their discourse is an issue that requires intellectual work. This issue is neither self-evident in the texts that students read nor immanent in students' transactions with texts; rather, it is a function of the critical resources that they bring as *writers* to their readings or reconstructions of texts. Graff's contention that certain contemporary critical approaches have a heuristic value that New Critical practice no longer enjoys offers a partial solution to the problem of invention, then, for having something to say about literature is clearly dependent on the literary-critical frameworks in which texts are read. Had the Hawthorne seminar incorporated theoretical discussions of narrative and allowed more time for secondary reading, for example, Karen might have felt better prepared to answer the question she had formulated. But I would caution against our seeing specific theories and approaches as a panacea to the problem of invention, for like literary texts themselves, critical theories "go only so far" in telling students what they're supposed to say about them, or more to the point, what they're to do with them and why. The exigencies which give rise to writing are no more inherent within critical approaches themselves than they are within the texts that students read. The issues which compel critical discourse must still be invented by a writer who has both a personal and professional stake in the criticism he or she produces. Karen and John, through their interactions with professors, sought not only to create a rhetorical context which would give purpose and meaning to their inquiries about Hawthorne and Dryden but to insert themselves within this context as authors or rhetors. However, so long as the questions of what to say and why it's important to say it remain confined to a pragmatics of reading—construed as a problematic of reader, text, and (theoretical) context but not writer, text, and (rhetorical) context—graduate students cannot locate themselves within the interpretive history of a literary work as coauthors or co-makers of this history. In other words, if students' writing is not perceived as an integral part of the study of a subject but only as a discursive exercise through which they demonstrate individual ability, they cannot fully participate in the critical and scholarly discourse that a graduate course is intended to engender. Chances are they will discover, like Karen and John, that they are not active agents in the construction of a scholarly tradition, a tradition that seems to go on independently of anything they might do.

Academic Genres

As my survey and case studies revealed, a term paper of at least fifteen pages is the most common writing assignment in graduate courses in English studies, the predominant mode of writing by which graduate students do their academic work. The fifteen-to-twenty-five-page term paper would seem, moreover, to be a distinctly (though not exclusively) graduate-level genre; the term papers which the four graduate students in my study reported that they wrote as undergraduate English majors generally fell into the eight-to-ten-page range, and all but one of the students said that they had never written a longer paper as undergraduates. Most likely, the term paper is the most frequently assigned writing task because it is perceived as preparatory to the scholarly essay or journal article, which requires research and a more complex and extensive treatment of a topic than a shorter paper allows. The term paper, in this sense, may be viewed as a kind of discursive "training ground," one in which graduate students gain practice conducting sustained inquiry into a topic. It is one of the ways that they learn the argumentative processes and bibliographic procedures that are the "tools of the trade" in literary studies. Also, such learning presumably has a cumulative effect: by writing a succession of term papers and reading different professors' responses to their work, students acquire knowledge of the formal features and conventions of literary criticism and enhance their skills in argumentative discourse.

But whether the term paper, as currently conceived and taught, truly has the effects which graduate faculty imagine and desire is a questionable assumption at best. For in truth, the term paper is not "taught" at all; it is assigned. This assignment is usually cast only in generic terms—a twenty-page research paper or a critical analysis—so that the work that students will do is already represented as a text, not as a process of inquiry. Whatever discursive practices are required to write the paper take place in what Patricia Bizzell has called a "black box," out of view of the professor (49). The professors who participated in my study, in fact, explicitly stated that such processes cannot or ought not be taught because discussion of the writing task would mean intervening in the writing process either in superfluous or counter-productive ways. One professor said he did not feel it was necessary to teach the term paper as a process of inquiry because "graduate students already know about such things"; another said that students learn the conventions of critical discourse "from their reading rather than having them spelled out"; and another said that to teach the term paper as a discursive practice would "inhibit students' creativity" and induce them to write "formulaic stuff." Perhaps because graduate faculty are accustomed to viewing their own scholarly and critical practices as acts of reading (or interpretation or criticism) rather than acts of writing, they naturally assume the role of readers (or critics or evaluators) of their students' texts rather than as teachers of the discursive processes by which texts are composed.[4] In any case, they commonly expect graduate students to have mastered the arts of discourse well enough to produce term papers "as easily and inevitably," in Bizzell's words, "as a hen lays eggs" (49).

From the students' perspective, writing term papers can be a gratifying and rewarding experience, a place to test out their own theories, to engage other critics' voices, to make discoveries and bring new challenges to the literary tradition. But the process of producing argumentative discourse (the predominant mode of discourse in literary studies) proves neither easy nor inevitable, as the reports of the graduate students who participated in my study reveal. To be sure, all of the graduate students I interviewed were able to say, in general, what constitutes a literary argument; in fact, all sounded remarkably similar: "You have to have a thesis, prove it with textual evidence, counter possible criticisms" and so forth. But the actual process of constructing a formal argument proved difficult when the students were engaged in writing sustained discourse on their chosen topics. Hank, one of the master's students in my study, had studied structuralism in a previous course and decided to write a term paper in his American Literature seminar on a certain "binary opposition" he had discerned in Sylvia Plath's short stories. But he said he needed to go to the library and get his professor's book to see how his professor "constructed an argument." The other master's student, Lisa, did considerable research in preparation of her term paper in the Shakespeare seminar, but she asked me and later her professor whether simply reporting on the various theories that have been advanced to account for *Othello*'s popularity in the Old South "constituted an argument." Karen said that her greatest difficulty in writing on the topic she had finally chosen for her term paper (the relation between Hawthorne's use of storytellers and his often ambiguous endings) was "interweaving disparate ideas into a coherent argument." In the professors' evaluations of the students' writing, the most frequently discerned problem was some flaw in the students' reasoning: Hank "tried to make his thesis do too many disparate things"; Lisa "didn't seem to understand what constitutes literary evidence"; the text "didn't warrant some of the claims that [Karen] made." Significantly, these comments came at the "end" of the students' writing, as evaluations of the students' finished texts, and at the end of the course, when students had no opportunity to revise or rethink the arguments they were trying to make for the actual reader of their work.

If we are searching for reasons why graduate students have difficulty with argumentation, we would do well to focus on the writing situation or context in which these arguments are composed. In the cases of the three students I have described here, this "context" was narrowed to the term paper itself. Each student had to produce a text-based form of argument, one which demonstrated its own logic rather than engaged an actual reader in a dialogical process. The students were not exchanging ideas with an interlocutor, in other words, but submitting a linear, fully formed argument to a textual critic, who then evaluated the argument's premises, evidence, and so forth. The product-oriented or formalist conception of argumentation evident in the professors' comments was also reflected in the students' own accounts of what constitutes an argument: the "thesis-proof" model to which each of the students pointed as the defining structural feature of the critical essays they were to compose. While this model may have "fit" neatly with the activities of close reading and explication that the students likely practiced at the undergraduate level, the longer paper that graduate students in literature are routinely asked to write calls for more elaborate and complex forms of argumentation, for a dialectical interplay of critical voices and perspectives—in short, for a discursive practice that goes well beyond the thesis-proof model with which they are most familiar. The problems the students encountered in drafting their arguments and the flaws the professors perceived in their students' texts might have been addressed more effectively had the students been given opportunities to engage in argument—to test their ideas, lines of reasoning, and evidence—with actual readers in the process of writing their term papers. But once again, such interventions were perceived by the professors in my study as either superfluous because students already know how to produce critical discourse or as impediments to students' individual creativity.

Those aspects and features of critical discourse that are not thought to be the function of already learned skills or a matter of inspiration are often assumed to be a function of the student's reading: students will learn to compose critical discourse by reading critical discourse and internalizing its structures, strategies, vocabulary, and style. While this assumption is no doubt true, Baldick's assertion that students compose "not tragic dramas, but essays in criticism" bears repeating here, for students in literature courses are reading and writing in two distinct genres. In most literature courses, graduate students read a set of literary works—for example, the complete works of Hawthorne, Twentieth-Century novels and poems, or Shakespeare's plays. They may or may not read "secondary" or non-literary works such as scholarly essays or critical reviews as part of the required reading of the course. (In one of the courses I observed, Twentieth-Century American Literature, students were instructed *not* to do outside reading for their term papers because other critics' notions might interfere with their own perceptions of the literary texts under study.) In their papers, however, graduate students are asked to produce a kind of discourse that bears almost no resemblance to the plays, novels, short stories, and poems they are writing about. Literary texts, the primary reading in most courses, assume an evidentiary role in the papers the students must compose. The texts that might serve as examples of the kind of critical work students are expected to emulate in their writing—critical reviews or scholarly essays on particular literary works—are not always read in class in conjunction with the literary texts themselves. And when secondary works are included in a course, they are not "read" as examples of the kind of work that professionals in English do. They are not analyzed for the way a critic frames an issue, establishes its significance, builds a case, and resolves the issue, but as further pieces of evidence the student might incorporate in his or her own argument. Thus, the literary essay, one of the predominant genres by which professionals do their work in literary studies, is not taught as such. We teach literary genres by asking students to read and analyze examples and variations of the kind, but we assume that the term paper, as both a mode of writing and a method of inquiry, teaches itself.

Reconceiving the Graduate Course

My study indicates that in the graduate curriculum, literature and composition are still represented as separate intellectual activities, the study of literary texts occupying center stage, the production of student texts a peripheral role at best. Graduate faculty tend to teach literature in the primary sense but assume that graduate students will master (or have mastered) the writing of scholarly and critical texts on their own. Literary criticism is still imagined as the "reading" an individual student produces rather than as a discourse he or she participates in. This individualized, privatized notion of reading and displacement of writing leaves students without a social context in which to develop and explore disciplinary issues, practice academic genres, or engage in argument with real (as opposed to idealized) others.

The persistence of product or text-oriented pedagogies of reading and writing in the graduate curriculum has implications, I think, both for students undertaking graduate study and for the profession itself. Such pedagogies tend to deny to the graduate student an active and defining role in shaping the critical and scholarly discourse of the discipline. And they contradict the very process approaches, including collaborative writing and peer response, that graduate teaching assistants are adapting in undergraduate writing courses.[5] If the purpose of graduate education is to train students in the roles they will assume as future practitioners of our profession, then our current modes of instruction are serving, in effect, to perpetuate the very models of inquiry and teaching that contemporary theories of reading and writing seek to displace at all levels of the English curriculum.

If we are to translate theory into practice, it will be necessary to revise text-oriented approaches to literature and practice ways of reading that call upon all of the resources available to the reader, including his or her experiences or "transactions" with the text in the act of reading. But though such a revision may represent a dramatic change in the way literature has traditionally been taught in the university, it still allows us to forget that criticism—the real content of literary studies—must be composed, that it is writing that ultimately defines graduate students' work and role in the academy. Along with text-oriented approaches to reading, then, we must also revise our view of composition as an art that graduate students have already mastered, for such a view gives rise to the currently dominant product-oriented model of composition that fails to recognize the social and constitutive nature of writing and commits us, at best, to a paradox: at the same moment we proclaim that literary texts are not self-interpreting, our practices reinscribe the belief that our students' interpretations are somehow self-generating.

The move from text-oriented to reader-oriented theories of literary criticism, in short, must be accompanied by a similar move from text-oriented to writer-oriented theories and pedagogies. It is not only the reader's relation to the text but the writer's relation to the texts and contexts of literary studies that must be the real "content" of English studies. If, indeed, interpretation is the only game in town, as Stanley Fish says, then the text the student writes must be the most important text in the class, the processes by which this text comes into being the real subject of any seminar. As Graff has observed, reader-response and pragmatic theories, which regard reading as the active construction of meaning, grant students an authority which was formerly held to be a property of the text "itself." And cultural criticism, feminism, and the new historicism, which concentrate on the social conditions and political circumstances under which texts are produced, offer graduate students more to say and exigencies for saying it. But it is not enough to grant authority to the reader nor to bring history and culture back into the classroom unless graduate students see themselves as makers of this history and culture through their acts of authorship.

Composition scholarship has shown that to become a practitioner of a discipline, one must not only learn the discursive terms of that discipline but must participate in its discourse as a rhetor, as an author whose texts have the power to alter knowledge in that field (see, for example, Bazerman). Graduate students must be able to reflect on their own work as developing scholars and critics, as members of a community who have an active role and stake in the knowledge generated by the course which formed the original occasion for inquiry. To become authorities on Shakespeare, Austen, Dickinson, or Derrida, students must first become authors, and their acts of authorship must occur in settings that are self-consciously rhetorical. The graduate course in English studies must be conceived as a scene of writing as well as a scene of reading, a discursive site in which literary history is truly conceived as history in the making.

Notes

1. I surveyed English departments at Florida State University, Ohio State University, Pennsylvania State University, the University of California at San Diego, the University of Oregon, and the University of Utah. I wish to thank both my colleagues and the graduate students at these institutions who assisted with the survey.

2. I have changed the names of the four graduate students who participated in this study to preserve their anonymity.

3. Early cognitive research in composition may have unwittingly contributed to this assumption via studies in which graduate students were placed in "expert-writer" control groups against which the writing of "novices" was measured.

4. The tacit hierarchy of discursive practices I discerned in the graduate seminars I observed—where the reading and in-class discussion of literary texts took precedence over the writing that students did about those texts—accords in many respects with the English apparatus Roberts Scholes has discerned and delineated in *Textual Power*. According to Scholes, consumption is privileged over production, reading over writing, and literature over non-literature; hence the greatest gap is between literature and composition—the reading (or interpretation or criticism) of literary texts and the writing of pseudo non-literature (or student essays). Scholes' schema serves to explain, in part, why literature

faculty more easily assume roles as readers and critics of the finished texts of their students than as readers or collaborators of work in progress: they are accustomed to seeing themselves as "consumers" of texts, as critics and scholars of the "already written" rather than as teachers of writing. The texts of their students, moreover, inhabit the area of pseudo-non-literature. But Scholes overlooks in his apparatus what graduate faculty overlook in their roles as teachers and readers of literature: criticism, including a book like *Textual Power*, must be composed. We do not merely "consume" literature; our readings, interpretations, and criticisms of literature and of the academy entail acts of production—of composition.

5. Irene Gale similarly observes that "many graduate courses, even in rhetoric and composition, are based on the presentational model, in that the professor lectures and requires one or two research papers due at the end of the term but offers no avenue for peer response to emerging papers." Arguing that it is "inconsistent to teach teaching assistants to teach writing as a process on the one hand while on the other to force them as students to magically produce finished products," she calls for graduate courses designed to let teaching assistants "deal with writing problems they face as students and professionals" (46-47).

Works Cited

Baldick, Chris. *The Social Mission of English Criticism: 1848-1932*. Oxford: Clarendon P, 1987.

Bazerman, Charles. "What Written Knowledge Does: Three Examples of Academic Discourse." *Philosophy of the Social Sciences* 11 (1981): 361-87.

Bizzell, Patricia. "Composing Processes: An Overview." *The Teaching of Writing*. Ed. Anthony R. Petrosky and David Bartholomae. Chicago: U of Chicago P, 1986. 49-70.

Gale, Irene. "Conflicting Paradigms: Theoretical and Administrative Tensions in Writing Program Administration." *Writing Program Administrator* 14 (1990): 41-50.

Graff, Gerald. "The University and the Prevention of Culture." *Criticism in the University*. Ed. Gerald Graff and Reginald Gibbons. Chicago: Northwestern UP, 1985. 62-82.

W.E. Mead. "Report of the Pedagogical Section," Proceedings for 1900, *PMLA* 16 (1901): xix-xxxii.

Punter, David. "University English Teaching: Observations on Symbolism and Reflexivity." *Demarcating the Disciplines*. Minneapolis: U of Minnesota P, 1986. 215-36.

Robinson, Jay. "Literacy in the Department of English." *College English* 46 (1985): 492-98.

Rosmarin, Adena. "The Narrativity of Interpretive History." *Reading Narrative*. Ed. James Phelan. Columbus: Ohio State UP, 1989. 12-26.

Scholes, Robert. *Textual Power: Literary Theory and the Teaching of English*. New Haven: Yale UP, 1985.

Slevin, James. "Connecting English Studies." *College English* 48 (1986): 543-50.

Sullivan, Patricia. "Writers' Conceptions of Audience in Graduate Literature Courses." *Reader: Essays in Reader-Oriented Response and Criticism* 21 (1989): 22-34.

Worlds in the Making: The Literacy Project as Potential Space

Nancy Welch

At the end of the first week of the Nebraska Literacy Project—a summer course offered at the University of Nebraska-Lincoln for K-12 teachers— Professor Roberts, the director of a similar course at another university, visited the classroom and made this observation to teachers:

> I've been comparing our two projects, and it appears that our literacy project seems to be, *is* more confrontational than yours. We have people standing up on the table and shouting at each other because they're impassioned. We're more theoretical. Here, I hear a lot of storytelling and conversation, and I see people sharing their writing and really working at it, and the atmosphere is very nice, but it's different, certainly, from what's going on in our project.

I start with this moment because it strikes me as what fiction-writer Eve Shelnutt calls a "radical experience" in which the teachers participating in the project and the teachers guiding it were confronted with what we had tacitly assumed to be the "good" of our activities—activities that included sharing writing and joining in conversation, activities that did not lead to standing-on-the-table shouting. It's a moment that made tensely visible our relationship to the larger, ongoing debates about literacy and the dichotomies reproduced in those debates: shouting/ sharing, theory/practice, challenge/safety, researcher/teacher.[1] I start with that moment too because participants repeatedly referred to it, speculated about it, and re-envisioned it in conversation, interviews, and journals throughout the five-week project.[2]

Kay, for example, who teaches elementary special education, wrote about initially feeling inadequate during Roberts' talk, in which he introduced a poem by Rilke, wanting participants to question the usual division between the poetic and the political. In her journal, Kay compared herself to the underprepared about whom Mike Rose speaks in *Lives on the Boundary* (a shared text in the project). She wrote that she kept silent when Roberts asked for class responses because she believed she was alone in not understanding the poem or the theme of "critical literacy" Roberts introduced. After all, she reasoned, six others in the class participated fully in that discussion; they must have had knowledge she did not. In the days that followed, Kay discussed and wrote about Roberts' visit with other project participants—participants like Martha, a high-school teacher, who wrote to Kay that while she felt annoyed by the "game of 'Guess what I'm thinking'" Roberts played, she was troubled too because "I know I do that sometimes, if not quite a bit, with my own students." Returning to her journal, in an entry she chose to read to the class, Kay wrote:

> I wonder how we as a group would be toward [Roberts] if he came back again. Would we verbalize our feelings more, as a group, instead of each one feeling inadequate or unknowledgeable about the poem and Roberts' questions?

In her journal and in discussions, Kay used that radical moment of Roberts' visit to look again at the systems that keep teachers divided, their classroom doors closed—each fearing that, especially in a political climate clamoring for "teacher accountability," she'll be called ignorant if she speaks; each knowing that in a university the knowledge she has isn't usually counted as knowledge at all. With Kay's questions about how that formerly silent group would respond now and with Martha's recognition of her own game-playing with students, these teachers also participate in the understanding of literacy that David Bleich works with in *The Double Perspective*: "a development of one's implication in the life of others" and the discovery and exercise of "*our mutual responsibilities*" (67).

Through writings, discussions, and revisions like this, Kay, Martha, and other participants in the literacy project offer me a way of seeing the writing and storytelling that went on as something other than merely "nice." They offer me a way of reconsidering those oppositions between sharing and shouting, practice and theory, a way of considering how critical literacy is fostered through the creation of "potential spaces." A potential space—a concept I take from child psychologist D. W. Winnicott and feminist revisions of his work—is one in which participants are able to consider and examine their external realities from a one-step distance. It's an intermediate arena that, neither immersed in nor divorced from contentious social debates, encourages questioning, experimentation, negotiation, and play. In potential spaces, Winnicott stressed, individuals don't learn to adapt to a culture, its practices, beliefs, and demands; nor do they experience complete freedom, the discovery of who they really are outside of institutions. Instead, in potential spaces individuals come together as Kay and Martha did to explore, examine, and imagine ways of intervening in, speaking back to, and shaping their institutions.

Bonnie Sunstein's recent *Composing a Culture*, a rich ethnographic study of a summer writing project at the University of New Hampshire, underscores for me the necessity of investigating the role of potential spaces in developing critical literacy and working for change in classrooms and in schools. In that project, Sunstein writes, participants came together to create a "liminal" or "temporary" culture, one in which storytelling played an important function. Through shared stories, Sunstein writes, teachers were able to "disrupt their own views of schooling" and develop "the personal principles" they would put into place in their own classrooms (232, 242). "Each time someone renders a draft and shares it, each time someone interprets a reading," Sunstein writes, "a literate re-invention takes place in the group and the process of personal and professional revision continues. Teachers learn responses and develop language to enable the others' continuing verbal creation" (242). According to Sunstein, however, this literate re-invention and the development of a language for talking about literacy remains undiscussed and unexamined within projects like the one she describes. "No one noticed," she writes, "that the stories were a necessary feature in the revision of a literate teaching self. And certainly no one noticed their stories fusing into a larger story about curriculum and literacy education" (232). As a result, teachers leave such a project feeling, perhaps, "more deeply and reflectively" themselves but also feeling more deeply "the oppression of the school day," the vast differences between the culture of the project and the culture of their schools (233, 232). Through such a project, then, the dichotomies of shouting and sharing, theory and practice, individual desires and institutional demands aren't questioned but reinforced. These teachers may "revise themselves as writers, readers, and as teachers," but they do not, according to Sunstein's analysis, discover that they can also, and probably must also, work for revision beyond themselves and beyond single classrooms (233).

In the literacy project I'll examine in this essay, participants and project leaders were also creating a kind of liminal culture in which our activities were never examined nor discussed—that is, until Roberts' visit. With Roberts' visit and the work of Kay, Martha, and others to make sense of that sudden, strange experience of conflict, teachers made, I believe, an important move from enjoying a temporary culture to creating potential spaces for examining moments of challenge, for articulating the revisionary potential of their own and each other's stories, for recognizing too that their stories were indeed fusing into a larger story about literacy education. More, recognizing that this larger story couldn't be kept out of their school hallways, staff rooms, and department meetings, they made an important move toward considering the potential spaces they must continue to create after the project's end. In this essay I want to examine these intermediate arenas participants created and planned, and I'll argue that it's through such potential spaces that teachers form the voices of critique and possibility they need to address both their classrooms and their institutions.

From Macro to Micro: Developing Literacy in Potential Spaces

In sharp contrast to ethnographic studies of literate cultures like Sunstein's, current discussions about literacy often take the form of taxonomies which categorize and define different orientations toward and agendas for reading, writing, and teaching practices. C.H. Knoblauch in "Literacy and the Politics of Education," for instance, distinguishes between a "liberal" or "personal-growth" conception of literacy and "critical" or "radical" literacy. According to Knoblauch, a teacher with a personal-growth understanding is often an advocate of open classrooms, whole-language learning, and personalized reading programs. He or she speaks "compassionately on behalf of the disadvantaged," while at the same time avoiding "the suggestion of any fundamental restructuring of institutions" (78). The personal-growth argument, Knoblauch writes, gives teachers the satisfaction of having effected some change in students' lives while leaving unchallenged the larger systems governing social relations and economic power. Critical literacy, on the other hand, actively seeks to challenge institutional structures and work for a society-wide redistribution of power through joining literacy development to the development of critical consciousness. Through programs of critical literacy like those of Paulo Freire and Henry Giroux, participants come to see how language has been used to dominate, suppress, and pacify them, and they learn to claim language as a means to gain entry into "the arena in which power is contested" (79).

While I find taxonomies like Knoblauch's genuinely useful—providing a macropolitical view of classroom practices and beliefs, telling me why I'm disturbed by Sunstein's emphasis on teachers' personal development divorced from the questions of institutional change, telling me too that I need to take a hard look at my own "rhetoric of moral sincerity" (78)—I also find them to be curiously a-contextual. In order to demonstrate literacy as multiple, situated practices, studies such as Knoblauch's run counter to the work of Sunstein, Shirley Brice Heath, Denny Taylor, and others. In their neatness, taxonomies suggest that, whatever the time or place, we each occupy one or another category exclusively, all of our beliefs and practices cohering to a single definition without conflict or contradiction. If privileged as the sole authoritative statement that can be made about literacy, taxonomies also lead to a sweeping dismissal of teachers' daily work and theoretical contributions; they can result, for instance, in the devaluing of whole-language curricula and personalized reading programs as *only* and *always* individualistic in practice, as uncomplicated by the differing contexts and positions of teachers and students. Such a macropolitical view can also plant us firmly in despair, Knoblauch seeing here little hope for enacting critical literacy:

> Although critical literacy is trendy in some academic circles, those who commend it also draw their wages from the capitalist economy it is designed to challenge. Whether its advocates will take [Jonathan] Kozol's risks in bringing so volatile a practice into community schools is open to doubt. Whether something important would change if they did take the risks is also doubtful. (79)

Skepticism about critical literacy as the latest fashion is needed to ensure that it keeps its political edge and is not neutralized by liberal ideology. But when skepticism slips into pessimism, the tone of our work *also* neutralizes the concept of critical literacy: shutting down all discussion; closing off avenues for further investigation, intervention, and action; discouraging risk-taking and revision at the local level.

Recently, Knoblauch and Lil Brannon have answered this pessimism with the final chapter of *Critical Teaching and the Idea of Literacy*, which, stressing the crucial role that teacher-initiated classroom inquiry must play in any reconstitution of education, puts context and teachers back into the picture. Yet, because they are primarily focused in this study on providing, again, a taxonomic view, along with examining and critiquing the belletristic elements of composition's "process" movement, Knoblauch and Brannon don't delve into the reading, writing, and revision *processes* that enable teachers to investigate, intervene in, and change their daily realities.

If we're to answer this tendency to separate theory and practice and if we're to think further, as Knoblauch and Brannon ask, about the place of teachers' inquiries and stories in making and remaking ideas of literacy, we need to turn to those theorists who can move us from the macropolitical to the micro, from theorizing critical literacy broadly to looking for its hints, suggestions, and contradictions in specific contexts. Teresa de Lauretis, for instance, asks us to seek out what she calls the "space-off"—"social spaces carved in the interstices of institutions" where we can witness "the micropolitical practices of daily life and daily resistances that afford both agency and sources of power" (25). Julia Kristeva considers the uses of metaphoric "exile" as a way out of the "mire of common sense" and as a means to become a "stranger" to one's usual practices and beliefs ("Dissident" 298). Mikhail Bakhtin examines the use of "familiar" and "popular" genres of writing as a kind of exile within which to scrutinize, experiment with, and dismantle social rules and doctrine (see "Epic and Novel" 21-23). And Joy Ritchie, in an essay about political divisions between secondary schools and universities, writes of the need for teachers from both institutions to "stake out a place on the margins of the trenches and the ivory towers" from which they can "question established assumptions, envision alternative structures, and work to create new forms of belonging and becoming" (120).

Despite differences in their historical positions and theoretical agendas, all of these writers focus on very much politicized self- and society-transforming processes of revision, the kind that critical pedagogy is especially concerned with. Significantly, these theorists also situate the possibility of revision within particular locations one step removed from the political fray: in the space-off, exile, carnivalized genres, margins, all providing me with metaphors through which to read the work of teachers in the literacy project and in their schools. All suggest, as Adrienne Rich writes, that for scrutiny of self and society to take place, for resistance and revision to be fostered

> a certain freedom of the mind is needed—freedom to press on, to enter the currents of your thought like a glider pilot . . . to question, to challenge, to conceive of alternatives, perhaps to the very life you are living at that moment. You have to be free to play around with the notion that day might be night, love might be hate. . . . (43)

Rich, de Lauretis, and Ritchie don't suggest that it's desirable to escape entirely from institutional structures or from arenas where an individual's words are continually contested—a suggestion that teachers in the literacy project, long used to being evaluated according to their students' success on standardized tests or being handed the latest in "teacher-proof" curriculum, would have little patience with. These theorists do, however, stress "a certain freedom of the mind" as a necessary—and, in critical pedagogy, often overlooked—ingredient for revision. I hear them invoking places and processes that allow a critical and creative one-step distance from, rather than immersion in, conflict and struggle—an intermediate and active arena that Winnicott and feminist revisionists of his work call a *potential space*.

Winnicott, a practicing psychotherapist, was particularly interested in child development and how children negotiate with "external reality" through constructing potential spaces. A child's blanket, for example, might be a potential space for such negotiation through a toy, which Winnicott calls a "transitional object." The transitional object isn't at all neutral; it's saturated with culturally shared meanings and uses. But pulled into the potential space of the blanket—a small bordered arena that offers the child both a view of the world around him or her and a space apart from that world—it becomes available for examination, play, and transformation, all structured and guided by the child. This learning-how-to-play, to use objects symbolically and to alter their meanings expands, Winnicott stresses, far beyond the space of the blanket and the early childhood years into what he calls "creative living": into lifelong play with and revision of individual beliefs and cultural forms (100-01).

In other words, unlike traditional psychoanalysis, which focuses entirely on psychosomatic processes, undifferentiated Oedipal narratives and so on, to the exclusion of environmental factors and cultural differences, Winnicott's practice focused on the interplay between "inner" and "outer," "me" and "not-me," prior experience, current context, and imagined future. Winnicott's theories differ radically, too, from the tenets of American ego psychology, which stresses the adaptation of individuals to external structures, and the normative educational practices that have arisen from its tenets: the construction of school playgrounds as "supervisable spaces" in which the child learns sanctioned forms of play under the "non-coercive moral observation of the teacher" (Hunter 47; see also Gore for a critique of the use of students' journals as a "supervisable space"); the construction of teacher-training programs in which teachers are presented and make a fit with a pre-formed classroom model (Bishop; Welch). Adaptation and compliance, Winnicott emphasized, brings a sense of "futility" and of "the world and its details being recognized . . . only as something to be fitted in with" (65). Instead,

Winnicott stressed play as a "basic form of living" through which individuals, in relationships of trust and dependability, discover their potential to participate in the *reconstruction* of shared reality, rather than merely comply, adapt, fit in (50).[3]

Because inherent in Winnicott's work are possibilities for creativity and transformation, for negotiation between individual desires and shared realities, feminist theorists such as Jane Flax have turned to and politicized his work as a means to examine what takes place in potential spaces of adulthood—feminist consciousness-raising groups, for instance. Winnicott's work is particularly attractive to feminist theorists, Flax writes, because unlike psychoanalytic theorist Jacques Lacan who views the gap between self and other as unbridgeable and castrating for women and men alike, Winnicott renames that gap as a space of activity and possibility, one without which no self and no culture, let alone cultural transformations, would be possible (Flax 126-27). More, with that renaming, Winnicott posits the existence of real and enabling relationships rather than viewing all relationships as more or less fictional projections of the narcissistic self or as entirely socially determined and imposed from without by the existing power apparati. This renaming, Flax writes, enables us to see how women (or here we might say teachers) "*can* creatively transform what is given" rather than view "Woman" (or "Teacher") as the uncontested product of technologies of gender (or of the educational system), as a "castrated, lacking 'empty set'" on which social meanings are inscribed (119, 117).[4] This renaming enables us to see, in short, how within the space of possibility between the "me" and "not me" cultural practices and institutions can be examined, questioned, challenged, and changed.

A potential space, Elizabeth Wright claims, can be one of resistance, a place from which "to challenge the parents' language" (99), to interrogate and dissent from received and naturalized meanings. A potential space is also one that, in the interstices of institutions, in daily micropolitical practice, allows one to "participate *with some equality* in the fun of meaning" and the "zest of experimentation" (Wright 99; emphasis added). Through such experimentation, participants in a potential space can imagine themselves out of positions of pessimism and paralysis and create from "tradition out there," as Winnicott writes, new forms for participating in social arenas. For such revisions to take place, however, with contributions from all participants, each working with some equality, words like "love," "trust," and "friendship" have to be taken seriously. Love, writes bell hooks, drawing on the work of Paulo Freire, is "a mediating force that can sustain us" in our work together to identify and change individual actions and shared systems of domination "so that we are not broken in this process, so that we do not despair" (26). Likewise, Winnicott stressed the need for relationships of trust and dependability, so that the participants in a potential space can work through the anxiety that necessarily comes with undoing as well as creating practices and beliefs (see 102-03). In a potential space, the construction and working through of relationships—the development and exercise, as Bleich says, of mutual responsibility—is serious and necessary work.

Especially with their valuing of relational work—considered an "oxymoron" in Western culture, Jane Flax notes, with relationship-building viewed as natural, womanly, not really "work" at all (87)—I find Winnicott and feminist revisions of his practice particularly responsive to the workings of the literacy project. In writings, discussions, and interviews, participants stressed words like "friendship," "support," and "trust" as central to their experience of the project, to their learning about literacy, and to the possibility of their sustaining and enriching this learning in the coming school year. It's that recognition of the need for ongoing relational work, the creation of intermediate arenas between challenge and response, that's missing from the writing project Sunstein describes. Teachers return to institutions that, Sunstein observes, aren't going to change and to colleagues who aren't going to understand, and they feel quietly "subversive" as they pretend to do what their schools expect while secretly doing something else behind closed classroom doors (231, 235). That idea of relational work is absent too from our taxonomic, decontextualized discussions of literacy—which don't imagine teachers, their schools, their students and colleagues at all and likewise construct institutions as impersonal and impervious monoliths. Relational work, however, is precisely what participants named as at the heart of their learning in the literacy project—learning through relationships how their individual stories join, disrupt, change, and are changed by the words of others, learning within potential spaces how to rename their relationships to institutions from one of compliance or alienation to one of collective, responsible, and creative participation.

The Literacy Project as Potential Space(s)

The five-week literacy project met for four half-days a week on the University of Nebraska campus and was collaboratively designed and guided by four teachers—a tenured professor in the English department, an assistant English professor whose doctorate is in Curriculum and Instruction, a junior-high language-arts teacher, and me, then a first-year doctoral student. The project's sixteen participants, fourteen women and two men, taught grades kindergarten through 12 in both city and rural school districts across the state. While half of the participants were English or language-arts teachers, the elementary teachers taught all subject areas, one in special-education. Another participant taught high-school German, and still another was an elementary-school principal.

Most of the teachers had participated before in the state writing project and said they signed up for the literacy project to "extend" or "refresh" their learning from that previous class, to find the "support" they'd experienced in the writing project and missed on a day-to-day basis in their schools, or—as in Martha's case—to figure out why the activities modeled in the writing project had not worked out in their classrooms. Martha, who had just finished her third year of teaching at a Catholic high school, said she'd had a "wonderful experience" in the writing project the previous summer and felt keenly frustrated that she'd been unable to create that same experience in her classrooms, her students only "cooperating" with the reading and writing workshop she tried to implement, viewing it as a "game" she directed. She described confusion too over how to make the writing project model work in her Advanced English class, which she'd taught in the past as preparation for students to take the standardized advanced-placement exam for college credit. By the end of the year, she said, "My beliefs were starting to crumble, and I was going back to the traditional way of teaching—the lecture, memorization, have a test over it."

In an early interview, Martha identified two problems that contributed to her classes becoming "just a jumble." First, she'd tried to copy the writing project activities "without seeing the whole picture and without maybe totally understanding why I was doing them." At the same time she was trying to copy those new activities, she'd also worried that dropping "traditional" instruction would leave her students unprepared for the next teacher, and so she attempted without success to combine a workshop format with her earlier practices—a required list of "classics," for instance, and a unit on New Critical analysis of poetry. "I wasn't sure how to mesh it all together," she said, "so that they'll get the stuff that everyone else expects them to read and so that I would still not have a major conflict with how *I* feel they should be learning."

For Martha, then, *both* the workshop format of the writing project and the traditional curriculum that her school encouraged were entirely a part of "external reality," outside of her experience, her understanding, and, especially, her control. Both pressed her, she felt, to assimilate to sets of assumptions she couldn't name and examine, and both pressed her to incorporate into her classroom pre-made sets of practices in direct conflict with each other. The literacy project, Martha hoped, would provide at least two intermediate arenas between her previous year's experience and the next: a place where she could talk with other teachers to see how they negotiate between institutionally-imposed curricula and their own conceptions of what students need to learn; a place where she could use writing to try to "figure out exactly" what she believed and identify "steps" she could take to support those theories in her classroom. In other words, Martha viewed the literacy project not so much as a place where she could become more deeply and reflectively herself, away from school-year questions and pressures, but as a place where she could both figure out what she believed *and* intervene in the gap between those beliefs and the practices of her school.

Jeri, an elementary-school principal, also came to the literacy project looking for steps she could take—not only to develop her own theories about literacy but also to encourage the teachers in her building to reexamine theirs.[5] Like Martha, Jeri expressed frustration about her failed attempts to put some of her beliefs to work in her school and to foster community and collaboration among its teachers—trying to create, for example, teacher-teams that would meet on a regular basis to discuss their classrooms, learn from each other, and initiate curricular change from those discussions. Like Martha's students, Jeri said, teachers in her building saw the team idea as a game she set up and that they must go along with: "They say, 'It's Jeri's new idea for this year, so we'll have to live with it. She'll discard it after she knows it isn't going to work.'" The team idea, Jeri said, was to be a way for teachers to intervene and work for change in an entrenched and hierarchical educational system that has stripped classroom teachers of voice and authority. "Until there's a revolution," Jeri said, "that says, 'We're the experts in education, we are going to regain that political edge,' we can't make a difference for kids." But Jeri recognized too that, far from seeing revolution, teachers saw her innovations as a further step toward denying them voice, yet another mandate imposed from above. In the literacy project, Jeri said, she hoped to observe a "literate" and "cooperative" environment while exploring what she could do to "nurture" such an environment in her school—and while considering too what she may be doing to "block" experimentation and action among its teachers. Jeri viewed the project, then, not only as a place to experience a range of literate practices and reflect on how those practices might become a part of her school; she also viewed the project as a place to consider why that gap between her and her teachers hadn't yet been changed to one of mutual, zestful activity.

Teachers in the literacy project like Martha and Jeri were very much aware of the pitfalls of courses which, like the graduate teacher-education class that Wendy Bishop observes in her ethnographic study *Something Old, Something New*, present participants with "ideal classrooms" they can export back to their own institutions. The presentation of ideal classrooms in the literacy project, Martha knew, wouldn't equip her to examine how those practices shape and are shaped by her particular context and to negotiate with others working within her conservative institution. Her own presentation of ideals, Jeri had learned, led only to acquiescence and the appearance of cooperation among teachers in her building. In addition, any presentation of one ideal classroom in the literacy project would have positioned the teacher-guides to suppress, rather than highlight, the different agendas, strengths, and institutional realities we knew informed each other's classroom teaching.

So instead of promoting one model classroom, the literacy project was designed to provide structures of participation through which teachers could explore together their own literacies and those of their students. Through writing and reflecting alone and with others, we believed, participants could de-naturalize and de-mystify their practices, beliefs, and institutional contexts, making them available for examination, critical questioning, and creative play. In Appendix A and B, I've sketched a description of some of those structures of participation and the outline of one class meeting, but here I want to stress that those structures (like those Sunstein describes in her study) didn't remain static, defined once and for all by the syllabus, the teachers entering into and using those structures in any predictable way. Into this arena teachers introduced stories from their schools and from their own educations, their questions and goals, their areas of expertise and their frustrations. They used the structures of participation to form different relationships to their prior experiences, to each other, and to their futures, those relationships far more numerous and complex than anything I could get down completely in my field notes. For example:

> Early in the course, Martha identifies Sue, who teaches in a one-room rural school, as someone "farther along" in enacting change in her classroom, and she begins exchanging weekly journals with her.

Martha also seeks out in class Meg, a high-school creative writing teacher, as someone who can teach her how to make time for the daily writing she needs to keep her next year's class from becoming a "jumble" of confused events and reactions.

Sue and a junior-high teacher, Steve, also exchange journals, both sharing histories of cultural censorship and silence, both examining their ambivalent, conflictual relationships to reading and writing.

Among other writings, Jeri examines side by side two essays—one that she wrote as a sixteen-year-old, just before her mother's death, about the primary and positive role her mother played in her life; the second, an essay she is composing now to her 11-year-old daughter, considering the many people who will shape her life and considering too for the first time that she has longed for but should not insist on holding the "number-one spot" in her daughter's life.

In her journal and in group discussions of her "parallel essays," Jeri extends this revision from her family relationships into her school, saying, "I feel very strongly that we *all* share in the responsibility of every kid that's in the building," but adding she recognizes too that she "hasn't quite accepted" not being at the center of responsibility and control—in both her daughter's life and among teachers in her school.

Jeri also joins up in class with Pam, who teaches in a Catholic elementary school, to learn how Pam has set up her whole-language classroom, how other teachers have responded to her revisions, and how she works to communicate her theories to other teachers and to her building administrators.

Kay writes a case study of a third-grader in her special-education classroom who struggled physically and painfully with speech, becoming frustrated, angry, and unwilling to try, until he formed a friendship with a deaf student and through that friendship, learned to converse in American Sign Language.

In response to Kay's reading from her case study, Martha writes in her journal, "This tells me again that literacy really is social, like Janet said in her town meeting." In her journal, Jeri wonders what she can do in her building to make the writing and examining of such stories from the classroom possible; she writes that she needs to "recognize" and be "sensitive toward" the differences in each teacher, as Kay demonstrates with this student, resisting her tendency to "put everything in *my* realm of experience" and "quickly make judgments."

> In Martha's small group, Peggy brings in drafts and revisions of a teaching philosophy to guide her next year's seventh-grade classroom, and Martha, considering with another teacher on the drive home from class "who we were and who we are becoming," writes a poem, "Stripping," in which she imagines herself moving from "Hiding behind my lectern in my two-piece gray suit of Armor" to walking, stripped of armor and lecture notes, among her students, "anticipating being caressed or cut."

In these ways and others, participants created in the literacy project numerous potential spaces for entering together into the "fun"—and the terror—of remaking their theories and their classrooms. Initially surprising to me, they also created potential spaces for learning from—rather than dismissing as irrelevant, as "not-me"—the many differences in their daily realities as teachers and in their culturally-shaped literacy histories.

For instance, during the first week of class, participants tended to talk and write about their students and about literacy in the sweeping strokes of what Knoblauch might call a personal-growth conception of literacy. Reading is a "good" and "positive" activity, and students are "apathetic" and show a "lack of effort" when they do not enter enthusiastically into classroom reading, wanting only to "escape" through reading "trash," if they read at all. Or society is to blame for "deadening children's curiosity" with TV, or else the nationwide educational establishment is at fault for insisting on measuring students' learning and teachers' success through standardized test scores. Such discussions always started in a fury, then quickly stalled with participants frustrated and silenced by this beyond-their-control external reality that opposed the values they believed they all shared.

In response to this trend in class discussion, Sue introduced in her "town meeting" (see Appendix A) at the end of the first week a very different relationship to literacy. Reading from a draft of her literate life history, she described this scene in which her father sat in a rocker, reading aloud from the Bible, while she, a child, sat on the floor and listened:

> I somehow got my bare foot underneath the rocker of my father's chair. I was sitting on the floor, and as he sat back, my foot was in the wrong place. The rocker came back and landed across my toes. My fear of my father was such that I didn't say anything, just let the weight of the chair rest painfully on my foot. I don't know how long I sat that way, but eventually he moved again, and I was free. The pain hasn't gone away,

> though. This memory came back as I was looking for memories of being read to as a child. I can't remember that sensation of closeness and safety that other people [in class] have described.

Relating this experience to class discussions of *Lives on the Boundary* and *Ways with Words*, Sue said that in her family and surrounding culture, reading outside of the Bible was "idleness" and storytelling was—as it was for the Roadville residents that Heath describes—boastful, selfish, and dangerously close to lying. Sue concluded by suggesting that the idea of escapist reading should not be dismissed; her own secretive reading-for-escape throughout childhood and adulthood had given her—like the familiar and popular genres Bakhtin explores—various ways for defining herself differently from the reality in which she lived.

Though there was nothing overtly confrontational in Sue's town meeting, it worked in the classroom as a powerful form of challenge and a model for dissenting from received and naturalized meanings. Her words, along with Heath and Rose, urged Martha to consider in her journal that what she had called "apathy" might be students' perception of school as "isolating" them from their families' values or as "seemingly meaningless" in the larger contexts of their lives. For Martha, a potential space for questioning and revision was created through the tension between her view of the uncontested, undisturbed good of reading and Sue's disquieting story. In this space Martha could consider the "not-me" of Sue's story and at the same time allow Sue's reading to tug at her own reading of her students. In that potential space created through the intersection of her world and Sue's, Martha *noticed* Sue's story as disrupting her beliefs about reading, *noticed* this story joining a larger story about literacy, *noticed* that something was happening in the here and now that could alter the stories she would tell about students in the future.

Sue's town meeting also led Martha to look again at her own literate life history and reexamine her statements, "I have always enjoyed reading" and "I have always had a joy and passion for reading." In her draft of that history she began to explore the contexts of her reading: the competitive atmosphere of her high school where "The only purpose of writing and reading . . . was to get good grades"; the university where she embraced a strict division between books that held "universal truths" and books that were "low" and "trash." She considered how during college, she "shoved into the closet" the popular romance novels she used to share with her sister, who had married as a teenager and, now divorced, was raising three children on ADC benefits. Remembering that the readings she and her sister once shared, Martha began to revise her belief in the rightness of high/low culture divisions, and in a project newsletter article she examined connections between "the welfare trap" and the "literacy trap," one dominant group in society "controlling literacy for their own agendas" and "subtly manipulating" people like her sister to "keep them in their place at the bottom of the economic and literacy scale." In her journal and in contributions to the project newsletter, she wondered what *Wuthering Heights* might have in common with a Harlequin romance or the impulse to spray graffiti on a bridge with that to write a tragic play.

Martha began, in other words, to consider what the "not-me" of Sue's story might indeed tell her about her own literate life history, her family, and her classrooms. And she began to revise through an act of reflection that wasn't quiet and solitary but populated with many competing, creative voices: the voices of Rose, Heath, Sue, her students, her sister, her college professors, her own as she's talked to and about students in the past, her own as she might talk to and about students in the future. More, moving from the journal to the project newsletter, she made this story of revision public and urged others to imagine how they might rethink familiar cultural categories.

But at the same time that Martha and the other participants used the potential spaces they created to reexamine their literacy histories and beliefs, they also looked ahead to the coming year—a looking ahead that, as in Martha's poem, created both a sense of play and disturbance. As Martha imagined transformations in her next year's class—turning her school's required reading of *Romeo and Juliet* and *Animal Farm*, for instance, into sites for her and her students to consider "stories of oppression and power"—she also wrote, "All of this sounds good in theory sitting in this class during the summer with people who enjoy writing, but how do I handle this when I return to school in the fall?" and "I'm not exactly sure how I'm going to do that yet, and that's very scary." Participants like Martha who had left the experience of the writing project enlivened and enthusiastic, only to see their ideas "crumble" during the school year increasingly voiced the concern that this history was about to repeat itself.[6] As Winnicott underscores, playing and negotiating need a place, a time, and an ongoing sense of encouragement and support. Especially given their experiences following the writing project, participants in the literacy project knew that the creation of a place, of time, and of encouragement would not just naturally happen.

The Literacy Project as Continuing Project

One response to this concern was provided by Jeri, who planned and led a literacy event that asked participants to list some of their beliefs about literacy, explore one in further detail, and then list and describe steps they knew they could take in one classroom to enact that belief. She then asked participants to describe the "literate culture" of their building or their department and list steps they could take to intervene in that culture. Finally, she asked participants to list activities and relationships from the project that were important to them and to form one goal for continuing that relationship or activity in some way.

In essence, Jeri was asking participants to reconsider their construction of "external reality" and move from the macro to the micropolitical, from being paralyzed by something "given" in their classrooms and in their schools to making goals to step in, play with, and maybe even transform some part of that reality. Goals participants formed ranged from continuing a journal partnership started in the project to planning—and implementing that fall—a new Curriculum and Instruction seminar, called "Classroom-Based Research," that would support teachers in researching and writing about their classrooms.[7] Martha considered that while it seemed an overwhelming task to learn about the varied literacies of 130 students or more, she could begin by asking them to compose and discuss scenes from their literate life histories, as she and others had done in the project. Two teachers discussed bringing into their teachers' lounges some form of "book talks" to change the nature of conversation there. Others formed the goal of proposing to their school administrators teacher-planned and teacher-guided in-service workshops. I made the goal of starting a journal-partnership with my officemate and initiating a lunchtime teaching discussion circle for TAs in my department.

With these goals, participants imagined potential spaces they could create beyond the boundaries of the literacy project—spaces not just of individual reflection but of cooperative activity, intermediate arenas they could form within the busy and often overwhelming social arenas of their schools. They recognized that their activities and discussions were not finished; through the literacy project their beliefs and lives were not neatly and completely transformed. As Jeri noted, "I can't say this experience is over and done with, my paper turned in, and now onto the next experience." Instead, teachers made plans to extend this course, and among the potential spaces they imagined were those that would support not only individual changes in particular classrooms but also collective challenges to institutional structures.

For instance, during Jeri's literacy event, Martha wrote that it seemed "a shame" to have three high schools in her area and yet no contact among the schools' teachers. Two days later, she met for lunch with three teachers, one from her school and the others from the two nearby public high schools. The purpose of the lunch, she wrote in a project newsletter article, was to "get to know each other better," "pool our resources," and, especially, plan for responses to the upcoming visit to their district by a conservative educational reformer. About that lunchtime meeting, she continued:

> We share the same distrust and doubt about his message and quick fix-it solutions to our nation's education. Linda is going to obtain his tape, and we are going to invite all teachers from our departments and others who would be interested to view this tape. . . . Our purpose here is to gain support to question his methods and solutions when he visits September 30. All of our administrators seem to be jumping on a bandwagon behind this man, and it frightens us that they are falling for his propaganda without examining his talks. Together, we can protect our right to literacy from top-down mandated "reform." We are tired of being talked at, and we intend to do some talking.

For Martha, who said during an earlier class meeting that she was reluctant to call herself an "authority" on anything, this writing marks a dramatic revision, and it's a revision not so much in her stance toward this reformer and his conservative "back-to-basics" movement in her school (such would have been her response from the project's start), as in her stance toward "external reality." At the project's start, Martha had spoken of her beliefs, her classroom practices, and her uncertainties as all pitted against a formidable, untouchable reality of recalcitrant students, indifferent colleagues, department-imposed curricula, a powerful test industry—an unbridgeable and disempowering gap between "me" and "not-me." But in the passage above, Martha's words suggest a fundamental change in her construction of and relationship to those external realities. She imagines relationships through which she can claim authority to talk back—not acquiesce, not shut her classroom door either—to building and district policy-makers. With that lunchtime meeting, she starts transforming the gap she's identified between her beliefs and what's happening in her school into a space of collective activity and possibility. More, she locates the possibility of transformation in particular literate practices: in discussion among a group of concerned teachers, in the "reading" of videotapes, in the writing of this account, in forums that encourage and support talking back.

Worlds in the Making

The literacy project did not offer teachers a set of beliefs and matching classroom practices, and their experiences in the course, as far as I can see in my notes and interviews, did not produce a move from one position to another on a scale of literacies. Class transcripts throughout the five weeks show a lot of slippage and tension among conceptions of literacy as participants and teacher-guides alike spoke, even within the same sentence, of reading as "survival," as "accepting other points of view," and "as maybe not just accepting other viewpoints but realizing that you really do have something to learn." If the goal for the entire course was to resolve this tension among functional, liberal, and critical conceptions of literacy and settle, once and for all, into a firm commitment to the latter, that goal wasn't met.

But, in fact, the work of teachers in the literacy project can teach us, I believe, to change the way we talk about literacy whether in a summer course for K-12 teachers, a seminar for graduate teaching assistants, or an undergraduate classroom. They can teach us to look for literacy development not in the occupation of a particular, stable position or in the claiming of a coherent, codifiable set of beliefs but rather in the imagining and carrying out of projects of revision: incomplete, always creative, and ever-renewing projects that Bakhtin calls a "world-in-the-making" (31), that Winnicott calls "creative living" (101), and that Martha calls, "Learning to look at the How and the Why as well as the What. How will I do this? What will it look like? What are the values I want my students to gain?" These teachers can teach us too that this literacy-development-in-the-making is the lifelong project—beyond a temporary summertime culture—of creating potential spaces in which we continue to join with others to support, challenge, nourish, and play with the questions of "How?" "Why?" and "What will this look like, what will this mean?"

In these intermediate arenas, conflict doesn't vanish, but our ideas about just what the conflict is *can* change as that gap between individual and institution, "me" and "not-me," is populated by other individuals, enriched by relationships, and complicated by recognitions that institutions aren't always "out there" but "in here," in our language, rituals, and assumptions. Especially with their emphasis on relational-work, such spaces can foster, rather than suppress, the "rhetoric of dissensus" advocated by John Trimbur and others: Sue's sense of trust and support through project activities and through her reading enabling her to call attention to and dissent from the group's dismissal of "escapist" reading; Martha's relationship with Sue enabling her to reexamine and critique what had been her "sacred beliefs" about literacy; Kay's reading of Mike Rose and her exchange of writing with others following Roberts' visit showing us all how a voice of difference can be constructed and made audible. In potential spaces, as these teachers demonstrate, we can revise our relationship to conflict from a two-way pull between acquiescence or flight to the opportunity to join in seeing how what is "given" can be examined, questioned, pushed against, changed.

"Meanings change as we think about them," Ann Berthoff writes, and Sue, Martha, Jeri, Kay, and others in the literacy project can tell us how both individual meanings and shared realities change as we enter into potential spaces that foster zestful, supported questioning and play (71). These teachers can tell us that we need in all classes (not to mention in the whole of our academic lives) to make *time*, make *space*, form *practices*, and form *relationships* for this kind of radical play. And, maybe especially, these teachers can tell us that we need to consider with our students and with each other ways to continue this work beyond the boundaries of five or sixteen weeks—into creative living, into active membership in our cultures, into the lifelong practice of revision.

Notes

1. For an examination of those dichotomies and their history, see Ritchie.

2. In this project, I followed ethnographic and case-study models for research, participating in and keeping field notes on all class activities, collecting writings from project participants, and conducting interviews with three participants twice during the five weeks, as well as meeting with two the following year. The purpose for this research was two-fold. First, since the literacy project was a new and experimental course, the University of Nebraska-Lincoln Composition Program wanted a thick description and multiple perspectives of the course to learn how participants described their experiences and to see what revisions in a future project should be made. Second, we wanted to model through my position and activities in the project one way in which a teacher could be a researcher in his/her classroom. I've fictionalized the names of participants in and visitors to the project throughout this essay.

3. This form of play to examine, question, and alter is very different from the passive notion of play prevalent in Western culture and used to reinforce, rather than reexamine, the status quo—as when a male co-worker, accused of workplace sexual harassment, responds by saying, "I was only *playing* around." That is *not* the kind of play Winnicott calls a "basic form of living," and that is not the idea of play I want to promote here or in my classrooms.

4. This renaming can also help those of us in composition studies revise the resistance/assimilation dichotomy that, as Peter Mortensen and Gesa Kirsch

have explored, has structured discussions about academic literacy and authority. It can open up a space between arguing for uncritical repudiation of academic conventions or arguing for equally uncritical acquiescence.

5. Jeri's presence in the literacy project, I think, prevented all of us from constructing our school administrations as the kind of monolithic and oppressive force that Sunstein describes in *Composing a Culture*. As project teachers worked to create relationships with Jeri, they had to question and complicate their representations of their own schools' administrators. As Jeri described wanting to encourage change in her school but meeting with quiet resistance from teachers, project participants had to reconsider their own forms of resistance. Teachers talked, for instance, about how they and their colleagues would sit, arms folded, in the back rows of in-service workshops they'd had no part in planning—and how they had never joined together to propose their own teacher-led in-service workshop. In this way and in others, Jeri helped point us toward renaming the wide gap between teachers and administrators as a space in which speech and negotiation might be possible, needed, collectively, to at least be tried.

6. Martha's narrative of heady enthusiasm and dramatic change through participation in the summer writing project, quickly followed by the "crumbling" of her new beliefs and practices, creating the increasing sense that she must now choose between being a teacher or having a life, tells me that we need to revisit the goals and activities of both writing and literacy projects. In "Lives on the Outside," Lil Brannon considers the self-sacrificing image of the female teacher who (as in Nancie Atwell's *In the Middle*) "writes to all 150 students almost daily, keeps daily detailed records on all students' work, holds daily conferences individually with every child, always smiling, always there for her students" (461). Such an ideal image, Brannon writes, insures that "no teacher can in fact be gifted or energetic or self-sacrificing enough" (461). Such an ideal image may also be what the National Writing Project and other teacher-education programs promote—setting up teachers like Martha for failure unless they are also introduced to the means for scrutinizing and revising such cultural constructions of the teacher.

7. That course, which enrolled nearly thirty teachers, including those who had been unable to participate in the summer literacy project, was repeated, at the teachers' urging, the following spring semester as well and has continued informally in monthly potluck meetings.

Works Cited

Bakhtin, Mikhail. "Epic and Novel." *The Dialogic Imagination: Four Essays*. Trans. Caryl Emerson and Michael Holquist. Ed. Michael Holquist. Austin: U of Texas P, 1981. 3-40.

Berthoff, Ann E. *The Making of Meaning*. Portsmouth, NH: Boynton, 1981.

Bishop, Wendy. *Something Old, Something New: College Writing Teachers and Classroom Change*. Carbondale: Southern Illinois UP, 1990.

Bleich, David. *The Double Perspective: Language, Literacy, and Social Relations*. New York: Oxford UP, 1988.

Brannon, Lil. "M[other]: Lives on the Outside." *Written Communication* 10 (1993): 457-65.

de Lauretis, Teresa. *Technologies of Gender: Essays on Theory, Film, and Fiction*. Bloomington: Indiana UP, 1987.

Flax, Jane. *Thinking Fragments: Psychoanalysis, Feminism, and Postmodernism in the Contemporary West*. Berkeley: U of California P, 1990.

Gore, Jennifer. *The Struggles for Pedagogies: Critical and Feminist Discourses as Regimes of Truth*. New York: Routledge, 1993.

Heath, Shirley Brice. *Ways with Words: Language, Life, and Work in Communities and Classrooms*. Cambridge: Cambridge UP, 1982.

hooks, bell. *Talking Back: Thinking Feminist, Thinking Black*. Boston: South End, 1989.

Hunter, Ian. *Culture and Government: The Emergence of Literacy Education*. London: Macmillan, 1988.

Knoblauch, C.H. "Literacy and the Politics of Education." Lunsford, Moglen, and Slevin. 74-80.

Knoblauch, C.H., and Lil Brannon. *Critical Teaching and the Idea of Literacy*. Portsmouth: Boynton, 1993.

Kristeva, Julia. "A New Type of Intellectual: The Dissident." Trans. Sean Hand. *The Kristeva Reader*. Ed. Toril Moi. New York: Columbia UP, 1986. 292-300.

Lunsford, Andrea, Helene Moglen, and James Slevin, eds. *The Right to Literacy*. New York: MLA, 1990.

Mortensen, Peter, and Gesa E. Kirsch. "On Authority in the Study of Writing." *College Composition and Communication* 44 (1993): 556-72.

Rich, Adrienne. "When We Dead Awaken: Writing as Re-Vision." *On Lies, Secrets, and Silence.* New York: Norton, 1979. 33-49.

Ritchie, Joy. "Between the Trenches and the Ivory Towers: Divisions Between University Professors and High School Teachers." *Farther Along: Transforming Dichotomies in Rhetoric and Composition.* Ed. Kate Ronald and Hephzibah Roskelly. Portsmouth, N.H.: Boynton, 1990. 101-21.

Rose, Mike. *Lives on the Boundary: The Struggles and Achievements of America's Underprepared.* New York: Free Press, 1989.

Shelnutt, Eve. *The Writing Room: Keys to the Craft of Fiction and Poetry.* Marietta, GA: Longstreet, 1989.

Sunstein, Bonnie. *Composing a Culture: Inside a Summer Writing Program with High School Teachers.* Portsmouth, N.H.: Boynton, 1994.

Trimbur, John. "Consensus and Difference in Collaborative Learning." *College English* 51 (1989): 602-16.

Welch, Nancy. "Resisting the Faith: Conversion, Resistance, and the Training of Teachers." *College English* 55 (1993): 387-401.

Winnicott, D.W. *Playing and Reality.* London: Tavistock, 1971.

Wright, Elizabeth. *Psychoanalytic Criticism: Theory in Practice.* 1984. London: Routledge, 1989.

Appendix A
Course Description

The syllabus for the literacy project outlined three goals: (1) to use our own histories as readers and writers to explore the contexts in which literate practices take place and the social meanings and values those practices imply; (2) to examine students' needs as developing readers and writers and the family and community literacies they bring with them to school; and (3) to examine the assumptions about literacy on which our teaching practices are based and how those assumptions are situated within a larger educational and cultural context. Shared texts for the course were *Lives on the Boundary*, *Ways with Words*, and *The Right to Literacy.* Optional texts available in the classroom included *Lessons from a Child*, *In the Middle*, *Insult to Intelligence*, *The Violence of Literacy*, and *Pedagogy of the Oppressed.*

The daily activities of the project included:

Literate Life History: In the literate life history, participants focused on one episode in their lives as readers and writers or recreated a range of episodes to help them consider their literate development, its relationship to their familial and cultural contexts, and the place of writing and reading in shaping their lives.

Literacy Case Study: In the case study, participants interviewed another person—student, family member, or friend—and examined that conversation with the goals of gaining insight into the complexities of literacy in another's life and becoming better observers of students in their own classes.

Reading and Observation Journal: The journal was defined as a forum for participants to respond to their readings and to class activities, as well as observe, record, and examine language use and literate practices in and outside of the classroom. In addition to the teacher-guides, participants gave their journals to one other person in class each week for reading and response.

Literacy Events: Literacy events, collaboratively planned and conducted by two project participants each day, asked the class to engage in a reading and/or writing activity and examine the activity's implicit assumptions and agendas.

Small Groups: During every session participants met in small groups to read drafts of their writing—literate life histories, case studies, journal observations, letters, position papers, poems.

Literacy Storehouse and Book Talks: Each class began with a participant reading from a text of his or her choice (for instance, *Writing without Teachers*, *Backlash*, *Ceremony*) and ended with one or two participants giving a review of a book they were currently reading.

Town Meetings: Town meetings provided forums for participants to speak for several minutes on an issue in literacy that they wanted the class to consider and discuss.

Newsletter: Each week participants put together excerpts from journals, case studies, writings generated during the literacy events, letters, and book reviews in a newsletter for the class.

Appendix B
Sample Class Outline

First Hour

Literary Storehouse: Louise (reading poem by Gwendolyn Brooks and excerpt from Adrienne Rich's "When We Dead Awaken: Writing as Re-vision")

Literacy Event and Discussion: Kay and Peggy ("Stepping Stones," a journal activity designed to help participants identify, examine, and compare life-shaping events)

Second Hour
Small Group Meetings

Third Hour
Literacy Event and Discussion: Donna (visitor to the project and professor in the English department and Women's Studies, leading reading and collaborative writing activity in examining roles of race, class, and sexual orientation in writing and reading; discussion of suppressions of those roles in classrooms, consequences, and means for resistance)
Town Meeting: Martha (a critique of the assumptions underlying the "Hooked-on-Phonics" approach to reading)
Book Talk: Nancy (on Peter Elbow's *What Is English?*)
Lunch: Linda's house

Part 2

Philosophical Issues

Interrupting the Conversation: The Constructionist Dialogue in Composition

Joseph Petraglia

In "Current-Traditional Rhetoric: Paradigm and Practice," James Berlin and Robert Inkster make the important point that epistemological assumptions underlie every conception of rhetoric and composition. They suggest that we cannot demonstrate what it means "to persuade" or "to explain" without a tacit belief in what it means "to know." I believe they are also correct in acknowledging a general neglect of these assumptions on the part of those of us who teach writing: it is fairly easy for instructors of composition (indeed, most teachers) to buy into a dominant theory of knowledge unquestioningly.

Nevertheless, though awareness of the ways in which written and oral discourse contribute to what people believe they know (that is, how rhetoric may be epistemic) may seem marginalized in the contemporary writing classroom, it has been a central issue for philosophers and rhetoricians since Plato and Aristotle. From that classical period to the contemporary writings of Burke, Perelman, and Young, Becker, and Pike, the tradition of investigating rhetoric's role in producing rather than merely transmitting knowledge has remained intact. Though it is not surprising that composition studies should follow in the wake of rhetoric and begin investigating the knowledge-generating capacity of language, the writing field seems to have carved out for itself the distinction, and perhaps the burden, of being the first discipline to bring to the fore questions of how this theory of knowledge relates to classroom practice.

A problem has arisen in the field, however, in that most of the rhetoric-as-epistemic arguments have settled on a rather eclectic and politicized conception of the issue and its relevance to the teaching of writing. Composition theorists, working within what appears to me to be a closed dialogue, downplay or completely ignore a wealth of critical thought available in related disciplines—speech communications and social psychology in particular. My use of the term "dialogue" is intended both as a convenient shorthand for "a-community-of-writers-in-composition-who-have-introduced-and-continue-to-popularize-*rhetoric-as-epistemic*," and as a way to convey my sense of that community's insularity from the criticisms and controversies surrounding "social construction," the somewhat generic term for social knowledge-production that composition has adopted in arguing for rhetoric's epistemic powers. In this essay, I'd like to suggest some of the basic premises that seem to underlie composition's conception of social construction, and to critique those premises from the perspectives of theorists in related disciplines that are investigating the relationship of discourse to knowledge.

Rhetoric-as-Epistemic(s)

Briefly (and broadly), a social constructionist argues that knowledge is created, maintained, and altered through an individual's interaction with and within his or her "discourse community." Knowledge resides in consensus rather than in any transcendent or objective relationship between a knower and that which is to be known. The choice of social constructionism as the contemporary composition field's most high-profile conception of rhetoric-as-epistemic is not for lack of alternatives; Michael Leff's "In Search of Ariadne's Thread: A Review of the Recent Literature on Rhetorical Theory" offers a number of candidates. Leff classifies perspectives on the knowledge-generating potential of rhetoric into four major groupings.[1] The first acknowledges rhetoric's weakest claim to knowledge generation: its ability to create a place in an already accepted paradigm for a new particular (cf. Perelman and Olbrechts-Tyteca's notion basing arguments on the structure of reality). The second argues a stronger case for rhetoric's knowledge-making capability in noting its role in establishing consensus in order to create a social knowledge which complements personal knowledge (cf. Bitzer's conception of "public knowledge"). The third perspective views rhetoric as establishing the knowledge necessary to mediate the limitations of formal logic. The last notion of rhetoric-as-epistemic suggests that knowledge *is* rhetorical. It is this last view, argued forcefully in Robert L. Scott's seminal "On Viewing Rhetoric as Epistemic," that basically forms what the discipline of composition has come to term "social constructionism."

The term "social construction," however, is the rubric under which a number of theories of social knowledge are subsumed; almost as many variations of social construction exist as there are rhetoricians, philosophers, sociologists, and anthropologists to promote them. Different writers serve as the principal gurus behind particular versions of a social theory. Although Thomas Kuhn and Richard Rorty appear to be most often cited in composition scholarship, social-construction's modern form has been variously attributed to sociologists Karl Mannheim, G.H. Mead and Emile Durkheim, anthropologists Franz Boas and Clifford Geertz, linguists Benjamin Lee Whorf and Edward Sapir, literary critic Michel Foucault, and Karl Marx, to name but a few.

The Constructionist Dialogue in Composition

Though cohesive (if problematic) theories of social construction can be found in disciplines such as the sociologies of science and knowledge, philosophy of science, hermeneutics, and history, no one theory of social construction from any one discipline has been adopted by the field of composition *in toto*. For this reason, the variety of social constructions presented in this paper is actually the result of many social constructionisms—a phenomenon that merits its own lengthy investigation, but not one with which this paper is concerned.[2]

This paper's stipulative definition of the dialogue's conception of social construction is limited to the manner in which its best-known advocates in the field have presented it, especially as explicated in Kenneth Bruffee's 1986 article in *College English* entitled "Social Construction, Language and Knowledge: A Bibliographical Essay" and James Berlin's article in that same journal entitled "Rhetoric and Ideology in the Writing Class." Though I am arguing that the dialogue's "core" is reflected in these two works, both Bruffee and Berlin have applied a constructionist stance to a broad range of topics of interest to English studies. These two significant articles are inclusive of, but are by no means limited to, the following premises, which I suggest form the basis of social construction in composition:

- Real entities ("reality") include knowledge, beliefs, truths, and selves.
- All reality is arrived at by consensus.
- Consensus, and thus knowledge, is "discovered" solely through public discourse (rhetoric).
- Reality changes as consensus/knowledge changes.

According to Bruffee, "A social constructionist position in any discipline assumes that entities we normally call reality, knowledge, thought, facts, texts, selves, and so on are constructs generated by communities of like-minded peers" (774). Without denying the existence of a physical reality, social constructionism is concerned solely with human perception of, and interaction with, that reality. To quote Bruffee again, "We generate knowledge by 'dealing with' our *beliefs* about the physical reality that shoves us around. Specifically, we generate knowledge by justifying those beliefs socially" (777). Thus, it is the social arena that produces what passes for knowledge, not "scientific inquiry" in any exclusively experimental sense. As linguistic interaction is necessary to establish and convey knowledge, rhetoric plays a central role in the discovery and solution of whatever problems a society believes it faces. Berlin's sketch of what he terms "social-epistemic" rhetoric summarizes the constructionist position as one which views reality as "located in a relationship that involves the dialectical interaction of the observer, the discourse community (social group) in which the observer is functioning, and the material conditions of existence" (488). The "observer," according to Berlin, "is always a creation of a particular and cultural moment" (489). Without explicitly *denying* the possibility of an individual's intellect existing apart from the communal public knowledge, social constructionists in English studies do not find a place for an individual who is not him or herself constructed by the environment.

For the teacher of composition, a social constructionist perspective has resulted in a focus on *discourse communities*—communities that share "values, objects of inquiry, research methodologies, evidential contexts, persuasion strategies and conventions, forms and formats, and conversational forms" in addition to conventions rooted in language (Reither 18). Much of the constructionist literature concentrates on the dynamics of such communities and the ways in which we as teachers can facilitate our students' entry into them (Bartholomae).[3] Consonant with Foucaultian and Freirean theories of knowledge as power, social constructionists in composition of all political persuasions have sought to promote access to knowledge-creating communities as a critical first step toward student empowerment. Compared to current-traditional and cognitive rhetorics which focus on the individual writer and how he or she can and/or should shape discourse to gain the audience's assent, one might say that constructionists focus on the ways in which the audience (that is, the community) shapes the discourse of its members.

An important theme in composition studies' dialogue is that a constructionist theory of knowledge heralds an overdue acknowledgment of a rheto-centric universe—a stance reminiscent of Kant's coronation of philosophy as "the queen of sciences" for its self-proclaimed ability to sit in judgment of the legitimacy of whatever knowledge sciences might produce. Bruffee has suggested that "it is possible to take the position that since knowledge is identical with language and other symbol systems, the problems presented by social constructionist thought are of a sort that humanists in general and English teachers in particular are especially well-equipped to cope with, if not solve" (778). The appreciation of rhetoric as a foundational discipline, critical for understanding any other academic enterprise, is thus a recurring theme in much constructionist literature, especially in English studies and rhetoric.

To speak of a constructionist dialogue is not to promote a conspiracy theory or to suggest that the political or pedagogical objectives of the dialogue's participants are identical or even similar. The theories of social construction held by Bruffee and Berlin do not overlap in many respects, particularly in terms of their sources.[4] Bruffee traces his ideas to Rorty and Vygotsky in order to provide a rationale for classroom collaboration; Berlin draws heavily on leftist literary theorists and Paulo Freire to advance the cause of "radical" pedagogy.[5] Instead, the term "dialogue" is meant to draw attention to the fundamental epistemic assumptions this conversation's participants appear to share as well as those they have commonly chosen to ignore. It is important to note as well that not all social constructionists in *rhetoric* are participants in *composition's* dialogue. Though writers such as Robert L. Scott and Barry Brummett are widely read in composition studies generally, they are not widely quoted by dialogists, nor do they in turn draw from the work of composition theorists to any great extent. The dialogue has no "card-carrying" members, of course, but one often associates social construction in composition with writers such as Berlin and Bruffee as well as Patricia Bizzell and David Bartholomae, as they are a few of the more frequent contributors.

In this paper, I make no pretense of critiquing any single dialogist, definitively characterizing any individual's full-blown conception of a theory of knowledge, trivializing any individual's contribution to our understanding of social construction, or taking a community of writers "to task." Rather, it is my belief that the constructionist dialogue (like *any* discourse among a fairly static group of participants), has a life of its own, especially from the perspective of people outside of the conversation. What I refer to as the "dialogue" is not the sum but a *subset*, a reduction, of its parts. It is this subset, these generalities, that have shaped the discussion of social construction in composition studies and which will be examined more closely. The remaining sections of this paper look at how each of the four constructionist premises listed above can serve as a focal point for critics seeking to resolve what they perceive as weak links in a social theory of knowledge.

An Issue of Ontology

Premise 1: *Real entities ("reality") include knowledge, beliefs, truths, and selves.*

In *The Strife of Systems*, Nicholas Rescher suggests that theories on any subject are comprised of premises which are independently plausible but inevitably inconsistent when taken together as a whole; theorists thus refine their disciplines by exploiting these inconsistencies. Premise 1 of social construction's definition presented here, however, demonstrates an instance in which a basic tenet of the theory has been criticized for being inconsistent within itself. Such a criticism comes from a viewpoint Richard Cherwitz and James Hikins call "perspectivist."

Cherwitz and Hikins note that the social constructionist claim that entities are created intersubjectively (through social interaction) requires an acceptance of the existence of objects (that is, the persons doing the "intersubjectifying"). But this leads constructionists to the "inherently solipsistic" conclusion that "other persons must be regarded as the product of meaning too" and that "in the absence of any account establishing the objective existence of other subjects, intersubjectivity collapses altogether" (254). Similarly, Jeffery Bineham states, "An intersubjective position traditionally is assumed to result from the collision and consequent refinement of two subjective positions. The subjective mind thus becomes primary in importance" (54). Thus, the status of the knower to the known is indeterminate if one takes literally the premise "reality includes knowledge, beliefs, truths, and selves."

Another variation on the chicken-or-egg riddle this first premise poses is the related ontological issue of whether, temporally, one can posit theories of existence and knowledge simultaneously. Earl Croasmun and Cherwitz argue that "any human system of ontological beliefs presupposes a valid epistemology. . . . A general theory of what should be granted the status of knowledge precedes the consideration of any specific ontological statement. . . . It makes no sense to suggest that we know something about the world unless we first determine what it means to 'know'" (8). Bineham too has suggested that the conflation of epistemic and ontological issues is one that will be central to future discussions of rhetoric-as-epistemic. Lack of a clear distinction between "reality" and "knowledge" is what many writers have discerned as social construction's most fundamental error.

The Need for Objective Reality

Premise 2: *All reality is arrived at by consensus.*

Criticism of premise 2 generally settles on the necessity of an objective reality or notion of transcendent "truth." At least three responses to this issue have surfaced in communications journals. Cherwitz and Hikins propose a perspectivist account of reality based on *relationality*. Cherwitz along with Croasmun offer a variation on the theme by resurrecting a notion of *objectivity* (as opposed to "objectivism"), and C. Jack Orr's suggestion that *critical rationalism* replace intersubjectivism offers a third articulation of the need for objective truth. A fourth argument relating to premise 2 does not make a case for objective truth, but instead goes further than the dialogists in the opposite direction: what can be called the hermeneutic perspective claims that not only reality, but *consensus itself*, is illusory.

The problem the first three positions find with a crude constructionist denial of objective reality is that it results in a relativist theory that ultimately must collapse under its own weight. As Orr makes clear, "Even if one insists . . . that the world we know is a rhetorically constructed, interpreted world, we wish to recognize, exchange, criticize, and improve upon our interpretations. This enterprise is made intelligible through the presupposition of an independent reality, a common target, toward which our interpretations are intended" (268). H. Gene Blocker argues, "It is the concept of an objective reality that enables us to acknowledge the limitation of the human standpoint to completely reproduce the world in thought and deed. We recognize our constructions of reality as constructs by making reference to an objective reality which our constructs fail to capture!" (qtd. in Orr 267). In this way, the argument follows, the articulation of any position, including that of a constructionist, assumes an appeal to some objective reality or notion of truth. Of course, thoughtful constructionists do not deny that material reality "exists," but neither have they really engaged the issue of representation versus materialism as philosophers of science routinely must. The problems encountered by endorsing subjectivism, even if the "subjects" are entire communities, are as recurring as they are counter-intuitive, yet it is seemingly unavoidable given a premise as all-encompassing as this second one. Though constructionists (with the notable exception of Scott in rhetoric) assiduously avoid using the "r" word, basing reality solely on consensus does not rule out relativism; it merely pushes it to a higher plane.

Cherwitz and Hikins critique a less strident form of social construction which they label "mitigated subjectivity" that attempts to moderate somewhat both premises 1 and 2 to escape the intersubjective dilemma. Its proponents, notably many philosophers of science, set up a dichotomy in which some realities/entities (such as objects of the material world) are independent of a subject's perception of them, while others (such as values and beliefs) are constructed intersubjectively. Mitigated subjectivists do not escape the brand of solipsism any better than their unmitigating counterparts for, according to Cherwitz and Hikins, they "embrace the dualist [Cartesian] position in their separation of mental and physical entities, without commenting on the philosophical problems which such dualism engenders. . . . How does one account for the influence of one realm on the other? How is it that two so qualitatively distinct worlds coexist and interact?" (254).

Cherwitz and Hikins suggest that perspectivism offers a way out of this bind. Central to perspectivism is the concept of *relationality*, originally formulated by sociologist Karl Mannheim (see Berger and Luckmann), or the notion that "entities in the universe are what they are solely because of the relationships in which they stand to other entities" (Cherwitz and Hikins 252). This position allows that individuals' accounts of the world are going to vary as their relationships to other entities are unique. In terms of classical rhetoric, one might say it comes down to a question of *stasis*. Disagreement does not result from the existence of different realities, for there is only one reality. Rather, people appear to disagree only because they stand in different relationships to reality. Once *stasis* is agreed upon and the other's relationship is understood, conflict is resolved: "On this account, the apparently contradictory judgments are really not contradictory at all, *since they are judgments about different aspects of the same object*" (264).[6]

Croasmun and Cherwitz develop further the distinction Cherwitz and Hikins make between *objectivity* and *objectivism* in the formers' "Beyond Rhetorical Relativism." Here, "objectivity" is defined as a concept that "frames an ontological assumption about the objects of reality, including discourse," whereas "objectivism" "characterizes a specific epistemological methodology for gaining knowledge of that reality. To embrace 'objectivity' is not necessarily to accept the tenets of objectivism" (3). This seemingly self-evident distinction enables them to preclude the relativism constructionists themselves would prefer to avoid. One can maintain that reality is objective and at the same time hold that knowledge of reality is subjective.

A third critique of premise 2, closely related to perspectivism in its retention of objective reality, is that of the *critical rationalists*, represented by Karl Popper and C. Jack Orr. Because crude constructionism refuses to entertain the possibility of objective truth, "truth" for them is dismissed as another construct, another social myth humans have invented to assuage our fear of relativism. Nevertheless, the utility of a notion of objectivity is seen by critical rationalists as too important to be discarded. By holding the objective existence of reality as a constant, they say, we are able to *criticize*, a faculty that intersubjectivity denies us. Orr states that critical rationalism is unlike the intersubjectivity of social construction theory in that, "critical rationalism retains the concepts of objective reality and truth. Therefore, it becomes possible to relate knowledge and truth dialectically, that is, to question each consensually validated claim to truth in the name of truth which is beyond consensual validation" (273). Of course, frameworks for knowledge will differ from knower to knower, but if we can engage each other in critical debate by appealing to an objective reality about which some propositions must ultimately be true, then, critical rationalists maintain, we can "take a constructionistic social theory at least several steps beyond the perils of intersubjectivism." Popper's influence is clearly felt here, as critical rationalism privileges the rendering of theories *falsifiable*, or subject to disproof.

Finally, perhaps the most troublesome critique of this second premise has its roots within the dialogue itself, in what might be seen as the hermeneutic "stance." Part of the baggage the dialogue takes on when it aligns itself with intersubjectivist philosophers such as Rorty (and, to a lesser degree, literary theorists such as Foucault and Jacques Derrida) is a belief in the significance of the interpretive act and the assumption that knowledge is not only constructed, but inevitably *mis*constructed insofar as language is rooted in idiosyncratic and unsystematic interpretation even as it is communalized. A strong hermeneutic stance, one might think, would prove especially problematic for constructionist theorists of composition, as they have a tacit investment in the systematic nature of consensual knowledge (that is, they want knowledge to be predictable enough to be of use in achieving some pedagogical end) and yet are intellectually indebted to theorists such as Rorty and Derrida whose conceptions of social construction are anything but "user-friendly."[7]

Rorty is less insistent than many of his followers in composition on tying reality to consensus by admitting, and even privileging, the existence of knowledge that operates outside of consensus, which in *Philosophy and the Mirror of Nature* he has termed "abnormal," though he is unclear as to the where and how of its origins. For Rorty, the goal of philosophy is to "keep the conversation going rather than to find objective truth" (*Philosophy* 377). In Rorty's ideal system, the paradigm would be dialectically challenged and undermined, never allowed to wallow in stultifying, "normal" discourse.

It is at this point that the strain of juggling the concerns of social construction with those of education are most apparent. Perhaps in an effort to make Rorty's perspective more operational, social constructionists in composition talk about "the conversation" (by which Rorty invites abnormal discourses to engage normal discourse in perpetual "edification"), while at the same time suggesting a more normative, systematic approach to knowledge—that based on the consensus of the discourse community. This seems logical; if social constructivists are to direct the teaching of rhetoric and composition toward any end, they cannot have students running about discoursing abnormally. As a correlate, educators have to assume they have some more or less stable knowledge worth imparting to students, knowledge that can be assimilated and used until it is tested and perhaps abandoned.

Thomas Kent underscores the tension the hermeneutic stance causes for constructionist teachers of composition when he notes that Davidson's and Derrida's "analyses of discourse suggest that (a) both writing and reading require hermeneutic skills that refute codification, and, therefore (b) neither writing nor reading can be taught as a systematic process" (25). For this reason, social constructionists in composition seem to make strange bedfellows with less-constrained, edifying philosophers who do not face similar occupational hazards. Put another way (and not too glibly, I hope), the educable unit that educators deal with is the individual student: we do not teach bodies of consensus-builders; we can only teach their members. The dialogue's pervasive preoccupation with consensus, it might be argued, is at odds with the teacherly focus on individual interpretation and agency to which it also subscribes.

Distinguishing among Knowledges

Premise 3: *Consensus/knowledge is "discovered" solely through public discourse (rhetoric).*

A key, perhaps *the* key, argument in the dialogue's constructivist theory of knowledge rests upon the presumption that all reality is mediated through language. As I noted earlier, such a premise is central to discussions of rhetoric-as-epistemic and makes it easy to understand social construction's appeal to those of us whose job it is to teach language skills. Critiques of premise 3 can be leveled from at least two slightly different perspectives. Many writers in speech communications as well as the cognitive sciences maintain that emphasis on the discourse within the social environment as *the* generator of knowledge ignores the ways in which the human brain "produces" ideas and perceptions. Other critics fault premise 3 for ignoring the non-social aspects of the "self." Both groups, basically, are making the case for widening the term "knowledge" to include forms other than the social.

Cognitivists would be critical of constructionists such as Berlin for not taking into account the varying abilities and idiosyncrasies of individuals in constructing meaning. Berlin seems to suggest that drawing attention to differences in cognitive abilities is politically expedient and has as its result, if not aim, the perpetuation of corporate capitalism (483). However, cognitivists would say that such differences can and do exist independent of their political desirability. George Steiner has noted that there are "such subconscious, deliberately concealed, or declared associations so extensive and intricate that they probably equal the sum and uniqueness of our status as an individual person" (qtd. in Gregg 137). To cognitivists it may seem paradoxical that a constructionist holds the opinion, on the one hand, that any given event cannot have a single, objective meaning, while maintaining on the other that individuals' processes of perception are identical or at least inconsequential. It is pointless, from a cognitivist perspective, to argue that qualitative (in terms of superiority) differences in cognitive abilities account for the variety of interpretations; equally capable people are still going to perceive things differently. These critics suggest, however, that it is likewise unreasonable to deny that individuals construct meaning based on private associations that may be withheld from public validation. Much of what I have already presented as the hermeneutic stance clearly ties into the positions of Steiner, Gregg, and others who argue for the primacy of individual cognition.

No contemporary cognitivist perspective that I am aware of supports an epistemology that could be labeled "positivist." Cognitivists generally concur that meaning is constructed both subjectively and socially and that there is a constant interaction between the environment of the mind and that of the outside world. There are psychological and physiological differences between individuals which suggest that neither associations nor knowledge can be constructed identically from subject to subject. Such features are crucial not only to personal knowledge but to social knowledge as well.

It is worthwhile, I think, to quote extensively from Richard Gregg's

"Rhetoric and Knowing: The Search for Perspective." Drawing heavily on research in psycholinguistics, Gregg, a strong advocate of acknowledging the distinction between individual and social knowledge, claims that "on the one hand, individual neurological structures are prerequisites for the development of social meanings, and on the other, the development of systems of social meanings will have concurrent consequences both for the further development of the neurological structure and other systems of social meaning. There is constant interaction between individual systems of meanings and a system of socially shared meanings, with neither system effacing the other" (136). To cut away the individual dimension of meaning making and to try to create a purely "'social knowledge,' or 'public knowledge' or 'explicit knowledge' is to artificially render static the active processes of meaning" (142). Gregg says Steiner has noted that "meaning is full of associative matter constructed from personal experience and the subconscious, and that such associative contexts will vary from person to person" (137). It is our ability to form idiosyncratic associations and our attendant capacity to generate personal knowledge which define our individuality. On a slightly different note, Gregg alludes to research that is discovering the impact *affective states* and *motivation* have on cognition and meaning making (I'll discuss such research shortly). He concludes: "if personal meaning is an inherent part of human meaning, we ought to avoid distinctions which preclude rhetoric scholars from being able to consider it" (138). Thus, Gregg finds the constructionists' rigid separation of personal and social knowledge (and their neglect of the former) both artificial and unproductive.

Whereas Gregg has argued against the premise that knowledge can only be generated through public discourse by suggesting that knowledge is not always *public*, research presented by Linda Flower and John Hayes challenges the notion that knowledge is always in the form of *discourse*. Their "multiple representation thesis" suggests that ideas and their articulation fall somewhere on a continuum ranging from sensory perception to formal prose. In studying how writers represent knowledge to themselves, Flower and Hayes discovered that "different modes of representation can range from imagery, to metaphors and schemas, to abstract conceptual propositions, to prose" (129). Thus, "As writers compose, they create multiple internal and external representations of meaning. Some of these representations, such as an imagistic one, will be better at expressing certain kinds of meaning than prose would be, and some will be more difficult to translate into prose than others" (122). In other words, meaning, and therefore knowledge, may be represented and brought to bear on problem-solving in the writer's mind without the aid of linguistic articulation. Research in cognition has suggested that non-verbal representations may be stored as a *visual image or pattern* that mimics its material referent, a *perceptual experience*, such as might be useful in determining whether the red lifesavers are cherry- or strawberry-flavored, or as a *procedure* "in which perceptual cues play a large share in 'knowing' something (e.g. how to dance your way across a crowded floor)" (130). If constructivists concede that these abilities count as knowledge, it cannot follow that all knowledge is socially constructed.

A dispute between two constructionists, Thomas Farrell and Walter Carleton, proves instructive. Farrell, a "mitigated subjectivist" in Cherwitz and Hikins' parlance, distinguishes between social and "technical" (perceptual) knowledge. Carleton argues that Farrell is resurrecting a dualism that social construction has sought to eradicate, and presents an extended syllogism which he believes logically precludes Farrell's notion of personal knowledge. The first five premises of the syllogism argue convincingly that "selves" have a social "dimension," but the subsequent three premises suggest:

> (6) The impossibility of being a wholly private self entails the impossibility of discovering or expressing wholly private knowledge.
> (7) Yet there is knowledge.
> (8) Therefore, the knowledge we have must be social knowledge. (325)

While the case that Farrell, Gregg, Flower and Hayes, and others make for the individual's potential to create knowledge is not undermined by the acceptance of social knowledge's existence, these scholars would suggest that Carleton's assertion—that as individuals are not wholly private beings, their knowledge is entirely social—fails to resolve the issues relating to the recognition of the role of individual cognition they have advanced.

Finally, research in social psychology is beginning to explore the relationship of affect to cognition and thus has created a whole new literature that undermines a conception of knowledge as entirely social. Although this scholarship is too extensive and varied to summarize adequately here, research on the ways in which emotion shapes knowing can be roughly categorized into three areas: emotion and perception, emotion and avoidance (both cognitive and behavioral), and emotion and memory. I will briefly touch on some key concepts in these areas that seem to have implications for a constructionist theory of knowledge.

The literature on emotion and perception is the least extensive but in some ways the most intriguing in that it focuses not on how individuals deal with or interpret information, but rather on the physical ability to acquire information itself. This research suggests that emotional arousal systems act to physiologically alter an individual's ability to use other sensory systems such as hearing and sight. Douglas Derryberry and Mary Klevjord Rothbart have called this phenomenon *perceptual defense*: "a tendency for stimuli of negative emotional tone to have relatively high recognition thresholds" (139). Psychologists have conducted a large number of experiments using very different designs to demonstrate that emotionally negative words, both written and spoken, more easily escape detection when placed subliminally in text than positive or neutrally toned words, suggesting that emotional (emogen) encoding prior to cognitive (logogen or imagen) encoding may circumvent the mind's cognitive perception processes. Thus, a sender's message is not only subject to personal interpretation, but to personal perception as well.

"Sensation-seeking and avoidance" is the term Marvin Zuckerman uses to describe the way affect motivates people to expose themselves, or avoid exposure, to information that enters cognition. Seeking or avoiding information is based on the "optimal level of arousal" theory proposed by Eysenck in 1967. Essentially, Eysenck, Zuckerman, and others have found that every individual has a level of emotional arousal at which he or she feels comfortable. When this "optimal" level is violated (that is, when the person feels over- or under-stimulated) cognition reacts accordingly by either seeking sensations to increase arousal to the optimal level, or avoiding sensation in order to reduce arousal to the optimal level. This affective-cognitive phenomenon has numerous implications, of course (see Pieters and Van Raaij), but for our purposes it suffices to note that every individual has his or her own level of arousal and thus seeks and avoids acquiring knowledge idiosyncratically, thus subverting the constructionist's tacit faith in discourse as the sole mediator of cognition.

The last area of research, emotion and memory, is the broadest and most complex literature in terms of the variety of claims and implications made by its researchers and theorists. Major contributors that composition and rhetoric theorists might find of most immediate interest include Gordon Bower, Margaret Clark, and Alice Isen and her coauthors. This area has witnessed tremendous growth over the last decade and continues to attract the attention of scholars throughout the field of psychology. A central theme in this literature is that of emotionally "toned" memory. As one might guess, the basic idea is that knowledge of words, situations, images, and so on may be encoded in long-term memory not only semantically, conceptually, and visually, but also emotionally. In other words, "cats" may be encoded in memory not only through the oral cue /kæts/ and other cognitive associations, but also in terms of one's emotional disposition toward cats. The memory of cats may then be retrieved through similarly emotionally-toned concepts; for instance, if one suffers from many phobias, being in a small, windowless room may invoke the thought of cats as the sensation of fear relates one's claustrophobia to one's aelurophobia. Though the *terms* that are being affectively linked (in this case "cats" and "enclosure") may ultimately be socially defined constructs, the link itself is not created through linguistic association. Clark's recent article "Moods and Social Judgments" demonstrates how such an emotional network may play a role in making simple judgments, but clearly such research has implications for more complex decision-making and knowledge-building.

The current research into affect is raising some exciting questions. Most fundamentally, it asks "what counts as knowledge?" If affect is not a discrete counterpart of cognition (as is commonly assumed) but actually *shapes* cognition by directing our attention to information and stimulating memory, what implications does this have for a conception of knowledge rooted in social discourse? It would seem to suggest that extra-linguistic phenomena play an enormous role in our mental lives. Though the realm of affect is by no means exempt from social construction in many respects, it certainly becomes more difficult to maintain an exclusively language-based theory of constructionism when affect is understood as critical to cognition.[8]

Questioning the Dynamics of Change

Premise 4: *Reality changes as consensus/knowledge changes.*

Central to social construction is the premise that reality changes as knowledge changes. Kuhn's phrase "paradigm shift" attempts to account for this change in the realm of science to an extent. As new observations and inexplicable phenomena challenge the existing paradigm, the paradigm must evolve so as to maintain the coherency and cohesiveness of the community. When the strain of the challenges becomes too great, however, the old paradigm crumbles, giving way to a new paradigm capable of commanding the community's allegiance. Though constructionism thus grants that consensus is subject to change, critics of this fourth premise suggest that a fairly loose intersubjective theory of knowledge, such as the one constructionists in composition promote, does not explain how *inter-communal* knowledges negotiate new consensuses. It makes sense that an outsider's opinion, either that of an individual or of some other extra-consensual entity, must serve as a catalyst for change; yet social constructionists do not explain how a minority's knowledge can exist in the face of consensus, much less alter that knowledge. From where do individuals derive unconventional ideas, and how can the expression of this "abnormal" discourse be tolerated?

Greg Myers raises a similar question when he points out that Bruffee fails to explain how knowledges evolve, differentiate, and come together again as consensus. He notes that "bodies of knowledge cannot be resolved into a consensus without one side losing something" (167). Though this conclusion may seem self-evident, the dynamics of consensus are neither specified nor alluded to in the dialogue which has generally played up the positive aspects of consensus-building. Like Kuhn, composition's constructionists are often content to confirm that inter-communal consensus is subject to change but do little either to show *how* competing communities arrive at all-important consensus or to acknowledge that consensus-building may not always be a progressive, "liberatory" process, that it could involve coercion instead.

Donald Cushman and Lawrence Prelli's "action theory perspective" takes the Wittgensteinian premise that "for an idea to count as knowledge, rules must be provided which allow agents embracing different ideological systems to share the same thoughts" and concludes that "knowledge, therefore, consists of those observations and ideas which remain stable under transformation" (275). At first glance, this definition of knowledge seems to preclude social construction altogether, but Cushman and Prelli suggest that it is by virtue of rhetorical action that understanding and rational consensus between ideologies is possible, again making consensus the focal point of knowledge, but providing at least a theory of how communities interact. Although the action theory perspective presumes a much less structured, theoretically "clean" conception of knowledge and of community than social constructionists do, their article (which is not a criticism of social construction *per se*) goes some way toward raising questions that a coherent theory of constructionism must address.

Conclusion: Resuming the Conversation

The purpose of this paper has been to look at social constructionism from the perspective of those that have found it lacking rather than from the perspective of its champions; naturally the resultant picture of constructionism is unfairly skewed to some extent. Also, I've purposely streamlined the constructionist argument so that it may be used as a springboard for exploring the scholarship of other fields. Even so, many of the questions these other perspectives raise seem important to composition but remain inadequately or inaccurately represented by those composition theorists who have taken the lead in importing the constructionist conversation to our own discipline. This is especially disturbing as the issues raised in this paper "against" social construction are hardly new; most if not all of the points made by communications theorists and psychologists have been fairly common currency in rhetoric for quite some time.

The question is not whether the field of composition can gain anything from a constructionist perspective; clearly it can and has. In a sense, the constructionist dialogue in composition is a welcome reaction, a counterbalance, to a field that has for too long accentuated the role of the individual writer and ignored the social forces that shape the writer's perception of reality. Current-traditional rhetoric enforced a long period of neglect of traditional social considerations such as audience and *kairos*, and subsequent rhetorics (including those emphasizing cognition) which tacitly acknowledge that the writer is only part of a broader social matrix, have been slow in examining the implications of this. A by-product of this reaction, however, seems to be that social construction has often been construed in such a way as to give further impetus to a political agenda, common in contemporary English departments, that centers on issues of social justice and empowerment even though there is little in constructionist theory itself that suggests a moral or political stance. Still, though the relationship of their social aims to a theory of knowledge might give one pause, constructionists in English have nonetheless succeeded in pushing concern for the social constraints imposed on the writer to the forefront of many theoretical debates—not a bad thing.

Social construction and its advocates in the field of composition have provided valuable insights into rhetoric's relation to knowledge. They undoubtedly will continue to raise critical questions about what we are doing in the composition classroom and in our research, and they have suggested many new areas of inquiry in interpretation theory, especially those having to do with discourse communities. What should be of concern to everyone, both inside and outside the dialogue, however, is that if the conversation sidesteps the difficulties it engenders in the belief that political or educational agendas are thereby furthered, it will become less responsive to other voices, ultimately to the detriment of those of us in rhetoric and composition who look to our journals for fresh ideas and critiques. In other words, the problem I find with the constructionist dialogue is not that its perspective is incomplete; *that* criticism can be easily and accurately leveled at any position. Rather, it is the threat of insularity of which we must be mindful. Insularity is bred, perhaps, whenever a theory becomes so closely identified as a vehicle for social, political, or pedagogical values that a call for a review or for a reframing of the theory becomes associated (unnecessarily) with a repudiation of those values. Primarily for this reason, I would argue, critical thinking about social construction in composition is in danger of falling victim to the aura of political-correctness often associated with it.

In an article on hermeneutics, Rorty speaks of a "preoccupation with 'radicalizing' the terms in which . . . problems are described." He goes on to say of hermeneutics what I believe can be applied with equal acuity to the constructionist conversation hermeneutics has helped to generate in English departments: "To the extent that 'hermeneutics' becomes the name of a movement which tells students 'These concepts are now old-fashioned; use these new ones—the recently discovered *right* ones—instead,' that movement betrays its own origins . . . it will eventually become as sterile as the tradition of positivistic scientism has become" ("Hermeneutics" 14). Conversing with its critics can spare the constructionist dialogue that fate.[9]

Notes

1. Jeffery Bineham similarly divides discussions of rhetoric-as-epistemic into four basic positions, each centered on either the "Objectivist Thesis," the "Critical Rationalist" position, the "Social Knowledge Thesis," or the "Consensus Theory." He argues that the four positions overlap in many ways, notably in their stance towards the "Cartesian" dichotomy pitting a Platonic conception of truth against unbridled relativism. Using Bineham's system of classification, I would place composition's dialogists in the Consensus Theorist camp along with Robert Scott, Barry Brummett, and Walter Carleton. Thus, Bineham's critique of the Consensus Theory from the perspective of the first three positions raises many of the same issues I am exploring here.

2. Kenneth Gergen's widely cited article "The Social Constructionist Movement in Modern Psychology" offers an interesting account of the interdisciplinary roots of social constructionism. Although, as the title suggests, Gergen is primarily concerned with how social psychology can be situated in a constructionist framework, the article provides ample references to philosophy and rhetoric. Of particular interest to readers of the present paper might be Gergen's brief critique of social construction's assumptions on pages 271-73.

3. The notion of "community" in composition studies has been reviewed by Joseph Harris. One of Harris' central arguments is that "one does not need consensus to have community" (20). The idea that communities are (to use his word) "organic" and rooted in the consensus of their members is commonplace in the constructionist dialogue, though Harris notes that "social theorists" in composition have begun to moderate their position on this issue. Nevertheless, I would argue that the characterization of communities as monolithic is so endemic to the dialogue (given its social and pedagogical commitments), that it is one that will continue to plague constructionists in composition whose emphasis remains on *inter*-communal conflict.

4. Kenneth Bruffee has complained that his notion of social construction has been mistakenly termed "a theory," preferring, instead, that it be understood as "a way of talking, a language, a vernacular" ("Response" 145). Presumably, then, he might argue that to critique constructionism is to miss the point. However, for most purposes (including that of this paper), I think that it is reasonable to present social construction as a theory, especially since it has been used to critique the theories of others and is sufficiently systematic and complete (especially in its compositionist incarnation) to bear critique of its own.

5. For a more detailed account of the sources of social constructionism and the various strains of antifoundationalism in composition studies, see Stanley Fish's chapter on composition in *Doing What Comes Naturally*. See also Patricia Bizzell's lengthier discussion and critique of both foundationalism and antifoundationism in rhetoric.

6. Rescher has termed the perspectivist position "syncreticism" (belief that every theory is true to some extent) in opposition to "skepticism," the position that doubts that anything can be true. The syncretic/skeptic dichotomy is one on which he elaborates extensively in his book and is, I think, an interesting alternative to the Cartesian dichotomy (Bineham) or the exogenic/endogenic dichotomy (Gergen) as a way of understanding the underlying tensions that spawn variations of social constructionism.

7. In interviews with the *Journal of Advanced Composition* conducted by Gary Olson, both Rorty and Derrida make clear that writing teachers adopt the strong hermeneutic program at their own peril. As Rorty puts it, "Higher education should aim at fixing it so the students can see that the normal discourse in which they have been trained up to adolescence . . . is itself a historical contingency surrounded by other historical contingencies. But having done that, whether they remain happily embedded in the normal discourse of their society or not is something teachers can't predict or control" (Rorty, "Social Construction" 8). Addressing this issue further, Thomas Kent's notion of "paralogical" rhetoric is an interesting attempt at reconciling interpretation with the exigencies of the classroom.

8. Rom Harré's *The Social Construction of Emotion* and Carol Stearns and Peter Stearns' *Emotion and Social Change* are two good sources for the constructionist perspective on affect. Chapters in both works demonstrate how

language and social norms play a major role in how individuals understand their feelings. Although a continuing debate surrounds the issue of whether affect is post-cognitive (that is, exists only after it is assessed) or pre-cognitive (exists as an arousal that leads to low-level preferences of some sort *prior* to appraisal), both sides in the argument maintain that a feeling's eventual appraisal is subject to social forces and then re-enters the cognitive process as a socially constructed "artifact" of experience.

9. I wish to thank Richard E. Young and Stuart Greene for their generous help and encouragement throughout the writing of this paper, as well as Gary Olson and Jasper Neel for their thoughtful and useful criticism of an earlier draft.

Works Cited

Bartholomae, David. "Inventing the University." *When a Writer Can't Write.* Ed. Mike Rose. New York: Guilford, 1985. 134-65.

Berger, Peter L., and Thomas Luckmann. *The Social Construction of Reality.* New York: Doubleday, 1966.

Berlin, James A. "Rhetoric and Ideology in the Writing Class." *College English* 50 (1988): 477-94.

Berlin, James A., and Robert P. Inkster. "Current-Traditional Rhetoric: Paradigm and Practice." *Freshman English News* 8 (1980): 1-14.

Bineham, Jeffery L. "The Cartesian Anxiety in Epistemic Rhetoric: An Assessment of the Literature." *Philosophy and Rhetoric* 22 (1990): 43-62.

Bitzer, Lloyd. "Rhetoric and Public Knowledge in Rhetoric." *Philosophy and Literature.* Ed. D. Burks. West Lafayette IN: Purdue UP, 1978.

Bizzell, Patricia. "Foundationalism and Anti-Foundationalism in Composition Studies." *Pre/Text* 7 (1986): 37-56.

Bower, Gordon H. "Mood and Memory." *American Psychologist* 36 (1981): 129-48.

Bruffee, Kenneth A. "Social Construction, Language, and the Authority of Knowledge: A Bibliographical Essay." *College English* 48 (1986): 773-87.

—. "Response to the ***JAC*** Interview with Richard Rorty." *Journal of Advanced Composition* 10 (1990): 145-46.

Carleton, Walter L. "What Is Rhetorical Knowledge? A Response to Farrell—and More." *Quarterly Journal of Speech* 64 (1978): 313-28.

Cherwitz, Richard A., and James W. Hikins, "Rhetorical Perspectivism." *Quarterly Journal of Speech* 69 (1983): 249-66.

Clark, Margaret Sydnor. "A Role for Arousal in the Link between Feeling States, Judgments, and Behavior." *Affect and Cognition* Ed. Margaret Sydnor Clark and Susan T. Fiske. Hillsdale, NJ: Erlbaum, 1982. 263-89.

—. "Mood and Social Judgments." *The Handbook of Psychophysiology*. Ed. Wagner and Manstead. Chichester, UK: Wiley, 1989.

Croasmun, Earl, and Richard A. Cherwitz. "Beyond Rhetorical Relativism." *Quarterly Journal of Speech* 68 (1982): 1-16.

Cushman, Donald P., and Lawrence J. Prelli. "Rhetoric and Epistemology from an Action Theory Perspective." *Central States Speech Journal* 32 (1981): 273-78.

Derrida, Jacques. "Jacques Derrida on Rhetoric and Composition: A Conversation." By Gary A. Olson. *Journal of Advanced Composition* 10 (1990): 1-21.

Derryberry, Douglas, and Mary Klevjord Rothbart. "Emotion, Attention, and Temperament." *Emotions, Cognition, and Behavior*. Ed. Carroll E. Izard, et al. Cambridge: Cambridge UP, 1984.

Eysenck, H.J. *The Biological Basis of Personality*. Springfield, IL: Thomas, 1967.

Farrell, Thomas B. "Knowledge, Consensus, and Rhetorical Theory." *Quarterly Journal of Speech* 62 (1976): 1-14.

—. "Social Knowledge II." *Quarterly Journal of Speech* 64 (1978): 329-34.

Fish, Stanley E. *Doing What Comes Naturally: Change, Rhetoric, and the Practice of Theory in Literary and Legal Studies*. Durham: Duke UP, 1989.

Flower, Linda, and John R. Hayes. "Images, Plans, and Prose." *Written Communication* 1 (1981): 120-60.

Gergen, Kenneth J. "The Social Constructionist Movement in Modern Psychology." *American Psychologist* 40 (1985): 266-75.

Gregg, Richard B. "Rhetoric and Knowing: The Search for Perspective." *Central States Speech Journal* 32 (1981): 133-44.

Harré, Rom, ed. *The Social Construction of Emotions*. Oxford: Blackwell, 1986.

Harris, Joseph. "The Idea of Community in the Study of Writing." *College Composition and Communication* 40 (1989): 11-22.

Isen, Alice M., et al. "Affect, Accessibility of Material in Memory, and Behavior: A Cognitive Loop." *Journal of Personality and Social Psychology* 36 (1978): 1-12.

Kent, Thomas. "Beyond System: The Rhetoric of Paralogy." *College English* 51 (1989): 492-507.

—. "Paralogic Hermeneutics and the Possibilities of Rhetoric." *Rhetoric Review* 8 (1989): 24-42.

Kuhn, Thomas S. *The Structure of Scientific Revolutions*. Chicago: U of Chicago P, 1962.

Leff, Michael. "In Search of Ariadne's Thread: A Review of the Recent Literature on Rhetorical Theory." *Central States Speech Journal* 29 (1978): 73-91.

Myers, Greg. "Reality, Consensus, and Reform in the Rhetoric of Composition Teaching." *College English* 48 (1986): 154-71.

Orr, C.J. "How shall we say: 'Reality is Socially Constructed Through Communication'?" *Central States Speech Journal* 29 (1978): 263-74.

Perelman, Chaim, and Lucie Olbrechts-Tyteca. *The New Rhetoric: A Treatise on Argumentation*. Notre Dame: U of Notre Dame P, 1969.

Pieters, G.M., and W.F. Van Raaij. "Functions and Management of Affect: Applications to Economic Behavior." *Journal of Economic Psychology* 9 (1988): 251-82.

Reither, James A. "Academic Discourse Communities, Invention, and Learning to Write." ERIC, 1986. ED 270 815.

Rescher, Nicholas. *The Strife of Systems*. Pittsburgh: U of Pittsburgh P, 1985.

Rorty, Richard M. "Hermeneutics, General Studies, and Teaching." *Synergos* 2 (1982): 1-15.

—. *Philosophy and the Mirror of Nature*. Princeton: Princeton UP, 1979.

—. "Social Construction and Composition Theory: A Conversation with Richard Rorty." By Gary A. Olson. *Journal of Advanced Composition* 9 (1989): 1-9.

Scott, Robert L. "On Viewing Rhetoric as Epistemic." *Central States Speech Journal* 18 (1967): 9-16.

Stearns, Carol Z., and Peter N. Stearns. *Emotion and Social Change: Toward a New Psychohistory.* New York: Holmes, 1988.

Zuckerman, Marvin. *Sensation-seeking: Beyond the Optimal Level of Arousal.* Hillsdale, NJ: Erlbaum, 1979.

Becoming Aware of the Myth of Presence

Reed Way Dasenbrock

It has been a fundamental axiom of writing instruction for generations that good writing is like speech inasmuch as it has "voice" and is aware of its audience. And this comparison seems to make sense, because both activities draw on a common reservoir of language skills. But why, then, do so many students have trouble writing when they seem to have so little trouble speaking?

The argument of this essay is that teachers of writing have in several crucial respects over-emphasized the similarities between speaking and writing and, in so doing, have reinforced what Jacques Derrida has called the "metaphysics of presence." Like most of Western culture, we have treated writing as if it were speech or essentially a substitute for it, even though the problems students have with writing are precisely with those aspects of writing that don't work like speech. Moreover, the relation between writing and speaking, as well as the methods by which we write and speak, are changing rapidly in response to technological innovations—computers, telecommunications, dictation systems, and the like. These innovations have changed the "scene of writing" in ways that teachers of writing need to be aware of. I want to argue that Derrida's critique of presence enables us to come to a sharper understanding of how these new developments affect the teaching of writing. I am not one of those who believe that Derrida can be "found everywhere," that the entire world can and should be read through lenses polished in Paris; in fact, the pedagogical model I want to develop finally is not one that Derrida would endorse. But I find Derrida's discussion of the relation between speech and writing (particularly in Part I of *Of Grammatology*, "Writing before the Letter") entirely relevant to current issues in the teaching and study of writing.[1]

Logocentrism: Privileging the Spoken Word

One of the key themes of Derrida's thought is the concept of *presence/absence*. Derrida sees the metaphysics of presence, which he also calls "logocentrism," as the dominant tradition in Western thought from Plato and Aristotle to the present. Logocentrism is the privileging of the *logos*, or spoken word, over the written word, and Derrida rather sweepingly asserts that the Western tradition has always privileged the spoken word or oral language over the written. In oral communication, the speaker is present to an audience, and, according to this tradition, this presence ensures full, unmediated communication; writing, in contrast, is seen as secondary to speech. As Rousseau has said, writing is "nothing but the representation of speech" (qtd. in Derrida, *Of Grammatology* 27). We resort to writing only when the more secure method of face-to-face communication is impossible—when the person we wish to communicate with is absent. Thus, writing is seen as a system for transcribing speech, a system that functions as a supplement to speech in the absence of the speaker, and the specific differences that exist between the written and the spoken codes are a function of the perceived difference between their natures.

Although Derrida has been faulted by his critics for ignoring examples which tend not to support his point, he has gathered an impressive array of passages in which key Western thinkers privilege speech over writing, presence over absence.[2] Plato's attack on writing as a falling away from the purity of speech is perhaps the *locus classicus*.[3] Aristotle also viewed writing as secondary to speech: "Spoken words are the symbols of mental experience and written words are the symbols of spoken words" (qtd. in Derrida, *Of Grammatology* 36). And Derrida has criticized such contemporary thinkers as Saussure, Levi-Strauss, and J.L. Austin for their analogous privileging of the oral over the written (*Of Grammatology* 27-73, 101-40; "Signature"). Moreover, a sense of the spoken word as vital is, of course, crucial to the Judeo-Christian tradition: "In the beginning was the Word." And "God *said*, 'let there be light.'"

It is difficult, perhaps, for many of us to share Derrida's agitation about this dominance of logocentrism. Derrida speaks of "the historical-metaphysical reduction of writing to the rank of an instrument enslaved to a full and originally spoken language" (*Of Grammatology* 29) as if writing were the victim of a nefarious authoritarian conspiracy. But, certainly, Derrida is correct in arguing that the way we customarily regard writing ignores the differences between writing and speaking, between reading and listening. I found it, for example, far more natural two sentences ago to write "Derrida speaks of" though I have never heard him say these words. We speak of what Shakespeare "says" in Sonnet 129 or of what an author is "telling us," and these metaphors are the marks of a metaphysics of presence that treats writing as if it were speech or, more precisely, that assimilates writing under a model of communication based on speech. Though the writer is absent when we read, we ignore that fact and treat the writer as if he or she were present, speaking to us in an unmediated way. This response ignores everything that is different (and much that is problematic) about writing, the essence of which is that the writer's writing functions in the absence of the writer. We see the differences between speaking and writing as contingent, not essential, as mere "devices" writing must use in order to approach the full, unmediated presence speech has unproblematically. The value of speech thus comes from its presence, and, in Derrida's view, the metaphysics of presence conflates speech and presence, thus automatically denigrating writing as absence.

Derrida argues that this metaphysics of presence, this logocentrism, utterly pervades the Western intellectual tradition; good evidence for this view is provided by the fact that even the discipline of the study of writing has continued in many important respects to be logocentric. For instance, the aim of one influential pedagogy—Zoellner's "talk-write"—is to increase students' written fluency by leading them from talking to writing.[4] Further, the tradition of rhetoric originated in the study of oral, not written, discourse, and the continuing influence of classical rhetoric on composition studies helps reinforce logocentric language and concepts. We find it more natural to refer to a writer's "awareness of an audience," as if the writer were on stage declaiming, than to refer to a readership; we also refer to the importance of a writer "finding his or her own voice," again as if the writer were speaking. Moreover, we teach writing orally and seem unaware of the resulting tension. Many of us conduct conferences, believing that comments given in person will be more effective than written comments even though our oral comments are about writing. Others work extensively with peer groups, in which a writer tries to say what he or she means and peers provide oral responses to the writing. In any of these situations, if the writer's meaning is unclear, we ask, "What are you trying to *say* here?"

Despite some important exceptions, much research in composition is also still enmeshed in logocentric assumptions. The relationship between speaking and writing is an important topic in composition studies, but the trend in these studies has been largely to emphasize the similarities—not the differences—between speaking and writing (for example, see Kroll and Vann). Moreover, armed with Derrida's critique, we can find traces of logocentrism in many other aspects of composition theory and practice today: in the methods of protocol analysis, in references to "inner speech," and in references to disciplinary or interpretive communities of discourse. However, it would be wrong to present all the approaches and theories in composition today as unequivocally logocentric. For example, in a spirit largely (if not totally) compatible with Derrida, those theorists who stress writing as a mode of learning—rather than as a mode of putting down on paper what one has learned—reverse the logocentric vision of writing as mere transcription.[5] But Derrida suggests that logocentrism is so pervasive that we must keep reminding ourselves that it is writing—not rhetoric, not invention, not inner speech—that we study and teach. All too readily, anyone working from Western cultural assumptions comes to see speech and writing as hierarchically related and, therefore, subsumes writing under a model of communication which privileges speech over writing, presence over absence.

Student Writers and the Metaphysics of Presence

Derrida's description of the metaphysics of presence also explains much about the state of mind of the average college writer. The "basic" writer, so Mina Shaughnessy and others have argued, is often overly aware of—and therefore intimidated by—the differences between speaking and writing. But the "average" college writer, sufficiently at ease with writing to have avoided the intimidation the basic writer experiences, far more often ignores these differences, treating writing as if it were speech or simply a device for transcribing it. A number of serious problems in student writing stem from this unarticulated premise about writing.

Most students, of course, have had much more experience with the spoken than with the written code, so it should come as no surprise that many of the most common errors found in student writing stem from excessive reliance upon the spoken code as a guide to writing. No one seems to know how to use an apostrophe anymore, largely because no one has ever spoken an apostrophe. Many spelling mistakes, and most of the frequent ones, arise from the same source: when in doubt about the spelling of a word, the student sounds it out and then writes it down as he or she hears it. This simple speech-based rule of thumb is often unreliable, so the student writes *piticular* instead of *particular*, *tempramant* instead of *temperament*. Other examples of common errors that arise from transcribing speech as writing are *most all* instead of *almost all*, *should of* instead of *should have*, and *suppose* and *use* as past-tense forms.

Punctuation, of course, is a feature of writing, not of speech, but four punctuation marks—the period, comma, exclamation point, and question mark—correspond fairly straightforwardly to the intonations and pauses of speech. And these are the forms of punctuation to be found in student writing. The dash, parenthesis, semicolon, colon—those forms of punctuation that cannot be indicated in speech—do not appear spontaneously in much student writing. But extensive reliance on the comma and the period does not mean that even these punctuation marks are used correctly. The punctuation errors that students make, unlike those concerning plurals and the apostrophe, do not typically arise from students' having forgotten the rules they were taught about comma use; these errors often come, on the contrary, from having learned one "rule" extremely well. For example, I hear semester after semester about a basic rule of comma usage taught across the nation: use a comma to indicate a pause. This rule is a wonderful example of the privileging of speech over writing: punctuation exists to indicate something in speech—pauses—that writing lacks. But, clearly, writing is richer, not poorer, than speech in this regard. Moreover (and this is the source of the problem), most of us pause for other reasons as well, and we do so quite haphazardly.[6] This means that following the punctuate-when-you-pause rule leads to some very oddly punctuated sentences.

These are some of the common mechanical and sentence-level errors that appear in students' writing, and we should be able to see the pattern in these errors. The pattern should tell us that our students make errors precisely where the connection or overlap between speaking and writing breaks down. Acting on the unarticulated premise that writing is simply transcribed speech, students make errors in those aspects of writing that require discriminations not found in speech. Where mastery of the spoken code suffices, the average college writer today does an acceptable job; it is where the written code works rather differently from speech that most student writing begins to manifest problems.

This phenomenon can be seen on a level beyond the surface and grammatical features I have described so far: in the problems students have creating a coherent text. The issue of how we produce formally coherent texts is, of course, enormously complicated, and I wish to point out only a few aspects of this problem here. One important means of creating coherence is the use of cohesive ties. Halliday and Hasan demonstrate that cohesion is realized by five means: reference, substitution, ellipsis, lexical cohesion, and conjunction. Though studies have shown that better writers use all of these cohesive devices more frequently than poorer writers do, the difference is largest, according to Witte and Faigley, in their use of conjunction (196; also see Gebhard). Conjunction is established primarily by what Halliday and Hasan call the "discourse adjunct," the conjunctive adverb or prepositional phrase (such as *consequently* or *on the other hand*) that signals the connection between sentences, and it is surely used less frequently in conversation. The "discourse adjunct" is under-utilized in student writing, I would argue, precisely because it is less frequently used in speech. The only conjunctive adverb students seem to use extensively in their writing is *however*, but even this word is usually used incorrectly as a conjunction. Even the simple word *nonetheless* strikes the student ear as unnecessary and foreign—unnecessary because it adds no new information about the referential subject and foreign because such an indication of the logical relation between two parts of a discourse is more a part of the mechanism of formal written discourse than part of the repertoire of conversational speech. But by refusing to employ devices that don't *sound natural*, students cut themselves off from fully learning the mechanisms of writing, some of which admittedly do not sound natural. Does anyone speak in footnotes?

The footnote is just one example of the devices employed in written texts but not characteristic of conversation and that, therefore, students tend to resist. Introductions, conclusions, transitional phrases, the apparatus of scholarship contained in notes and in bibliographies—all are part of the formal repertoire of writing and deliberately call attention to their written formality as a way of signaling the coherence, the *integritas*, of a written text.[7] Students, by and large, have difficulty with these devices, preferring a more purely referential, subject-oriented prose that calls much less attention to itself as writing.

Though our students run into many different kinds of problems creating coherent texts, a remarkable number of these problems are traceable to a common root: they are not characteristic of the conversational speech our students have mastered. And as long as our students have not mastered the facets of writing not found in speech, they are going to continue to have problems in all these areas, from "surface" conventions like the apostrophe to larger whole-discourse units. Another way of putting this is that our students' problems are a function of their logocentrism, their privileging of oral over written discourse. And it is difficult to make students aware of their logocentrism because it is part of the much larger culture of logocentrism Derrida has described. Our students regard writing as a transcription of speech, a supplement to speech that we resort to only when face-to-face communication is impossible, because they have been taught—consciously or unconsciously—to regard writing this way. They see writing this way, in short, because their culture does. Understanding this phenomenon is helpful in itself because it can lead us, instead of uselessly blaming our students' mysterious recalcitrance about apostrophes, to see how and why these errors are reinforced by the culture as a whole.

Articulating the Myth

In the writing classroom, therefore, we must discuss the myth of presence, make our students conscious that we all subscribe to such a myth. We need to articulate for our students a more complex and sophisticated view of writing, showing them that writing is not a supplement to speech but a different form of language in its own right, with advantages over speech as well as disadvantages. But such theoretical teaching must complement—not displace—the more concrete teaching of the specific problems that result from the myth of presence. Only a combination of the two will really do the job.

How can this be done? How can we make students aware of the myth of presence? (Here, beyond giving us a useful theoretical framework, Derrida is not going to help us very much.)[8] First, we can lead students to see from their own experience how writing can be of use in its own right and not just as a form of communication to resort to when face-to-face communication is impossible. The difference between letters and conversations on the telephone is one useful example. Even, or especially, if they do not receive many letters, most students feel that a letter "means" more because of its permanence and because, as reluctant writers themselves, they think that more work went into it. Love letters, for instance, have a value that conversations on the telephone do not exactly replace. Complaint letters provide another useful example; everyone has had to complain to someone about something, and it is easy to see that to get results one has to complain by letter, because organizations seldom keep accurate records of the phone calls they receive. And almost every student has had a similar experience with job applications. By means of such examples within their experience, most students can be brought to see the distinctiveness and usefulness of writing as a system of communication in its own right and not just a device for recording speech.

Ironically, perhaps, the use of oral presentations and formal public-speaking practice can also help make students conscious of the myth of presence. A good presentation is almost always scripted and written in advance; a terrible presentation is one that partakes of the spontaneous, disorganized nature of everyday conversation. So the introduction of such elements in a writing course suggests that writing may, on occasion, be prior to speech, not the other way around.

I also think it important to insist on students' typing (or now, word processing) formal essays precisely because typed text looks more foreign to the student than the student's own handwriting. That foreignness brings home the lesson of absence. It enables the student to see his or her own work more as others would see it, which means that the student sees its errors and weaknesses more readily and, more importantly, that he or she realizes *that* others might see it: "Someone could read this who doesn't know me at all, who doesn't even know that a 'me' wrote it." Writing, students will see, is indeed a different activity from having a conversation with a friend. It can also be valuable to discuss these matters in class as well as have students experience them; I always speak in my writing classes about what it feels like to see my own work in print and how I often see errors at that point that I never saw before. Mature writers as well as immature ones have to grapple with the problems of absence; such problems are, indeed, part of the nature of writing.

A Pedagogy of *Absence/Presence*

But, of course, introducing examples from public speaking and discussing differences between writing for ourselves and writing for publication reveal that the presence/absence distinction is not exactly the same as the speaking/writing one; they are at least partially—and also usefully—distinguishable. There are, however, *intermediate cases*, kinds of writing close to the presence of speaking—a note to a friend or a note to oneself, for example. In these kinds of writing, we can use the code we often use in speech because we are not concerned with the intelligibility of our message to a large audience and may, in fact, be trying to prevent such intelligibility. Our almost-present audience may indeed welcome and certainly won't mind the more personal and intimate writing which behaves like speech. And in these situations in which we can write more the way we talk, more colloquially and informally, correctness is no longer an issue. Thus, the problems of absence are not part of the nature of writing as much as they are part of the broader category of communicating in the absence of the recipient. There are also intermediate forms of *speech* which have some of the characteristics I have been ascribing to writing. In public speeches, for example, the audience—though physically present—is relatively absent in much the same way readers are. This absence means that the language used in public speech falls between that appropriate for face-to-face communication and that appropriate for writing. Indeed, as I have already said, such speeches are generally written in advance, though written from the idea of being spoken, and this perfectly establishes public speech as an intermediate case.[9]

Moreover, the presence/absence concept just sketched is being radically transformed by new technologies of communication. Something as simple as Post-It notes, in making writing detachable and readily disposable, creates a new kind of writing more like speech in its impermanence. Electronic mail makes writing radically present even across great distances; other electronic media, particularly television and video storage, make public speech possible in contexts of absence—despite a powerful illusion of presence. In contrast, audio mail and dictation/transcribing technologies (recently studied in Halpern and Liggett) present speech situations in which speech functions much like writing or is designed to be transformed into writing.

It is impossible to predict the effect these new technologies will have on writing, since we are experiencing transformations we cannot see the end of. But I want to relate Derrida's thoughts on presence/absence and speech/writing to these new technologies. On the one hand, the new technologies demonstrate incontrovertibly that we need a partial distinction between speaking/writing and presence/absence. On the other hand, Derrida's distinctions—modified in this way—give us a powerful theoretical perspective on the new technologies. The new technologies help shatter or deconstruct any simplistic speech/writing model and help blur the overly neat speaking/writing distinction that this essay began with and that most research in this field assumes (and that is represented by the disciplinary distinction between departments of English and departments of speech and communication). This blurring means that if we stick to the old speaking/writing problematic, we won't be giving our students the distinctions that will help them cope with and adapt to the changing scene of writing. We need to shift our thinking from speaking/writing to presence/absence because our students are writing in a world described more adequately by the presence/absence problematic. And Derrida has given us the terms with which to describe this new world of writing.

What our students need to learn, in short, is to move from presence to absence, not just from speaking to writing. And showing that the writing/speaking difference is less fundamental than the presence/absence difference is a crucial part of leading our students to negotiate both differences. Playing a random set of messages left on a telephone answering machine, for example, quickly shows students how this form of communication shares some characteristics with writing. Communicating successfully here requires a very different sense of language than does conversation; normal context-dependent or presence-oriented speech doesn't work well in this context. In contrast, Post-It notes circulating among departmental colleagues are largely unintelligible removed from their original context, in just the way comparable snippets of conversation among the same people ("What did you decide about that thing I gave you?") would be. Such presence-oriented, contextually-dependent notes are far easier to compose than are messages left on the answering machine of a stranger. This observation helps show students that their writing problems are only partially a function of their inability to master the specific conventions of writing as opposed to those of speech; and, probably more importantly, it shows that these problems are partially a function of their inability to master the general conventions of communicating in the absence of a recipient.

It is not writing that is so difficult for our students but communicating in the absence of a reader. The aspects of writing that give them trouble are not there to give English teachers things to find wrong with their writing but to ensure communication in a situation of absence. When communicating to someone who is absent, one must master two skills not necessary for those who communicate in the presence of their audience. First, one's communication must partake of certain formal characteristics which mark it as a coherent piece of discourse; second, it must be error-free because an absent audience has none of the tolerance for error allowed a present speaker. Students need to see this, not only to learn to write but also to learn other modes of communication characterized by absence. And they will learn these modes of communication more quickly if they encounter them aware of what these modes have in common with writing as well as of how they differ.

Notes

1. The essays collected by Atkins and Johnson avoid this issue altogether, focusing instead on the relationship between reading and writing. Crowley's early essay is the pioneering work to explicitly relate Derrida's critique of the metaphysics of presence to issues in the teaching of writing, although she emphasizes less the speaking/writing issue than the related one that language is not primarily a representation of ideas and therefore should not be valued only for its clarity or transparency. Derrida is never mentioned in Kroll and Vann or in either of Tannen's collections of essays.

2. Schafer provides considerable support for Derrida's claim. In an excellent summary of the work that has been done on the similarities and contrasts between speech and writing, Schafer shows how until quite recently linguistics neglected this topic because it took the spoken word as primary and, thus, as its principal object of investigation.

3. Connors has recently argued that Plato's attack on writing (in the *Phaedrus*) lines up with his attack on rhetoric (primarily in the *Gorgias*) and on poetry (primarily in *The Republic*) because all three are one-way modes of communication "that cannot be questioned" (55), as opposed to the dialectical reasoning Plato wants opened up through the insistent questioning of Socrates. This argument redraws Derrida's distinction but doesn't obliterate it. What Socrates represents is the presence of dialogue; and, to anticipate a point made later, the public speech of rhetoric and poetry would, in this view, approach the condition of writing in relative absence.

4. Liggett's useful bibliography lists a number of studies influenced by Zoellner's work.

5. See Emig and Elbow, for example. I say "not totally" both because of Elbow's insistence on the importance of voice in writing and also because both writers would agree with the reservations about Derrida's position explained in note 8 below.

6. Shaughnessy subscribes to the speech-based notion that writing is primarily a way to transcribe speech when she suggests that "the writer perceives periods as signals for major pauses and commas as signals for minor pauses." But she goes on to provide an excellent summary of the different reasons for pausing when we speak: "Pauses mark rates of respiration, set off certain words for rhetorical emphasis, facilitate phonological maneuvers, regulate the rhythms of thought and articulation, and suggest grammatical structure" (24).

7. Schafer suggests that the problems inexperienced writers have with transitions and with opening and closing their texts comes from the fact that in conversation we get help from the other party in these acts (23-37). Writing, a monologue not a dialogue, requires the writer to do these things alone.

8. I say this because Derrida's position is that, because of its acontextuality or "iterability" (the fact that writing can be significant fully stripped of its originating context), writing can never unequivocally transmit authorial intention; it can never work in quite the way its author would want. This is, of course, a hotly disputed position; my sense, which I assume most teachers of writing share, is that this is not a view likely to be enabling in the writing classroom, however useful and enabling Derrida's discussion of the absence/presence distinction can be. A number of people disagree with me, however; see the Atkins and Johnson collection.

9. Hirsch cites radio broadcasting and writing to oneself as examples that blunt the absoluteness of the distinction between speaking and writing:

> From the structure of these speech situations, it is evident that the distinctive features of written speech do not depend on its merely being written down. A radio talk is, functionally speaking, written discourse. A private note is, functionally, oral speech. Moreover, we encounter utterances which belong equally in the two functional categories, for instance, a rather formal conversation, or a very informal and elliptical letter to a close friend. As with most generic distinctions in speech, one

discovers a continuum where one had hoped to discover definitive classifications. *But a good reason for keeping the functional distinction between speech and writing is that the typical, privative character of written speech creates the main difficulties in teaching and learning composition.* (22; emphasis added)

Works Cited

Atkins, G. Douglas, and Michael L. Johnson. *Writing and Reading Differently: Deconstruction and the Teaching of Composition and Literature*. Lawrence: UP of Kansas, 1985.

Connors, Robert J. "Greek Rhetoric and the Transition from Orality." *Philosophy and Rhetoric* 19 (1986): 38-61.

Crowley, Sharon. "Of Gorgias and Grammatology." *College Composition and Communication* 30 (1979): 279-84.

Derrida, Jacques. *Of Grammatology*. Trans. Gayatri Chakravorty Spivak. Baltimore: Johns Hopkins UP, 1976.

—. "Signature Event Context." *Glyph I* (1977): 172-97.

Elbow, Peter. "The Shifting Relationships between Speech and Writing." *College Composition and Communication* 36 (1985): 283-303.

Emig, Janet. "Writing as a Mode of Learning." *College Composition and Communication* 28 (1977): 122-28.

Gebhard, Ann O. "Writing Quality and Syntax: A Transformational Analysis of Three Prose Samples." *Research in the Teaching of English* 12 (1979): 211-31.

Halliday, M.A.K., and Ruqaiya Hasan. *Cohesion in English*. London: Longman, 1976.

Halpern, Jeanne W., and Sarah Liggett. *Computers and Composing: How the New Technologies Are Changing Writing*. Carbondale: Southern Illinois UP, 1984.

Hirsch, E.D. *The Philosophy of Composition*. Chicago: U of Chicago P, 1977.

Kroll, Barry M., and Roberta J. Vann, eds. *Exploring Speaking-Writing Relationships: Connections and Contrasts*. Urbana: NCTE. 1981.

Liggett, Sarah. "The Relationship between Speaking and Writing: An Annotated Bibliography." *College Composition and Communication* 35 (1984): 334-40.

Schafer, John. "The Linguistic Analysis of Spoken and Written Texts." Kroll and Vann 1-31.

Shaughnessy, Mina P. *Errors and Expectations: A Guide for the Teacher of Basic Writing*. New York: Oxford UP, 1977.

Tannen, Deborah, ed. *Coherence in Spoken and Written Discourse*. Norwood: Ablex, 1984.

—., ed. *Spoken and Written Language: Exploring Orality and Literacy*. Norwood: Ablex, 1982.

Zoellner, Robert. "Talk-Write: A Behavioral Pedagogy for Composition." *College English* 30 (1969): 267-320.

Hall of Mirrors: Antifoundationalist Theory and the Teaching of Writing

David W. Smit

Over the past ten years or so, a significant number of scholars in composition and rhetoric have argued in support of what has come to be known as antifoundationalist theory. Although these scholars emphasize different aspects of antifoundationalism and its implications for teaching writing, they might agree with the basic distinction between foundationalism and antifoundationalism made by Stanley Fish in an article entitled "Anti-Foundationalism, Theory Hope, and the Teaching of Composition." In that piece, Fish defines foundationalism as "any attempt to ground inquiry and communication in something more firm and stable than mere belief or unexamined practice"—that is, in such "objective" things as "God, the material or 'brute act' world, rationality in general and logic in particular, a neutral-observation language, a set of eternal values, and the free and independent self" (342-43). Antifoundationalism, on the other hand, is the theory that

> questions of fact, truth, correctness, validity, and clarity can neither be posed nor answered in reference to some extracontextual, ahistorical, nonsituational reality, or rule, or law, or value; rather anti-foundationalism asserts, all of these matters are intelligible and debatable only within the precincts of the contexts or situations or paradigms or communities that give them their local and changeable shape. (344)

Foundationalists argue that despite a number of epistemological problems we can rely to a certain extent on such things as the "real world," the referential nature of language, and human rationality and intersubjectivity. After all, most of us live and act as if the real world exists and that we can depend on it; we never seriously doubt that in the foreseeable future the sun will continue to come up in the east, and we depend on the fact that our homes will still be there when we come back from vacation—or if they are not, we assume that there will be clear signs as to why they are not: ashes, for example. Moreover, most of us rely on some sort of stable references for certain words. When we ask family members, friends, and waiters to bring us a glass of water, there is hardly ever any problem with what we mean: we are usually brought a glass of water. And when we argue certain points or express our opinions, our audiences often knowingly nod their heads or they get a fire in their eyes and try to interrupt us with opposing arguments. So it would seem obvious by everyday-ordinary common sense that "a material or 'brute act' world" exists and that some words in our language refer to objects in this world. And it would seem equally obvious that we share some form of rationality, some form of subjectivity, with our fellow human beings.

However, antifoundationalists argue that our understanding of the material world is mediated through our language and our individual historically conditioned and culturally determined world-and-life views and that as a result there is no *necessary* connection between the words of our language and what they refer to. And because our individual world-and-life views are so historically conditioned and culturally determined, we cannot assume that all forms of human reason and all forms of intersubjectivity have a great deal in common. As a result, antifoundationalists often seem to imply that our language and knowledge of the world is an infinite hall of mirrors, in which diction and syntax, rules of grammar, the neurological structure of the human mind, and what we call reality reflect upon one another with no ultimate source for all the shifting mirror images. Pressed to account for how we do seem to understand one another to some extent, antifoundationalists often rely on the idea of an interpretive community or social convention to explain how we know and understand and how we use language.

Now, the discussion of foundationalism and antifoundationalism in our discipline strikes me as curious for two reasons. The first reason is the sheer onesidedness of the argument: scholars in composition and rhetoric are overwhelmingly antifoundationalist—this in spite of the fact that common sense would seem to tell us that antifoundationalism is extremely problematic. Indeed, scholars who study rhetoric in departments of Speech Communication have long argued the implications of a much wider range of philosophical positions than we have in composition and rhetoric (see for example Cherwitz). These positions include realism, the belief that we can know and rely on our sense of an objective material world. The main arguments these scholars advance in favor of realism are the apparent *givenness* of our sensory experience and the necessity of a knowable objective reality in order for us to have any coherent sense of truth at all (Hikens).

In addition, scholars in literary theory, such as Gerald Graff and Kathleen McCormick, have pointed out the difficulties of relying on interpretive communities as a basis for a theory of knowledge: such a concept does not sufficiently distinguish between the kinds of strategies that people may use in understanding; nor does it explain how individuals within a community acquire these strategies or how they may move from community to community and develop new strategies. In addition, the philosopher Donald Davidson has made a convincing case against the very idea that conventions explain anything about language. And yet, despite its many conceptual problems, antifoundationalists have carried the day in our books and journals without any organized or serious opposition.[1]

The second curious thing that strikes me about all the antifoundationalist talk in our discipline is that its relevance to the teaching of writing has never been very clear. Two early arguments using forms of antifoundationalism as a rationale for specific pedagogical practices—for teaching a self consciousness about the forms of discourse and for using collaborative teaching methods—have either been severely qualified or they have been shown to be very problematic. The latest version of antifoundationalism to be presented in our journals—an argument based on the work of Donald Davidson—suggests that writing cannot be taught in any systematic way, especially in schools. We might wonder then whether antifoundationalism has any relevance to the teaching of writing.

One way antifoundationalism has been used to justify a particular pedagogical practice in writing is exemplified in the work of Patricia Bizzell. In a 1982 essay entitled "Cognition, Convention, and Certainty: What We Need to Know about Writing," Bizzell argues for "teaching about academic discourse (the 'theoretical perspective on situationality') as a way of demystifying academic discourse and giving students more control over their use or rejection of academic discourse" ("Response" 243).[2] Fairly or unfairly, Fish seized upon Bizzell's article as one of a number of arguments which claim a natural affinity between antifoundationalism and "a process-oriented or rhetorical approach to composition," and which Fish in turn identifies with such things as "process over product, the replacement of a standard of correctness by the fluid and dynamic standard of effectiveness, the teaching of strategies rather than of rules and maxims" ("Anti-foundationalism" 346-47).

However, Fish argues that an antifoundationalist epistemology cannot be used to justify a process pedagogy because whatever we believe, we will always be situated in a particular context which will determine the language we use and how we communicate. If we subscribe to an antifoundational epistemology, we can only increase our self-consciousness of our own situatedness; we cannot transcend it:

> What one must remember is that circumstantiality—another name for situatedness—is not something one can escape by recognizing it, since the act of recognition will itself occur within circumstances that cannot be the object of our self-conscious attention. . . .
>
> To put the matter in a nutshell, the knowledge that one is in a situation has no particular payoff for any situation you happen to be in, because the constraints of that situation will not be relaxed by that knowledge. ("Antifoundationalism" 350-51)

It follows, according to Fish, that teaching our students about discourse conventions and writing strategies rather than, say, rules of grammar and conventional genre formats will make no difference in their ability to learn how to write because any particular piece of information has to be contextualized, and information about discourse conventions and writing strategies will in the end be just another kind of knowledge which our students will have to apply to particular situations. If antifoundationalism is correct in asserting that all knowledge is contextual, then even the awareness that we have to apply conventions and strategies in context is contextual and our awareness of that fact will not be helpful. In the words of the Nike ads, we just have to *do* it.

Thus, according to Fish, all instructors can do to teach writing is help students work through the problem of communicating in specific situations:

> However, I do believe in training of a kind familiar to students of classical and medieval rhetoric—training, let's say, of the Senecan kind, in which one is placed by one's instructor in a situation: you are attempting to cross a river; there is only one ferry; you have to persuade the ferryman to do this or that, and he is disinclined to do so for a number of given reasons—what do you then do? That kind of training, transposed into a modern mode, is essential. I don't think it need be accompanied by any epistemological rap. (Olson 258)

It is noteworthy that Bizzell now accepts this argument and agrees that "talk about academic discourse cannot be meta-discursive," although she does hold out the possibility that teaching students the conventions of academic discourse can "help students to understand it better, practice it more fluently, and work to change it more creatively, without having to claim that this kind of perspective on the discourse constitutes critical 'distance' of the kind Fish disallows" ("Response" 243-44). In other words, Bizzell admits that she can no longer use antifoundationalism to privilege her pedagogy.

Another theorist, Kenneth Bruffee, uses antifoundationalism to provide a philosophic rationale for collaborative learning. In two major articles "Collaborative Learning and the 'Conversation of Mankind'" and "Social Construction, Language, and the Authority of Knowledge: A Bibliographic Essay," Bruffee, relying heavily on the work of Fish, Thomas Kuhn, Richard Rorty, and Clifford Geertz, argues that "thought is internalized public and social talk," that writing is "internalized social talk made public and social again," and thus that knowledge is "socially justified belief" ("Collaborative" 651). Bruffee concludes that only some form of collaborative learning as a pedagogical method can capture the social nature of language and knowledge, that collaborative learning ought to be intrinsically better than other methods in teaching people to write. However, as I have pointed out elsewhere, because Bruffee argues that *all* language is social, it does not follow that collaborative learning is inherently more social or more able to capture the social nature of experience than any other pedagogical method. In Bruffee's own terms, lecturing is social and recitation classes are social, all methods of teaching writing are social, and we must therefore find additional reasons for supposing that collaborative learning is a superior way to teach writing.

Finally, another antifoundationalist, Thomas Kent, in a series of articles, argues that we may not be able to teach writing systematically at all. In "Paralogic Hermeneutics and the Possibilities of Rhetoric" Kent follows Donald Davidson in arguing that all communication is a matter of interpretation. To Kent—and Davidson—each act of interpretation is so dependent on the idiosyncracies of a particular context that generalizations and systematic descriptions of how language works cannot help interpreters do their job. Interpretation is primarily a matter of sympathy, luck, and skill, not general knowledge:

> Because they require (1) skill that cannot be codified and (2) skillful guessing that cannot be reduced to a formal method or technique, both discourse production and discourse analysis include a crucial hermeneutic act that is unsystemic, nonconventional, and paralogic in nature. (30)

In "Beyond System: The Rhetoric of Paralogy" Kent argues that the idea of convention cannot adequately account for interpretation. Again relying heavily on the work of Davidson, Kent demonstrates that no convention can identify completely how a particular sentence is employed, whether for example it is an assertion, a joke, or a question. Likewise, no convention can identify the intention of the speaker of an utterance or clarify whether that intention is sincere. As a result, according to Kent:

> Radical interpretation means that we employ our knowledge of a language to make guesses about what speakers and writers desire to communicate, and no formal method may be established to ensure that our guesses will be correct. A knowledge of conventions—linguistic or otherwise—only helps make us better guessers. (502)

And in "Externalism and the Production of Discourse" Kent again follows Davidson's lead and argues that notions about thought and mental processes are less important to a theory of communication than the nature of "public and external communicative interaction" (66). Such public interaction involves Davidson's concept of charity, the presupposition that "an interpreter will assume that we intend him or her to hold our sentences true, and in a reciprocal manner, we will attribute beliefs to the interpreter that agree with our own" (65); his idea of triangulation, that public forms of interaction are the basis for internal states; and his idea of a passing theory, that communication requires "on the spot interpretation that cannot be reduced to a schematic cognitive process or to any kind of epistemological system" (67).

How then, according to Kent, should we go about teaching writing? In "Paralogic Hermeneutics" he resorts to Fish's advice that students just have to practice: "A student may only learn *how* to employ his background knowledge—and learn how to expand it at the same time—by entering into specific dialogic and therefore hermeneutic interactions with others' interpretive strategies" (37). These dialogic interactions cannot be artificial. Teachers cannot be mock audiences, for they do not have enough background in specific areas to hold up their side of the dialogue. Likewise, case study methods are inadequate because they are too detached from the conversations in specific disciplines and contexts. Real dialogic interactions must involve, Kent says, an opportunity for the writer to engage in collaboration with others in the context of specific disciplines. However, discipline-specific courses are not enough: "no practical writing course like technical writing can teach an engineering student to write" (39). This seems to suggest that students can only learn to write like engineers by *being* engineers, an idea which may be true but which begs the question of how students learn to write as engineers.

Finally, in "Externalism" Kent opposes process-oriented instruction and dialectical methods that lead students to "the truth." Such methods, he says, can be used to teach a body of knowledge, such as grammar, methods of analysis, and theories of communication, but they cannot be used to teach writing. His only suggestion is that we "drop our current process-oriented vocabulary, and begin talking about our concrete social and public uses of language" (70). The problem, of course, is that talking about such social and public uses of language may become another form of knowledge, which Kent has ruled out ahead of time as being useful for learning how to write. We seem to be back to Stanley Fish's position: students can only learn to write by *doing* it, albeit in the context of some specific real-world domain for which academic disciplines are not an adequate substitute. One possible interpretation of Kent's position is that writing cannot be taught in schools.

However, we may contrast Kent's conclusions with another compositionist sympathetic with Davidson's theories, Reed Way Dasenbrock, who reaches a conclusion much different from Kent's. From studying Davidson, particularly Davidson's notion of triangulation, Dasenbrock concludes that learning the public forms and conventions of discourse, presumeably in a systematic way, is absolutely essential. Dasenbrock quotes Davidson—"thought is necessarily part of a common world"—and goes on:

> In a Davidsonian vision, we can adopt a much more balanced attitude towards the received conventions of usage: they are not threats to the autonomy of the soul nor are they projections of a class bent on domination. It remains a basic fact of communication that we must master the public structures of meaning before what we say is intelligible, indeed before we have anything to say. . . . So a Davidsonian approach to composition would, I think, teach usage and received forms in a resolutely descriptivist spirit—not you must follow this form to show you know the rules nor you must break this form to show your spirit, but this is the rule and break it or respect it as you will. (29)

So according to Dasenbrock, we must teach rules, conventions, received forms—the *knowledge* of these things—and rather rigorously and systematically at that, if only to give our students the choice of either following the rules or breaking them. It would seem then that even among dedicated antifoundationalists there is no unanimity about the implications of the theory for particular practices.

What then are we to make of all this? Is antifoundationalism convincing when it argues for a hall of mirrors and against the reliability of the material world, human rationality, and the referential nature of language? And whether it is convincing or not, does antifoundationalism have any practical implications for the teaching of writing?

The major difficulty in discussing these matters is that the conversation about antifoundationalism in our discipline has been greatly oversimplified. We have been presented with only a few of the many arguments involved in a major philosophical problem that goes back to ancient times and is still intensely controversial in current philosophical circles. The reasons for this state of affairs in composition/rhetoric, I think, are two: the relative newness of our discipline and our overwhelming desire and need to be practical, to apply philosophical positions to the business of teaching writing. As a result, we do not have the tradition of philosophical inquiry that exists, say, in departments of Speech Communication, and the tradition we do have is skewed by our desire for practical applications. In our desire to apply philosophical theory to the teaching of writing, we tend to look for metaphors for instruction rather than to analyze a particular theory for its strengths and weaknesses.

Although I am sympathetic to what we generally call antifoundationalist positions, it seems to me that antifoundationalist theory faces a number of major difficulties, difficulties with which it has not yet come to grips. For one thing, it has not yet given an adequate account of how we rely on the material world and how we learn and use language to refer to that world in ways which are consistent and useful. As Davidson has put it, ". . . there must be some connection [between belief and truth] if we are to relate the truth of utterances to their use. The question is what that connection can be" ("Structure" 305). For another, if antifoundationalism is to have any relevance to composition and rhetoric, it must offer some convincing suggestions about how we ought to teach writing, suggestions which seem to be organic or integral to the theory.

So in the interest of furthering the conversation about antifoundationalism, I would like to address both of these issues: First, the problem of relating what we know, our beliefs, to the material world, using language. Davidson's theories are an excellent point of reference—it is no accident that he has been getting so much attention in composition and rhetoric—because his work is at the cutting edge of current philosophical thinking on matters of language, knowledge, and belief. What I find encouraging about Davidson's work—but what has not been sufficiently pointed out, however—is the degree to which Davidson tends to blur the distinction between foundationalism and antifoundationalism and seek solutions that transcend these pigeonholes. Nor has much attention been given to the problems in Davidson's theories. Although Davidson has made a strong case for relying on our sense of an external reality—primarily by arguing against traditional empiricism and the notion that we have internal conceptual schemes that mediate reality—he has yet to go the next step and specify more concretely what the connection can be between belief and truth. So I would like to point out the difficulties of Davidson's position and still note that his solution may be the best we can hope for.

Secondly, I would like to explore how we use philosophical theory in composition/rhetoric as a model or metaphor for instruction. Since there may be no other way to use theory in praxis, I offer Davidson's theory of triangulation as a more fruitful model in ways that Kent or Dasenbrock have yet suggested. And I note that Davidson's reliance on theories of language acquisition to explain his theory of triangulation may be a profitable suggestion for us in continuing to think about these matters.

Davidson's Theory of Triangulation

Davidson is not the only contemporary philosopher who is trying to account for how we know about "the material or 'brute act' world"—hence, such positions as internal realism, unlimited realism, metaphysical realism, and any number of theories as to how language reflects both the material world and our beliefs (see for example Putnam, especially chapters 1-3). The arguments for or against the various positions have such a long and complicated history that most philosophers settle on a position as lightly as a bee on a flower, carefully noting the difficulties of their chosen position and delicately assaying its strengths and weaknesses.

Among contemporary philosophers, however, Davidson is somewhat unique in that his theories finesse the entire problem of how much we can trust our sense of the material world. Although he calls himself a "nonfoundationalist" ("Myth" 167), Davidson assumes that the world is in some sense knowable—it is just not knowable in any way that will convince a skeptic—and that epistemic views—that is, views in which our perception and language *constitute* the world—are false ("Structure" 304).

The main theory that Davidson offers to explain how we know the world is what he calls triangulation:

> Well, the idea of triangulation is partly metaphorical, but not wholly. The basic idea is that our concept of objectivity—our idea that our thoughts may or may not correspond to the truth—is an idea that we would not have if it weren't for interpersonal relations. In other words, the source of objectivity is intersubjectivity: the triangle consists of two people and the world. Part of the idea is this: if you were alone in the world—that is, not in communication with anybody else—things would be impinging on you, coming in through your senses, and you would react in differential ways. Now, here's where the metaphor comes in. If you were to ask, "Well, when you're reacting a certain way, let's say to some pleasant taste, what is it that pleases you?" We would say, "It's the peach." However, in the case of the person who has no one with whom to share his thoughts, on what grounds could you say, "It's the peach that pleases: rather than the taste of the peach, or the stimulation of the taste buds, or, for that matter, something that happened a thousand years ago which set all these forces in motion which eventually impinged on the taste buds. There would be no answer to that question at all: nothing for him to check up on, no way to raise the question, much less to answer it. So, the idea of triangulation is this: if you have two people both reacting to stimuli in the world and to each other—that is, to each other's reactions to the stimuli—you've completed a triangle which locates the common stimulus. (Kent, "Language Philosophy" 7-8)

In short, triangulation is a theory of how human beings come to use words to refer to a common reality in a similar way: only by using words in response to "common stimuli" can they get any sense of how another person might be using the same words in the same way.

Now, Davidson's notion of triangulation carefully sidesteps two major theoretical problems. First, by asserting that language is one way we respond in common to external stimuli, he avoids the problem of reference, the precise way in which language reflects reality. Note that Davidson does *not* say that the objects of our perception *correlate* with any particular aspect of our language, that there is any necessary correspondence between the stimulation of our senses and any objects in the material world. He only argues that human beings share a way of talking about common stimuli in common situations. Thus, in Davidson's theory, when we use language we may be using words to refer to vastly different things in vastly different ways. All we know for certain is that we share a common language in certain situations and that this common language gives us some sense of the material world. Just what that sense is Davidson does not say, although he says we can rely on it.

Secondly, in developing a holistic theory about common stimuli in common situations, Davidson avoids the problem of empiricism and how we develop concepts, our "picture of the world," out of more primitive sense data. In effect, Davidson rejects the entire empirical tradition of grounding our knowledge in what we receive through our senses. He will only assert that our language is based in common experience, not in sense data. Thus, Davidson also rejects the notion that we constitute the world by building up our own internal beliefs as if we were putting together a grand mental structure using external sense data as the basic pieces. In fact, he argues the opposite view: that our internal beliefs and the language we use are somehow directly related to the beliefs and language of others. Again, just *how our* language and beliefs are related he does not say, but he is adamant that we can assume they have something in common because of how we learn language in the first place and use language together in common circumstances.

One great advantage of Davidson's theory is that he can refute an argument made by a number of antifoundationalists that if the world is independent of our minds, it is theoretically possible that all our beliefs could be false and or that there may be "one, complete, true description of the world against which all other accounts are to be measured" (Crumley 363). On the contrary, Davidson argues that we hold the beliefs we do because, as Jack Crumley puts it, "at least some of those beliefs are conditioned to events and objects in the world" and this conditioning is reflected in our language (365). Crumley goes on:

> In holding that the meaning of a sentence or the content of a belief is inextricably tied to the causal conditions productive of that belief, Davidson is not saying that the truth conditions are constituted by our *recognition* of those conditions. Rather our recognition of such conditions is but a consequence of those conditions obtaining in the first place...
>
> We have the beliefs that we do precisely because at least some of those beliefs are conditioned to events and objects in the world. (365)

Another great advantage of Davidson's theory is that it rejects any notion that something comes between, as it were, our experience of the world and our beliefs about that world. No socially-conditioned conceptual scheme or individual power of interpretation or self-awareness mediates between our experience of the world and our understanding of it. All we need for an adequate theory of language is the notion of triangulation: that the way we learn language in common situations reflects something truthful about the world.

> Anyone with thoughts, and so in particular anyone who wonders whether he has any reason to suppose he is generally right about the nature of his environment, must know what a belief is, and how in general beliefs are to be detected and interpreted. These being perfectly general facts we cannot fail to use when we communicate with others, or when we try to communicate with others, or even when we merely think we are communicating with others, there is a pretty strong sense in which we can be said to know that there is a presumption in favor of the overall truthfulness of anyone's beliefs, including our own. So it is bootless for someone to ask for some *further* reassurance; that can only add to his stock of beliefs. All that is needed is that he recognize that belief is in its nature veridical. ("Coherence" 314)

However, the fundamental weakness of Davidson's theory, as Richard Rorty is at great pains to point out, is that it does not give an adequate description of how language and the material world are related. Davidson takes truth as "primitive" ("Coherence" 308). Rorty glosses Davidson's argument this way:

> That there is no third thing relevant to truth besides the meanings of words and the way the world is—is the best explanation we are going to get of the intuitive force of . . . the idea that "truth is correspondence with reality. . . ."
>
> If this is indeed what Davidson is saying, then his answer to the skeptic comes down to: you are only a skeptic because you have these intentionalistic notions floating around in your head, inserting imaginary barriers between you and the world. Once you purify yourself of the "idea idea" in all its various forms, skepticism will never cross your enlightened mind. (344)

On the other hand, if Davidson is correct—and I think his solution to the problem of the relation of truth and belief is very attractive—we need not be as dogmatic about our antifoundationalism as Fish, Bruffee, and Kent suggest. As Wittgenstein pointed out earlier, we can choose to play a believing game or a doubting game, and no amount of evidence can convince a person who insists on playing the doubting game. Indeed, there is a school of what David Ray Griffin and others call "constructive postmodern philosophers"—Peirce, William James, Bergson, Whitehead, and Hartshorne—who argue that we should trust our basic beliefs about the world primarily because there is little *practical* reason to doubt them:

> Constructive postmodern philosophers hold that some beliefs are privileged in the sense that, once we become conscious of them (through

> whatever method), we should have more confidence in their truth than in the truth of any other beliefs from which their falsity could be deduced. The beliefs in question are *those that we inevitably presuppose in practice, even if we deny them verbally.* Whitehead formulates this principle as "the metaphysical rule of evidence: that we must bow to those presumptions, which, in despite of criticism, we still employ for the regulation of our lives." (Griffin 26-27)

This is not foundationalism in Fish's definition by any means—it does not guarantee ultimate "objectivity," whatever that might be—but it does suggest that our "mere beliefs" are more firm and stable than radical antifoundationalists suggest. Although such a position may not be sufficiently "grounded" to convince skeptics, it may be all we can ask of any theory of the relationship between belief, language, and the material world. The theory of triangulation does not provide a necessary and sufficient ground for us to trust our language, our reason, and our sense of the world, but it does suggest we have good *reasons* for doing so.

Triangulation as a Metaphor for Instruction

The primary way in which theorists in composition/rhetoric seem to use philosophical theories is as models or metaphors for how we ought to teach. Each of these theorists argue that if a certain theory of language and belief is convincing in accounting for how we communicate, then we ought to teach writing using methods modeled after that theory:

> Bizzell: Because all communication is situated, we should teach our students to be "meta-aware" of their situatedness.
>
> Bruffee: Because all language is social, we should teach our students to use collaborative methods which are more social than other ways of learning to write.
>
> Kent: Because all communication is contextual and dependent on luck, skill, and sympathy, we as teachers can only teach writing by providing contexts for real communication.

Now, it is important to recognize that even if a theory seems to accurately describe some aspect of the way language works or the way language reflects the material world, it does not necessarily follow that the best way to teach is to model instruction after that theory. A certain state of affairs may not necessarily be the best model for how to teach others *about* that state of affairs. Similarly, a certain kind of behavior may be a goal of instruction, but simply having students engage in that behavior may not necessarily be the best way to teach it.

For example, Fish may be right that in an ultimate sense all knowledge is contextual, that we cannot escape being "situated." But it does not follow that because all knowledge is contextual and we cannot escape being situated, no particular awareness of our situation will ever help us in learning to write. Our knowledge of our particular situation may be limited, but what we know and how we apply that knowledge will have consequences, and we can prefer and choose one situation over another.

Take, for instance, Fish's famous example of the sign on the door at the Johns Hopkins University Club: PRIVATE MEMBERS ONLY (*Text* 275). If we were to hear these words spoken aloud with the usual falling intonation after the word "private," most of us would spontaneously understand them to mean that only certain members of the Hopkins faculty are allowed in the room behind the door. And even without that spoken intonation, I suspect that most of us, passing quickly down the hall at Hopkins and glancing at the door, would understand the sign in the same way. But with a little training and practice in noting multiple meanings, especially in written language where we do not have the help of intonation, we can start to understand things differently. We begin to notice the ambiguity, the indeterminacy of the language we use all the time—with the same spontaneity that we used to understand things with single meanings. In the case of the sign on the door at Hopkins, we can understand the sign in any number of more suggestive and comic ways.

Fish would argue that in learning to understand and notice the indeterminacy of language, we have not transcended our situation; we have simply substituted one situation for another. And this is true. But I would argue that being able to recognize the ambiguities and indeterminacies of language is a superior position to be in. Not all situations are of equal value; knowing that language is indeterminate and often ambiguous can help us to recognize indeterminacies and ambiguities. And in many cases, for many people, it is better to be able to recognize such ambiguities than not. For many people in many situations, it is better to know more than less; it is better to recognize a range of possible meanings than to be limited to one—of course, not for everyone in every situation, but for many.

The same argument holds for Bizzell's teaching her students to be aware of the conventions of academic discourse. Such talk may not be "meta-discursive" or privileged in any ultimate sense, but it may produce the results she wants: students who are more self-aware about what they are writing and who have a better sense of how to go about manipulating the conventions of academic discourse for their own purposes. Bizzell's only difficulty may have been that she felt compelled to justify her instruction on something metaphoric of Fish's theory in the first place.[3]

Similarly, Kent's notion that writing cannot be taught systematically may be the result of Kent's trying to apply Davidson's theory of radical interpretation a little too literally. Even if we do learn to write in ad hoc and unsystematic ways, it does not necessarily follow that we should not teach writing systematically. Indeed, it seems intuitively obvious that systematic instruction might make unsystematic learning easier simply by providing a wider range of helpful information, guidance, and response over time. There is no reason why we cannot learn a host of things we bring to every writing situation in a "systematic" way, among them the way the language works and a knowledge of what we might call the principles of communication: the importance of context, various strategies for both producing prose and understanding certain kinds of discourse. And we can learn how to apply what we know systematically by practicing how to use different rhetorical strategies in different situations.

In short, we can insist on applying particular philosophical metaphors with such rigor that we ignore other aspects of our experience. The trick may be to keep our metaphors as rich and complex and true to our experience as we can make them. One of the major conclusions of Fish's antifoundationalism is this: If we know things to be true "only within the precincts of the contexts or situations or paradigms or communities that give them their local and changeable shape" (344), then arguments cannot be conducted primarily by referring to some independent "objective" reality; rather arguments can only be conducted by using persuasion, appealing to the "local and changeable" warrants and beliefs of those we want to persuade. When we choose a particular method of teaching writing, then, the question naturally arises: what makes a particular method convincing? If we decide with Bizzell that our students need to know the "meta-discourse" of academic prose, if we decide with Bruffee that our students need practice in collaborative learning, if we decide with Kent that our students need to write primarily as practitioners of a particular discipline, on what grounds do we make these decisions?

Obviously in any particular situation we make these decisions for a host of reasons, dependent on our background and experience, our situation, the nature of our curriculum, the kinds of students we are teaching, the resources at our disposal. But it may be useful to think that we use any particular teaching method primarily for one of two reasons. First of all, we may find the theory on which our teaching is metaphorically based to be convincing; that is, we intuitively recognize that, say, Fish's description of our situatedness is inherently true to our experience, and we want to capture the truth of that experience in our teaching. And secondly, we apply a particular method over time, and after a while we recognize that in some way it works; that is, we recognize that it actually produces good writers or good writing. What strikes me about the scholarship in favor of antifoundationalist pedagogies is the remarkable lack of much discussion about whether these methods of instruction actually produce good writers or good writing.

I am not suggesting that antifoundational writing theorists need to justify their pedagogies by using the empirical methods that were popular in our discipline in the 1950s and 60s. I recognize that empirical studies are certainly not "objective" and have their own theoretical problems. But it seems to me that ever since Stephen North, among many others, pointed out the conflicting assumptions and methods of various schools in our discipline—including the "lore" of practitioners who recognize in their students' work the success of how they have been teaching—we have been very uncomfortable talking about what makes our instruction successful, preferring to talk about philosophical metaphors rather than how we recognize that our students have become better writers or that their writing has improved. I sense that Bizzell, Bruffee, and Kent *know* that their methods are effective; they just haven't yet discovered a language to talk about their successes with broad acceptance in our discipline.

I wonder if philosophical metaphors are any more appealing to the wide range of practitioners in composition/rhetoric than various empirical methods of research or even practitioner lore, indeed any language that talks about how we recognize the success or failure of our instruction. In any case, it seems to me that sooner or later we will have to again bring back the success or failure of our instruction as a major part of the arguments in favor of various pedagogies in our discipline, whether they are antifoundationalist or not. After all, philosophical theories can be applied in many different ways with many different results, and any number of theories may produce methods of instruction which seem to those involved to be successful. The question is whether we can develop a way to talk about our successes and failures which appeals to a broad spectrum of scholars and practitioners.

Here again I find Davidson suggestive. Davidson has looked to theories of language acquisition to buttress his theory of triangulation:

> Let us start with what it is we know or grasp when we know the meaning of a word or sentence. It is a commonplace of the empirical tradition that we learn our first words (which at the start serve the function of sentences)—words like "apple," "man," "dog," "water"—through a conditioning of sounds or verbal behavior to appropriate bits of matter in the public domain. The conditioning works best with objects that interest the learner and are hard to miss by either teacher or pupil. This is not just a story about how we learn to use words: it must also be an essential part of an adequate account of what words refer to and what they mean.
>
> Needless to say, the whole story cannot be this simple. On the other hand, it is hard to believe that this sort of direct interaction between language users and public events and objects is not a basic part of the whole story, the part that, directly or indirectly, largely determines how words are related to things. ("Myth" 163)

Most theories of language acquisition now emphasize the nature of the active learner who develops internal hypotheses about how language works and constantly tests them against her experience. Young learners—or learners of a second language, for that matter—must work out their own private sense of the way language works, gradually approximating the language of adult speakers. Many composition theorists, such as Frank Smith and James Britton, have applied theories of language acquisition to how we learn to write.

What is interesting about Davidson's use of language-acquisition theories is that he invokes the empirical tradition to suggest that his theory of triangulation may be valid and useful. In doing so, he suggests that we too may combine the best of our knowledge and experience from a wide range of philosophical assumptions and points of view in thinking about how writing should be taught. For example, both the theory of triangulation and theories of language acquisition suggest that what will be most helpful in learning to write and in teaching writing is attention to those aspects of the world, those aspects of human behavior, those conventional aspects of discourse which we can name together and use in common ways. Thus, our instruction ought to pay overt and systematic attention to the ways we correlate our writing behavior with "the events and objects [we find] salient in the world" and the common conventions of language and written discourse we find salient in our communication (Davidson, qtd. in Kent, "Externalism" 65).

If this way of looking at Davidson seems useful, we may think of the concept of triangulation as philosophical support, a useful metaphor, for justifying the instructional methods of a number of composition theorists in the empirical tradition: those promoting sentence-combining (see Kinneavy) and those using what George Hillocks calls the environmental mode and focus on inquiry. Each of these methods focuses on activities which clarify a target concept or an aspect of written discourse—an object or event salient in the world or a convention salient in discourse—before providing for controlled application and practice using the target concept or aspect of writing. And like Davidson, we need not worry about whether these target concepts are "objective"; we need only recognize that such objects and events are what other people refer to when they communicate, that such aspects of discourse are indeed what people use when they communicate, and that novice writers need to have these things made salient for them so that they too can participate in the process of triangulation, of developing shared concepts and practices.

One major reason why the pedagogies noted by Kinneavy and Hillocks have not received more broad-based support in composition/rhetoric may be that their persuasive appeal is based on research in the empirical tradition of pre- and post-tests, a language which many of us view with suspicion. Perhaps if these theorists based their appeals on philosophical metaphors, they might make their pedagogies more attractive.

The larger question for our discipline to address is this: What kind of evidence would we accept that a particular pedagogy was successful? Any theory of language and communication will have its strengths and weaknesses; the point is to recognize the value of any particular theory and how it attempts to capture the truth of our experience. Ways of talking about the success and failure of our instruction, theories of evaluating writers and writing, are by no means objective and privileged, but they do provide us with one way to get at the heart of our instruction: whether it works. I doubt if any argument in favor of a particular method of instruction will win broad-based support in our discipline if it does not provide both a philosophical justification and evidence of its successful application.

Conclusion

The fascination of compositionists with antifoundationalism may or may not prove to be very useful for the teaching of writing in the long term. I suspect that most of us do not feel lost in a hall of mirrors: we feel comfortable in the material world and trust that our perceptions about it are generally true. We also manage to understand one another quite well enough, thank you, and whatever the quality of our instruction, our students do manage to learn to write, although of course some of them learn to write better than others. Although I too am fascinated by the arguments in favor of antifoundationalism, I believe that as a discipline we need to seriously examine the claims and arguments of the wide range of antifoundational theories and we need to evaluate their relevance to the teaching of writing. Most of the varieties of antifoundationalism are still a matter of lively debate in professional philosophy. They ought to be matter of lively debate in composition/rhetoric too.

In addition, I think we need a great deal more discussion of the metaphors we use to guide our instruction and the ways in which we can evaluate their effectiveness. Fish refers rather sarcastically to "theory hope," the belief that theory can help us out of the hall of mirrors. Davidson's theory of triangulation may not provide a necessary and sufficient rationale for believing in the objectivity of a material world, the language we use to talk about that world, and our own rationality; but the theory of triangulation does give us reason to trust the experiences we have in common, to believe that there is something *there* for our language to capture, and to trust in some small way the language we develop to talk about those situations. The question remains whether the theory of triangulation or any antifoundational philosophy can provide us with a useful language for talking about writing or provide us with convincing reasons for teaching a particular way in the hall of mirrors.

Notes

1. The only systematic critique of antifoundationalism in composition/ rhetoric I know of is by Royer, although Foster makes a few similar points in his criticism of Bruffee.

2. This is Bizzell's own summary of the earlier article, which is reprinted in *Academic Discourse and Critical Consciousness*, 75-104.

3. I have dealt with my reservations about Bruffee's metaphoric use of theory in "Some Difficulties."

Works Cited

Bizzell, Patricia. *Academic Discourse and the Critical Consciousness*. Pittsburgh: U of Pittsburgh P, 1992.

—. "A Response to 'Fish Tales: A Conversation with "The Contemporary Sophist." ' " *Journal of Advanced Composition* 13 (1993): 241-44.

Britton, James. *Language and Learning*. Coral Gables, FL: U of Miami P, 1970.

Bruffee, Kenneth A. "Collaborative Learning and the 'Conversation of Mankind.'" *College English* 46 (1984): 635-52.

—. "Social Construction, Language, and the Authority of Knowledge: A Bibliographic Essay." *College English* 48 (1986): 773-90.

Cherwitz, Richard A., ed. *Rhetoric and Philosophy.* Hillsdale, NJ: Erlbaum, 1990.

Crumley, Jack S. "Talking Lions and Lion Talk: Davidson on Conceptual Schemes." *Synthese* 80 (1989): 347-72.

Dasenbrock, Reed Way. "The Myths of the Subjective and of the Subject in Composition Studies." *Journal of Advanced Composition* 13 (1993): 21-32.

Davidson, Donald. "A Coherence Theory of Truth and Knowledge." In Lepore. 307-19.

—. *Inquiries into Trust and Interpretation.* Oxford: Clarendon, 1984.

—. "The Myth of the Subjective." *Relativism: Interpretation and Confrontation.* Ed. Michael Krause. Notre Dame, IN: Notre Dame P, 1989. 159-73.

—. "A Nice Derangement of Epitaphs." *Philosophical Grounds of Rationality.* Ed. Richard E. Grandy and Richard Warner. Oxford: Clarendon, 1986. 157-74.

Fish, Stanley. "Anti-Foundationalism, Theory Hope, and the Teaching of Composition." *Doing What Comes Naturally: Change, Rhetoric, and the Practice of Theory in Literary and Legal Studies.* Durham: Duke UP, 1989. 342-55.

—. *Is There a Text in This Class?: The Authority of Interpretive Communities* Cambridge, MA: Harvard UP, 1980.

Foster, David. "More Comments on 'Social Construction, Language, and the Authority of Knowledge: A Bibliographic Essay.'" *College English* 49 (1987): 709-11.

Graff, Gerald. "Interpretation of Tlon: A Response to Stanley Fish." *New Literary History* 17 (1985): 109-17.

Griffin, David Ray. "Introduction: Constructive Postmodern Philosophy." *Founders of Constructive Postmodern Philosophy.* Ed. David Ray Griffin, et al. Albany, NY: State U of New York P, 1993. 1-42.

Hikens, James W. "Realism and Its Implications for Rhetorical Theory." In Cherwitz. 21-77.

Hillocks, George. *Research on Written Composition.* Urbana, IL: NCTE, 1989.

Kent, Thomas. "Beyond System: The Rhetoric of Paralogy." *College English* 51 (1989): 492-507.

—. "Externalism and the Production of Discourse." *Journal of Advanced Composition* 12 (1992): 57-74.

—. "The Hope of Communication." *Journal of Advanced Composition* 12 (1992): 427-30.

—. "Language Philosophy, Writing, and Reading: A Conversation with Donald Davidson." *Journal of Advanced Composition* 13 (1993): 1-20.

—. "Paralogic Hermeneutics and the Possibilities of Rhetoric." *Rhetoric Review* 8 (1989): 24-42.

Kinneavy, James L. "Sentence Combining in a Comprehensive Language Framework." *Sentence Combining and the Teaching of Writing.* Ed. Donald A. Daiker, Andrew Kerek, and Max Morenberg. Conway, AR: L & S Books, 1979. 60-76.

Lepore, Ernest, ed. *Truth and Interpretation: Perspectives on the Philosophy of Donald Davidson.* New York: Blackwell, 1986.

McCormick, Kathleen. "Swimming Upstream with Stanley Fish." *The Journal of Aesthetics and Art Criticism* 44 (1985): 67-76.

North, Stephen. *The Making of Knowledge in Composition.* Upper Montclair, NJ: Boynton, 1987.

Olson, Gary A. "Fish Tales: A Conversation with 'The Contemporary Sophist.'" *Journal of Advanced Composition* 12 (1992): 253-77.

Putnam, Hilary. *Reason, Truth and History.* New York: Cambridge UP, 1981.

Rorty, Richard. "Pragmatism, Davidson and Truth." In Lepore. 333-55.

Royer, Dan. "New Challenges to Epistemic Rhetoric." *Rhetoric Review* 9 (1991): 282-97.

Smit, David W. "Some Difficulties With Collaborative Learning." *Journal of Advanced Composition* 9 (1989): 45-58.

Smith, Frank. *Writing and the Writer.* Hillsdale, NJ: Erlbaum, 1982.

Wittgenstein, Ludwig. *On Certainty.* Ed. G.E.M. Anscombe and G. H. von Wright. Trans. Denis Paul and G.E.M. Anscombe. New York: Harper, 1969.

Rhetoric and Hermeneutics: Composition, Invention, and Literature

George L. Pullman

Rhetoric and hermeneutics are clearly if variously related disciplines. They are historically related because they developed simultaneously in ancient Greece (Eden 60). They are professionally related in that many journals publish essays relevant to both disciplines (*PMLA, College English, Quarterly Journal of Speech, Rhetoric Review, Critical Inquiry, Rhetorica*, and the *Journal of Advanced Composition*, for example). They are pedagogically related because the burden for teaching both falls largely on English departments. And they are theoretically related because they are, or at least they are assumed to be, reverse sides of the same communication coin (Schleiermacher 74): one provides reading instruction while the other provides writing instruction. Despite (and because of) this clear relation between rhetoric and hermeneutics, composition and literature are generally disassociated.

In the last fifteen years or so, a great many people have suggested various ways of integrating these two disciplines (for overviews and related arguments, see for example: Booth, Clifford and Schilb, Comprone, Hartman, Horner, Kaufer and Waller, Lanham, J. Hillis Miller, Susan Miller, Salvatori), and yet, as Patricia Sullivan observes, even at the graduate level "literature and composition are still represented as separate intellectual activities" (296). This disassociation is primarily caused by matters of "attitude and history" (Horner 8), and one of the longest standing, most divisive attitudes is the theory/practice dichotomy (Jarratt 94) which assumes that theory and practice operate in separate realms: the one of abstract, intellectual knowledge; the other of concrete human activity. While each may inform the other, they are distinct and essentially different. The distinction between theory and practice adumbrates the subjects of rhetoric and hermeneutics, reinforcing beliefs and attitudes about the relative function and value of literature and composition. After all, for a majority of traditional English department faculty, literature is studied while composition is taught. They are categorically different enterprises, best dealt with by different kinds of people, but they are related activities and so best housed in the same department. One coin, two sides.

Schleiermacher's assertion that "hermeneutics and rhetoric are intimately related in that every act of understanding is the reverse side of an act of speaking" carries with it an obvious, almost intuitive plausibility (74). As with all plausible appearances, however, this one relies on several significant assumptions. If one assumes, as Schleiermacher's text suggests, that rhetoric is the art of transforming thoughts into signs while hermeneutics is the art of transforming signs into thoughts, and if one assumes, as Schleiermacher asserts, that "hermeneutics deals only with the art of understanding, not with the presentation of what has been understood," then obviously rhetoric and hermeneutics are reverse sides of the same coin (73). These assumptions about the nature and function of rhetoric and hermeneutics, however, have a disciplinary effect on English departments. By associating hermeneutics with the search for abstract thoughts and rhetoric with the presentation of concrete signs that momentarily stand in for abstract thoughts, one associates hermeneutics with abstract thinking and rhetoric with the physical, at most managerial, act of writing. Because the academy generally considers the production of knowledge (thinking) superior to the dissemination of knowledge (writing), the reverse-sides metaphor ultimately subordinates rhetoric to hermeneutics and composition to literary studies, polarizing members of the English department into those who love either literature or composition and tolerate the other as either an indulgence or an unfortunate necessity. The subordination of rhetoric to hermeneutics has also had the more seriously harmful effect of creating an underclass of composition instructors, a situation that nearly everyone deplores, but which is also difficult to correct. Although I do not for a minute imagine that a new understanding of the relation between rhetoric and hermeneutics is going to solve a largely financial problem, I do think that reevaluating the relation between the two disciplines may improve the relative attitudes of those who find themselves (schizophrenically) on opposite sides of the same coin.

Instead of accepting Schleiermacher's metaphor of reverse practices, which assumes that the discovery of ideas precedes rhetorical activity on the interpreter's part, the practical understanding of interpretation that I am describing and promoting on these pages presents hermeneutics as a specialized application of topical invention. The topics have traditionally been understood as the places where subjects for discourse can be located (*loci* is the Latin translation of *topoi;* both the Greek and the Latin words are usually translated into English as places, but they must not be confused with common places, which most people associate with hackneyed ready-mades, the compositional equivalent to prefabricated houses). As the location of arguments or subjects for discourse, they form the core of invention, and to the extent that invention is central to rhetoric, the topics are a critical practice. Aristotle differentiates between special and general topics in his *Rhetoric* (1358a 20-35). General topics are patterns that may be applied in any field. "Superfluities are better than bare necessities," for example, "and sometimes also preferable. For living a good life is better than merely living" (*Topica,* 118a 6-8). Special topics, on the other hand, are primarily discipline-specific sites of argumentation. Every field has its own set of acceptable topics. Literary interpretation is no exception. These patterns are not merely containers for words, but interpretive conventions, ways of understanding, and ways of locating relevant subjects for discourse. By understanding the production of literary studies as an application of topical invention, a general rhetorical technique that can be taught in composition courses but that can be specified in any field where writing is relevant, we can associate composition and literary studies as the general to the specific.

Although my insistence on the centrality of invention for interpretation may seem arbitrary to some, placing invention at the center of interpretive activity is critical to a practical hermeneutics because the current division of labor in English departments is the result of a hermeneutics that considers understanding non-rhetorical and rhetoric non-inventional. It is, however, the canon of invention that gives rhetoric its substance; without it, rhetoric merely arranges, clothes, and dispatches the arguments and observations other disciplines have discovered. Without invention, rhetoric is not an epistemic activity, and as such it can never hold anything but a secondary place in the English department (to say nothing of the academy at large). If, on the other hand, invention is part of the way interpretations are performed, then literary studies are epistemologically connected to rhetorical theory. The value of this practical hermeneutics is that it eschews the hierarchy that subordinates composition to literature because it describes interpretation as a creative effort to compose an understanding. It may appear as though I am simply trying to subsume literature under the heading of composition. My intention, however, is to level the hierarchy, not invert it. I am simply trying to specify by means of a practical hermeneutics one inventional aspect of the composition of literary interpretations.

To make this argument I will review, schematically, the historical origins of the arrangement between hermeneutics and rhetoric that makes Schleiermacher's misleading metaphor plausible. I will then indicate how the reverse-sides metaphor and the theory/practice split it reinforces disassociate composition and literary interpretation. Penultimately, I will recount the changes in hermeneutical thinking, which I call the rhetoricization of hermeneutics, that mark one current move in the humanities away from an apparently passive appreciation of literature toward a performance-centered hermeneutics. It is from this recent hermeneutical center that the possibility of an inventional approach to interpretation becomes plausible. In recounting these changes in interpretive thinking I am not so much arguing in the sense of attempting to demonstrate the validity of a theoretical position as I am narrating a segment of a tradition to suggest that a new turn in the narrative is appropriate given the prevailing intellectual climate. This is a *kairotic* rather than a demonstrative proof. Finally, I will provide a partial list of literary topics which will illustrate how patterns of reading can configure interpretation.

A History of the Subordination of Rhetoric to Hermeneutics

It is possible to trace the lineage of our current configuration of rhetoric and hermeneutics—one that understands hermeneutics as theoretical, rhetoric as practical, and the former as superior to the latter—back to Plato's configuration of rhetoric and dialectic in the *Phaedrus*. In that dialogue, the art of incrementally distinguishing knowledge from appearance or opinion (*episteme* from *doxa*) is called dialectic, whereas the art of tailoring opinions to a specific audience in order to improve that audience's soul is called rhetoric. This dialogue actually concludes with a wholesale rejection of all written compositions as not worth "serous attention," thus setting a precedent for the denigration of writing generally (278a). We might explain Plato's preference for dialectic over rhetoric in the following way: ideas are the unmediated apprehension of a portion of divine reality (knowledge). Thought is the internal representation of ideas; thought produces opinions. Any representation of an idea is instrumentally inferior to the idea itself, just as any representation of a thing is instrumentally inferior to the thing itself: a picture of a glass of water only increases thirst. Any representation of an idea is also ontologically inferior to the idea itself because even a fragmentary portion of divine knowledge is superior to any human opinion. Thoughts are therefore ontologically and instrumentally inferior to ideas. Opinion is inferior to knowledge. Speech is a representation of thought. Therefore speech is inferior to thought and even more inferior to ideas. Moreover, because speech is externalized thought, it is debased even further by the fact of its being in the world of unstable perceptions, in the cave of human existence where sounds and images are distorted by imperfect conditions. Speech removes thought even further from the realm of ideas.

Rhetoric, when understood in the Platonic sense as the techniques of effective speaking, translates divine ideas into human opinions because humanity in general is incapable of understanding divine Truth. Dialectic, when understood in the Platonic sense as the techniques of effective thinking, provides human knowledge that approximates ideas because even philosophers cannot completely grasp divinity. What is instrumental in a superior realm is superior to what is instrumental in an inferior realm. Therefore, dialectic is superior to rhetoric. This hierarchy is responsible for rhetoric's divorce from theory. Because ideas are *a priori* and divine, they are superior to any human invention. Ideas are glimpsed by introspection (*theoria*, a looking at, beholding, viewing, knowing). They are seen for what they are in themselves, not constructed or construed by human activity. Such introspection is purely theoretical; that is, it no more manipulates the objects of its apprehension than the eye distorts the images it perceives clearly. Because dialectic translates these ideas into thoughts, dialectic is a practical activity, but it is more theoretical than rhetoric because it creates knowledge while rhetoric merely organizes opinions for dissemination. Rhetoric is as far removed from theory as it is removed from knowledge. It is therefore extremely practical.

The Platonic "rhetorical" tradition was translated from a primarily oral culture to a primarily literate one by St. Augustine, who attributed invention to hermeneutics, while presenting rhetoric as merely a collection of strategies for effective preaching. He begins the first book of *On Christian Doctrine* with the following assertion: "There are two things necessary to the treatment of the Scriptures: a way of discovering those things which are to be understood, and a way of teaching what we have learned" (7). Of the four books, the first three are dedicated to the techniques of discovering textual truth in the Scriptures—dedicated, that is, to hermeneutics; only the last discusses homiletics, or the art of preaching. Because he divides his subject in this way, he suggests that discovery (invention) belongs to hermeneutics, and thus all that remains of rhetoric is merely a collection of rules or strategies for preaching the Truths that hermeneutics has discovered. This division between learning and teaching, with its consequent reduction in the scope of rhetoric, subordinates writing to reading: "Those with acute and eager minds more readily learn eloquence by reading and hearing the eloquent than by following rules of eloquence. . . . And he will learn eloquence especially if he gains practice by writing, dictating, or speaking what he has learned according to the rule of piety and faith" (119). Thus, in the pursuit of eloquence, reading precedes writing just as for Plato knowledge must precede rhetoric. This organization of hermeneutics and rhetoric suggests that not only is writing nonepistemic, it is actually ancillary to any epistemic activity. The substance of discourse and the means of discourse are separate entities that must be learned at separate moments, and because rhetoric is insubstantial, it is a secondary academic concern from an intellectual standpoint. According to this division of hermeneutics and rhetoric, when writing finally does come into play, it is predicated not on rhetorical knowledge or practice, but on piety and faith. One must pray, or (a secular alternative) seek one's muse for divine inspiration. Thus, writing instruction is theoretically impossible, not just irrelevant to this kind of hermeneutics. The rhetorician may offer a few general rules and some techniques regarding the presentation of knowledge, but that is all rhetoric has to offer a writer.

Thus, Augustine believed, just as Plato did before him and Schleiermacher did after him, that rhetoric was epistemologically insignificant. Hermeneutics discovers what to say while rhetoric merely suggests how to say it. The two disciplines are mutually dependent because thought without expression is useless, and expression without thought is vacuous. It is from this perspective that rhetoric and hermeneutics can be construed as opposite sides of the same coin. One must think before one speaks, and one must know before one thinks. The corollary of this is that one must understand a book before writing about it. Thus, reading and writing are mutually dependent but entirely different activities—two sides of the same coin. If one accepts this argument, then one is committed to reading and writing instruction as they are currently provided in the traditional sort of English department where the honors and perks go to those who teach literature while those who teach writing teach nothing intellectually significant and are rewarded accordingly.

The survey of contemporary exclusivist positions that follows is offered as an indication of how the theory/practice dichotomy configures the relation between reading and writing, and also as an indication of how the hierarchy of disciplines that the split between theory and practice creates remains active even among arguments favoring the interrelation of reading and writing.

Disassociations

For those writing specialists who consider literary studies inappropriate for composition, literature is too specialized a form of discourse to warrant its inclusion in courses where the emphasis is largely on developing basic rhetorical skills. Literary discourse is considered an unapproachable model for students, one that creates impractical expectations about the purpose and nature of the kind of prose that almost all of them will be called upon to write both in their academic careers and in life after graduation. Earl Britton, for example, has argued that first-year composition courses predicated on literary study develop skills antithetical to professional writing. More recently, Edward Corbett has argued that literary texts distract students "from the objectives of a writing course" (183). Even more recently, Erika Lindemann has offered five more reasons why "using literature in freshman English is inappropriate" (313). If the goal of all nonfiction writers is to convey information linearly, in simple declarative sentences, with adequate forecasting so that the reader can understand effortlessly, then reading William Faulkner or Virginia Woolf would seem to be counterproductive. If one argues in this fashion, that literary texts are opaque while nonliterary texts are transparent, then literary interpretation is an impractical activity that should remain separate from composition. Although it is no doubt true that some students may be intimidated by literary texts as composition models and others misled into assuming that a good technical manual should be constructed like a gothic novel, completely separating composition from literary interpretation suggests that understanding a literary text must be fundamentally different from composing a more mundane text. Moreover, it suggests that the composition of literary interpretations is a non-rhetorical activity. Thus, this position contributes to the valorization of literary studies even as it champions the autonomy of composition precisely because it associates composition with practicality and literary studies with something impractical.

Conversely, some literature specialists believe that the practical concerns of composition instruction confound literary interpretation. Hephzibah Roskelly records a telling example of this kind of literary exclusion of rhetoric. She observes Geoffrey Hartman's complaint in *The Fate of Reading* that reading considered as a precondition for writing, "where interpreters read only to find topics for their own discourse," destroys the "dream of Communication" that was once the foundation of writing and reading (Roskelly 138). Hartman seems to believe, at this moment at least (he is more conciliatory at others: "Understanding Criticism"), that introducing rhetoric into literary studies, encouraging the integration of composition and literature, could subvert effective interpretation because it would encourage people to appropriate what the author said. In other words, integrating composition and literature would stage an interpretive coup by supplanting the authority of the author with the voice of the critic or interpreter. Writing about a text before one completely understands it seems to disrupt communication the way speaking before thinking makes communication dangerous. This position suggests that the production of a literary interpretation is dissimilar to the comprehension of a literary work because understanding is non- or pre-linguistic. Thus, literary interpretation would seem to be divorced from rhetorical practice and, therefore, better left separate from composition. The difficulty with this position is that it relies on a hermeneutics of piety similar to Augustine's and Plato's. If the process of understanding is a form of supernatural magic, then there is nothing to teach in a literature class, and literature has nothing to offer apart from the spontaneous appreciation of powerful works. The literature specialist becomes a museum curator and the English department a museum piece. This splendid isolation excites some kinds of non-activist literary scholars but leaves the more issue-oriented literary scholars "doing theory." It also invalidates rhetorical study, offering "rhetoric" as nothing more than a service to the academy at large in return for financial support.

This division between theory and practice is resilient even to positions that address it directly. Robert Scholes, for example, argues that "reading and writing are complementary acts that remain unfinished until completed by their reciprocals" (20). Writing, or expression as he calls it, is critical to the development of understanding. Thus, reading and writing are inseparable. This position goes a long way toward redressing the theory/practice split. Interpretation offers the opportunity for a social construction of textual reality, where interpretation is a process that produces its own market in the process of its production. Thus we would teach interpretation in order that our students would learn how to insert their own texts in the spaces they have created in other people's texts. But Scholes also argues that literary interpretation and discourse production are reciprocal practices (16), a mathematical equivalent to Schleiermacher's numismatic metaphor. This configuration threatens to reassert the theory/practice dichotomy, which makes the division between composition and literature inevitable. I may seem to be quibbling here. What difference does it make if a theory has a dichotomous tendency? The answer is that the theory/practice dichotomy is not a theoretical infelicity. It is rather an event, an attitude that has serious consequences for the distribution of labor and respect in English departments.

The problematic nature of Scholes' configuration of rhetoric and hermeneutics is most apparent when he explains that reading is a process of decoding "the codes that were operative in the composition of any given text and the historical situation in which it was composed" (21). He composes this position by explaining how he teaches a Hemingway piece to a group of historically ignorant students. Basically his practice is to inform his students of the sedimented meanings of the terms around which pivot the kind of interpretation that would be performed by a person of Hemingway's generation, culture, and gender—a traditional hermeneutic recuperation of the text. Hence his concern to "rehabilitate reference itself" (85). Such a position continues to privilege the past, suggesting that meaning is buried in language that has become opaque because of the passage of time. The interpreter thus becomes a cataloguer of semiotic references that can be applied to a text the way solvents are applied to dusty windows. The purpose of interpretation is to make language a transparent window on the thoughts of (dead) authors. A person who writes interpretations, therefore, uses interpretation only to efface the changes that language undergoes in time, employing rhetoric simply to present the discoveries made by interpretation. If the interpretation is properly constructed according to the rules of "rhetoric," then it is itself not in need of interpretation. Interpretations are thus instrumentally different from literary texts, and rhetoric is understood as a set of techniques for presenting information unmediated by authorial assumptions. Because each literary text contains a historically accurate interpretation (the meaning of the text) and the role of hermeneutics is to recover that meaning, meaning precedes any rhetorical activity on the interpreter's part. Composition is used to communicate what interpretation discovered. Interpretation produces knowledge and composition expresses that knowledge. The theory/practice dichotomy is momentarily removed, but the hierarchy it created remains. Writing is merely the expression of thought. And so the wall between literary theory and rhetorical practice remains even when the desire to talk about reading as writing and vice versa motivates the discussion.

Perhaps the most successful approach to removing the theory/practice dichotomy has been presented under the sign of deconstruction (see the essays collected by Atkins and Johnson for a sample of different perspectives). J. Hillis Miller has argued, for example, that "reading is a kind of writing" (41) and that rhetoric is a form of de- composition or analysis (42). By associating rhetoric with the creation of new understandings, he elevates rhetoric beyond mere expression. But Miller also argues that writing is a "trope" for reading. Like Scholes', this intersection of rhetoric and hermeneutics indicates just how resilient the theory/practice dichotomy can be, even for rapprochement theories of reading and writing. If writing is a trope for reading, then writing is still a secondary practice, a translation or an alteration of the literal. Writing can thus be returned to the level of that which presents but does not invent meaning.

In each of the arguments I have just recounted, either the preponderance of a theoretical or practical orientation in one discipline distinguishes it from the other to such an extent that the two must be held separate, or the hierarchy that subordinates composition to literary studies remains intact even when reading and writing (theory and practice) are considered inseparable. Theoretical activities are and have been associated with knowledge production, while practical activities have been associated with the dissemination of knowledge. Thus, the theory/practice line divides literary interpretation from composition and creates the potential for the hierarchy which privileges literary interpretation. The separation of these two disciplines, then, is the result not only of the theory/practice dichotomy but also of the relation of inequality that the dichotomy sets up between rhetoric and hermeneutics.

The persistent segregation of composition and literature might end, therefore, if the hierarchy that holds composition inferior to literary interpretation could be leveled. In order to do this, hermeneutics and rhetoric have to be understood as something other than reversely or even reciprocally related disciplines, as two sides of the same coin, so that it is impossible to associate one with theory and the other with practice exclusively. If we recognize the rhetorical nature of interpretive processes as a topical form of invention, then literary interpretation is simply a special instance of a general practice of invention. This argument connects literature to composition at the site of invention rather than expression, unites theory and practice (reading and writing), and eliminates the hierarchy of texts. I am not arguing that *King Lear* and a college junior's interpretation of it are equally valuable to the world, only that the production of any text, even the production of a text about a text, requires the application of special topics and, therefore, that composition and literary studies are positively related subjects.

This topical approach to literary interpretation is historically grounded in a Renaissance hermeneutic, which, according to Victoria Kahn, considered interpretation and rhetoric indistinguishable (Kahn 39). The Renaissance humanists understood interpretation as a re-presentation of a verbal artform that offered the manuscript writer the opportunity to embellish, to amplify, to read, and even to write between the lines of a previously composed text (Bruns 101-02). Meaning, from this perspective, is created by interpretive activity. It does not reside in a text the way an artifact lies buried in the dust. A text is not a repository of meaning, but rather a potential opportunity for discourse. Meaning is continually reinvented, not originally given to be recovered. Interpretive validity is no longer determined by an isomorphic relationship between an idea and its linguistic representation, by a metaphysical goodness-of-fit test. There is no absolute standard of evaluation for interpretive propositions because interpretation happens within informal, open systems. Unlike mathematics and formal logic, where propositions can be evaluated by absolute standards because the words that construct these systems are entirely formal, interpretation involves words and systems of thought that cannot be codified and formalized. Thus, interpretive propositions cannot be evaluated according to an absolute standard. From this perspective, rhetoric is significantly involved in interpretation at two different levels. Rhetoric not only advises people how to arrange arguments and choose words, it provides the framework of informal argumentation that is necessary for evaluating interpretive propositions. This Renaissance rhetorical hermeneutic has recently been reinvented by Continental and American hermeneuts, as well as by scholars who "do theory." Despite its success in these fields, its implications seem to be ignored by English departments at large because the opinion that one must re-write a text in order to read it is inconsistent with the disassociation of reading and writing. Thus, a fast overview of the rhetoricization of hermeneutics is warranted.

Rhetoricization of Hermeneutics

Before 1970, hermeneutics was primarily dedicated to the discovery of features in a specific text that indicated an essential meaning and to developing universal principles that could guide the discovery of essential meanings in any text. The concepts of authorial intention and literal meaning, for example, were thought to anchor interpretation outside language (in the psyche or the world) and so necessarily demonstrate the accuracy of an interpretation, or at least to provide the hope that interpretive certainty could approximate scientific certainty (Hirsch; Hoy 32). A literary author could use rhetoric if he or she wished, but an interpreter could not permit rhetoric to interfere with interpretive method because he or she sought knowledge of the text in question. Rhetoric would be additionally irrelevant when it came time to present that meaning because knowledge must be demonstrated rather than proven. In other words, rhetoric was unacceptable as a method of inquiry and even as a method of composition. Although the attitude that rhetoric is an underhanded technique employed when authorial ambition outstrips the available evidence is slowly being eradicated, you will know that some strain of it is alive and well wherever you hear someone say something like, "I liked that lecture (or article); it wasn't full of rhetoric."

The prevalence of this attitude toward rhetoric began to diminish when Richard Palmer introduced the hermeneutic thought of Heidegger and Gadamer to America. Palmer argues that the separation of time and place that holds readers and writers apart is the natural and inevitable effect of the fact that written discourse outlasts the context of its composition. He concludes, therefore, that the hermeneutic purpose is to overcome this separation, to revivify the text (14), to breathe life back into the empty words, as it were, so that they may say what they were composed to say. This hermeneutic task of returning a text to immediate (aural) experience is, according to Gadamer, what makes "the rhetorical and hermeneutical aspects of human linguisticality completely interpenetrate each other" ("Scope" 25). Interpretation "resembles more the art of the orator than the process of listening," he says (24). The interpreter must amplify a text in order to "hear" it as it once was spoken. This perspective leads Palmer to argue that understanding a text is more like interpreting a piece of music than deciphering a code in that one's abilities improve with practice rather than with the application of universal laws (15). Hermeneutics, in other words, is closer to *phronesis* than it is to *theoria.* It is more practical than theoretical. Demonstrative validity is therefore an inappropriate criterion for hermeneutic evaluation.

Although this perspective helps integrate composition and literature by arguing that rhetoric and hermeneutics are both practical activities, it privileges the spoken word in a way that reinforces the idea that rhetoric is essentially an oral practice, which would seem to render it ancillary in a textual age such as our own (an assertion which Gadamer himself makes: "Hermeneutics" 55). More importantly however, Gadamer's logocentricity privileges the Platonic epistemology that relegates rhetoric to the art of dissemination and so removes invention from the rhetorical canon. The rhetoric of interpretation is thus limited to the art of amplification, of increasing or improving the reception of what is already there. Thus rhetoric is disassociated from the production of knowledge and relegated to the practical sphere of broadcasting. Nevertheless, by making interpretation a performative rather than a purely analytical activity, this perspective does suggest that rhetoric and hermeneutics are both practical activities.

Palmer also inaugurated the transition from an object-oriented hermeneutics to a process-oriented one by arguing that literature was an experience rather than an object and a conscious practice rather than an effect. Incidentally, he argued hermeneutics is an iterative process, just as writing is. Palmer laments the trend in American criticism to treat interpretation as though texts were objects indifferent to the intentions of their writers and the attentions of their readers (5-7). Thus he offers his phenomenological hermeneutics as a move toward an interactive understanding of interpretation that follows the examples of Gadamer and Heidegger. The concepts of effective history and fore-having suggest that the interpreter and the object of interpretation are not independent of each other as subject from object can be in controllable experimentation. Because hermeneutic understanding is understood as a circular and holistic process involving a shuttling back and forth between part in relation to whole and whole in relation to part, the context of consumption has to be considered in addition to the context of production. Adequate understanding, therefore, does not consist solely of placing a text in its historical context, but also of placing the interpretive process in its historical context and considering the interrelation of the two processes. This reflection on the process of interpretation is meant to ensure that the truth of the subject that inspired the text is no more obscured by present conditions than historical changes necessitate. Although this hermeneutic insists that some interpretive influence is unavoidable, and so does not construe a text as an object about which absolute knowledge is available, it retains a metaphysical goal, and so reasserts the divine/human dichotomy which generates the theory/practice dichotomy, from which descends the literature over composition hierarchy.

So while the rhetoricization of hermeneutics has not entirely endorsed the idea that rhetoric in an epistemic activity and so has not yet provided members of the traditional English department with a way of recognizing the intellectual integrity of rhetoric, it has re-presented hermeneutics as a performance-centered form of argumentation, the validity of whose propositions cannot be necessarily proven by demonstrative reasoning, and thus it has understood interpretation as a broadly based, socially significant form of informal argumentation. It has, in other words, concluded that rhetoric has a lot more to do than just dispense the knowledge that hermeneutics produces on its own. But if contemporary hermeneutics informs literary studies as to the significance of rhetoric as a paradigm of argumentation, it also informs compositionists that hermeneutics is not an abstruse derivative of esoteric philology, but rather an unavoidable activity of life in general.

Hermeneutics is sometimes mistakenly understood to occur only when obscurity, ambiguity, alienation, or misunderstanding render immediate recognition impossible. Metaphorically speaking, it is, from this limited perspective, the set of tools used to restore the Sistine Chapel. Thus, it would seem to be an irrelevant practice when clarity, uniformity, immediacy, or previous understanding make recognition instantaneous and unnoticeable. In other words, it would seem to be irrelevant to technical writing and exposition in general. Since the publication of Gadamer's *Philosophical Hermeneutics*, however, the processes of interpretation have been generalized to cover all situations, immediate and foreign. One interprets even when doing so is effortless because one must filter sensations or be overwhelmed by them, just as one who wears an unsophisticated hearing aid may not hear a conversation for the sound of the refrigerator, the computer monitor, and the rumble of cars outside until he or she learns to consciously "tune out" the extraneous noise. All of these sounds attend the conversation but cannot be attended to without a loss of understanding. Interpretation is an unavoidable activity: just as one cannot not communicate, one cannot not interpret; the world is always already constructed by selection and arrangement of material. Interpretation is therefore just as relevant when writing a process description for an extrusion plant as for illuminating a Chaucerian Tale. If one accepts the tenets of contemporary hermeneutics, then interpretation is an unavoidable part of practical wisdom (*phronesis*), a purposive activity rather than a spontaneous psychological mechanism or objective technique that produces absolute knowledge (*episteme*). From this perspective, then, interpretation is a form of rhetorical argumentation. If we add to this an inventional component, then we will have a rhetorical hermeneutics that does not distinguish between learning and writing.

Topical Hermeneutics

The virtue of understanding interpretive practices as an application of special topics is that it affords the practitioner a level of conscious control over how he or she will construe a text, and thus some measure of control over how he or she will both construe and be construed by others. Because meaning is not given in a flash of insight but created, invented out of existing but differently composed materials, writing and reading are inseparably linked. They both require invention. An additional virtue is that there is no effort to describe the process of interpretation in such a way that one topic is always privileged over all others, as it is, for example, when meaning is understood as authorial intention or a single stable meaning is assumed available to a particular methodology (or a multiple, ethereal collection of disparate readings, for that matter). This makes interpretation more versatile, more able to suit various situations and needs. This makes some of what is learned in a literature classroom relevant to other endeavors without rendering literature subservient to other practices. One can still enjoy the power of a great piece or consider the ethical implications of a great work. One simply has a broader range of ways to write about these topics.

From the perspective of topical invention, the purpose of writing is not to represent thought in words or to convey abstract meanings to others by means of words, but rather to exert power over experience—to re-form what had been formed before. Interpretation is understood not as a psychological event or metaphysical quest or a methodical reconstruction of a historical consciousness, but rather as a conscious effort to apply formalizing principles to previously formed matter. Just as an interpretation of a piece of music creates another piece of music, one that bears a family resemblance to its parental score, so the interpretation of a text produces another text. When reading and writing, as in all other aspects of life, one considers what one can do with what one has found. From this perspective, then, rhetoric is significant to interpretation because it advises interpreters how to arrange and clothe arguments; it provides the argumentative framework for evaluating the relative plausibility of various interpretations; and, most importantly, it provides a practical method for discovering how to provide interpretations—for inventing meanings, in other words.

Literary Topics

The special topics of literary interpretation have in the past been chosen more or less by practice, habit, and inheritance, or because a particular topic was thought to lead to an undeniably true interpretation differentiated from other interpretations by the denomination meaning, but the topics of interpretation may also be chosen self-consciously. Just as one versed in rhetorical invention can deal effectively and immediately with new situations by at first dividing the new experience into familiar categories and then branching out, so can an interpreter create a useful encounter out of a new text by starting with traditional special topics and then considering topics from elsewhere. Some traditional literary topics are intention (or anti-intention), structure, context, influence, origin, significance, implication, sublimation, signs of ideological issues and conflicts, form and substance, ambiguity, indeterminacy, etymology, figurality. Any particular instance of interpretation might require any number and hierarchical configuration of these.

Literary topics, like all special topics, are contextual in two ways. They are associated with a particular endeavor. Although they may be transported from one endeavor to another, they will carry with them residue of the first context. Intention, for example, comes from law (as do many traditional hermeneutic practices) and carries with it the aura of vindication (or vilification) and contractual agreement. Special topics are also contextual in that each one (or each collection) is more fitting and appropriate in certain circumstances (determined by audience, desire, ethos, institutional context) than in others. It is important to underscore the contextuality of interpretation because doing so makes interpretation a real-world event rather than a metaphysical quest which exceeds all temporality, or, at the other extreme, a schoolbook exercise performed for the sake of a grade. One is not searching for either the Meaning or the Being of a text, but rather for what can be said about it and for reasons to write in the first place.

Intention, for example, is used when the obvious meaning is inefficacious for an interpretive purpose. The rap singer Ice-T's defense of himself when his song "Cop Killer" created a pubic outcry was that he was merely personifying an attitude. In other words, he defended himself from the accusation of inciting violence toward authority by distancing or disassociating himself from the words he sang. He was requesting (perhaps belatedly) that his rap not be interpreted literally, but obliquely, as the dancing of an attitude, as Burke might say. A similar, although more subtle, defense may be given for the author of "A Modest Proposal." The fact that the intentional defense is only rarely required of Swift (in cases where the audience has no idea who Swift was, or when the audience does not understand the idea of double reading, or misses what are normally considered cues) does not make the topic different for Swift than for T, even though most of the people who readily understand Swift as ironic would blanch at T's rap simply because they miss the cues or refuse the ones offered. What is alien is frightening and so must be normalized by some means. One of the purposes of interpretation is to naturalize the alien, and intention is a topic that can be used to vindicate an author just as it can be used to defend someone accused of a crime. One may also interpret for the opposite reason, however. Defamiliarization makes immediate and apparently effortless interpretations unpersuasive and alien, while rendering obscure interpretations plausible. Because, as Roland Barthes once said, for every inclusion there is an exclusion, it is always possible to redirect compositional attention, to locate a group of people who have been unfairly represented or an ill-conceived attitude behind a well-meaning explanation. Description reveals the writer, not the world. This topic is useful when an audience seems complacent about the validity of a particular interpretation, or when a work is locked into a single mode of interpretation—when, for example, an audience refuses to "see" any ideological component to what it calls a fairy tale, but which you can perceive as a vehicle for promoting unquestioned opinions: a young woman must obey her father; wolves are terrestrial sharks. The topics that support defamiliarization in general are ambiguity, indeterminacy, etymology, and figurality. These may be chosen and arranged in different ways to accomplish different interpretations. Ideological critique, for example, the topic of locating a social injustice beneath a fair semblance, is a politically specified form of defamiliarization. By promoting indeterminacy and then "discovering" ambiguity, one can create an interpretive space between immediate understanding and a preferred understanding. Thus, one can use defamiliarization whenever something different needs to be said but there does not appear to be any place to say it.

A related literary topic is that of ethics. The "great works" tradition of literary scholarship argues that people who are exposed to canonical literature develop an improved ethical sensibility. The opposite is also true, according to this hermeneutic: people are ethically corrupted by inferior works, pulp fiction and pornography. From within this hermeneutic, all texts are read and evaluated in relation to an abstract standard of conduct that is supposed to be universally valid. All authors are preachers. To apply this topic, one has to assume that the text is presenting what the author believes is a correct mode of being in the world. Does the text provide an accurate description of human behavior while maintaining a proper attitude toward that behavior? This topic was employed, for example, by the people who condemned *Madame Bovary* on the grounds that it depicted immoral behavior. They were assuming that the central figure of a text was necessarily the heroine and was offered as a model to be emulated. The same topic was used against Ice-T and, perversely, against Reverend Swift. Although many people interpret all works of art as sermonic, a more versatile understanding recognizes that some texts may be more valuable if understood from some other topic, whereas books already considered artistically valuable can be revalued if read according to a sermonic hermeneutic. A topical approach to interpretation does not remove the ethics of interpretation. It suggests that ethics is a topic worth pursuing in some circumstances for some works, but it also points out that the topic implies (as all topics do imply) certain assumptions—that human behavior is generalizable, that ethics are not purely situational, that authors are priests. With these assumptions in mind, one may be better able to choose the topic wisely. One would also be much less likely to apply the topic blindly, as when one thinks that Swift had to have been a barbarian.

Another special topic is to use a narrative about the historical context of a textual production as a method of analysis and argumentation. This topic is employed almost exclusively by those who would recuperate the true meaning of a text. Even if one is inclined to reject the hermeneutics that posits reading as a metaphysical quest, one might still consider historical context of production in order to generate a discourse that relates the past and the present, using a particular text as a locus or point of intersection. The interpreter's goal of establishing the meaning of a text as a psychological event in the author's head is abandoned and replaced by the effort to locate a text's participation in social configurations as a result of how it was construed at the time it was published. This is the approach that Steven Mailloux has used for *Huckleberry Finn*. The goal in this particular case is to explain the social function of a text and thus to explain how various meanings could be attributed to it at a particular time. Whereas underscoring the importance of context is a universal tenet of the new historicism, a topical hermeneutics considers context a text in itself. It is a narrative frame or a lens that may be used to recompose interpretations of a given text. In other words, context is thus a compositional option rather than an Archimedean point for accurate interpretation. If it were an absolute criterion, then it would not be susceptible to infinite regress—each context being supplemented by another context that fails to completely explain the previous one, until it too has been explained by a context, *ad nauseam*.

Influence as a literacy topic is a specification of the general topic of cause and effect. Influence studies are (like causal studies) out of fashion these days because continuity has been replaced with discontinuity as a special topic of historiography. The heterodox composition of contemporary society renders emphasis on difference (equal but different) more plausible than similarity. Thus, a study that posits direct lineage between ages or cultures is more likely to be objectionable now than when people believed that there was essentially one culture and that it descended in a straight line. Influence studies might return, however, if lineage became important again. If one were trying to collect a disparate group of works under a single term or idea, then tracing a connection to a previous term or idea might be an effective technique. The topic of influence is also just one example of how topics act as subliminal ideological arguments, as rhetorics in the sense of persuasive events. By demanding that a work or a practice have an identifiable origin, and, as it were, a pedigree, we demand that all narratives conform to a humanist paradigm. By arguing, for example, that the origin of rhetoric can be attributed to Corax and Tisias responding to political changes, that they influenced Gorgias, and that he influenced Plato (negatively), we place human action at the center of change. Thus, the topic of influence is also an ideological argument, albeit a very indirect one. All topics have allegiances and rely on assumptions that they simultaneously promote when they are "successfully" interpreted, that is, when they are interpreted as true or right.

Gender bias is another special literary topic of considerable ideological importance these days. One begins with an intense set of expectations about how individuals should or should not behave as a consequence of their gender and then critiques a text based on its fit with or remodification of those expectations. One assumes that the piece describes the world, prescribes others' perceptions of the world, or signifies a past understanding of the world. If texts were closed systems, their prejudices would be quaint or irrelevantly obscene, but not dangerous and in need of critique. Thus, it would be highly difficult to nest a gender topic within a formalist topic unless the formalism was itself gendered. If one were arguing that prose style or argumentative style is a function of gender, for example, then one could nest formalism and gender. But again, the writer's purpose and her or his circumstances would influence the application of these topics.

This list of special topics is by no means complete, and the actual group and configuration of topics will be changing constantly as local exigencies change. I have provided this brief sketch simply to show how literary topics can be implemented. Each one provides a way of reorganizing a text, of finding new things to say about it, of inventing knowledge in the sense of producing a text that elaborates textual understanding.

The interaction of these topics will provide compositional possibilities. They may be hierarchically arranged, as when, for example, Hirsch distinguishes between significance and intention and then privileges the latter. In the face of that pattern's popularity, one might need to revise the hierarchy if one felt compelled to provide a modern interpretation of an ancient text (if the audience one were addressing were aligned with contemporary hermeneutics). This is what Richard M. Weaver does when he concludes his interpretation of the *Phaedrus* by replacing the topic of intention with the topic of structure:

> No one would think of suggesting that Plato had in mind every application which has here been made, but that need not arise as an issue. The structure of the dialogue, the way in which the judgments about speech concentre, and especially the close association of the true, the beautiful, and the good, constitute a unity of implication.
>
> (Johannesen et al. 82-83)

He is able to make this move because his understanding of textual interpretation is subtle and dynamic, attuned to local interpretive needs (in this case the contemporary application of one brand of ancient rhetoric) and not confined to a single method of interpretation. The critical point for a topical hermeneutics is that any interpretive hierarchy that would valorize one topic and subordinate another, like intention over significance, is usefully understood as a momentary effect of argumentation rather than an accurate description of a permanent truth.

Conclusion

It seems to me that a topical approach to interpretation enables us to refute many of the arguments used to separate composition and literature. Once a writer progresses beyond grammatical instruction, the discovery and application of special topics is a basic rhetorical skill and so not alien to the composition at any level, undergraduate, graduate, or professorial. Because literature offers a reasonably interesting source of topics and because most English teachers practice written interpretation anyway, literary interpretation may be a useful composition practice. Literature need not be the only place in which to develop the practice of discovering and using topics, but, because the interpretation of literature requires the application of a general theory of invention, it is a legitimate area of composition. Although it may be a special form of discourse, it is not interpreted in an entirely unique way. For the same reason, the gap between first-year composition and technical writing will be less broad if the idea and practice of topical invention is regarded as integral to all writing activities.

The fear that rhetoric's practical orientation spoils communication is more difficult to allay. But if communication is considered a congeries of several topics, intention and context primarily, and as an argument rather than an event, then perhaps the fear may abate somewhat. A topological hermeneutic emphasizes the work involved in producing interpretations and so seems to de-emphasize the experience of direct communication, but it does not eliminate communication, only exchanges the conduit metaphor of direct transmission for an argumentative paradigm: communication is ascribed rather than prescribed; it is a rhetorical construct, not an experiential or cognitive phenomenon. One cannot deny another's communication by appropriating a text because the textual possibilities that a text enables do not belong to the individual who signed that text; each text is simply a figurative space that one may attempt to lay partial claim to, a space from which to work with other figurative spaces. From the perspective of a topical hermeneutics, the truth of one's interpretation is simply equivalent to the cogency of one's argument as determined by anyone who interprets the piece. To argue that there is a True Meaning of a text is to employ specific topics in order to limit the method of interpretation employed by one's readers. It is, in other words, a rhetorical effort to control a textual situation. From within a topological hermeneutic, Meaning is simply a primary topic in the hermeneutics of recuperation. It is an option, not a necessity.

Plausible objections to topological theory of interpretation are no doubt numerous. From within the framework of a paralogical hermeneutics such as Thomas Kent offers, a list of special literary topics might seem an excessively codified approach to interpretation. Indeed, unless one takes a pragmatic attitude toward topics, an attitude such as Quintilian offers (V 10.119- 20), for example, then the practice of interpretation would become uselessly rigid. And, although a certain amount of rigidity argues against interpretation as a metaphysical activity, against a quest for epiphanic meaning, and so highlights the hard work of writing that interpretation requires, too much rigidity could reduce interpretation to a plodding application of rules that would produce formulaic and uninteresting interpretations.

Another related objection is that topical interpretation seems to remove natural purpose from interpretive activity. If all topics are equally possible, as they appear when presented schematically as they are in this essay, then "why pound the keyboard?" There are two responses to this objection. First of all, the topics are not purely interchangeable. They are hierarchically arranged by social conventions so that some topics will be convincing under certain social circumstances while others will not. Second, by rejecting the metaphysical concept of a single, stable, and universally available (if partially obscured) meaning, one foregrounds the labor of composition and so makes conscious the effort to manipulate and control, to participate, in other words, in the conversation. While we lose the innocent commitment to discovering the truth behind a given collection of words, we gain an active ability to consciously influence the collection. We interpret, not to tell the truth or to amplify a faint sound, but to gain (or relinquish) control over the world and our place(s) in it.

Works Cited

Aristotle. *Rhetoric* and *Poetics*. Trans. W. Rhys Roberts and Ingram Bywater. New York: Modern Library, 1954.

—. *Posterior Analytics* and *Topica*. Trans. Hugh Tredennick and E.S. Forster. Cambridge: Harvard UP, 1989.

Augustine. *On Christian Doctrine.* Trans. D.W. Robertson, Jr. New York: Macmillan, 1958.

Atkins, G. Douglas, and Michael L. Johnson, eds. *Writing and Reading Differently: Deconstruction and the Teaching of Composition and Literature.* Lawrence: UP of Kansas, 1985.

Booth, Wayne C. "The Common Aims that Divide Us." *Profession 81.* New York: MLA 1981. 13-17.

Britton, Earl W. "The Trouble with Technical Writing is Freshman English." *Journal of Technical Writing and Communication* 4 (1974): 127-31.

Bruns, Gerald L. *Inventions: Writing, Textuality, and Understanding in Literary History.* New Haven: Yale UP, 1982.

Clifford, John, and John Schilb. "Composition Theory and Literary Theory." *Perspectives on Research and Scholarship in Composition.* Ed. Ben W. Mclelland and Timothy R. Donovan. New York: MLA, 1985. 45-67.

Comprone, Joseph J. "Literary Theory and Composition." *Teaching Composition: Twelve Bibliographical Essays.* Ed. Gary Tate. 2 ed. Fort Worth: Texas Christian UP, 1987. 291-330.

Corbett, Edward P.J. "Literature and Composition: Allies or Rivals in the Classroom?" *Composition and Literature: Bridging the Gap.* Ed. Winifred Bryan Horner. Chicago: U of Chicago P, 1983. 168-84.

Eden, Kathy. "Hermeneutics and the Ancient Rhetorical Tradition." *Rhetorica* 5 (1987): 59-86.

Gadamer, Hans-Georg. "The Hermeneutics of Suspicion." *Hermeneutics: Questions and Prospects.* Ed. Gary Shapiro and Alan Sica. Amherst: U of Massachusetts P, 1984. 54-65.

—. "On the Scope and Function of Hermeneutical Reflection." *Philosophical Hermeneutics.* Trans. and Ed. David E. Linge. Berkeley: U of California P, 1977. 18-43.

Hartman, Geoffrey H. "Understanding Criticism." *Writing and Reading Differently: Deconstruction and the Teaching of Composition and Literature.* Ed. G. Douglas Atkins and Michael L. Johnson. Lawrence, UP of Kansas, 1985. 149-68.

Hirsch, E.D. *Validity in Interpretation.* New Haven: Yale UP, 1967.

Horner, Winifred Bryan, ed. *Composition and Literature: Bridging the Gap.* Chicago: U of Chicago P, 1983.

Hoy, David Couzens. *The Critical Circle: Literature, History and Philosophical Hermeneutics.* Berkeley: U of California P, 1978.

Jarratt, Susan C. *Rereading the Sophists: Classical Rhetoric Refigured.* Carbondale: Southern Illinois UP, 1991.

Johannesen, Richard L., Rennard Strickland, and Ralph T. Eubanks, ed. *Language is Sermonic: Richard M. Weaver on the Nature of Rhetoric.* Baton Rouge: Louisiana State UP, 1970.

Kahn, Victoria. *Rhetoric, Prudence, and Skepticism in the Renaissance.* Ithaca: Cornell UP, 1985.

Kaufer, David, and Gary Waller. "To Write Is to Read Is to Write, Right?" *Writing and Reading Differently: Deconstruction and the Teaching of*

Composition and Literature. Ed. G. Douglas Atkins and Michael L. Johnson. Lawrence, UP of Kansas, 1985. 66-92.

Kent, Thomas. "Paralogic Hermeneutics and the Possibilities of Rhetoric." *Rhetoric Review* 8 (1989): 24-42.

Lanham, Richard A. *Literacy and the Survival of Humanism.* New Haven: Yale UP, 1983.

Lindemann, Erika. "Freshman Composition: No Place for Literature." *College English* 55 (1993): 311-16.

Mailloux, Steven. *Rhetorical Power.* Ithaca: Cornell UP, 1989.

Miller, J. Hillis. "Composition and Decomposition: Deconstruction and the Teaching of Writing." *Composition and Literature: Bridging the Gap.* Ed. Winifred Bryan Horner. Chicago: U of Chicago P, 1983. 38-56.

Miller, Susan. "What Does it Mean to be able to Write? The Question of Writing in the Discourses of Literature and Composition." *College English* 45 (1983): 219-35.

Palmer, Richard E. *Hermeneutics: Interpretation Theory in Schleiermacher, Dilthey, Heidegger, and Gadamer.* Evanston: Northwestern UP, 1969.

Plato. *The Collected Dialogues of Plato.* Ed. and Trans. Edith Hamilton and Huntington Cairns. Princeton: Princeton UP, 1961.

Quintilian, Marcus Fabius. *The* Instituio Oratoria *of Quintilian.* Trans. H.E. Butler. 4 Vols. Cambridge: Harvard UP, 1920-22.

Rickman, H.P. "Rhetoric and Hermeneutics." *Philosophy and Rhetoric* 14.2 (1981): 100-11.

Roskelly, Hephzibah. "A Marriage of Convenience: Reading and Writing in School." *Farther Along: Transforming Dichotomies in Rhetoric and Composition.* Ed. Kate Ronald and Hephzibah Roskelly. Portsmouth, NH: Boynton, 1990. 137-48.

Salvatori, Mariolina. "Reading and Writing a Text: Correlations between Reading and Writing Patterns." *College English* 45 (1983): 657-66.

Schleiermacher, Friedrich Daniel Ernst. "Foundations: General Theory and Art of Interpretation." *The Hermeneutics Reader: Texts of the German Tradi-*

tion from the Enlightenment to the Present. Ed. Kurt Mueller-Vollmer. New York: Continuum, 1988. 72-97.

Scholes, Robert E. *Textual Power: Literary Theory and the Teaching of English.* New Haven: Yale UP, 1985.

Sullivan, Patricia A. "Writing in the Graduate Curriculum: Literary Criticism as Composition." *Journal of Advanced Composition* 11 (1991): 283-99.

Part 3

Cultural Studies and Composition

After Progressivism: Modern Composition, Institutional Service, and Cultural Studies

Michael Murphy

Education in America, especially literacy education, has always been marked by a peculiar faith in social progress. From the establishment of the first universities in the New World with the mission to build an American New Jerusalem, to the Whitmanian determination to create a wholly literate and enlightened populace to oversee the functioning of an idealized democracy of intellectual and social equals, to the technocratic dream behind the founding of the "new university" at the turn of the century which looked toward the erection of a self-evidently fair and rational "meritocracy" administered by benign Science, to (especially important for modern composition as a university discipline) the Cold War imperative for "Space Age" national "advancement" in education, Americans have regarded the schools as perhaps the most important agents in fulfilling a whole host of manifest destinies. In *The Composing Process of Twelfth Graders*, Janet Emig bears witness to the implication of English teachers in this sense of mission when she quips of the five-paragraph theme—which she identifies as a kind of pedagogical monolith of the American secondary-school, "so indigenously American that it might be called the Fifty-Star Theme"—that its very discussion should invoke echoes of "Kate Smith singing 'God Bless America' or the piccolo obligato from 'The Stars and Stripes Forever'" (97). Indeed, it is hard to overestimate the power and regularity with which such echoes have informed generations of dutifully committed teachers of that formula and a host of other similar formulas—teachers placed by proverb in the very "trenches" of the "fight" for progress, whose work needed always (and still needs, it seems) to be underwritten by just such a compelling sense of purpose in order to alleviate its well-documented laboriousness.[1] In the light of such purpose, service in the institution—a vocation, we should note, clearly inscribed in and reinforced by composition's powerful institutional gendering as something like housewife/schoolmarm in the male-dominated English department—by simple immediate extension works to represent service in the progress of the social organism as a whole.

And yet as composition struggled to begin to come of age as a self-conscious academic discipline in the late 1960s and early 1970s, it seemed anxious to mark itself a certain distance, even if sometimes somewhat tentatively, from this still largely intact sense of the educational institution as enrolled in some greater mission of social progress, and especially from the sense of its own institutional service as part of that mission. And since then, in fact, as the first waves of exhilaration over modern composition's then newfound, Sputnik-inspired institutional legitimacy finally began to flatten out, it has been fashionable for self-conscious teachers of writing to show a "healthy" cynicism about, sometimes even disdain for, composition's role as an institutional servant, or at least about the ends toward which that service has typically been directed.[2] Even, say, since James Britton and the "growth model" theorists began in the middle and late sixties to challenge the traditional American grammarian's emphasis on propriety—along, at least implicitly, with its corollary ethic of good citizenship (an ethic which served to ally that tradition of grammatical propriety powerfully to the new institutional forces of cognitivism and classical rhetoric through their respective associations with technocratic first-citizen science on the one hand and the very roots of Western civicism on the other)—it seems to me that it has been part of the discipline's set of implicit agreements, only seldom expressed openly, that "compositionists" need to qualify their presumed complicity with the goals of the general university community in order to take themselves seriously as practicing intellectuals.[3] Those goals, that is, were coming to be implicated more and more frequently, and on occasion even quite explicitly, in what Richard Ohmann, for example, began calling "the military-industrial complex" in an indictment of conventional writing instruction as crudely transparent "rhetoric for the meritocracy" (93, 97).

Of course, the exercise of this sort of obligatory qualification has not been taken up monolithically in every disciplinary quarter. One need look no further than Carnegie-Mellon's continued success conducting federally-funded empirical research in cognitive psychology—as well as the number of dissertations and published papers invested each year in Carnegie-Mellon-style scientism—to see that the matrix of power relations behind modern composition's original institutional legitimation which had begun to crystallize even in the early 1960s still exists and still generates a network of negotiable institutional currencies.[4] But it seems to me that a clearly recognizable strain of composition scholarship, growing in the 1970s and 1980s all the time more definitive of the disciplinary mainstream, trades much on the signs of its often only partially articulated opposition to this matrix. Literacy-for-the-war-effort-style social utility has long since been confronted by a competing disciplinary currency, so that by and large institutional legitimacy has been defined increasingly in the last twenty years in very different terms, even when unconsciously or half-consciously. That is, the traditional American progressivist sense of education in the service of highly generalized social goals—through which, as I have suggested, the American academy has traditionally drawn its cultural power—can be seen to have reached a certain frenzied apogee in the defense department's attempted commandeering of the literary academy in the 1960s.[5] But after the waning of general enthusiasm over this recognition and embrace by the educational and social establishment sometime in the late sixties and early seventies, it became increasingly difficult, and remains difficult, to mark one's professional seriousness in composition studies without demonstrating some form of antagonism to one or another of those ostensibly universal social goals, or at the very least without cultivating a certain cynical self-consciousness about enlistment in their service.

In fact, it seems to me that this impulse can be seen to have manifested itself to some degree or another in a remarkable share of the different agendas brought to composition studies over the last twenty-five years (after the formative big three scientisms, that is, of cognitive psychology, classical rhetoric, and post-Chomskyan linguistics)—though this is a manifestation easily overlooked, from within the climate of recent composition scholarship. Such scholarship, that is, has often been anxious in its admirable enthusiasm for a heightened intellectual rigor in composition to dismiss much of this work (which admittedly can now be seen as significantly reactionary) without, nonetheless, having sufficiently acknowledged its contexts and purposes. It should not be difficult to recognize the brashly anti-grammar-and-style "vitalists" of the early 1970s, for instance, as significantly formed by radical anti-service and anti-establishment inclinations, such vitalism's now potentially offensive and much-critiqued romance of the autonomous creative individual notwithstanding. As spirited proponents of an "authentic voice," such vitalists saw literacy as the key much rather to a heightened humanity than to any sort of conventional civic propriety and complained that the mechanized bureaucracy of the university and the stifling conventionality of traditional prescriptive "English" instruction stunted their students' real intellectual development. Ken Macrorie's notorious comma-splice-eliminating, five-paragraph-theme-manufacturing composition monster, "Engfish," a sort of a Nurse Ratchett for the academy, effectively blanched and regularized its healthily spirited and idiosyncratic university students into proper and insipid automatons exactly suitable for the purposes of domination by the boorish and sometimes brutally exploitive powers that be (like the anti-Civil-Rights racists Macrorie continually chides, or the university president who ruthlessly squashes a student protest in the book's prologue). In this way, Macrorie clearly connects service in the traditional academy with the larger goals of a repressive culture, effectively implicating them both, in fact, in a "conspiracy of silence" carried out simultaneously against both pre-Civil-Rights "blacks" and the "slaves in my classes" (54). Expressivist-affiliated scholars like Anne Berthoff and James Miller, whose work had influence not only on the process, revision, and group-work movements but also on the imperative for connecting writing to "critical thinking," either ignored or openly disavowed the set of sciences (cognitivism, empirical research, transformational grammar, structuralist linguistics) that had been used to authenticate composition's practical usefulness in something like "the real world." And this was true even when the expressivists would embrace science as an "abstract" principle, separate as much as possible from the smack of such real-world pragmatism carried by science's association with technology (as Berthoff herself does with her unswerving faith in the composing process as a sort of holistic manifestation of a scientistic natural order[6]). In "The Problem of Problem-Solving," her much-cited attack on Janice Lauer's call for the use of cognitive psychology in composition research, Berthoff openly berates those she calls "the technologists of learning" for pedagogical and scholarly "approaches which are politically not above suspicion," pointing with great censure to the traditional "alliance between the needs of commercial interests and what the American public schools offer" (237, 239). And old-guard literary-trained compositionists like W. Ross Winterowd, whose orientation in rhetoric served as a kind of home base from which to write on composition impulses as diverse as speech-act theory, discourse analysis, and invention heuristics—while still convinced of composition's social utility in a conventional way ("all of my somber . . . moralizing about commitment, authority, and service" [335])—could still be seen to rail (both openly and implicitly by way of a self-consciously elegant, literary prose style) against the simplicity and theoretical naivete of the volumes of practical advice on writing and teaching writing that served to demonstrate that utility: "an endless string of pedagogical tips:

teaching without teachers; teaching with tape recorders; teaching writing with or without writing; teaching writing through immersion in TV game shows; teaching games through an immersion in writing; infinite variations on the touchy-smelly-looky-listeny-writey model" 329). Even if composition could still perform an indispensable service to the university community, such scholars decided, nearsighted allegiance to the performance of that service had resulted in a shameless anti-intellectualism.

So by the middle seventies (though it's easily forgotten lately) vanguard composition scholarship had settled into an orthodoxy of what might be called controlled institutional dissent—or at least a measured rejection of the old earmarks of composition's institutional function—clear enough, though often only indirectly expressed: an at least vague sense of dissatisfaction with the writing teacher's traditional role in the institution became an important badge of pedagogical and scholarly purposefulness. Even a book as soberly scientistic in tone and as invested in the utility of training in all the old institutional proprieties that defined "acceptable" prose as Mina Shaughnessy's *Errors and Expectations* had by 1977 developed a sophisticated squeamishness about the suggestion carried by such proprieties of an uncritical alliance with the implied goals of the institution. Shaughnessy carefully marks her reservations about those goals, conceding almost obligatorily:

> When one considers the damage that has been done to students in the name of correct writing, this effort to redefine error so as to exclude most of the forms that give students trouble in school and to assert the legitimacy of other kinds of English is understandable. Doubtless it is part of a much vaster thrust within this society not only to reduce the penalties for being culturally different but to be enriched by that diversity. (9)

Without question, then, a certain smack of unholiness began to pervade the original founding alliance—powerfully seductive to the new compositionist struggling to take him or herself seriously in the 1960s—between composition as an independent discipline and its surrounding academic and social institutions.

And of course, more recent expressions of composition's frustration with and uneasiness about this alliance, like perhaps most notably Patricia Bizzell's groundbreaking work in such essays as "Cognition, Convention, and Certainty" and "What Happens When Basic Writers Come to College?" or James Berlin's now almost standard "Rhetoric and Ideology in the Writing Class"—fueled by the explosion of structuralism and sign theory into the contemporary radicalisms of knowledge/power relations and ideological critique—are the direct heirs to this general anti-service impulse, though they are clearly far more explicit, emphatic, and incisive about the dangers of composition's traditional role as institutional and social servant, as well as about the insidious process by which composition has been interpellated as such a servant. They worry openly about the indoctrination of students into the socially oppressive terms of traditional academic discourse, about how to enable students to become "resisting, negotiating subjects within positions of power in the dominant culture" (Berlin, "Contemporary" 50) and about "the school's function as an agent of cultural hegemony" (Bizzell, "Cognition" 237). And of course they have even been—quite rightly, if on occasion somewhat nearsightedly—vocal in their insistent dissatisfaction with the limits of the work of their anti-service predecessors, whose pedagogies, they point out, were always ultimately disabled by an insufficient understanding of the ideological constructedness of language and the writing subject. The battle-lines, then, have emerged even more clearly under the influence of "cultural studies": there is nothing indirect about the way this new generation of compositionists has announced its rejection of old-style institutional service, in which (in its crudest form) teaching students clarity and grammatical correctness would, it was supposed, somehow manifest itself unproblematically in the good of the social organism as a whole. Berlin and Bizzell—along now to some degree or other with a whole range of different figures from John Schilb to Henry Giroux to Victor Vitanza to Linda Brodkey to Charles Schuster—have taken up composition's post-Sputnik-era tradition of submerged anti-establishmentarianism and made its active, self-conscious articulation the cornerstone of new cultural-studies-informed pedagogies.

Indeed, it is difficult at this moment in the development of the discipline not to read the history of modern composition as the story, carried out across all composition's major phases in the last twenty years, of a continual evolution ever closer to a refined and effective critical rejection of the institutional and social role concretized for it in the 1960s, a narrative having come to its conclusion in some sense with cultural studies' recent foregrounding of politics in the academy. Composition, it seems, has finally begun to throw off the oppressive yoke of its tangled institutional archaeology (through which, as we have seen, it always rooted and rerooted itself in the grand American myth of progress and service) and has become an autonomous, self-conscious field of inquiry on its own terms, now fully the equal of (and no longer the ostensibly insipid housewife to) that centered in the "English" department, at the same time empowering its students similarly in the classroom. Never has the imperative for composition to renounce its traditional role as a "service" discipline, then—which as we have seen ended in producing (among other things) uncritical pragmatism, science-as-totem, and blind participation in the often oppressive project of the institution—seemed so pressing or so nearly fulfilled.

Progress, "Expressionism," and Disempowerment in the Institution
And yet it is difficult at the same time—in the crudest possible terms, for example, when ostensibly professionalized "compositionists" typically still teach four courses a semester—not to wonder if all these attempts to mark a distance between composition as an intellectual project and the overwhelming smack of institutional and social enlistment implied by composition's formative keeping-up-with-the-Russians impulse haven't themselves all ultimately been coopted by the residue of that impulse in a way that renders them largely harmless.[7] Avant-gardes of all sorts, especially academic ones, have a long history of disappointingly partial successes. Even if the categories set up by composition's latest coming-of-age narrative (institutional service and intellectual independence) seem powerfully convincing, it is still easy to imagine that the sense of disciplinary arrival they imply may seem suspect. At least implicitly, composition, even at its avant-garde fringes, by and large still conceives its project in the same service-oriented terms that it has staked so much of its own sense of intellectual legitimacy on rebelling against.

And of course the persistence of these terms is especially clear in the earlier manifestations of what I have called the anti-service impulse, which have been under fairly constant attack for different, though parallel, reasons recently by that impulse's more contemporary representatives. As I have already suggested, we have been reminded often in the last ten years or so of the politically disabling effect of the "humanist" cult of art and the autonomous creative individual in the academy, as well as of the overwhelming humanist orientation of the bulk of the earliest composition pedagogies implicated in what I have tried to identify as a generalized implicit resistance to composition's traditional designation as a service discipline.[8] What it seems to me hasn't been adequately considered, though, is that this often-noted political disability, normally articulated simply as the artist's general withdrawal from the social, worked not only (as we have so often heard) to de-politicize the humanist-aestheticist English classroom in a larger ideological sense, but also in a much more local sense to effectively disable composition's own attempts in the 1970s to rebel against the politics of institutional service.

Probably the most notable of these now familiar critiques of the humanist-aestheticist tradition within the field of composition itself have been James Berlin's, made public for an especially wide disciplinary audience in *College English*.[9] Berlin perceptively summarizes the reasons for the social and political ineffectuality of what he calls "expressionism" (while acknowledging its intention of political committedness)[10] by explicating the epistemological assumptions on which it is founded:

> The underlying conviction of expressionists is that when individuals are spared the distorting effects of a repressive social order, their privately determined truths will correspond to the privately determined truths of all others; my best and deepest vision supports the same universal and external laws as everyone else's best and deepest vision.
>
> ("Ideology" 486)

Hence, of course, the function of the expressionist composition classroom as a social sedative by which knowledge in general is rendered politically neutral through the elision of cultural difference and ideological constructedness.

But as I have suggested, such an epistemology can also be seen—less obviously, perhaps, but just as powerfully—to accomplish the resurrection of composition's service ethic, even from within expressionism's often explicitly anti-service position (just as its explicit claims to "empower" students through "personal growth" and "self-discovery" can be seen ultimately to disable them with its implication of "universal and external laws"): universally recognizable social goals and duties still exist for "expressionist" teachers as they did in the traditional service model, even though one must now be able to see through "the distorting effects of a repressive social order" in order to recognize them. While "expressionist" writing teachers are no longer enlisted (as in the old Sputnik-era model) in the service of a standing institution which was taken unproblematically to reflect a body of universally recognizable truths, they nonetheless come to be enlisted in a similarly compelling (and coopting) service—this time, the service of a set of nobler and more cryptic truths which are accessible only through the cultivation of "personal" literacy and which have by and large eluded that institution. In this way, Berlin's "expressionists" establish a sense of professional order that corresponds perfectly to the theoretical assumptions behind their pedagogical order, even though it fulfills their "anti-service" impulse only quite problematically. That is, the social goals of the enlightened teacher in this model (usually somewhat contrary to those of the institution) are still, like the work of their students, validated by reference to an unchanging and universal if somewhat mysterious internal reality in something like artistic truth (even if instead of to a simple consensus in common sense, as the scientism of the traditional service model would have it). "Expressionist" composition, then, has no better chance of achieving an effective critical position in the arena of institutional politics than its students do of seeing, as Berlin says, that the expressionist vision "in fact represents the interests of a particular class, not all classes" (487). Ideological constructedness, including the constructedness of the terms of the academic enterprise itself, are cloaked under a deified essentiality, figured ultimately as "art."

Indeed, then, vanguard composition scholarship's strategy of institutional resistance in the 1970s was clearly compromised—as Linda Brodkey has also suggested provocatively in "Modernism and the Scene(s) of Writing" (though again at the level of the individual student in the classroom and not at the level of the discipline in the institution)—by its intuitive adaptation of the high modernist strategy of cultural resistance, played out in its cult of the individual artistic genius. And this intuition is not surprising given that the literary training of most second-generation compositionists asked them to see the appreciation of enactments of this strategy as their primary professional vocation. That the New Criticism was invented as a technology of consumption for the products of high modernist culture is hardly a new idea, and that New Critically-trained "compositionists" brought the baggage of the high aestheticist's withdrawal from a compromised culture into the Self with them as they confronted the problems of professional legitimation in an emerging discipline is understandable.[11] They would resist an institutional alliance they found problematic in the terms they knew best, the same terms in which the modernist artist (as it is so often explained) resisted the industrialized culture that alienated him or her.[12] So it is not without significance to note the connection here to how powerfully and how often teaching came to be figured as high art in composition scholarship in the 1970s: like the noble modernist alone in a garret, the enlightened compositionist would cultivate truth and beauty as a form of resistance in the cloister of the classroom.[13]

And yet the ultimate political effectivity of such a gesture of resistance, as critiques like Berlin's and Brodkey's have made clear at the student level, should not be overestimated. For both the modernist aesthete withdrawing as a mode of resistance into high art and what James Berlin calls the "expressionist" teacher of composition to whom modernism eventually gave indirect intellectual animation, the epistemological commitment to essentialized ideals, at any level of accessibility, implied a faith in progress easily more powerful than their respective senses that their work was implicated in a "politics" that needed critical engaging: even if it were only for the enlightened literate, there was still illumination above ideology and discourse to move toward. The attempted replacement of science by art as twentieth century high culture's animating discourse has done little to achieve the sort of liberatory radicalism it seemed to promise.[14] Beyond the momentary, though not altogether inconsiderable, sobering effect provided by their respective shock values, the rebellion against the politics of progressivist institutional service implied by Ken Macrorie's attempted reinvigoration of the mechanical and anti-intellectual "Engfish" monster seems in the end little more effectively subversive than the more general revolt, say, against the politics of progressivist technological "advancement" taken up explicitly by T.S. Eliot's intensive *l'art-pour-l'art* cultivation of aesthetic form, both of which ultimately get reenlisted in progressivist service on another *merely somewhat less conventional* level. In the end, then, composition's wide reaction in the 1970s against the mindless assumption about social progress embodied by the traditional service ethic, a reaction launched under the banner of high aesthetic anti-institutionalism largely at the residual impetus of the abating New Criticism, could be only a decidedly partial success.[15] Clearly, its implied sense of social progress was entirely as real as the traditional and explicit allegiance to the sort of old-fashioned, for-the-good-of-all progress it defined itself largely against; and its ultimate effect, in fact, was the invocation of what it seems to me hard not to recognize precisely as modern composition's golden age of "progressive" thinking.

Progress, Cultural Studies, and Disempowerment

If the disabling effect of this implicit recuperation of the progress ethic seems striking, the degree to which its residue quite openly marks composition's most significant contemporary expression of resistance to institutional service is perhaps shocking. Indeed, it could well be argued that composition's cultural studies movement is itself largely coopted by the same progressivist discourse that we have seen embodied in the expressionist pedagogy that cultural studies seems most self-consciously poised against: even while it has articulated an effective alternative to the compromising epistemology it critiques so thoroughly, the progressivist trappings of that epistemology often remain disturbingly uninterrogated in the new orthodoxy of radical composition scholarship. In the earliest, most tepid articulations of the new epistemology for composition, these trappings were sometimes painfully obvious: Richard Young, Alan Becker, and Kenneth Pike—peculiarly situated between a cautious theory of anti-foundationalist rhetoric and various affiliations with the positivist establishment—argued for a kind of happily enlightened scientism in tagmemics, a system of cognitive principles designed as a kind of exhaustive science of language use and yet based on the conviction that knowledge is shaped by arbitrary distinctions embedded in different languages.[16] And later, even in an institutional climate generally more agreeable to the aims and methods of critical theory, composition scholars as serious and as intellectually energetic as C.H. Knoblauch and Lil Brannon proposed their own "New" rhetoric largely as a way of giving new urgency to all the now traditional 1970s progressivist pedagogical themes which had by then crystallized into an easily recognizable cluster: process-over-product, grammatical relativism, group work, non-quantitative evaluation, freedom from generic and formal constraints, exhaustive revision, decentered classroom authority, writing across the curriculum, and so on.[17]

But more startling is the sort of casual obliviousness with which recent cultural-studies-oriented critiques of progressivist pedagogy (by all accounts considerably more self-conscious and militant) seem prone to fall into progressivist discourse themselves, threatening in this way to coopt cultural studies as simply the latest in composition's long line of ultimately moderationist liberalisms. We have seen, for example, the committedness of James Berlin's critique of "expressionism." Invoking Louis Althusser and Michel Foucault by way of Swedish Marxist sociologist Goran Therborn, Berlin argues that "Ideology is . . . inscribed in language practices, entering all features of our experience" ("Ideology" 479) in order to press still-expressionist-invested composition scholarship "to place the question of ideology at the center of the teaching of writing" (492). He goes on from this first principle toward such an objective by claiming that "A rhetoric can never be innocent, can never be a disinterested arbiter of the ideological claims of others because it is always already serving certain ideological claims" (477), and then by attacking what he sees as composition's two main rhetorics on this basis: the rhetoric of cognitivism for "claiming for itself the transcendent neutrality of science" and the rhetoric of "expressionism" (as we have seen) for obscuring ideology with a "creative realization of the self, [which] exploit[s] the material, social, and political conditions of the world in order to assert a private vision" (478, 487). Instead, he offers what he calls "social-epistemic" rhetoric, which, "self-consciously aware of its ideological stand" (478), eliminates "arguments from transcendent truth since all arguments arise in ideology" (489). So he is scrupulous in his anti-foundationalism and insists that only such scrupulosity can effectively empower the reading and writing subject.

Nevertheless, it seems to me as if in a kind of unconscious mouthing of composition's apparently immanent progressivist heritage, Berlin goes on to take "democracy" as just such a transcendent truth, as an absolute value (here an "ethical" one) which requires no justification or explanation. And his anti-foundationalism starts sounding strangely compromised in order to accommodate the unblinkingness of this value.[18] Though knowledge-as-ideology is inescapably a matter of "linguistically-circumscribed" possibilities, it nonetheless turns out, it seems, also to have certain features which are somehow inherently democratizing: "ideology is always pluralistic, a given historical moment displaying a variety of competing ideologies and a given individual reflecting one or another permutation of these conflicts" (489, 479). That "all arguments arise in ideology," he continues with newfound tautological verve, "thus inevitably supports . . . democracy. . . . Because there are no 'natural laws' or 'universal truths' that indicate what exists, what is good, what is possible, and how power is to be distributed" (489-90). That particular ideologies are culturally dominant and that subjectivity is ideologically constructed, then (the ostensible basis of "social-epistemic" rhetoric and its accompanying pedagogy), is apparently no longer important: knowledge is no longer a "never innocent" matter of "ideological conflict," but an unproblematic manifestation of something like "free competition" in which all positions of subjectivity have equal dialectical chances (492, 489). Democracy bubbles up from nowhere, erupting in the progressivist rhetoric of pluralism and egalitarianism, which of course sits more than a bit unevenly with Berlin's stated concern over "the interpellations of subjects" which "are always already ideological" (490). He speaks of promoting "self-fulfilling behavior" which would serve to flesh out one's "full humanity," even though "There is no universal, eternal, and authentic self," and "selves" are "social construct[s]," the ideological "creation[s] of a particular historical and cultural moment" (490, 489). He invokes "the greater good of all" (490) with similar fervor—even though knowledge of such ostensibly universal good is attained only by way of highly subjective and suspect "socially-devised definitions" (489)—just as he vigorously holds onto the idealist orthodoxy of "false consciousness" (490) while his "social-epistemic" rhetoric is said to be founded immovably on "the inherently ideological nature of rhetoric" (489) and thus the unavoidable "falseness" of *all* consciousness. And he argues passionately for "the liberatory classroom," as if it were somehow above ideology and indoctrination, even though "a way of teaching is never innocent" (491, 492).

All that is potentially radical about Berlin's deployment of "social-epistemic rhetoric," then, seems to me in this way quickly coopted by its implicit association with composition's progressivist baggage. The progressivist discourse of educational democracy—along with its allied senses of duty ("our responsibilities as teachers and citizens" [493]) and social welfare ("the greater good of all" [490])—is so fundamental a part of the language of composition scholarship that it can effectively underwrite the work of even as guarded an anti-foundationalist as Berlin.[19] Very much, in fact, as in the "expressionist" model Berlin critiques so thoroughly, both student and teacher are pressed into the service of an absolute which works to represent the establishment, in this case the apparently self-evident value of "democracy." The goals of the classroom and the goals of the social organism at large, it seems, are once more essentially the same, just as the progressivist ethos insists they must be.

Not surprisingly, this leads Berlin back to an espousal of a kind of happy Freireanism (the circle-up-the-desks progressivist idyll), in which the classroom serves as the ultimate enactment of the birthright democracy in which the committed pedagogue hopes to empower students to participate. In the same way, then, that Berlin's discourse of essentialized democracy reenlists composition in the service of the institution by ignoring differences between contesting social interests in favor of some "greater good of all," his corresponding vision of classroom practice also serves, I think, largely to make students impotent in the larger economy of cultural politics: when we pretend that the institutionally inherent differences between teachers and students don't exist (even though teachers write syllabi, choose readings, assign grades), students are both deceived about the politics of the classroom and encouraged to ignore such differences between cultural affiliations outside the classroom in favor of a happy faith in the inherent cultural authority and personal integrity of their own free "opinions." Patricia Bizzell gets at the problem perceptively in another context:

> Ultimately, I am calling for the inspection of what some curriculum theorists have called the "hidden curriculum": the project of initiating students into a particular world view that gives rise to the daily classroom tasks without being consciously examined by teacher or students. If we call what we are teaching "universal" structures or processes, we bury the hidden curriculum even deeper by claiming that our choice of material owes nothing to historical circumstances. To do this is to deny the school's function as an agent of cultural hegemony, or the selective valuation and transmission of world views. ("Cognition" 237)

In his establishment of democracy as a transparent value, a matter of political "ethics," then, Berlin ignores the problematics of discourse and ideology he theorizes so finely and insists on so stubbornly. Freireanism not only "hides" but positively *denies* that such implicit curricula exist: a course's focus is to be created by equal participation inside the classroom, just as meanings, one must assume, are to be generated outside it somehow "freely" in culture at large. Indeed, as Bizzell suggests, the institution's "function as an agent of cultural hegemony" must be taken responsibility for—and not be made even more insidious than such cultural functions already are through any pretense of "natural" democracy—if students will be saved paying a crippling cultural price for it. Once more, even for as focused a critic of the establishment as James Berlin, the compositionist is enlisted in the service of a transcendent good embodied in the proper function of the institution, and the composition student is left, once again like the discipline itself, inadvertently but undeniably disabled.

Progress, Disciplinary Archaeology,
Critical Literacy, Politics-as-Ethics

It seems to me fundamentally important for those interested in radicalizing composition as a cultural force, then, to recognize the powerful disciplinary heritage in the context of which the cultural studies movement in composition must make its play for disciplinary authority, a heritage from which that movement characteristically sees itself as having effected a fairly breathtaking secession. In this context, I should make clear that I do not wish by any means to single out James Berlin for critique, to suggest that he has been less than one of the most important and clearly committed voices in the struggle to bring cultural studies meaningfully to composition, or to diminish his obvious contribution to composition's development as a critical intellectual project. But I do hope to make the presence of the latent and largely disabling residue of progressivist libertarianism in Berlin's work suggest the difficulties inherent in any attempted radicalizing of composition. If even Berlin's very deliberate, self-conscious, and carefully theorized assault on the cultural orientation of traditional composition pedagogy can be in some way implicitly shaped by the spirit of that orientation, then it is clear that we need to develop and maintain a special fastidiousness about the discourses that enable our own critical formations as participants in such a dialogue. All that we can speak in our attempts to contribute to the development of the project that composition has become must necessarily be framed by an extraordinarily complicated institutional archaeology, one out to enlist us in projects of its own from the start.

What this paper amounts to, then, is a call to composition's cultural studies contingent to maintain a diligent self-consciousness about the ways in which the shape of the discipline itself implicitly but powerfully asks that contingent to construct its commitment to the social. And such a self-consciousness, I think, should begin with a recognition of the peculiar power that the discourse of progress has been made to wield for composition, a power consolidated by a narrative in which all new disciplinary developments become stages in an evolution toward something like a discipline effectively engaged in the service of the essentialized general good of the social organism. First science, then art (and now social justice) have been made to serve as the essentialized goal—in Saussurian terms, the transcendental signified—that makes that narrative meaningful, the absolute toward which progress is taken to be directed. But if we have come to accept the deployment of some theory of anti-foundationalist rhetoric as the single useful mode of contemporary resistance—and I think such acceptance is definitive of all serious manifestations of the cultural studies/ideological critique impulse in the academy—then models of making composition a site for meaningful cultural engagement simply cannot allow themselves to be underwritten by any such transcendental signified even as "ethics." If all knowledge is, as Berlin says so eloquently, "an arena of ideological conflict" (489), then "progress's" implication of a finally useful goal—even if a mysterious and ultimately unattainable goal, as in aesthetic fulfillment, or an ostensibly enlightened goal, as in social justice—can only serve to perform a dangerous effacement of that conflict. It is vital, then, to recognize the monumental historical significance of the ongoing play for power made by progress as a concept: meaning is always a matter of problematic, contestatory difference; never simple reference, as progress would have it.

So the real urgency of cultural studies' commitment to the social is animated not by the invocation of any timeless code of democracy or even ethics—as so much of the cultural studies contingent in composition, like Berlin, have had it, and as composition's traditional urge to justify itself as an academic discipline by making some sort of contribution to the general project of the social organism would suggest—but simply because the production and distribution of knowledge is *inherently* a matter of social contest, one in which we are always already positioned at the moment we consider opening our mouths to speak. Indeed, the contemporary theoretical fetishization of ethics (only the latest in a long line of powerful essentialist mystifications) is what the example of Berlin suggests most graphically as we begin to think in the early 1990s about the sorts of effects cultural studies can have on academic practice: politics-as-ethics is only the dangerously moderationist pseudo-radicalism to which contemporary cultural studies has been propelled by the academy's progressivist residues, which we need to remember wield special power in composition.[20] We do not need to invoke the moral to speak of power/knowledge relations and of participation in the "ideological arena" of knowledge: as readers and writers we simply have no other choice. If we accept that meaning is always cultural and ideological, then textual action *is* political action, so our insistence on the importance of intervening in the production and distribution of cultural meanings needs no justification by way of moral right; such intervention happens unavoidably whenever we open our mouths to speak. As makers of and traffickers in knowledge, that is, we necessarily find ourselves always already engaged (and *positioned*) in the ideological contest of culture at large, and not propelled into the fray by some innate sense of any timeless principle of "justice" or "fairness." In fact, to recognize the promotion of, say, democracy as this sort of unconditional, *unconstructed* "ethical" imperative is actually to effectively tame all that is potentially radical about cultural studies' anti-foundationalism, no matter what smack of political "involvement" it may carry; simply, it amounts to the restoration of the essentialized referent. As Victor Vitanza has insisted, the great "narratives of emancipation" clung to by "social-consensual theory-hopeful rationalists, who through social reengineering and instrumental reason . . . want to cure society and make the world into a great, good place," ultimately "only further remystif[y] and disempower students and us all" (143, 142). Such categories as the scientific, the aesthetic or the politically ethical cannot be left uninterrogated. Instead, we need to ask tirelessly what cultural forces provide the imperative behind the constitution of those categories, and what the effects of such constitution are, especially when the categories in question serve as the grounds for other knowledge. And the progress ethic in which composition has been steeped for at least thirty years refers us constantly, as we have seen, to such ostensibly self-evident grounds for knowledge, replacing one for another ingeniously as each outlives its rhetorical utility.

This, the deft and constant deferral of serious critical engagement behind reference to apparently self-evident absolutes which defy interrogation, is progress' great insidiousness. It also suggests the challenge presented by the composition studies tradition to the critical integrity of cultural studies's commitment to the social. Progress has a vital interest in seeing cultural studies represent this commitment as a matter of "ethics": even if invoked to provide an imperative for investigating knowledge as an "ideological contest," ethics posits the same sort of final, universal ground for knowledge—the greater good of all—that is at the center of progress' cultural powerplay *precisely by serving to obscure that contest.* If as I argued earlier, then, the political disability of much of traditional composition pedagogy has to do with its implication in "modernist" strategies of resistance, then this essay can also be understood as a call for composition to become a cannily "*post*modern" discipline—that is, to carefully interrogate and disclaim the effects of the essentialist epistemology on which modernism—and modern composition, in turn—was largely founded.

It is only in this way, I argue, that composition can accomplish either of the imperatives which were beginning to be set for it at least implicitly as early as 1965 by what might meaningfully be called its first avant-garde: the liberation of the discipline itself from uncritical service in the academic institution and the liberation of the student from uncritical service in the arena of culture at large. As I have suggested, it seems to me vital to recognize that both depend on the assumption of the same critical posture and that neither can be achieved successfully without the other: composition studies cannot become politically effective, either as a discipline within the academic institution or as a pedagogical technology for its students within their larger cultural spheres, without stubbornly resisting the urge to defer critical interrogation by positing an essentialized reality of some sort or other, an urge made frighteningly manifest in the great American (and modernist) fantasy of "progress." The mindless institutional service effected by such deferral on one front—in the hierarchy of disciplines within the academy—is destined to replay the larger mindless cultural service effected by that same deferral on the other—in the classroom. And the recent movement to bring cultural studies to composition has only partially succeeded in establishing the resistance to such service that it seemed to promise. We can only stop being a "service" discipline when we begin taking intelligent, self-conscious account of the ideological conditions that have enabled us. Indeed, effectively renouncing blind institutional and cultural service means sensitively and assiduously sorting out, delineating, and critiquing composition's complicated intellectual heritage—carefully accounting for the ideological forces that have enabled its erection as a discipline—exactly what essentialist allegiance to the idea of "progress" makes impossible. Critical intellectual work, literacy even—both inside and outside the classroom—can mean nothing else.

Notes

1. It is difficult, for example, for any teacher of college composition, struggling to think through the implications and presuppositions of his or her practice critically—while teaching, say, four sections of first-year composition—not to take as emblematic Berlin's report of "four teachers and two graduate assistants" at Michigan in 1894 who "were responsible for 1,198 students" in a day when convention dictated the writing of daily or near daily themes ("Reality" 22), or in turn not to rally around Stephen North's observation of the tendency in English departments to write composition off as "academic dirty work" (13).

2. See Chapter 1 of North for a thorough discussion of Cold War nationalism's crucial role in shaping modern composition as an academic discipline. Albert Kitzhaber's 1966 call for "a 'New English' to take its place alongside the 'New Mathematics' and the 'New Science' now being taught in many United States schools," though, pointed out recently by Harris, serves to suggest the contours of that role pretty plainly (635). See also note 5 of this paper.

3. There are notable exceptions—like W. Ross Winterowd and Louise Phelps, who self-consciously combine a high theoretical seriousness (largely unallied to the disciplinary forces of science and classicism which would capitalize most clearly on the Cold War sense of educational crisis) with a willingness to understand—sometimes even with a profound commitment to—the cultivation of literacy as a public service performed in a spirit of republican, even classically modeled civic responsibility. But such scholars seem to me decisively outnumbered by those who would lay claim to such seriousness by way of an at least partial (or even implicit and unarticulated) repudiation of the role of institutional servant. In fact, theorists like Winterowd and Phelps, despite their allegiance to some form of the service ideal, are typically most troubled by

those composition scholars who embrace institutional service least problematically.

It is worth noting, too, that Phelps has pointed out a potentially serious problem with my enterprise in this paper on a related score: she reminds me that academic work (and work in general) is necessarily *always already* implicated in a context and is thus unavoidably enlisted in the "service" of certain interests. I do not at all mean by calling attention to the ways in which it seems to me that composition has been intellectually and institutionally disabled by "service" in such projects that "service" in the abstract can be escaped. Much to the contrary, my project is fundamentally based on this very problematic, and I do not intend to give the impression that I endorse disciplinary "liberation" in any naively Romantic way. Instead, I argue only that critical engagement, literate intellectual work, means being as self-conscious and savvy about this process of enlistment as possible—only that service, that is, should at all costs never be blind, and that such blindness makes for the crudest kind of ideological indoctrination.

4. See Lauer and Asher for a sense of the still formidable marketability of different forms of empirical research in contemporary composition studies.

5. If this language seems extreme, witness for example the almost rabid rhetoric of civic duty that marks documents like the NCTE's 1961 *The National Interest and the Teaching of English* ("Only a quality education will prepare our youth for the test" [136]) and the Commission on English's 1965 *Freedom and Discipline in English* ("The commission was fully aware of the importance of [its] objective for the students who will be the future citizens of a great democracy" [viii])—documents which were clearly direct responses to establishment culture's new eagerness to embrace English studies as something like a "national priority," a matter even of national security (an eagerness manifested materially in the advent of "Project English"). Or see the barely submerged us-and-them nationalist sensibility so important to a book like Corbett's omnipresent 1965 *Classical Rhetoric for the Modern Student*, which is rife with Cold War language and categories and which from the perspective of 1990 often seems even crudely and frighteningly propagandistic, especially in the simple casualness with which its ostensibly arbitrary and innocent examples of logical forms and moves invoke the terms of Cold War conflict as generic content. In this way, the book works powerfully to legitimize the apparent importance of those terms even when applying them to examples of specious argument. It includes, for example, exercises in the logical evaluation of such syllogisms as "No Russians are democratic. All Americans are democratic. [Therefore] All Americans are Russians" and "Since only radicals want to subvert the duly constituted government of a country, this man can't be a radical because he wants to preserve the government of the country" (60, 61).

6. See, for instance, Berthoff's suggestion that "Interpretation is a branch of biology" (*Making* v).

7. Slevin outlines the managerial practices by which compositionists are

effectively de-professionalized, denied, for example, the time and job security needed to participate in professional development as a scholar given as a matter of course to faculty in other disciplines.

8. Most notably, see one of the introductions to teaching critical theory published in the last ten years, such as Catherine Belsey's *Critical Practice*. More incisively, see recent articulations of the problematics of radical Marxism in the Humanities in the work of such figures as Stanley Aronowitz, Henry Giroux, and Peter McLaren, or on a somewhat different radical left, Mas'ud Zavarzadeh and Donald Morton (see especially "Theory Pedagogy Politics: The Crisis of the 'Subject' in the Humanities" and the recent collection of the same name).

9. Here I will quote from "Rhetoric and Ideology in the Writing Class"; see also "Contemporary Composition: The Major Pedagogical Theories." For a significantly more thorough treatment of the same ideas, see Berlin's *Rhetoric and Reality*.

10. Berlin concedes, "Most proponents of expressionistic rhetoric during the sixties and seventies were unsparingly critical of the dominant social, political, and cultural practices of the time," and he even offers Peter Elbow as an example of this sort of outspoken though ultimately impotent political consciousness (485). Also, it's worth noting the other less strictly theoretical grounds on which Berlin makes his critique of "expressionism": the disabling effect of its suggestion that "effective resistance can only be offered by individuals, each acting alone," its reification of "entrepreneurial virtues" like "private initiative" and "risk taking," and the way it promotes "a variety of forms of consumer behavior" by making leisure (and never work) the only possible site of "self-discovery and fulfillment" (487). Though these are astute and useful readings of expressionism's various social utilities, I have confined myself to Berlin's sense of the theoretical limits of expressionist epistemology (even though it is perhaps less thoroughly articulated than the rest) since these theoretical limits will figure most prominently in what I will argue about composition and the progress ethic.

11. See, for instance, Eagleton's *The Function of Criticism*, where he speaks of "the liberal humanist consensus which was, in effect, criticism's sole rationale" in the age of "New Criticism's cloistered aestheticism" (86, 85).

12. Of course, it is something of an over-simplification (and a popular one) to reduce as undeniably varied and complicated a cultural impulse as "modernism" to a single aesthetic-epistemological tenet in this way, just as it smacks of over-simplification to explain New Criticism in turn wholly as a manifestation of such an impulse. And even though one might name a good number of writers, artists, intellectuals, and so on commonly identified as "modernist" who neither advocated nor enacted any withdrawal from the social into high art—what Andreas Huyssen has called an aestheticist "anxiety of contamination" (vii)—it is not without value to see the phenomenon of "modernism" *more generally* as born significantly out of the need for just this kind of withdrawal. I do not

intend to suggest that there were either no modernist aesthetes (consider Pound) or no New Critics (remember New Criticism's self-consciously political roots in Agrarianism) who had political preoccupations or who were willing to see their aesthetic positions as politically conditioned and implicated. I argue only that the general modernist impulse for aesthetic cultivation can be seen ultimately to represent a strategic shrinking from what modernism conceived as "administered" culture through the cultivation of a profound and compelling (though ultimately disabling) individuality.

13. For a sense of this conjunction (of writing and teaching writing behind art in humanist-aestheticist circles) see the work of William Coles.

14. It is useful to consider, for example, how vigorously a voice as steeped in modernist discourse as, say, I.A. Richards in *Science and Poetry* (1926) can be seen to have insisted on conceiving its modernity as a manifestation of the early twentieth-century assertion of idealist art against empiricist science. For a sense of the failures of modernism as this sort of project, Jameson's observations on Wyndham Lewis are typical of similar critiques articulated from various lefts:

> The most influential formal impulses of canonical modernism have been *strategies of inwardness*, which set out to reappropriate an alienated universe by transforming it into personal styles and private languages [and which] have seemed in retrospect to reconfirm the very privatization and fragmentation of social life against which they meant to protest (2; emphasis added).

Also see Huyssen, Krauss, Eagleton (*Against*), Lyotard, and Foster.

15. It would be a grave over-simplification, of course, to understand all the 1970s composition scholarship that I have called "progressivist" as animated wholly by New Critical aestheticism. I claim only that progressivism's strategy of institutional resistance devolved mainly from a sense of the culturally liberating effects of art, played out most importantly in the academy for composition scholars like Britton, Macrorie, and Coles by the grand institutional specter of the New Criticism. This does not mean that the theoretical implications of this strategy of resistance were played out with any kind of consistency in the other aspects of progressivist practice. Very general disciplinary impulses like the ones I have named aestheticism and scientism are seldom manifested in categorically distinct ways. Science, for instance, once allied very powerfully to classicism and what I see as the first generation of modern composition "progressivism" in the post-Sputnik era via the Aristotelian sense of rhetoric as a descriptively exhaustive and perfectly logical taxonomy (as in, say, Lauer's determination to use empirical research in order to arrive at a finally prescriptive and exactly *correct* cognitive model of composing), quickly becomes a convenient ally for the second-generation "progressivist" fixation on process, despite the same group's celebration of art (see, for example, Britton's commitment to painstaking empirical research in order to demonstrate the pedagogical urgency of teaching "expressive" writing). Composition's discourse of development is

invested with a similarly curious and complicated disciplinary currency as is writing across the curriculum. This, in fact, is why I will come to insist later in this essay on the vital importance of acute theoretical self-consciousness for meaningful composition scholarship.

16. See especially Chapters 1 and 2, where the authors argue that reality is "a creation that reflects the peculiarities of the perceiver" and that a language is "a theory of the universe, a way of selecting and grouping experiences" (25, 27).

17. For a fairly detailed explication of the intellectual archaeology behind the alliance of these themes, see Bizzell's reading of what she calls "personal-style pedagogy" ("Composing").

18. I will focus here on Berlin's attempts to provide a theoretical justification for his sense of democracy as a natural right, but I should note that he seems aware of the essentialist implications of such a sense in as much as he is tempted at times to avoid it by simply begging the question and claiming his embrace of democratic idealism as something like a frank admission of his own ideological orientation. The real issue for a social-epistemic rhetorician, of course, would be to account for the cultural reasons behind such an orientation. Anything less amounts to what I find my students doing all too often: deferring serious discussion by claiming what they call "a right to my own opinion."

19. It's worth noting that the pattern suggested by "Rhetoric and Ideology in the Writing Class" is representative of almost all Berlin's other work as well, though admittedly a bit less plainly so in more recent essays. It is characteristic, that is, for Berlin to invoke anti-foundationalist rhetoric in order to argue in strikingly dutiful, sometimes even baldly patriotic terms for "democracy, [which] ordinarily provides political and social supports for open discussion, allowing for the free play of possibilities in the rhetorics that appear" (*Reality* 5) and for a politically interested pedagogy as "an effort to prepare students for critical citizenship in a democracy"—or even to appeal without irony to the ostensible authority of "leaders in government, business, and industry" ("Composition 51, 53) as reliable evaluators of this capacity for "critical citizenship" in students. That his more recent work represents what seems a self-conscious (if only partially successful) attempt to suppress this rhetoric of democratic fervor is similarly suggestive: the movement from pronouncements of "the greater good of all" promised by democracy ("Ideology" 490) to the somewhat less energized and more theoretically careful "rigor and promise of a dialogic rhetoric in a democracy" ("Composition" 54) does a good deal to indicate the palpability of this contradiction between cultural studies' radical anti-foundationalist imperative and composition's residual progressivist discourse.

20. I hope in disavowing "ethics" in this way that I do not seem to prudishly assume what Bizzell has recently so eloquently denounced as the "posture of frozen horror at the operations of the ethical binary" typical of "American intellectuals" ("Marxist" 68). I certainly do not mean this paper to be a call to inaction, and I am in fact not ultimately unwilling to reunderstand "ethics" in an aggressively post-foundational, "dialectical" manner like the one Bizzell hints

at. But then ultimately, I would argue, why bother? I have to wonder, that is, not only about the philosophical problems but even about the simple practical *utility* of salvaging "ethics" as a key animating principle for "political" intervention (even if it serves to make certain social issues raised by ideological critique more, say, popularly compellingly and thus broadly accepted, what can ethics do in the end to make critique and the deployment of such sentiment finally more *incisive and useful*?). And I worry significantly, on the other hand, about what seem to me the likeliest effects such a salvaging might have on the possibilities for cultivating what I think of as *a more truly enabling critical self-consciousness*, at both individual and institutional levels.

Works Cited

Belsey, Catherine. *Critical Practice.* London: Metheun, 1980.

Berlin, James A. "Composition and Cultural Studies." *Composition and Resistance.* Ed. Mark Hurlbert and Michael Blitz. Portsmouth, NH: Boynton, 1991. 47-57.

—. "Contemporary Composition: The Major Pedagogical Theories." *College English* 44 (1982): 765-77.

—. "Rhetoric and Ideology in the Writing Class." *College English* 50 (1988): 477-94.

—. *Rhetoric and Reality: Writing Instruction in American Colleges, 1900-1985.* Carbondale: Southern Illinois UP, 1987.

Berthoff, Anne E. *The Making of Meaning: Metaphors, Models, and Maxims for Writing Teachers.* Upper Montclair, NJ: Boynton, 1983.

—. "The Problem of Problem-Solving." *College Composition and Communication* 22 (1971): 237-42

Bizzell, Patricia. "Cognition, Convention, Certainty: What We Need to Know about Writing." *Pre/Text* 3 (1982): 213-43.

—. "Composing Processes: An Overview." *The Teaching of Writing.* Ed. Anthony R. Petrosky and David Bartholomae. Chicago: U of Chicago P, 1986. 49-70.

—. "Marxist Ideas in Composition Studies." *Contending with Words: Composition and Rhetoric in a Postmodern Age.* Ed. Patricia Harkin and John Schilb. New York: MLA, 1991. 52-68.

—. "What Happens When Basic Writers Come to College?" *College Composition and Communication* 37 (1986): 294-301.

Britton, James, et al. *The Development of Writing Abilities (11-18)*. London: MacMillan, 1975.

Corbett, Edward P.J. *Classical Rhetoric for the Modern Student*. New York: Oxford UP, 1965.

Eagleton, Terry. *Against the Grain*. London: Verso, 1986.

—. *The Function of Criticism: From the Spectator to Post-Structuralism*. London: Verso, 1984.

Emig, Janet. *The Composing Process of Twelfth Graders*. NCTE Research Report No. 13, 1971.

Foster, Hal. *Recodings: Art, Spectacle, Cultural Politics*. Seattle: Bay, 1985.

Freedom and Discipline in English: Report on the Commission on English. New York: CEEB, 1965.

Harris, Joseph. "After Dartmouth: Growth and Conflict in English." *College English* 53 (1991): 631-46.

Huyssen, Andreas. *After the Great Divide: Modernism, Mass Culture, Postmodernism*. Bloomington: Indiana UP, 1986.

Jameson, Fredric. *Fables of Aggression: Wyndham Lewis, the Modernist as Fascist*. Berkeley: U of California P, 1979.

Knoblauch, C.H., and Lil Brannon. *Rhetorical Traditions and the Teaching of Writing*. Upper Montclair: Boynton, 1984.

Krauss, Rosalind E. *The Originality of the Avant-Garde and Other Modernist Myths*. Cambridge: MIT P, 1985.

Lauer, Janice M., and J. William Asher. *Composition Research: Empirical Designs*. New York: Oxford UP, 1988.

Lyotard, Jean-François. *The Post-Modern Condition: A Report on Knowledge*. Trans. Geoff Bennington and Brian Massumi. Minneapolis: U of Minnesota P, 1981.

Macrorie, Ken. *Uptaught (A Professor Discovers His Students on the Way to a New University)*. Rochelle, NJ: Hayden, 1970.

The National Interest and the Teaching of English: A Report on the Status of the Profession. Urbana: NCTE, 1961.

Ohmann, Richard. *English in America: A Radical View of the Profession.* New York: Oxford UP, 1976.

Richards, I.A. *Science and Poetry*. London: Kegan, 1926.

Shaughnessy, Mina P. *Errors and Expectations: A Guide for the Teacher of Basic Writing*. New York: Oxford UP, 1977.

Slevin, James F. "The Politics of the Profession." *An Introduction to Composition Studies*. Ed. Erika Lindemann and Gary Tate. New York: Oxford UP, 1991. 135-59.

Vitanza, Victor J. "Three Countertheses: Or, A Critical In(ter)vention into Composition Theories and Pedagogies." *Contending with Words: Composition and Rhetoric in a Postmodern Age*. Ed. Patricia Harkin and John Schilb. New York: MLA, 1991. 139-72.

Winterowd, W. Ross. "Getting It Together in the English Department." *ADE Bulletin* 55 (November 1977): 28-32.

Young, Richard E., Alan L. Becker, and Kenneth L. Pike. *Rhetoric: Discovery and Change*. New York: Harcourt, 1970.

Zavarzadeh, Mas'ud, and Donald Morton. "Theory Pedagogy Politics: The Crisis of 'The Subject' in the Humanities." *boundary 2* 1986: 1-22.

Social-Process Rhetorical Inquiry: Cultural Studies Methodologies for Critical Writing about Advertisements

Bruce McComiskey

> Critique involves stealing away the more useful elements and rejecting the rest. From this point of view cultural studies is a process, a kind of alchemy for producing useful knowledge . . .
>
> Richard Johnson

There is mounting evidence that composition studies has recently experienced a "social turn," and, according to John Trimbur, this social turn is the result of an increasing disaffection among certain composition teachers with the radical individualism promoted by the early writing-as-process paradigm.[1] In the mid 1980s, fueled by emerging debates about academic discourse, professional writing, and writing across the curriculum, scholars such as Patricia Bizzell, Lee Odell, and James Reither, among many others, began to question the individualism implied in previous articulations of the writing process, arguing instead that different institutional contexts for writing (academic, professional, disciplinary) require different writing processes. And I believe that the best way to convey this contextual character of writing processes is to teach students the social nature and function of writing, both of the texts they produce in class as well as those they encounter everyday outside of class.

In my experience, those who practice social approaches to composition studies expand the notion of the writing process from its current linear (and recursive) model to a cyclical model. In the linear model, the writing process begins with invention, progresses to revision, and ends with a final product. Of course, these stages in the process are recursive: we may decide during revision that we need to invent more details to support a weak argument, etc. But it is difficult, using this linear model of the writing process, to account for where topics and invented details come from and where essays go when they are finished—and to what effect. As David Bartholomae points out, "If writing is a process, it is also a product; and it is the product and not the plan for writing, that locates a writer on the page, that locates him in a text and a style and the codes and conventions that make both of them readable" (144). The recent interest among composition scholars in professional writing, writing across the curriculum, and academic discourse represents a renewed concern for written products (though no less concern for writing processes), especially insofar as they facilitate and constrain the production of texts, provide socio-discursive contexts for texts, and demand of writers a certain critical literacy as a precondition to entering ongoing conversations in any discourse community.

Thus, as an alternative to the linear (and recursive) process model currently in vogue, a model that I believe gives students the wrong idea about what happens when writers write, I propose a cyclical model of the writing process, one that accounts for the composing strategies of individual and collaborative writers as well as the socio-discursive lives of texts. And I represent this model in the form of a "*social-process*" heuristic for rhetorical inquiry based on the cycle of cultural production, contextual distribution, and critical consumption, a colligation of cultural studies methodologies for critiquing social institutions and cultural representations. Invention heuristics based on this cycle encourage students to understand language and culture as socially constructive forces (production) conditioned by contexts (distribution) and negotiated by critical subjectivities (consumption), and later in this essay I will illustrate one such heuristic designed for use in an advertising analysis unit, perhaps the most common context for critical writing in cultural studies composition classes.

Through using the terms "cultural production," "contextual distribution," and "critical consumption," I intend both to invoke and transform the traditional Marxist concepts from which they derive. In his "Introduction to a Critique of Political Economy," Karl Marx describes the cycle of production, distribution, exchange, and consumption: "In the process of production members of society appropriate (produce, fashion) natural products in accordance with human requirements; distribution determines the share the individual receives of these products; exchange supplies him with the particular products into which he wants to convert the portion accorded to him as a result of distribution; finally, in consumption the products become objects of use, i.e., they are appropriated by individuals" (193-94). And Marx completes the link in the cycle by arguing for a reciprocal understanding of production and consumption: "Production leads to consumption, for which it provides the material; consumption without production would have no object. But consumption also leads to production by providing for its products the subject for whom they are products" (196). Marx's own uses of the terms that I appropriate in this essay ("production," "distribution," and "consumption") are, of course, decidedly modernist: production results in material goods; distribution (and exchange) refers to the portioning out of the produced goods and the money that *re*-presents them (in the modernist sense); and in consumption, subjects make use of the produced goods, possibly to produce other material goods, in turn creating a need for further production of the original products.

Postmodern cultural theory problematizes Marx's materialist description of the cycle of production, distribution (and exchange), and consumption, opening up this useful heuristic to new interpretations and applications. In the postmodern age of mass production, material goods are, for the most part, no longer produced to satisfy the needs of consumers. Instead, goods exist as potentialities, and the real work of production is the creation of desire in consumers for the potentially producible goods; the physical production of goods becomes less important than the rhetorical construction of desire for them. Cultural production, then, is the creation of social values which manifest themselves in institutional practices and cultural artifacts. Within this postmodern framework, the distribution (and exchange) of material goods becomes secondary to the contextual distribution of the cultural values that construct desire in consumers. Distribution, then, comprises the contexts of cultural values as they are manifest in particular institutional practices and cultural artifacts: some corporations, for example, serve as distributing contexts for particular personnel policies that perpetuate racist cultural values; and some magazines serve as distributing contexts for particular advertisements that perpetuate sexist cultural values. Critical consumption refers to the social uses to which "readers" put their interpretations of produced and distributed cultural values. Finally, the link that completes the cycle relies on the culturally productive power of critical consumption and the precondition of critical consumption for effective cultural production.

A few scholars in composition have adapted specific cultural studies methodologies for use as social-process guides to rhetorical inquiry, yet these few methodologies are limited in their theoretical and practical scope, engaging students in short-sighted concentration on just a single "moment" in the cycle of cultural production, contextual distribution, and critical consumption. In "Composition and Cultural Studies," for example, James Berlin describes an invention heuristic for rhetorical inquiry based on cultural studies methodologies drawn primarily from Roland Barthes' work on advertising and John Fiske's work on television. In Berlin's composition classes, students generate critical essays about the production of cultural meaning in advertising using the following cultural studies heuristic for rhetorical inquiry:

> The major devices used to undertake this analysis [of advertisements] were three simple but powerful semiotic strategies that function as heuristics. The first of these is the location of binary oppositions in the texts—that is, the nature of the boundaries that give terms meaning. The second is the discovery of denotation and connotation as levels of meaning that involve contesting. The third is the reliance on invoking culturally specific narrative patterns—for example, the Horatio Alger myth or the Cinderella plot. These served as exploratory devices that enabled students to investigate semiotic codes as persuasive appeals, paying particular attention, once again, to the reliance of these codes on culturally specific categories of race, gender, and class. (51)

While Berlin's heuristic does draw on a number of established cultural studies methodologies, it does not encourage students to move beyond critiquing the production of cultural meaning in advertisements. Berlin's invention heuristic, particularly as it relates to advertising analysis, helps students gain a solid understanding of how texts produce certain social meanings. However, students using this heuristic are not encouraged to explore how the semiotic contexts of advertisements (the magazines, the television shows, etc.) condition the connotative meanings of key terms or how these contexts influence readers to invoke certain binary oppositions and social narratives over others; and students using this heuristic are not encouraged to formulate particular critical stances toward (or subject positions in relation to) the key terms, oppositions, and narratives they find represented in social institutions and cultural artifacts. Berlin's heuristic, in other words, leads only to "production criticism"—the examination of how cultural meaning is produced without concern for the semiotic force of its distributing context or the political force of critical consumption.

James Porter has also developed a heuristic that emphasizes a particular aspect of writing processes in cultural context. In *Audience and Rhetoric*, Porter describes his "forum analysis" heuristic as a method for exploring distributing contexts. Forum analysis offers a *text*-based alternative to the more common heuristics based on sociological ("real-reader") views of audience and community. Drawing primarily on

Foucault's theory of discursive formations, Porter describes a "forum" as a "textual system," a "concrete locale, a physical place for a discourse activity"; and forum analysis "assumes that audience is defined by the texts (oral and written) it produces and that the writer needs to systematically explore this textual field in order to produce acceptable discourse within it" (106, 95, 112). Porter's forum analysis heuristic has two main sections: under "background," students answer questions about the organizational affiliation, purpose, membership, origin, and reputation of the forum in question; and under "discourse conventions," students answer questions regarding who is allowed to speak or write in the forum, to whom they speak or write, what issues or topics are addressed in the forum, and in what form and style these issues are addressed (114-45). Forum analysis encourages writers to examine in detail the texts that constitute a particular discursive formation, and the knowledge gained through this brand of textual criticism is vital for rhetorical effectiveness. However, in isolation, forum analysis is incomplete; knowledge of the background and discourse conventions of a discursive formation does not necessarily enable a critical understanding of how cultural meaning is produced in particular texts, nor does it encourage participants in discursive formations to adopt critical subject positions in relation to particular discourses. Forum analysis teaches writers the importance of understanding the rhetorical flow of a discursive formation, but its short-sighted emphasis on distributing contexts leaves writers with an incomplete understanding of specific rhetorical practices used both in the production and consumption of texts.

Students who engage in detailed heuristic exploration of all three moments in the cycle of cultural production, contextual distribution, and critical consumption develop the sense that culture itself is a constantly changing process and that their own writing can influence some of the changes that cultures undergo, and social-process rhetorical inquiry brings these processes of rhetorical intervention consciously to bear on students' own critical writing. It is my goal in this essay to develop a more complete social-process approach to composition by proposing a conception of rhetorical inquiry based on the complete cycle of cultural production, contextual distribution, and critical consumption.

The Cycle of Cultural Production, Contextual Distribution, and Critical Consumption

The cycle of cultural production, contextual distribution, and critical consumption has given rise to powerful writing in cultural studies, and I believe it holds similar potential to elicit powerful writing in response to cultural studies composition assignments. In "What Is Cultural Studies Anyway?" Richard Johnson, former director of the Birmingham Center for Contemporary Cultural Studies (BCCCS), describes the cycle of production, distribution, and consumption as a "heuristic" for understanding a wide variety of social phenomena, and this heuristic focuses attention on the complex interactions among encoders, texts, and decoders (all broadly defined) in the act of generating cultural meaning. The value of this cycle to composition studies is that, when viewed as a heuristic for rhetorical inquiry, it encourages students to understand both writing and culture as dialectical social processes through which they can derive a degree of agency. Cultural production, contextual distribution, and critical consumption represent three crucial "moments" in the process of developing social relations in lived cultures, and although I discuss each moment separately in the pages to come, a certain critical veracity is sacrificed if we lose sight of the cycle as a complete process. Each "moment," in other words, relies on the others for critical power and is indispensable to the cycle as a whole.

The first moment in the cycle isolates *cultural production* as the object of critical study. Studies of cultural production assume that social practices are conditioned by cultural values encoded into and decoded from texts. It is crucial, then, that students understand the ways in which encoders inscribe texts with "preferred readings," because as John Fiske points out, "the preferred reading *closes* off potential revolutionary meanings" and conditions readers to adopt subject positions that fulfill the economic, political, and social desires of encoders (111). In the context of advertising, cultural production is the creation of desire to consume, and this desire is achieved when advertisers promote certain preferred cultural values over others and associate their products with those values. Cultural values are produced through combinations of signs that function as associations, socialized links (often unconscious) between words and visual images and their subjective meanings, and they usually imply "ideal" consumer-audiences and social practices. Visual images in advertising signify associations between products and subjective desires. For example, most people associate stately mansions and expensive jewelry with upper class lifestyles; and when Liz Claiborne portrays mansions and jewelry in her perfume advertisements, the audience associates these products with their desire for wealth, and their consumption of Liz Claiborne perfume superficially and temporarily satisfies that desire. These associations between Liz Claiborne perfume and an upper class lifestyle imply a number of possible cultural values, one of which is: "Ideal wealthy women own mansions, diamonds, and Liz Claiborne perfume." Words in advertising also signify associations between products and subjective desires. For example, when the CEOs of the Coca-Cola corporation realized that New Coke was a failure, they changed back to its original recipe and advertised the new/old product as Coca-Cola "*Classic*." The word "classic," of course, invokes images of the best things in life that have stood the test of time, and the Coca-Cola corporation wants its customers to associate this new/old "classic" product (actually the result of a disastrous marketing decision) with their nostalgic desire for the good old days when quality—not profit—was the top priority. The associations between Coca-Cola Classic and a desire for the uncomplicated past imply a number of possible cultural values, one of which is: "Ideal nostalgic cola consumers commemorate the past by drinking Coca-Cola Classic (instead of Pepsi, the choice of a new generation)." Images also function to limit the polysemy of meanings words might invoke in readers (the word "dry" signifies different values when accompanied by images of deodorant or moisturizing cream), and words function to limit the polysemy of meanings an image might invoke (the silhouette of a naked female figure signifies different values when accompanied by the words "sensual" or "natural"). These different kinds of associations in advertisements construct cultural values that encourage preferred readings, particular meanings that encoding advertisers want decoding consumers to attribute to the advertised products.

Most advertising cultural values construct readers as ideal identities and encourage certain ideal social practices over others, and they relate these ideal practices to particular products. Cultural values have the surface appearance of descriptive statements; however, they operate culturally as prescriptive behavioral directives that position readers within certain advantageous subjectivities: "if *you* want to be an ideal progressive young adult, then you *should* drink Zima malt beverage," or "if *you* want to be an ideal rugged man, then you *should* smoke Marlboro cigarettes." The element missing from cultural values is the reason for which particular ideal practices are favored over others; the motives that generate cultural values are often selfish and work against the best interests of many people whose lives they influence. For example, cultural values in advertisements for expensive products are often directed toward middle and low income families who cannot reasonably afford the advertised merchandise—e.g., Nike ads selling the dream of escaping ghettos through sports, and state lottery ads selling the dream of financial security through "sure thing" odds. Although cultural values are inevitable and essential aspects of any social arrangement, the ones that result in marginalizing and oppressive cultural practices can be recognized through critical reading and revised through careful rhetorical interventions into the institutions and artifacts that construct and maintain these values, and this is one goal students strive to achieve in advertising analysis essays. Yet it is naive to assume that texts such as advertisements—in and of themselves—contain pure meaning and that readers consume this meaning through direct and uncritical identification with the texts. We can't, therefore, revise cultural values until we understand their modes of contextual distribution and critical consumption.

The second moment in the cycle isolates *contextual* distribution as the object of critical study. It is important to examine the distributing contexts of cultural values because, as Johnson points out, "context is crucial to the production of meaning" (62). When we critique a distributing medium, we examine "the subjective or cultural forms which it realizes and makes available" (62). In advertising, then, contextual distribution is the location (the specific magazine, television show, radio program, etc.) in which the cultural values of particular ads are presented to potential consumer audiences, and this location further limits the polysemy of meanings advertisements might invoke. Media contexts construct their own cultural values through associations, socialized links between recurring key words, hot topics, and visual images and their subjective meanings, and they usually imply "ideal" audiences and social practices. Every element of every magazine contributes to the construction of associations—the cover design, table of contents, editorials, letters to the editor, regular columns, feature articles and their accompanying photographs, personals, and advertisements, etc. Associations link magazines with preferred readings and cultural values, some of which may conflict—popular magazines rarely represent a monolithic discourse. In *Esquire*, for example, certain key words (media, fashion), hot topics (electronic gadgets, Armani), and prominent visual images (handsome single men wearing designer casual suits) construct subjective desires in young men for financial excess and casual European good looks, which imply a number of possible cultural values: "ideal young men own the latest technologies and understand their (elitist) social significance," and "ideal young men wear designer clothes for confidence and comfort (not necessarily for romantic purposes)." Through associations, distributing media promote certain cultural values over others, and these values either support or subvert the cultural values in the advertisements they contain. For example, the predominant cultural values in *Self* magazine—e.g., "ideal healthy women enjoy active lifestyles achieved through safe exercise and nutritional diets"—both subvert a Baileys Light ad (alcohol slows human metabolism making exercise difficult and often leading to weight gain) and also support it (Baileys Light has 33% fewer calories and 50% less fat than Baileys Irish Cream, so it is a healthier option when you want to relax with a drink).

As Johnson points out, "narratives or images always imply or construct a position or positions from which they are to be read or viewed," and certain media—popular magazines in particular—"naturalize the means by which [subject] positioning is achieved." The purpose of cultural studies is to render these processes of subject positioning "hitherto unconsciously suffered (and enjoyed) open to explicit analysis" (66). In their advertising analysis essays, students critique the subject positioning engaged in by the medium that distributes the advertisement they have chosen as the focus of their critical essays, and they compare and contrast the cultural values in their advertisement with the values in its distributing medium, looking specifically for consistencies and contradictions.

The third moment in the cycle isolates *critical consumption* as the object of study. Here the focus turns from the cultural values produced in texts and their distributing media to the subjectivities who encounter the produced and distributed values. When we study consumption, we study the impact media messages have on us as "readers." While Johnson acknowledges the powers distributing media have to construct subject positions for their readers, he is careful to point out that readers also possess the powerful agency to construct alternative narratives and images: "human beings and social movements also strive to produce some coherence and continuity, and through this, exercise some control over feelings, conditions and destinies" (69). And this control is achieved through "critique," which "involves stealing away the more useful elements [of media cultures] and rejecting the rest" (38). Critical analysis helps students problematize the subject positions constructed for them in texts, and cultural studies writing assignments encourage students to exert pressure on the construction of their own subject positions from which they might solve social problems for the benefit of communities.

In "Encoding/Decoding," Stuart Hall, also former director of the BCCCS, argues that media generate meaning using a "dominant hegemonic" code, a metalanguage that inherently promotes the cultural values of those already in power; and media texts are encoded with preferred readings (selected from the dominant hegemonic code) that construct subject positions for consumers of media messages.[2] As Dave Morley points out, "texts privilege a certain reading in part by inscribing certain preferred discursive positions from which its discourse appears 'natural,' transparently aligned to 'the real' and credible" (167). Uncritical audiences accommodate preferred readings, and they adopt subject positions constructed for them in media by dominant groups. The cultural values inscribed in media representations appear to these audiences as universal truths, inscribed in nature, beyond the realm of critical questioning. Although advertisements and their distributing contexts do at times promote positive cultural values (e.g., many of the new computer animated Levi's ads suggest that ideal women are independent and creative), too often as readers we accommodate marginalizing values uncritically and accept them as objective facts. When we accommodate cultural values without interrogating them, we allow the media that perpetuate these values to interpret our worlds for us, and we accept their interpretations without questioning the often self-serving social motives implicit in their assumptions. However, as Lawrence Grossberg argues, "the fact that texts encode certain preferred readings does not guarantee that they are read accordingly; that is, we cannot assume effects simply from origins" (138); and Morley agrees that a preferred reading "cannot be the *only* reading inscribed in the text, and it certainly cannot be the only reading which different readers can make of it" (167).

Some communities, often sub-cultures, establish what Hall refers to as "oppositional" codes, metalanguages that inherently resist the hegemonic cultural values of those in power; and media texts, encoded with "dominant" preferred readings, are rejected for promoting values that contradict those of the interpreting community. Based on oppositional codes, audiences deliberately decode media representations according to resistant logics. Audiences resist cultural values when they consciously understand the underlying messages in advertisements and their distributing contexts, yet they refuse to accept the cultural implications of these values and messages. From an "oppositional" perspective, media messages are perceived as "dominant" and therefore oppressive, and they are consumed according to (often marginalized) counter-cultural logics which subvert the dominant hegemonic code. Environmentalists, for example, may consume dominant cultural values in advertisements extolling the convenience, comfort, and economy of disposable diapers through oppositional codes, arguing instead that convenience, comfort, and economy are poor excuses for the systematic destruction of entire ecosystems. But resistance from oppositional subject positions can lead to reactionary rhetorical practices; and oppositional rhetoric elicits oppositional audience responses that often smother the potential for social change.

Most decoding operates according to "negotiated" codes, metalanguages that take the place of the dominant hegemonic code when it is unable to account for situated cultural values. Negotiated codes are not oppositional; they function as contingent correctives to the dominant hegemonic code when dominant cultural values no longer serve the socio-political interests of certain populations. We negotiate cultural codes in advertisements when we invoke specific circumstances from our own social experiences to which the dominant cultural values in advertisements do not necessarily apply, and this act of negotiation may affect our desire for—and use of—the advertised products. Some working class families, for example, may negotiate ads for Fancy Feast cat food, accommodating the desire for a comfortable lifestyle but resisting Fancy Feast's promotion of excessive consumption for its own sake. Some women may negotiate ads for Revlon Fire and Ice perfume, accommodating their desire for feminine sensuality while resisting Revlon's implication, in their use of anorexic models, that the ideal female body is thin. Some African Americans may negotiate ads for Lustrasilk Luxury Care relaxing cream, accommodating the desire for straight hair yet resisting Lustrasilk's representations of ethnic neutrality—the models pictured in the ad have light brown skin—by styling their hair in distinctively Afrocentric fashions. As Elizabeth Ellsworth points out, negotiation requires audiences who "are not passive recipients of the communications of others. Rather, they actively, and unpredictably, construct diverse and sometimes contradictory meanings for the same text" (61). And audiences' individual and collective cultural experiences generate these divergent readings. According to Morley, "At the moment of textual encounter other discourses are always in play other than those of the particular text in focus—discourses which depend on other discursive formations, brought into play by the subject's placing in other practices—cultural, educational, institutional" (163). These "other practices" account for divergent negotiations of advertisements, and they comprise the predominant critical focus of advertising analysis essays.

Johnson and others theorize cultural production, contextual distribution, and critical consumption as a *cyclical process*, necessitating a forward-looking link between critical consumption and the future production, distribution, and consumption of cultural values. The cultural production, contextual distribution, and critical consumption of cultural values in all new texts change, in different ways and to varying degrees, the character of the cultures (and the individuals within the cultures) that consume them, and each instance of critical consumption generates new exigencies for different styles of production, distribution, and consumption; as cultures change with the accommodation, resistance, and negotiation of cultural values represented in texts, new economic, social, and political values arise, requiring new texts to address emergent cultural needs. It is in this link between critical consumption and the future production, distribution, and consumption of cultural values where composition studies lends practical effectivity to cultural studies, which remains primarily an academic discourse. Specific concerns in rhetoric and composition for matters of audience, purpose, and style illuminate the importance of practical rhetorical interventions based on the critical knowledge gained through advertising analysis. Thus, while cultural studies is indeed "an alchemy for producing useful knowledge" (Johnson 38) derived through critical consumption, composition studies is a process for transforming "useful knowledge" into *shared knowledge* that influences the future production, distribution, and consumption of cultural values. Critical consumption alone does not, in and of itself, lead to social reform; only careful rhetorical interventions into this cycle make possible the reforms that cultural studies seeks.

In the context of the advertising analysis assignment that I describe in appendix A, students create links between their critical consumption of advertisements and the future production, distribution, and consumption of cultural values by writing letters that attempt to solve some of the problems they discover in their heuristic inquiries and describe in their critical essays, and they direct their letters to *at least* one of three possible audiences: representatives of the company that either makes the product or offers the service advertised (cultural production audience); editors of the magazine that distributes the advertisement (contextual distribution audience); and/or consumers who encounter the advertisement or its distributing medium on a regular basis (critical consumption audience). Before writing these letters, students consider the *quantity of knowledge* each audience might have regarding the cultural values promoted in the advertisement, and the *quality of attitude* each audience might have toward potential reform in the future production, distribution, and/or consumption of the cultural values promoted in the advertisement. These two considerations are crucial to the success of the letters, since they determine students' rhetorical aims (informative when audiences know little and/or have positive attitudes toward reform, and persuasive when audiences know much and/or are resistant toward reform; most of the letters, however, contain mixtures of informative and persuasive discourse). Having explored the knowledge and attitudes of each audience, students then decide which audience(s) would, having received an effective letter, most likely influence the future production, distribution, and consumption of cultural values within the context of the advertisement in question. This process of rhetorical intervention into the cycle of cultural production, contextual distribution, and critical consumption transforms "useful knowledge" into shared knowledge and enhances the potential for social change, change that is less likely to occur if students end their composing processes with critical essays.

Extensive heuristic exploration of *all three* "moments" in the cycle of cultural production, contextual distribution, and critical consumption—and, most importantly, rhetorical intervention into the cycle (in the link between critical consumption and the future production, distribution, and consumption of cultural values)—is crucial to the practice of social-process rhetorical inquiry. Heuristics that foreground only one of these moments, as Johnson points out, apply only to "those parts of the process which they have most clearly in view," and these heuristics, like those described by Berlin and Porter, are "incomplete, liable to mislead, in that they are only partial, and therefore cannot grasp the process as a whole" (46). This "process," of course, is the cycle of developing social relations that cultural studies seeks to critique, and unbalanced attention to just one moment in this process leads to short-sighted conclusions which may inhibit the potential for political action. Johnson explains the need for an integration of these isolated criticisms into a whole-process approach to the study of culture: "All cultural products, for example, require to be produced, but the conditions of their production cannot be inferred by scrutinizing them as 'texts.' Similarly all cultural products are 'read' by persons other than professional analysts (if they weren't there would be little profit in their production), but we cannot predict these uses from our own analysis, or, indeed, from the conditions of production" (46). Social-process rhetorical inquiry incorporates *all three* moments in the cycle of cultural production, contextual distribution, and critical consumption into focused and balanced heuristic exploration of the entire process of developing social relations.

Social-Process Rhetorical Inquiry

In Appendix A, I present an advertising analysis assignment with two parts, a critical essay and a practical letter. This assignment is intentionally abstract, since students will develop their own responses as they engage the invention heuristic in Appendix B. As the assignment suggests, students should first choose a magazine with which they are familiar; it helps if they already know the "code(s)" from which the magazine draws. I encourage students to select magazines with clear audiences, such as *Seventeen*, *GQ*, *Rolling Stone*, *Self*, *Muscle*, *Hot Rod*, etc. Magazines like *Newsweek*, *Time*, *Us*, and *People* are indeed directed at certain kinds of readers, but because they target broad audiences they tend to draw from a number of divergent "codes," which can confuse students in their critiques of the cultural values in media. Once students have chosen a magazine for the assignment, I ask them to read it cover-to-cover, paying careful attention to everything: the cover design, table of contents, editorials, letters to the editor, regular columns, feature articles and their accompanying photographs, personals, and, of course, advertisements. As they read, students look specifically for recurring key words, hot topics, and prominent visual images that associate the magazine with certain preferred readings and cultural values. The goal here is to give students a "total experience" with the magazine, not just a selective experience with a few articles and ads. Once students have oriented themselves to the "code(s)" within which the magazine operates, their task is to select one advertisement from the magazine; this ad will become the focus of their critical and practical essays. Selecting the ad is critical since not all are equally right for the advertising analysis assignment. The best advertisements have a fairly balanced mixture of visual images and written text that promote cultural values. Ads that are imbalanced toward either visual or textual representations do not highlight the *interaction* of these elements in the construction of cultural values.

While students are reading their magazines and selecting an ad for their critical essays, I spend two class periods (on a Tuesday/Thursday schedule) helping students apply the heuristic in Appendix B to a specific magazine and a few of its advertisements. Since these magazine and ads are the objects of class discussion, they are then off limits for the students' advertising analysis essays. During the first class period, I bring in several (as needed) identical copies of a single magazine with a well defined audience. I have students examine the magazine issues in groups, working through the "contextual distribution" questions in the Appendix B heuristic. I give student groups about thirty minutes to examine every aspect of the magazine, after which we discuss the associations and values promoted in the medium. During our class discussion of the magazine, I have students generate lists (which I write on the board) of the recurring key words, hot topics, and prominent visual images. We usually fill the chalk board with words, topics, and images, some of which may contradict others in the lists, serving to demonstrate the polysemous codes within which magazines operate. Having filled the chalk board with lists, students then generate the subjective meanings and desires that the recurring key words, hot topics, and prominent visual images in the magazine imply. If there is enough room on the chalk board, I try to write the meanings and desires below our lists of words, topics, and images so that students can clearly see their interrelationships.

Students then generate cultural values implied in the magazine, and I take this classroom opportunity to discuss what makes a good statement of cultural value. Effective statements of cultural value have two components: ideal identities and ideal social practices. First students ask from the perspective of the magazine in question, "What ideal identities do the key words, hot topics, and visual images in the magazine construct?" As we have seen, the key words, topics, and images in *Esquire* construct "young men" as its ideal audience, and the key words, topics, and images in *Self* construct "healthy women" as its ideal audience. Some magazines may construct two or three different identities. Next students ask, again from the perspective of the magazine, "What ideal social practices do the key words, hot topics, and visual images in the magazine construct for that ideal audience?" The key words, topics, and images in *Esquire* construct purchasing high tech gadgets and designer clothing as ideal social practices for young men, and the key words, topics, and images in *Self* construct safe exercise and dieting as ideal social practices for healthy women. Most magazines construct multiple ideal social practices for their ideal audience(s). We then consider the relevant questions from the "critical consumption" section of the heuristic in Appendix B, critiquing each cultural value (arguing for our accommodation, resistance, and/or negotiation of it) and its association with the magazine under examination.

During the second class period, while students are reading their magazines and selecting an ad for their critical and practical essays, I have students collaboratively choose two or three ads from the magazines we examined during the previous class period. Here we discuss the differences between balanced and imbalanced ads, and the class votes on which few they would like to critique for the rest of the class period. With the ads chosen, and examining them one at a time, students begin to generate lists of associations among the words and images in the ads and the subjective desires they imply. Again, I write these lists of associations on the chalk board so that students can look at them as they begin to formulate the statements of cultural value implied by the associations. In formulating these statements of cultural value, first students must ask from the perspective of each advertisement in question, "What ideal identities do the words and visual images in the ad construct?" In IBM laptop computer ads, for example, words and images imply that ideal consumers are successful CEOs; in Calvin Klein jeans ads, ideal consumers are sexy women; and in Gerber baby food ads, ideal consumers are doting mothers. Some ads may construct two or three different ideal identities. Next students ask from the perspective of the advertisement, "What ideal social practices do the words and visual images in the ad construct for that ideal audience?" IBM's ideal successful CEOs work late hours on (IBM) laptop computers; Calvin Klein's ideal sexy women wear close-fitting (Calvin Klein) jeans; and Gerber's ideal doting mothers stay home with their kids and feed them (Gerber) baby foods. Some ads may also construct multiple ideal social practices for their ideal audience(s). We then consider the relevant questions from the "critical consumption" section of the heuristic in Appendix B, critiquing each cultural value (arguing for our accommodation, resistance, and/or negotiation of it) and its association with the advertised product.

We end this second class period exploring each potential audience for our own rhetorical interventions into the cycle of cultural production, contextual distribution, and critical consumption. For example, students might decide to write a letter to IBM executives explaining that their advertisements encourage husbands and fathers to neglect their families, which could be damaging to IBM's long-term public reputation, and recommending that they discuss a different promotional campaign with their advertising department; students might write a letter to the editors of *Esquire* magazine, a medium that distributes the IBM advertisement, explaining that the ad contradicts *Esquire*'s values regarding casual lifestyles, and recommending that they discontinue the ad in future issues; finally, students might write a letter to *Consumer Reports* magazine (or a local newspaper for a local ad) describing to other potential consumers the damaging cultural values promoted in IBM advertisements, and recommending that consumers boycott IBM products until it changes its advertising practices. In most instances, a three letter combination is the best rhetorical choice for enacting changes in product/service advertising. However, there are audiences that will decode such letters oppositionally; often, in these cases, sending just one or two letters to potentially receptive audiences is the best rhetorical choice. "Potential impact" is an important consideration in students' choice of audiences. I always encourage students to send their letters to the audiences they most want to reach, and we discuss the responses as they arrive throughout the rest of the semester. Many of the responses are oppositional and reactionary, and students learn quite a bit about tone and purpose from critiquing them; they also learn valuable political lessons about the effectiveness or ineffectiveness of their own rhetorical choices. Other responses, however, acknowledge the problems students have pointed out in their letters, describing a potential course of action, and the students take pride in knowing that their writing has affected for the better their own cultural lives and the lives of others.

This kind of hands-on classroom practice gives students the confidence they need to fully engage the difficult heuristic questions in Appendix B, and individual teachers may spend more or less class time on heuristic exploration as the need arises. It is crucial for a social-process approach to rhetorical inquiry that students engage the heuristic cycle of cultural production, contextual distribution, and critical consumption *collaboratively*, since students working in isolation may: 1) view advertisements and their distributing media as monolithic, true, universal representations, leaving accommodation as the only viable critical stance; or 2) view advertisements and their distributing media as monolithic, false, particularized representations, leaving resistance as the only viable critical stance. Collaborative heuristic inquiry, on the other hand, highlights the plurality of cultural values promoted in advertisements and their distributing media; in class, students argue among themselves about what cultural values advertisements and magazines represent, and they argue even more about their own negotiations of these cultural values. Even when teachers assign the advertising analysis critical and practical essays as individual projects, initial collaborative heuristic inquiry demonstrates to students the polysemous discourses represented in the advertisements and magazines they will critique, and this knowledge results, I believe, in more complicated critical writing than when students do not collaborate.

The advertising analysis assignment works best when it is preceded with collaborative heuristic inquiry, but it is most successful, in my own experience, when the entire assignment is written collaboratively by groups of three or four students. Here social-process rhetorical inquiry is best served because students must reconcile their differences in the critical essay (many of which are left graphically represented as dialogue) into a single rhetorical purpose in the practical essays. Collaborative heuristic inquiry into the cycle of cultural production, contextual distribution, and critical consumption generates polysemous readings of ads and magazines; however, this polysemy must be constrained if students' rhetorical interventions are to succeed.

The advertising analysis assignment I describe also works equally well with or without research. Students can use research in a number of ways in critical essays and rhetorical interventions to improve their skills in conducting primary and secondary research and incorporating sources into their writing. Under "cultural production," for example, students might find print sources on the company that makes the product or offers the service: they might, for example, research the Philip Morris company to explore its own cultural values as a tobacco company and to what extent those values are manifested in their ads for Marlboro cigarettes. Under "contextual distribution," students might find print sources on the company that owns and distributes the magazine that contains the ad in question: they might, for example, research Condé Nast Publications to explore its own cultural values as a communications corporation and to what extent those values are manifested in the pages of *Glamour* magazine. Under "critical consumption," students might interview different populations regarding their reactions to the cultural values promoted in the advertisement or magazine in question. Here students might gather and record reactions from "cultural groups" to their advertisement: they might explore a variety of responses from different ethnicities, social classes, genders, sexual preferences, religions, political affiliations, educational backgrounds, geographical regions, etc. These different responses, like the earlier collaborative heuristic explorations, complicate critical consumption by highlighting the polysemous character of cultural values, and they foster a more inclusive ethic in students' critical writing.

The cultural studies methodology for rhetorical invention described in Appendix B is a *social-process* heuristic precisely because of its cyclical character. Not only does it encourage students to understand writing as a process, but it also encourages students to understand culture itself as a process that is open to change through careful rhetorical intervention. The heuristic gains its most significant power when students critically consume the production and distribution of cultural values with an eye toward producing their own values to be distributed and consumed in particular discourse communities. In other words, once students have examined an advertisement in terms of its production of cultural values and its distribution in a semiotic context, and they have explored their own critical consumption of the produced values in both the ad and its context, then they must continue the cycle through specific rhetorical interventions into the processes of developing social relations—they must produce texts of their own for specific distributing contexts and for consumption within particular communities, which in turn elicit further texts, contexts, and critical readings, etc. And these rhetorical interventions are most effective when cultural values have been negotiated through dialectical rhetorical practices that incorporate multiple perspectives on social problems.

Conclusion

I propose a movement in writing instruction toward what I have called *social-process* rhetorical inquiry, and this movement requires further pedagogical adaptations of cultural studies methodologies into invention heuristics for critical inquiry. These heuristics, however, should provide students with guides for careful rhetorical inquiry through the complete cycle of cultural production, contextual distribution, and critical consumption, and they should help students explore means for rhetorical interventions into this cycle. Invention heuristics for critical inquiry based on cultural studies methodologies help student writers tap into the knowledge they already possess about their own cultural experience, thereby demystifying critical writing for many students who might otherwise precipitously adopt "oppositional" perspectives in relation to cultural studies composition pedagogies.

Notes

1. Even typically asocial rhetorical theories have gravitated toward the study of culture as a context for teaching writing: in *The Construction of Negotiated Meaning*, for example, Linda Flower describes a "social-cognitive" theory of writing in which she examines the cultural forces that shape human thought processes in the acquisition of literacy; and in *Romancing Rhetorics*, Sherrie Gradin articulates a "social-expressivist" approach to teaching writing, describing subject formation as a dialectical interaction of social and individual forces. No more than a decade ago, the terms "social-cognitive" and "social-expressivist" would have been considered oxymorons, but in recent years they have become commonplace.

2. It is important to note, however, that a dominant hegemonic code is only dominant from a particular perspective; in other words, what is dominant in one social arrangement or discursive formation (environmentalist codes in Demo-

cratic discourse on preserving the environment) may be marginalized in another social arrangement or discursive formation (environmentalist codes in Republican discourse on reducing government excess). Unfortunately, much cultural studies still theorizes media as a monolithic discourse, encoding a single "dominant" ideological perspective into all media messages, and it still theorizes media audiences as the duped "masses." While such theories, developed in the 1940s and 1950s by members of the Frankfurt Institute for Social Research, helped explain Nazi crimes against humanity, these totalizing theories are overly simplistic when applied to the complex polysemy characteristic of postmodern media.

Works Cited

Bartholomae, David. "Inventing the University." *When a Writer Can't Write: Studies in Writer's Block and Other Composing Process Problems.* Ed. Mike Rose. New York: Guilford, 1985. 134-65.

Berlin, James A. "Composition and Cultural Studies." *Composition and Resistance.* Ed. C. Mark Hurlbert and Michael Blitz. Portsmouth, NH: Boynton, 1991. 47-55.

Ellsworth, Elizabeth. "Educational Media, Ideology, and the Presentation of Knowledge through Popular Cultural Forms." *Popular Culture, Schooling, and Everyday Life.* Eds. Henry A. Giroux and Roger I. Simon. New York: Bergin and Garvey, 1989. 47-66.

Fiske, John. *Introduction to Communication Studies.* 2nd ed. Studies in Culture and Communication. London: Routledge, 1990.

Flower, Linda. *The Construction of Negotiated Meaning: A Social Cognitive Theory of Writing.* Carbondale: Southern Illinois UP, 1994.

Gradin, Sherrie. *Romancing Rhetorics: Social Expressivist Perspectives on the Teaching of Writing.* Portsmouth, NH: Boynton, 1995.

Grossberg, Lawrence. "Strategies of Marxist Cultural Interpretation." *Critical Perspectives on Media and Society.* Eds. Robert K. Avery and David Eason. New York: Guilford, 1991. 126-59.

Hall, Stuart. "Encoding/Decoding." *Culture, Media, Language: Working Papers in Cultural Studies, 1972-79.* Eds. Stuart Hall, Dorothy Hobson, Andrew Lowe, and Paul Willis. London: Hutchinson, 1980. 128-38.

Johnson, Richard. "What Is Cultural Studies Anyway?" *Social Text* 6 (1987): 38-80.

Marx, Karl. "Introduction to a Critique of Political Economy." *A Contribution to the Critique of Political Economy.* Trans. S. W. Ryazanskaya. Ed. Maurice Dobb. New York: International, 1970. 188-217.

Morley, Dave. "Texts, Readers, Subjects." *Culture, Media, Language: Working Papers in Cultural Studies, 1972-79.* Eds. Stuart Hall, Dorothy Hobson, Andrew Lowe, and Paul Willis. London: Hutchinson, 1980. 163-73.

Porter, James E. *Audience and Rhetoric: An Archaeological Composition of the Discourse Community.* Englewood Cliffs, NJ: Prentice, 1992.

Trimbur, John. "Taking the Social Turn: Teaching Writing Post-Process." *College Composition and Communication* 45 (1994): 108-18.

Appendix A

Advertising Critical and Practical Essays: Assignment

In this essay, you will examine the culture of "advertising" critically. We all encounter hundreds of advertisements every single day, whether we are conscious of them or not. Advertisements bombard us in our cars, at work, at school, and—most of all—in our homes during leisure time. It is crucial, therefore, that we develop a critical understanding of how advertisements affect us and our surroundings. Only then do we have the power to choose consciously whether to accommodate, resist, or negotiate the cultural values each advertisement promotes.

Your first task in this assignment is to choose a magazine with which you are already familiar, and get a recent copy of it (you will turn the copy in when you turn in your final advertising critical and practical essays). Next, choose an advertisement within the particular magazine issue you have bought or borrowed; it should have an equal mixture of visual and verbal elements. This advertisement will be the primary focus of your critical and practical essays.

The Critical Essay

You have two options for the general structure of your advertising critical essay: you might organize your critique around the concepts in the invention, slightly altering their order to contextual distribution, cultural production, and critical consumption; or you might organize your critique around the dominant cultural values that you find in the advertisement and the magazine.

The Practical Letter

Attempt to resolve one or two problems that you describe in your critical essay by writing *at least* one formal letter for which there are three possible audiences and purposes:

a letter to the company that makes the product or offers the service advertised, providing specific and viable alternatives to their present advertising practices.

a letter to the editors of the advertisement's distributing medium, pointing out contradictions between the medium and the advertisement it contains.

a letter to the editors of *Consumer Reports* magazine, warning other potential consumers about the advertising practices of the company and/or medium in question.

Appendix B

A Cultural Studies Heuristic for Rhetorical Inquiry into Advertising

The following heuristic is designed to help you explore the cycle of cultural production, contextual distribution, and critical consumption as it relates to magazine advertisements.

Cultural Production

Explore the advertisement's production of cultural values ("ideal" audiences and social practices) through associations:

List associations between the predominant images in the advertisement and their subjective meanings.

List associations between the key words in the advertisement and their subjective meanings.

What cultural values do the associations in the advertisement imply?

Circle the cultural values with which you feel uncomfortable.

Contextual Distribution

Explore the cultural values of the magazine that distributes the advertisement you have chosen to critique:

List associations between the key words in the magazine and their subjective meanings.

List associations between the hot topics in the magazine and their subjective meanings.

List associations between the predominant visual images in the magazine and their subjective meanings.

What cultural values do the associations in the magazine imply?

Mark with an asterisk the cultural values of the magazine that directly contradict the cultural values of the advertisement.

Circle the cultural values of the magazine with which you feel uncomfortable.

Critical Consumption
Critique (accommodate, resist, and, most importantly, negotiate) the cultural values in the advertisement and its distributing medium:

Identify cultural values *in the advertisement and the magazine* that you accommodate, and explain based on your own personal experience why you accommodate those values.

In the case of each cultural value that you accommodate *in the advertisement*, explain whether or not you believe the value is legitimately associated with the advertised product.

Identify cultural values *in the advertisement and the magazine* that you resist, and explain based on your own personal experience why you resist those values.

In the case of each cultural value that you resist *in the advertisement*, explain whether or not you believe the value is legitimately associated with the advertised product.

Identify cultural values *in the advertisement and the magazine* that you negotiate, and explain based on your own personal experience why you negotiate those values.

In the case of each cultural value that you negotiate *in the advertisement*, explain whether or not you believe the value is legitimately associated with the advertised product.

Rhetorical Intervention as Cultural Production
Compose effective rhetorical documents challenging the cultural values that do not serve the interests of a community to which you belong:

> **Cultural Production Audience:**
> Do representatives of the company (that either makes the product or offers the service) know that the cultural values in their advertisement have negative effects on you and other consumers?
>
> What is the company's attitude toward these negative effects?
>
> **Contextual Distribution Audience:**
> Do the editors of the magazine know that the cultural values in the advertisement contradict the cultural values of their medium?
>
> What is the editors' attitude toward these contradictions?
>
> **Critical Consumption Audience:**
> Do other consumers know that the cultural values in the advertisement and/or the magazine have negative effects on them?
>
> What are consumers' attitudes toward these negative effects?

Articulation Theory and the Problem of Determination: A Reading of *Lives on the Boundary*

John Trimbur

The narrativity of an individual life is a literary trope that figures across a range of genres. From memoirs, biography, the journalistic profile, and the celebrity story to the autobiographical novel and *bildungsroman*, the narrativity of a life is a familiar and apparently altogether consumable literary convention, turning up in bestsellers such as *Iacocca: An Autobiography* and popular magazines such as *People*. Other forms of writing, too—popular psychology books such as Gail Sheehy's *Passages* and the gamut of self-help and popular advice tracts that line bookstore shelves—seem to take it for granted that an individual life not only can be narrated but that such narration can make a life intelligible and thereby subject to control and change.

Harvey Kail suggests that composition theory and textbooks likewise rely on the narrativity of a Student Writer's life by projecting mythic quests for students to take on their road to advanced literacy. In "Narratives of Knowledge: Story and Pedagogy in Four Composition Texts," Kail argues that we can read out the plots of standard textbooks such as Becker, Young, and Pike's *Rhetoric: Discovery and Change*, Ann Berthoff's *Forming/Thinking/Writing*, William E. Coles, Jr.'s *Teaching Composition*, and Kenneth A. Bruffee's *A Short Course in Writing* in order to identify their underlying narratives and the tales they tell of the formation of a personality through emergence into literacy. According to Kail, these narratives are familiar ones, based on Christian and social traditions deeply rooted in American culture, such as the search for identity, salvation, self-improvement, and knowledge. By paying attention to these narratives, moreover, Kail suggests an alternative way to represent composition studies, not just as a series of discrete theoretical positions on a taxonomic grid (Becker, Young, and Pike are "cognitivists," Berthoff a "neo-Cassirerean," Coles an "expressivist," Bruffee a "social constructionist") but as a series of conjunctures that link scholarly and pedagogical discourses and practices to culturally sanctioned narratives, to the interests, institutions, and identities these narratives call up, and to the way these narratives make the meanings of reading and writing intelligible to students and teachers alike.

By and large, however, composition studies has paid relatively little attention to its own narrativity, to the way in which composition theory and practice are articulated to the master narratives that charter belief and action in American culture. This may appear to be surprising because the notion that knowledge is invariably authorized by its narrativity has become something of a commonplace in postmodern thought. Richard Rorty, Jean-François Lyotard, and others, for whatever differences may otherwise divide them, seem to agree that what we have traditionally called knowledge is in fact a "fiction," a manufactured account that legitimizes itself precisely to the extent that it holds its readers in the thrall of persistent and unexamined metaphors and metanarratives.

There has, of course, been a recent turn toward narrative in composition studies, in part following Jane Tompkins' call to "unlearn" the critical essay and write in a more personal and autobiographical style. In the work of Donald McQuade, Nancy Sommers, and others, however, narrative remains separate from "thesis-driven" exposition. It figures as an academically devalued genre capable, its advocates hold, of redeeming prose by replacing the authoritarian, masculinist, and hierarchical strategies of arguing for a position with the immediacy and authenticity of lived experience rendered narratively. This turn to narrative, thus, has largely limited itself to counterposing narrativity as a way of knowing to argumentative strategies, instead of probing for the connections between narratives and other discursive forms and cultural practices—or, as Kail might put it, how the discourse of composition studies joins together with available culturally authorized narratives and the social contexts in which these narratives arise.

In this essay, I want to suggest, in the broadest sense, the usefulness of investigating the conjunctures at which discourses and practices in the field of composition studies are linked to discourses and practices outside of it. I will be looking in particular at how the narrativity of an individual life in Mike Rose's *Lives on the Boundary* is articulated to wider cultural narratives. I have chosen to focus on *Lives on the Boundary* in part because it makes its own narrativity so explicit by relying on autobiography to tell the story of what the book's subtitle calls the "struggles and achievements of America's educational underclass." But I am also interested in *Lives on the Boundary* because its use of such a popular genre to narrate its concerns makes the book more problematical than has usually been acknowledged.

The Problem of Narrativity in *Lives on the Boundary*

Since *Lives on the Boundary* appeared in 1989, it has been hailed as the book composition studies was waiting for. Addressed to the general public, as well as to education and composition specialists, *Lives on the Boundary* seemed to do the kind of cultural and ideological work needed in the Reagan/Bush era of educational retrenchment by providing an eloquent and moving case for expanded educational opportunity, multicultural curricula, enlightened pedagogy, and the educability of all Americans. At last, it appeared that someone had succeeded in translating the hard-won experience and expertise of writing teachers, and especially of basic writing teachers in open admissions programs, into a popular idiom capable of affecting public opinion. *Lives on the Boundary* was greeted as the book to give composition studies a public voice and visibility to counter bestsellers such as E.D. Hirsch's *Cultural Literacy* and Allan Bloom's *The Closing of the American Mind* and commission reports from William Bennett, Diane Ravitch and Chester Finn, and Lynne J. Cheney.

To bring his case to a broad audience, Rose has chosen to devote a substantial part of the book to his own life. Rose tells the story of his "passage from South Vermont [the working-class neighborhood where he grew up] to Loyola," where Rose was an undergraduate and, as he puts it, "entered the conversation" (67). We follow Rose on a kind of pilgrim's progress, from his struggles as a high-school student who arises, miraculously, from the slough of Voc-Ed despond, through college and the temptations of literary studies in graduate school to his redemptive work as a teacher of the neglected and underprepared. This narrative, of course, possesses enormous cultural resonance, recalling such autobiographies as Richard Wright's *Black Boy* and Richard Rodriquez's *Hunger of Memory*. But because the tale of a poor or working-class youth's rising from his humble origins is such a familiar one, it also contains some political risks I think have not been adequately accounted for. To put it as directly as I can, the risk is that readers will take *Lives on the Boundary* to be another comforting American success story of an individual who, through the power of education and the guidance of more experienced teacher-mentors, takes the predictable road to self-improvement and upward mobility, from the mean streets of Los Angeles to the halls of

UCLA. Such a narrative, furthermore, would seem to fit right in to what Harvey Graff calls the "literacy myth": the moral consensus that has dominated the meanings of literacy since the mid-nineteenth century by representing the ability to read and write as a social explanation of success and failure in class society, a token of middle-class propriety, and a measure to divide the worthy from the unworthy poor.

The issue I am concerned with here is whether Rose's decision to use the narrativity of a life backfires on him. Despite Rose's obvious intentions to argue for fundamental reforms in American education, the question needs to be asked whether the autobiographical impulse in *Lives on the Boundary* inevitably locates the book for its readers within what Kristin Ross calls the "exemplary bourgeois cultural project" of narrating a life, individualizing a person's fate, and positioning readers as witnesses to an edifying tale of individual initiative and the transformative powers of education and literacy. But before I consider whether Rose's life history is absorbed, inadvertantly or not, by the cultural narrative it articulates, I want first to define more precisely the notions of conjuncture and articulation I will be using to read *Lives on the Boundary*.

Taxonomies and Conjunctures

For the most part, literature reviews and histories of writing instruction have used a taxonomic strategy to order composition by dividing and classifying its various pedagogies, rhetorics, and research programs into categories, with perhaps the discontinuity of a Kuhnian paradigm shift to demarcate one approach from another. Like any rhetorical strategy, taxonomies both enable and constrain their users, bringing some things to light while suppressing others. Taxonomies, in other words, need to be seen not so much in terms of their truth value as their uses and what they make possible.

The standard taxonomies in the field, such as James A. Berlin's expressionistic, cognitivist, and social-epistemic rhetorics, Lester Faigley's expressive, cognitive, and social views of composing, and Stephen North's division of the field into researchers, historians, scholars, and practitioners are useful for the ordering functions they perform and the differences, both practical and theoretical, they bring to the surface. Particularly for a young and emerging field such as composition studies, taxonomies can codify positions that might appear otherwise to arise spontaneously from the pressures of practice. In this regard, Berlin's and Faigley's taxonomies especially have contributed to the professionalization of the field by giving it a shape, by identifying central issues, and by lifting the study and teaching of writing from the shared activity of a few like-minded individuals at the margins of English departments into the realm of scholarly controversy where a set of standard positions defines the context of issues and establishes the terms of ongoing discussion. From this perspective, we might say that without taxonomies it would be difficult to think and speak composition studies at all. By dividing and classifying, taxonomies create a unity of differences as the terrain of composition studies.

At the same time, such division and classification tends to make instances of intellectual work into synechdoches or labels for trends and currents in the field. The work of David Bartholomae, for example, and in particular his essay "Inventing the University," is often cited as a founding statement of a social constructionist, academic discourse approach to writing instruction. Although, as Carolyn C. Ball argues, this conventionalized view may actually ignore or suppress expressionist or cognitivist currents in Bartholomae's writing, the treatment of "Inventing the University" as a kind of shorthand token seems virtually to be called for by the generic function of the literature review and the scholarly convention of locating one's work in relation to prior work, as the ground to validate new inquiries or a foil to establish counter-tendencies.

However, as Susan Miller says of North's division of composition studies into humanistic "scholars" and empiricist "researchers," taxonomies are based not on "logical, but political, differences" (37). Taxonomic categories need to be seen not just as the formal defining terms of a field of study but as the result of particular conjunctures that ascribe certain cultural meanings and political valences to ideas and practices. Unlike the categories of a taxonomy, which reside in the space of logic, conjunctures are located in actual historical time. A conjuncture designates those moments when ideas (whether in the form of theories or narratives or other genres) are joined to other ideas, practices, institutions, interests, and subjectivities. Conjunctures constitute the temporal and temporary moments at which ideas take on particular social weight, cultural meaning, and rhetorical effect not because of their intrinsic or essential identities (as specified categorically) but because of the way these ideas are articulated concretely by specific men and women and take on specific identities in specific historical settings and social contexts.

To give a brief example: from a conjunctural perspective, the emphasis on the value of personal voice and individual sincerity in the work of Peter Elbow cannot be reduced simply to a category of expressionistic rhetoric that distinguishes it, say, from the emphasis on academic discourse and the kind of imitative ventriloquy Bartholomae notes in students' efforts to appropriate the institutional voices of the university. The sincerity of self-revelation that Elbow struggled to teach young men writing statements of conscientious objection during the Vietnam War carries a quite different political meaning from the usual practice of sincerity in expressionistic rhetorics. Berlin, correctly I think, sees these rhetorics as critical of "the dehumanizing effects of industrial capitalism" but at the same time indebted to "the entrepreneurial values capitalism most admires: individualism, private initiative, the confidence for risk taking, the right to be contentious with authority (especially the state)" (487). The point here is that apparently identical ideas and practices can take on quite different cultural meanings and political valences depending on the conjuncture at which (and to which) they are articulated. The rhetorical effect of ideas and practices is produced not only by reference to their logical features but also by the practical joining together of discourse, institutions, and interests that social utterances and performances inevitably enact. When sincerity of expression is linked to mass movements against war, as occurred during the Vietnam War, or invoked as a means to give voice to those who have been systematically silenced, as during the Black Expressionist movement of the 1960s (see Leroi Jones/Amiri Baraka's classic "Expressive Language"), an expressionistic rhetoric can indeed be oppositional in effect. At other times, however, in "normal" classrooms of middle-class students, expressionistic rhetoric may well serve simply as a form of personal protest that, as Berlin notes, is "easily coopted by the very capitalist forces it opposes" or, at best, a limited means of "creative realization of the self" (487).

What I am suggesting is that there is no way to tell on the basis of a taxonomic categorization, to predict with certainty the effects. Unlike the categories in a taxonomy, which are meant to have a predictive value, the notion of a conjuncture suggests that nothing can be guaranteed ahead of time strictly according to formal or textual qualities alone. Rather effective meaning is a matter of what happens: practice takes place in historical time and social space.

Stuart Hall's Theory of Articulation

The notion of a "conjuncturalist" approach to the relationship between ideas, practices, and social formations might be seen as an attempt to formulate a neo-Marxist model of determination. As Raymond Williams notes, "No problem in Marxist cultural theory is more difficult than that of 'determination'" (83). Part of the difficulty may be attributed in the first place to the writings of Marx and Engels, which seem at times to presuppose a fixed correspondence among the existing stage of material production, social relations, and consciousness. In *The German Ideology*, for example, Marx states quite clearly that the "mass of productive forces accessible to men determines the conditions of society" (18). There is a tendency in Marx's writings to see human activity and historical development as governed by scientific laws of determination, a tendency that objectifies the social process and, as Engels indicates in a letter to Bloch in 1890, reads human will and agency out of history. "The historical event," Engels writes, may "be viewed as the product of a power which works as a whole unconsciously and without volition. For what each individual wants is obstructed by everyone else, and what emerges is something that no one willed" (476). At the same time, of course, one can also find equally authoritative passages that seem to affirm the creativity of human agency, even if it operates within particular constraints. Probably the best-known statement of this view is Marx's famous remark that "people make history but in conditions not of their making."

According to Williams, the confusion surrounding the problem of determination results in part from the "extraordinary linguistic complexity" of the term "determine" (84). While the term has certainly been colored in its uses within the Marxist tradition by scientistic biases and a typically nineteenth-century postivist quest for certainty, the root sense of "determine," Williams says, refers not only to an external force or authority—whether history or God—that decides or controls the outcome of an action but also to the way limits are set and pressures exerted by the momentum of the social process itself. According to the latter sense of the term, Williams says, "'Society' is then never only the 'dead husk' which *limits* social and individual fulfillment"—as it sometimes appears in orthodox Marxisms that hold to an abstract determinism based on isolated and autonomous forces acting upon the social formation from outside. Instead, for Williams, society "is always also a constitutive process with very powerful *pressures* which are both expressed in political, economic, and cultural formations and, to take the full weight of 'constitutive,' are internalized and become 'individual wills'" (87; emphasis added).

Perhaps the fullest exploration of the problem of determination in contemporary Marxist thought occurs in Stuart Hall's theory of articulation. Like Williams, Hall wants to develop a model of determination based not upon the implacable and predictable laws of history but upon the limits and pressures of specific historical, social, and cultural conjunctures. Situating his theory of articulation within past and current critical discourses, Hall has attempted to formulate a model of determination that avoids, on the one hand, the traditional Marxist view of a fixed and necessary correspondence between cultural practices and social structures and, on the other, more recent poststructuralist views of the indeterminancy or necessary non-correspondence and incommensurability of discourses, practices, and structures. By looking at how particular ideas, discourses, and practices are linked—or articulated—to particular conjunctures in the social formation, Hall has sought to define a "Marxism without guarantees," a guide to action that relies not on the predictive certainties of classical Marxist theory but on a reading of those linkages and how they articulate, at specific times and places, interests, subjectivities, and social forces.

Hall's theory of articulation was developed as part of a larger project to define the meaning of cultural studies in relation to what Hall calls "culturalist" and "structuralist" paradigms of critical thought. Cultural studies is often seen as the effort of the Birmingham (UK) Center for Contemporary Cultural Studies, under Hall's directorship, to balance the culturalist work of Williams, Richard Hoggart, and E.P. Thompson from the late 1950s and early 1960s (the period of the emergence of the British New Left) against the impact of more recent poststructuralist and postmodernist trends on Marxist thought in the 1970s and 1980s, as embodied above all in the influence of Althusser's structuralist Marxism. The usual version holds that a balancing act between the two paradigms was achieved by turning to Gramsci and his notions of hegemony and a war of positions in civil society—to account, on the one hand, for the empirical specificity characteristic of Williams and, on the other, the importance of difference that emerges from Althusser. This is a fair portrayal in a general sense but somewhat unnuanced. Cultural studies, at least in Hall's representation of it, is not so much an effort to locate a middle ground between the two paradigms as to use the two paradigms themselves as limits and pressures on each other—to hold them in dynamic tension as forms of reciprocal interrogation. To see how Hall's theory of articulation derives from this dynamic tension, we need now to look more closely at the way Hall reads the two paradigms against each other and the effect of this reading on Hall's model of determination.

First of all, the culturalist work of Williams, Hoggart, and Thompson registers a break from the reductionist economic determinism of orthodox Marxism in the direction of a Marxist or socialist humanism that emphasizes the creativity of cultural practices and the authenticity of working-class experience. In various ways, Williams, Hoggart, and Thompson argued that the popular culture of the working class is not simply a form of false consciousness imposed from above in the interest of ruling elites but rather is a way of life and shared subjectivity that resists as much as it accommodates the dominant order. According to this view, precisely because the formation of subjectivities is linked to class position, the lived experience of the working and subordinate classes offers a grounds to measure the distorting effects of ideology against reality. The culturalist paradigm, in other words, severs the ties of the left to the mechanical materialism of traditional Marxism but preserves a necessary correspondence among class position, cultural practices, and forms of consciousness as the framework of determination.

In contrast, the structuralist paradigm argues that there is no essential subjectivity at the center of experience but that experience of the "real" is itself made available and intelligible only as an effect of ideology, already preshaped by the categories, classifications, and frameworks of culture. In this sense, the structuralist paradigm loosens the ties in culturalism between cultural practice and social position by thinking of the social formation as a unity which is constructed through the differences of relatively autonomous practices rather than an expressive totality of corresponding practices. In Hall's view, Althusser's notion of the social formation as a structure in dominance of relatively autonomous practices and institutions that cannot be reduced to a system of homologous correspondences typifies the structuralist paradigm. These structures, as Althusser has it, "hail" or "interpellate" subjects by creating subject positions which speak and place individuals in capitalist social relations. Subjects, as Hall says, are by this account "bearers of structures" rather than "active agents" in making their own history.

Hall's strategy is to use these two paradigms as limits and pressures on each other. Hall takes Althusser and the structuralist paradigm as a way to reread Williams and the culturalists, to retain the creative subject by turning it into a subject positioned not by an essential class location but by mediating social and cultural forces, a subject in ideology who lives, as Althusser puts it, in and through imaginary relations to the real and contradictory conditions of existence. Althusser's understanding of the social formation as a complexly overdetermined structure instead of a simple or monolithic one allowed Hall, as he says, "to live in and with difference," to imagine a social formation determined by a totality of relatively autonomous institutions and practices (in, say, education, culture, mass media, the rituals of everyday life, and so on) which can be reduced neither to forms of each other nor to reflexes of the economic order but which still cohere as a unity in difference. For Hall, there is no necessary correspondence between cultural practices and social structures that can be referred to the determinations of class position or authentic experience.

At the same time, Hall also wants to put a break on certain poststructualist tendencies, arising in part from Althusser but certainly exceeding him, to think that there is not only no necessary correspondence but rather that there is a necessary non-correspondence that makes it analytically impossible to relate practices, beliefs, discourses, identities, and institutions to each other in determinate ways. According to Hall, Foucault and other post-Althusserians take the emphasis on difference in Althusser's relative autonomy of overdetermined practices in the direction of a radical heterogeneity, incommensurability, and the absolute autonomy of practices that refuses to think of determination as anything other than local and specific contingencies. In other words, Hall is prepared to follow the poststructuralists by thinking that cultural and social practices can be read as if they were textual or linguistic events. But by reaching back to the culturalist emphasis on lived experience, Hall also wants to resist what he sees as the typically postmodern abandonment of any appeal to the "real" or to experience outside of discourse. Hall holds on to the Marxist project of theorizing a complex unity of the social formation—but not by relating base to superstructure or latent to manifest content in a structure of necessary correspondence. Instead, Hall is proposing a fractured or articulated totality in which people make their own history, only under conditions not of their making.

Hall's theory of articulation conceptualizes the conjunctures at which people knit together disparate and apparently contradictory practices, beliefs, and discourses in order to give their world some semblance of meaning and coherence. Articulation theory, in other words, describes how people make a unity which is neither necessary nor previously determined. So, if Hall uses Althusser to set limits on the essentialism of class identity in the culturalist paradigm, by the same token he uses Williams and draws upon Gramsci to put pressure on what he calls the "creeping functionalism" in Althusser's structuralism, the tendency to see ideology as performing the function required of it by reproducing the social relations of production without countertendencies. In Hall's view, Althusser's "ideological state apparatus," the famous ISA, collapses the state and civil society, precisely the gap through which Hall sees the pressures of ideology from below running, in the tensions and conflict between the people and the ruling bloc. This domain of the popular is not strictly imposed from above but rather is negotiated in a contested arena where the struggle for hegemony and consent takes place. By using Gramsci's theory of hegemony and Ernesto Laclau's argument that the political connotation of ideological elements has no necessary belongingness to class or social location, articulation theory, Hall says, "enabled us to think how an ideology empowers people, enabling them to make some sense or intelligibility of their historical situation, without reducing those forms of intelligibility to their socio-economic or class location or social position" (53). The point for Hall is that one can connect cultural practices to the social formation—only not in advance. Articulation is always a matter of struggle in a war of positions where nothing is certain ahead of time but rather a matter of practice. No outcome can be guaranteed, as it is in orthodox Marxism, by the laws of history but must be determined concretely at specific conjunctures of history.

By refusing the scientistic metanarrative of orthodox Marxism and denying the necessary correspondence between practice and class location, Hall poses instead the quite practical yet crucial analytical question: "under what circumstances can a connection be forged or made" among particular ideologies, political subjects, cultural practices, and social movements and institutions? The double meaning of articulation—to put into words and to yoke together physically—offers both "a way of understanding how ideological elements come, under certain conditions, to cohere together within a discourse, and a way of asking how they do or do not become articulated, at specific conjunctures, to certain political subjects" (53). The workings of articulation, as Hall describe them, are simultaneously discursive and social: articulation names those historical moments at which certain ideas are uttered and combined (sometimes by severing ideological elements from their conventional uses and recombining them with other elements) into material forces capable of binding subjects together in social identities and movements.

Articulating *Lives on the Boundary*

From the perspective of articulation theory, the question to ask of *Lives on the Boundary* is how Rose puts into words the narrativity of his own life and how this articulation is thereby linked to other discourses, practices, subjectivities, and institutions. Rose has chosen to narrate his life history, as a student and a teacher, both to indict an educational system that wastes the intellectual curiosity of young people and adults and to demonstrate the possibilities of individual growth and development within America's educational underclass. Rose wants readers to see, and to feel, how such class-based educational practices as testing and tracking produce the desire of poor and working-class students not to excell and get ahead but to be "average," to distance themselves emotionally from a reward system that neglects their talents and potential. And he wants readers to understand how the intervention of caring teachers can mobilize and cultivate the intellectual resources of non-mainstream students. This is a story worth telling, especially at a moment in our collective history when "reform" movements in education are calling for higher standards, national testing, teacher accountability, discipline, and a return to a canonical curriculum. It is a story to break the prevailing silence in public discourse about education by speaking of democratic aspirations to increase access, to open opportunity, and to remove educational barriers to the poor and working class.

The problem, though, is whether the narrativity of a life in *Lives on the Boundary* is adequate to Rose's purposes, whether it can adequately represent the social processes of illiteracy and school failure in contemporary America and project a compelling vision of needed change. As I have already suggested, as a coming of age narrative, *Lives on the Boundary* might be read as an instance of the "exemplary bourgeois cultural project" of narrating a life. What makes the narrativity of a life so "exemplary" as a class-based tale is the fact that just to have a life—to experience oneself as possessing a life that can be narrated in the first place—is itself a particular historical development, inseparable from the emergence of individualism and the authority and autonomy ascribed to the bourgeois subject in class society. The narrativity of a life, in other words, is not something that is naturally given but rather is a strategic trope for what C.B. Macpherson calls the ideology of "possessive individualism," in which the individual emerges as a social subject by taking on a proprietary relationship to his or her own life. The autobiographical impulse to narrate a life, therefore, is not a straightforward one but rather the result of a particularly bourgeois cultural project of making and owning a sovereign and inalienable life, free from the ascriptions of birth, status, and social obligation in traditional society.

The classic coming of age narrative, however, tends to naturalize this struggle to fashion a self-created life and an individual personality by representing the passage from youth to maturity not as the formation of a particular kind of subjectivity in class society but as a timeless biological and psychological process. The rhetorical effect is an ostensibly universal subject whose life is narratable because its meanings transcend historical circumstance by expressing general laws of development and human nature. What is disguised or mistaken to be a natural desire to tell one's own story is, in fact, a critical moment in the bourgeoisie's growing self-consciousness and cultural self-confidence, as it entitles its members to author their own life histories and to inscribe the formation of the bourgeois personality in literature and popular culture as the normative story of growing up.

Such a coming of age narrative has a fairly predictable and formulaic narrative pattern. The plot typically recounts the adventures and crises of an alienated youth and how these youthful exploits and the wisdom of older and more experienced adults enable the youth to reconcile his or her identity to the constraints of class society. Readers are often offered a vicarious experience of the transgressions and marginality of youth, but only so that such disruptions of adult order and common sense will enable readers more surely than ever to define the boundaries of the normal. In this sense, what we call the coming of age narrative enacts not only a rite of passage from youth to maturity but also a ritual of inversion that permits formulaic moments of violation in order to contain their subversive force within the hierarchical patterns of mature order and authority.

According to Marxist critics such as Georg Lukács and Jean-Paul Sartre, the classic coming of age narrative tells how the disruptive desires and the turbulence of youth are contained by class society as the central character achieves maturity by taking on a professional calling and joining the adult world of full-fledged citizens. An atmosphere of calm typically pervades the narrative, the result of what Lukács sees as the social optimism of the rising bourgeoisie and the narrative transformation of a troubled youth into a well-adjusted and idealized bourgeois subject. For Sartre, this calm is a matter of the distanced lucidity of the narrator who represents the desires of youth as an "adventure" and a "brief distraction which is over with" (134). As the turbulent events of youth are situated narratively at the remove of time, they are relieved of their convulsive energies by the narrator's achieved stability and maturity. For this reason, the formation of a personality, as Sartre says, "is told from the viewpoint of experience and wisdom; it is listened to from the viewpoint of order" (134).

For Lukács and Sartre, the subject is shaped not only archetypally by the passage from youth to maturity and innocence to experience, but also practically by reconciling his or her youthful desires to the alienated adult world of work. In a typical coming of age narrative, a youth will wander through bohemia, want to be a writer or a painter, experiment with drugs and sexuality, travel to exotic places—and then settle down by choosing a profession, a calling, a *metier*. In other words, in the classic tale of the formation of a bourgeois personality, a youth comes into maturity by internalizing the necessity of work in the capitalist division of labor as a matter of personal choice, and the narrative represents this choice as a moral lesson learned from the errors and enthusiasms of youth. As Sartre says, "Neither the general nor the doctor impart their memories in a raw state: they are experiences that have been distilled, and we are warned as soon as they begin to speak that their story has a moral" (134).

Readers will recognize the classic features of the coming of age narrative in *Lives on the Boundary*. The book does indeed narrate a rite of passage, from a turbulent adolescence in South Los Angeles through a youthful flirtation with Beat culture and a brief literary romance with graduate studies in English to Rose's mastery of the secrets of the academy brought about by his acquisition of an identity and professional expertise as teacher and researcher. Rose's struggle, for himself and his students, to crack the code of the university appears in this narrative both as an affirmation of the (adult) authority of academic discourse and its institutions and as an act of benevolence toward the underprepared, from whose ranks Rose has risen. The question then is whether, or to what extent, *Lives on the Boundary* enacts the kind of reconciliation to the party of order and maturity that Lukács and Sartre find characteristic of the classic coming of age narrative.

The question of the social allegiances of *Lives on the Boundary*, I believe, hinges on the problem of determination I have been concerned with in earlier sections of this essay. Lukács and Sartre link the coming of age narrative, historically and culturally, to the formation of the bourgeois subject as the owner and operator of an exemplary life, an act of self-creation that culminates in the moralization of professional work as an explanation of success and failure in class society. From this perspective, the cultural practice of narrating a life seems to fit neatly with class location, and one might therefore postulate a necessary correspondence between the genre and the reproduction of capitalist social relations. There are, of course, other ways of narrating a life, as Sartre's admiration for Jean Genet in *St. Genet* indicates, that hold on to a position of marginality, criminality, and transgression that will not be reconciled to the dominant order. Mike Rose's book, however, is not written from such an outsider's perspective. But it is not written from the inside, either. Rather, as the title tells us, the book is located at the boundary of the dominant culture, at the points of intersection where the lives of the dispossessed encounter an educational system that sorts individuals into a capitalist division of labor, allotting life chances by separating mental from manual labor, the upwardly mobile from those stuck in place.

Lives on the Boundary is more than just an account of how Rose slips through the system, more than a tribute to the initiative (and luck) of the few who make it. What allows Rose to evade the class-bound limits of the self-made coming of age narrative—and what distinguishes his book from Wright's and Rodriquez's autobiographies—is his refusal to separate himself from the lives on the boundary and to take on the kind of distanced lucidity that Sartre finds characteristic of the genre. For Wright and Rodriquez, the cultural trajectory of personal development alienates them from their indigenous communities. In a very real sense, each confirms the adage that you can't go home again, that you can only look back. Wright and Rodriquez become professional writers, men of letters, and take on cosmopolitan identities that lead them to view their places of origin in terms of a cultural deficit, a lack of sustaining social and intellectual resources. Rose, however, despite his journeys into the wider world and his standing as a successful professional, never quite leaves his neighborhood or his youth behind. He remains open to the pressures of the milieu in which he grew up—the frustrated aspirations and ambitions of the people he knew along the way. As Rose discovers through his interactions with underprepared students and adult learners, the narrativity of his own life is articulated in terms of other lives. The veterans Rose teaches in a special program at UCLA figure as his "Voc-Ed comrades reincarnated" (137), and his work with Concepcion Baca (a student who drops out of UCLA, goes to work, and then returns to complete her degree and go on to graduate studies) causes him to register "how much of myself I saw in her" (204). Rather than calling attention to the distance between himself and America's educational underclass, as Wright and Rodriquez do, Rose repeatedly uses the story of his own personal success as a sign of the educability of all those others who have fallen through the systemic cracks in American schools.

The point is that Rose does indeed use a conventionalized and formulaic coming of age narrative, but he diverts it from the usual pattern of the self-made success story and the edifying tale of maturity to articulate another set of social, cultural, and educational interests that offer a democratic vision of education for all. In this sense, Rose rearticulates one of the most basic of American myths by severing the cultural meaning of personal success and professional achievement from its usual conservative functions. Rose's own professional expertise appears in *Lives on the Boundary* not as a reconciliation to work in class society or an exemplary lesson in maturity but as a practice that links his own labors to those of students and adult learners at the margins of the educational system and to the popular pressures from below that have struggled to extend educational opportunity. Like Mina Shaughnessey and Kenneth A. Bruffee in the days of open admissions at CUNY and David Bartholomae and Patricia Bizzell, Rose re-makes himself as a teacher and researcher, joining his expertise in close reading to the social force of protest movements of the late 1960s and early 1970s that fought to open higher education to those who had been excluded and, in effect, created the historical conjuncture from which the figure of the basic writer arises in composition studies.

By the account I offer here, Rose's professional expertise is not just the result of individual initiative, the accumulation of credentials, and the creation of a career. Instead, professional expertise is articulated with and to political subjectivities and social movements. Expertise is certainly coded by the cultural narratives of maturity and distanced lucidity as a particular determination of consciousness and class position. If professional practices and discourses typically represent the dispossessed as a client population in need of the intervention of expert benefactors, the political valence and cultural meaning of professional work nonetheless cannot be guaranteed in advance as an accommodation to the dominant culture and its division of specialists and laypersons. Professional expertise, as I believe *Lives on the Boundary* demonstrates, can also articulate a sense of solidarity with the aspirations and purposes of the dispossessed. It all depends on practice.

Rearticulating Literacy

But if the effects of professional work depend on practice, it is not the case that professional practices are themselves offered freely; nor can they be enacted simply by an act of will. While the conditions of professional work are not predetermined in a final and fixed sense, they are determinate—the result of how they are joined together with other practices in an ensemble of overdetermined social relations and cultural realities. This point is worth mentioning because one of the dangers of professionalism is its tendency to generalize the conditions of its own work into causal factors that determine success and failure in class society. On the one hand, the relative autonomy of professional work—what professionals experience daily as a series of individual decisions and responsibilities—can lead them to cast success and failure as a matter of volition and individual effort. On the other hand, professionals, especially in education, often make the forms of literacy they have mastered into causal factors that explain the fate of individuals and social formations.

Rose comes close to this occupational hazard of professionalism when he claims that his work with veterans made him realize that "education has the power to equalize things" (137). One might justifiably worry that Rose has slipped into the peculiarly American view of education as a social panacea—the great American literacy myth that the ability to read and write determines the outcome of people's lives. At least according to revisionist currents in literacy studies, this might well appear to be exactly what Rose has done.

From Lévi Strauss in *Tristes Tropiques* to J. Elspeth Stuckey's recent and provocatively titled *The Violence of Literacy*, revisionist critics have held that literacy is not primarily a means of intellectual development and upward mobility. Instead, as Lévi Strauss says, the "only phenomenon with which writing has always been concomitant is the creation of cities and empires, that is the integration of large numbers of individuals into a political system, and their grading into castes or classes" (337). Stuckey is even more direct when she says that "literacy is a system of oppression that works against entire societies as well as against certain groups within given populations and against individual people" (64). From this perspective, to speak of the transformative powers of literacy for the individual, as Rose does, at best is naive and at worst reproduces a discourse of equal opportunity and predictably unequal results, thereby turning systematic inequality into the result of differences in individual effort and talent, not of social determinations.

Stuckey is right to emphasize the connections between literacy and the way individuals are ranked in an unequal social order. At the same time, however, she seems to argue that there is a necessary correspondence between the cultural practices of literacy and social structures. According to Stuckey, people like Rose fail to see how the "violence of literacy is the violence of the milieu it comes from, promises, recapitulates. It is attached inextricably to the world of food, shelter, and human equality" (94). Literacy, for Stuckey, is determined by—or "attached inextricably" to—the reproduction of class relations in advanced capitalist society. Literacy has a locked-in, guaranteed-in-advance class character.

In contrast, Rose avoids the mechanical determinism in Stuckey's account by offering a sense of how literacy is articulated in variable and sometimes unpredictable ways to the social formation. In *Lives on the Boundary*, we do see the violence of literacy Stuckey describes. Rose's profile of the adult learner Millie and her struggle with a multiple-choice reading comprehension test demonstrates how schooled literacy disconnects underprepared students from their practical knowledge of the world and leads educators thereby to label them as cognitively deficient (216-20). Literacy does indeed function, as Rose shows, as an instrument to pathologize subjects. But, for Rose, literacy can also function in a variety of other ways that evade the surveillance of a class-based educational apparatus. "Consider the sources of literacy," Rose says, "among the children of El Monte: shopkeeper's signs, song lyrics, auto manuals, the conventions of the Western, family stories and tales, and more" (236). What Rose sees here is how literacy is not only a tool of a class-based ranking system but also a cultural resource embedded in and persistently available through the "pop cultural flotsam" that pervades the American landscape—"television and *People* magazine," "the Bible and . . . American media illusion" (237). For Rose, literacy is a matter not simply of the limits of an oppressive social order. It is also a quite concrete pressure and sensuous activity that surrounds all Americans and can be tapped for the purposes of human development and liberation. Whether that happens or not, I have tried to suggest throughout this essay, depends not on a fixed or necessary correspondence between literate practices and the social formation but rather on how individuals and groups articulate literate practices to institutions and subjectivities.

In this regard, Rose's sense of how "education has the power to equalize things" can be useful precisely to the extent it is detached from its usual political meaning of giving everyone an equal chance (when unequal class-based outcomes can be predicted in advance) and rearticulated as a political pressure to change the standards and practices that are used to evaluate and rank students in the first place. Investing education with "the power to equalize things" can avoid being simply another version of the literacy myth to the extent that it articulates redefined standards and practices of literacy that are capable of promoting a more equal social order. Rose's account of the popular and everyday sources of literacy begins imagining such a redefinition and thereby contests not only the traditional view of what makes a person literate but also the current neoconservative monopoly of the public discourse on educational standards. What Rose suggests is that it is not enough just to change or expand our sense of literacy to include non-canonical and unauthorized forms of writing—and then continue to evaluate and rank students in the same old ways. Rose also wants to appropriate the "literacy crisis" from the Reagan/Bush camp, to rearticulate it as a matter not of whether standards are high enough but rather of how standards can be reconceived to serve popular aspirations and democratic goals.

Lives on the Boundary takes a lot of risks. To recount his life, Rose turns to the familiar coming of age narrative that has historically and culturally been encoded with the entrepreneurial values of individual initiative, professional maturity, and personal success. Rather than presenting a critical analysis to demystify the genre (as radical theorists typically do), Rose has sought to rearticulate the narrative from the inside—to disconnect its cultural meanings and political valence from its usual ideological function of reproducing capitalist social relations and instead to join together the narrativity of his own life to the ongoing struggle for democracy and social justice. In this regard, Rose's use of such a popular genre as autobiography not only allows him to speak to the public as well as to specialists; it also allows him, strategically, to locate *Lives on the Boundary* in the current cultural wars of position to secure popular consent and social allegiance. In *Lives on the Boundary*, Rose has chosen to speak in the idiom of what Gramsci calls the "national-popular," the constellation of common sense, ideological elements, and everyday practices that shape the subjectivities of civil society. What Rose thereby seems to suggest is that the task of radical democracy is not just to speak as critics against the master narratives of American culture but to speak as rhetors through them—to rearticulate the social and ideological force of the American *mythos* in the name, the voices, and the interests of the many.

Works Cited

Ball, Carolyn C. "The Politics of Citation." CCCC Convention. Cincinnati, 19 Mar. 1992.

Bartholomae, David. "Inventing the University." *When A Writer Can't Write: Research on Writer's Block and Other Writing Process Problems.* Ed. Mike Rose. New York: Guilford, 1985. 134-65.

Berlin, James A. "Rhetoric and Ideology in the Writing Class." *College English* 50 (1988): 477-94.

Elbow, Peter. "A Method for Teaching Writing." *College English* 30 (1968): 115-25.

Engels, Friedrich. Letter to J. Bloch, 1890. *Marx and Engels: Selected Correspondence*. New York: International, 1935. 476.

Faigley, Lester. "Competing Theories of Process: A Critique and a Proposal." *College English* 48 (1986): 527-42.

Hall, Stuart. "On Postmodernism and Articulation: An Interview with Stuart Hall." Ed. Lawrence Grossberg. *Journal of Communication Inquiry* 10.2 (1986): 45-60.

Jones, Leroi (Amiri Baraka). "Expressive Language." *Home*. New York: William Morrow, 1966. 166-72.

Kail, Harvey. "Narratives of Knowledge: Story and Pedagogy in Four Composition Texts." *Rhetoric Review* 6 (1988): 179-89.

Lévi Strauss, Claude. *Tristes Tropiques*. Trans. John and Doreen Weightman. New York: Pocket Books, 1977.

Lukács, Georg. *The Theory of the Novel*. Trans. Anya Bostock. Cambridge: MIT P, 1971.

Macpherson, C.B. *The Political Theory of Possessive Individualism*. New York: Oxford UP, 1962.

Marx, Karl, and Friedrich Engels. *The German Ideology*. New York: International, 1970.

McQuade, Donald. "Living In—and On—the Margins." *College Composition and Communication* 43 (1992): 11-22.

Miller, Susan. *Rescuing the Subject: A Critical Introduction to Rhetoric and the Writer*. Carbondale: Southern Illinois UP, 1989.

North, Stephen. *The Making of Knowledge in Composition: Portrait of an Emerging Field*. Upper Montclair, NJ: Boynton, 1987.

Rose, Mike. *Lives on the Boundary*. New York: Penguin, 1990.

Ross, Kristin. *The Emergence of Social Space: Rimbaud and the Paris Commune*. Minneapolis: U of Minnesota P, 1988.

Sartre, Jean-Paul. *What Is Literature?* Trans. Bernard Frechtman. New York: Harper, 1965.

Sommers, Nancy. "Between the Drafts." *College Composition and Communication* 43 (1992): 23-31.

Stuckey, J. Elspeth. *The Violence of Literacy.* Portsmouth, NH: Boynton, 1991.

Tompkins, Jane. "Fighting Words: Unlearning to Write the Critical Essay." *Georgia Review* 42 (1988): 585-90.

Williams, Raymond. *Marxism and Literature.* New York: Oxford UP, 1977.

Meditations upon Hypertext: A Rhetorethics for Cyborgs

Pamela K. Gilbert

> And behind all these questions, we would hear hardly anything but the stirring of an indifference: "What difference does it make who is speaking?"
>
> Michel Foucault

> Insofar as evaluating does occur . . . it is usually helped by knowing where the author is coming from. What the fallacies of relevance reject, I value.
>
> Joyce Trebilcot

The rhetoric surrounding electronic text resounds with terms like "freedom" and "democracy."[1] Promising to narrow the gap between reader and writer, universalize information access, and dethrone authoritarian hierarchy in favor of collaborative networking, electronic text ought to sound like the postmodern feminist's dream come true.

Electronic text has the potential to do all its proponents promise, and more. What it actually is or will be doing immediately may be a quite different story. Hypertext is a technology.[2] The liberatory potential of such technology is only actualized to the extent that the human user is able to do so. Our ability to actualize that potential is limited by the lack of an adequate theory of hypertext reading which accounts for ethical and political issues of identity or subjectivity. I would then like to identify some examples of this problem and speculate on some responses; specifically, I would like to consider what sort of reader and/or reading practices hypertext requires.

Critics have pointed to hypertext as the actualization of postmodern theoretical ideals. Antihierarchical by nature, according to these critics, hypertext explodes conventional notions of closure and textual boundaries and radically disperses author-ity, extending it to the reader in the very act of reading. It seems almost as though theory has not only anticipated hypertext, but demanded it. However, as Landow and Delany point out, "hypertext creates an almost embarrassingly literal reification or actualization" of theoretical fantasies (10). Those who deal with a hermeneutics of specificity, in particular, may find the dispersal of the author problematic.

For good or ill, gender and ethnicity specialists have often worked from assumptions about subject positioning and intentionality linked to author identity. Foucault defines the author-function as a temporal and idiosyncratic set of boundaries which serve to limit the freeplay of the text in a particular corpus. The author function has historically, particularly in gender and ethnicity studies, played itself out as *ethos*. In hypermedia, these assumptions are simply not workable. Even if an assumed (performative) subject position is identified by a networker, we face the question of performative competence, motive, and so forth, which refer us back to the issue of identity.

Who's Online?

Identity politics enter a new phase of complexity on the network. As things now stand, users work within a politics of performativity, rather than essences, although some may choose to "perform" a particular "essential" role, e.g., I might self-consciously position myself as a white U.S. American woman. Although most netters use their own names and legal identities, many choose "handles," and some netters have several such identities. I know women who use gender-neutral or masculine-sounding handles on the Net for a variety of reasons. (The one most usually given is that one gets more respect that way.) A colleague of mine in sociology used an electronic bulletin board to extend class discussion in a class concerned with race and ethnicity in which the participants were racially mixed. She reported that participants, often choosing to be anonymous, were able to discuss issues much more freely—not simply because their names weren't known, but because their racial/ethnic identity could be acknowledged or ignored (or perhaps even disavowed) post by post (Schleiter). I have found that in private electronic conversations, ethos is clearly important to many netters, who will, in a first communication, often baldly ask their interlocutor to identify sex, age, ethnicity, etc. On an academic list, one listmember responded to a discussion of whether e-messages should be more formal and carefully edited by affirming the pleasures of "reading between the lines" and "seeing a personality profile" emerge from a history of several postings.[3] Assessment of ethos also often drives responses to bulletin boards and lists (does a post represent a legitimately held, if extreme, opinion, or merely flame-bait?). Often a netter's handle, or history of previous postings (which constitute a "body of work" within which an author function is perceived) will provide the basis for the decision—that is, for an assessment of the ethos of the post.

A longstanding and reasonably graceful means of eliding these questions is to "shift grounds" from individual to cultural identity. As many critics of hypertext have noted, Bakhtin's "polyphony" gives us a way to talk about the many-voicedness of hypermedia. Again, however, we are returned to a similar quandary. When Bakhtin speaks of Dostoevski as polyphonic, we are still working through Dostoevski as the organizing identity.[4] We know what culture is being represented. The Net has no such narrowly defined identity, and what it does have is changing daily. *Currently,* however, we can make some general statements about Net culture.

Net culture is global, transcending national boundaries. However, Net culture does not currently transcend class boundaries evenly. That means that, although theoretically international, the Net is now overwhelmingly first-world, white, and culturally or economically elite. It is also technologically adept, which in combination with the above descriptors adds the further current descriptor, male. Plans under debate to make the internet a pay-per-message service would eliminate most academics, students and working class netters, or at least substantially reduce the volume of their networking (especially for non-subsidized hypertext productions), reducing Net culture to its other major constituency; business people. In short, although the potential for democratic information creation and access across all boundaries exists in the technology, just as it did in early print culture, it is presently only potential, just as it was in early print culture. As Landow pointed out in 1992, "[D]ividing the world into the informationally rich and informationally impoverished . . . would produce a kind of techno-feudalism. . . . Now is the time to protect ourselves from such a future" (*Hypertext* 199). Unfortunately, although still fluid enough to change, this is essentially the structure we now have.

As a technology is being developed, the groundwork for its uses, its representation to and within a culture, and its politics are conceptualized with it and become part of it. As Barthes, Derrida and many others have pointed out, the subversive potential of print culture has always been enormous. As Showalter, Gallagher, McDowell and many others have also pointed out, that potential took a long time to even begin to be actuated because of assumptions built into the production and dissemination of print culture that reinforced the hierarchical organization of the general culture.

"Space—The Final Frontier"

The rhetoric surrounding the Net, the Web and hypertext is fascinating, consisting (as does any complex discourse) of many base metaphors. Many of these metaphors are collaborative and anti-hierarchical (e.g. networking, the Web). However, given the culture of the Net, sketched out in the broadest possible strokes above, one very dominant metaphor deserves particular attention: the metaphor of movement through space. Net-discourse is riddled with it: the information superhighway takes us through cyberspace; we used to go into gopherspace to find out the best site to telnet to; now we walk (or crawl) the Web, etc. Hypertext is organized in space rather than time—instead of a linear narrative, we shift planes, jump into other areas, go through a window into another screen. Instead of "then X event happened," we have "then [the reader] went to X location in the Web." Often, the rhetoric of netting reminds one of colonial narrative—stories of exploration, expansion, acquisition and cooptation. Coover describes the multiple choices of hypertext in terms reminiscent of early twentieth century imperialism—"the allure of the blank spaces of these fabulous networks, these green-limned gardens of multiply forking paths" (qtd. in Landow, *Hypertext* 105).[5] Bolter has written persuasively and in detail about the spatialization of electronic textuality, arguing that "in place of hierarchy, we have a writing that is . . . 'topographic.'" And Landow conceives the problem of composing hypertext to be largely an issue of providing (imposing?) spatial orientation for (on?) the reader: "Designers . . . confront two related problems, the first of which is how to indicate the destination of links, and the second, how to welcome the user on arrival to that destination" (*Hypertext* 25, 188-89). When those who decide what that seductive space is to be filled with—what information will be "mapped" there and how—are the global elite, the politics of inclusion become highly charged. As Landow points out, in a medium in which many texts are easily available, a text that is not on the Web falls even farther into the margin and out of sight (188-89). Further, the need to organize information by lexias, and the desire to present them in a form which makes sense in a screen-by-screen format inevitably shapes the ways in which information is presented according to the biases of the "authors." Even if the dissenting voices of Others link to existing lexias, their inclusions are shaped by the texts that prompt them. This, of course, is true of any medium, but it may be less obvious in a medium that has pretensions of all-inclusiveness and polyphony. The rhetoric of democracy and access often seems to be more about the future inclusion of Others in a preexisting space already mapped than about the inclusion of those Others in a process of creation.

The spatial metaphor is pernicious. Ulmer quotes Hinton and Anderson, perhaps to raise exactly this point: "The connectionist model, however, offers a completely different conception, in which information is not stored anywhere in particular. Rather it is stored everywhere. Information is better thought of as 'evoked' than 'found'" (148-49).[6] An interesting question is why the "docuverse" is described spatially in the first place. It may have to do with the Net's problematic blending of public and private—the fact that one may be seated in one's bedroom in a bathtowel having a casual conversation with several hundred people. Perhaps we define it as space simply because of the dichotomy between public and private space; because there is no "room" to understand the experience of the Net in the overdetermined spaces we already inhabit, we must assume it exists "elsewhere."

All That Was Solid Melts into Metaphorical Anachronisms

These issues are, at least in part, issues of transition. Part of the problem is that, inevitably, hypertext pioneers are still thinking in structures codified by print. Hence Landow's emphasis on the reader's "not getting lost" in hyperspace, the notion of the map, the link that "makes sense"—in short, the whole notion of hypertextual coherence. In truly hypertextual reading, one cannot "get lost" because there is no particular place one is going in the first place; there is no destination to "get to" other than the screen(s) in which you are. Harpold recently pointed out that the language of navigation is negative—it implies the possibility of displacement and loss, and that the "accidents" of reading hypertext are part of the "general condition of the hypertext as *text*" ("Contingencies" 127, 137). Moulthrop has questioned the appropriateness of hyperhetorics to date, noting that hypertext rhetoric must be "founded not on coherence and order but on instability and 'chaos,' an understanding of structure not as an imposition from without but as spontaneous development from within" (155). Even here, however, Moulthrop resorts to a model of Pynchonian "paranoia" which creates a totalizing coherence in which all things are linked and in which the reader's task is simply to uncover the hidden significance of the connection. Yet, as Rosello has pointed out, "screeners' fear of disorientation may be a metaphorical anachronism" (139).

Moulthrop does not consistently remain beyond his assumption of a necessary coherence because we are working with the notion of a certain kind of narratee for hypertext. This narratee is a highly skilled reader in conventional print and film forms and assumes that materials which are proximate to each other (either sequenced or linked) have a meaningful relationship. This narratee fills those gaps which Bolter found in the links, almost by default. This narratee expects an overall unified meaning in all materials which such proximity, and will seek a closure that is structural, if not narrative.

None of these assumptions will work in the docuverse envisioned for hypertext. Links can be extended almost indefinitely. There will be no closure other than that created by the reader's decision to stop interacting with the text—which will mean the demise of formal argument as we know it, since that is driven by closure. Suasive rhetoric in general may go the way of recent political campaigning—into the sound bite or single screen—since the control of the extended structure and sequence of the reader/audience's exposure to data on which complex suasive texts or performances have traditionally depended will not be available to the author. It will also not be necessary to invest links with meaning, unless the reader is motivated to. It will be just as valid to interpret lexias discontinuously as to perceive them as coherent. Another possibility is that "real" authorship will be defined as the creativity of the implied meaning in links between divergent texts authored by others, and that the links themselves are what will be "read" with most aesthetic interest while the linked documents will be subordinated to the linkage structure. As Ulmer points out, hypertext structures meaning like collage—conductively rather than in- or deductively, like exposition (160-61).

Who *Else* is Online

In any case, given the historical differences between women's and men's relationship to space, particularly public space, the metaphors of exploration (historically linked to domination) should give us pause. As Mireille Rosello rather indignantly responds to Bolter's notion of writing as the exploitation of space, "To exploit indeed," agreeing with Ulmer's critique of hypertext metaphors inappropriately redolent of colonization—to which we might add a reference to the gendered associations of that "virgin territory" (129).

Given the historical tendency of collective nouns like "culture" to elide and suppress women's and minorities' voices while seeming to "speak for them," critical positions built on decades of painstaking retrievals of individual voices must now include strategies for approaching the much heralded "dispersal" of textual and authorial boundaries and identities. Although hypertext allows a reader to move from one "voice" to another with ease, it is also possible that a reader's sense of distinctions between those voices may be blurred, or at least subordinated to the form which dominates the reader's encounter with those voices. Landow argues that although "the capacity of hypertext to initiate the novice into a disciplinary culture suggests that this new medium has an almost totalitarian capacity to model encounters with texts, . . . the intrinsically antihierarchical nature of hypertext counteracts such a danger," since the reader controls the path s/he takes (Landow and Delany 23). I find this unconvincing. Harpold observes that the reader comes to experience the links as relatively seamless (like the suturing of a well-edited film): "Narrative suture is what shores up the gaps in hypertextual discourse; it's what makes credible the link's function as a marker of connection and integration, rather than one of division and fragmentation." As Harpold goes on to argue, however, describing the links as a kind of knotting, "if you take apart a knot, there is nothing inside it" ("Threnody" 177). I would suggest that the links function much as Iser's gaps do: they invite the reader to invest them with meaning. In so doing, however, they create a false continuity between documents that, in their original contexts, might work from radically different epistemological or political stances. Experience tells us whose voices tend to be coopted by powerful narrative structures.

Writings on hypertext so far have tended to collapse the political issues of representation into the fairly simplistic one of canon-formation. Although this is certainly important, it fails to directly address issues of readership; that is, it is not only what is offered to the reader, but how it is offered.[7] It is also often argued that as the userbase grows, elitist interpretation will self-correct—that is, that as more "marginal" voices are added to the Net, elitist, racist and sexist representation and interpretation will not go unchallenged. However, as theorists like Ngugi wa Thiong'o and Patrocinio Schweickart point out, there is a colonization of the mind far more subtle and potent than that of the bookshelf—although it can certainly include the bookshelf—or CD Rom. As Schweickart argues, the problem is not merely that women's literature is not read, but that women are taught to become "good" readers by reading like males—according to male standards and adopting male worldviews. Wa Thiong'o makes a similar point regarding the enculturating/colonizing effects of colonial and postcolonial education on the colonized subject.[8] Certainly the work of Belenky or of Robin Lakoff would tend to indicate that there are strongly marked gender differences in Western culture in the ways in which women and men respond to verbal aggression, in their willingness to challenge others' perceptions and in their assessments of the potential value of their own ideas and responses. Hypertext may provide a medium for challenge of these enculturated differences—in the relative "privacy" of electronic conversation, a woman (or other minority) may feel less intimidated. Certainly a computer will not engage in the unconscious gender-selective reinforcement that we know teachers and other caretakers fall into, which reinforce children's (and adults') differential assessments of the relative merits of their contributions to discussion. However, to assume that hypermedia will automatically empower marginalized speakers/writers is dangerously utopian. Hypertext may also, in its "almost totalitarian capacity to model encounters with the text," simply be an extraordinarily efficient tool to immasculate and colonize the marginal subject.[9]

Perhaps the most basic example of critical blindness is its disinclination to deal with the materiality of hypertext and its supporting hardware. Nowhere in the celebration of hypertext's polylogic inclusiveness is the acknowledgement of the muteness encoded into the electronic component's very existence—that of the overwhelmingly "Third World" female work force who produces it, working under conditions few of the people who actually use computers would be willing to accept.[10] The refusal to address the material conditions of electronic and therefore hypertextual production as integral to any attempt to theorize the nature of hypertext is in some ways analogous to the suppression of the body in Western thought—it dooms the project to a partiality which is tantamount at least to a kind of naivete and at worst to a kind of totalitarianism.

Wreading

Thus, hypertext's "inclusiveness" really refers to an elite group. Within this group remains an issue of hierarchy emerging from the subject positions of the user in the larger social context, of which the Net is a part. And within that hierarchy remains the gap—narrowing fast—between author and reader. It is precisely the issue of the reader's control which I would like to address. While singing the praises of a mode of reading which liberates and empowers the reader, dispersing the author, most hyperhetorics have focused (paradoxically enough) on the author's control over the text and obligation to the reader as comparatively helpless—easily "lost" and frustrated. (This may result in part from the focus on pedagogic uses for hypertexts.) However, if we really believe that the reader is given equal authority in the brave new docuverse—both as re-creator/reader and as creator/author—in short, if we really see the collapse of the distinctions between author and reader, then the rhetoric of hypertext must call for an intensely self-reflective reader/writer who is always meta-reading the self as s/he "reads" the hypertext, because the only ethos s/he can reliably read there will be her/his own.[11] In short, the reader, in all ignorance of the ethos of the multiple authorship of Net culture, must take sole responsibility for critical distance from the information offered there, for the appropriateness of paths chosen, and for the creation of new paths to reflect her/his own subjectivities. For the user to produce coherence in her/his re/creation (no longer separable terms), s/he will have to maintain, for the duration of one interfacing, meta-awareness of a coherent subjectivity which s/he uses to organize the experience of the text. Author-ity devolves upon the user, and with it comes the responsibility to know the self that is reading, its goals and values—and to perform it consistently (35).[12] Secondly, s/he must assume that s/he is moving not through space or across a unified topography of text, but between and through different voices, which each requires recognition. Thus, we are talking about an ethics which, since the reader and writer have lost distinction, is also a rhetoric—a rhetorethics of hypertext.

It is precisely this rhetorethics that reading theory and writing theory—that had been converging even without hypertext—have logically demanded, just as postructuralism logically demanded hypertext without knowing it existed. A readerly text leads us back to Iser, Fish et al., and gender/ethnicity/colonialism theories lead us inevitably to the politics—and ethics—of subjectivity.[13]

This reader must, as a starting point, be highly literate—electronically literate, that is. This reader must be as competent in the creation of hypertext as in its recreation, or we see no true phenomenological change, only an expanded version of print reading; after all, the reader who is only free to follow paths created by others, regardless of how multiple those choices are, still has little ultimate author-ity over the text, except as s/he recreates it. Even a resisting reader does not have the authority of the author; a peace protester may "reread" the law, but that will not provide the protester with the status of the legislator or even judge—a point that becomes painfully obvious at sentencing hearings.

The Political Cyborg

The notion of a rhetorethics of hypertext can hardly be discussed without reference to Haraway's foundational "Manifesto"—"an argument for *pleasure* in the confusion of boundaries and *responsibility* in their construction" (174). It is surprising that the early key printed works on hypertext and literary theory (e.g. Landow in 1991 and 1992, or Bolter in 1991) do not address Haraway—or, indeed, feminist theory generally. In fact, these printed works deal almost entirely with issues of structure, reducing political components to issues of canon formation. The political uses of deconstructive theory (as exemplified by Barbara Johnson, for example) are ignored; in fact, Bolter suggests that hypertext ends the deconstructive project: "An electronic text already comes to us in pieces, as a tentative, fluid collection of words: why seek to deconstruct it further?" (165). Bolter's argument in this strange section of his book, the (il)logic of which is not replicated elsewhere in his fine analysis, is basically that since hypertext does not "take itself seriously," the need for a rigorously critical, subversive reading disappears. Haraway's essay (originally published in 1985) is the answer which anticipates Bolter's question—as subsequent theorists such as Turkle, Rosenberg and Stone have recognized. Her "cyborg"—which easily fits as a definition of the ideal hypertext naratee envisioned by Landow, Bolter, Moulthrop, and, insightfully, Ulmer—"is resolutely committed to partiality, irony, intimacy and perversity. . . . No longer structured by the polarity of public and private, the cyborg defines a technological polis. . . . Nature and culture are reworked; the one can no longer be the resource for appropriation by the other. [So much for Coover's "green limned paths."] The relationships for forming wholes from parts, including those of polarity and hierarchical domination, are at issue in the cyborg world" (Haraway, 175). Haraway's thumbnail sketch of the "informatics of domination" is too important to be summarized here (better to link the whole article). Haraway argues that the cyborg, lacking the Edenic origin-narrative, is not crippled by a totalitarian utopian vision.[14] I would argue that the cartological musings of those who would turn hyperspace into a landscape are precisely efforts to create an Edenic "garden" within which reading moves away from linear narratives of loss, mortality and castration toward an oceanic (and on to navigational tropes) polymorphous perversity—from the father to the mother, so to speak.[15] (Although Harpold argues persuasively that links within hypertext act as fetishes, providing an acceptable simulation in place of the castrated phallus, within a cyborgian model of interaction, simulation may be more potent than reality ["Contingencies" 134].) The trouble here is that the pleasureable confusion of boundaries here indicated has no "responsibility"; it regresses to the totalizing solipsism of the infant.

The cyborg reader must resist not only the traditionally utopian impulse being mapped on to hyperspace, but also the utopian impulse of a cynicism that does not admit its vulnerability. As Flynn notes, critical reading takes place when one is neither wholly dominating the text nor dominated by the text, but at that liminal point between absolute credulity and unthinking rejection. The oscillation that hypertext creates between the user's awarenesses of medium and message has been cited as a way to maintain a qualified distance from the text. But one might as well say that the act of turning pages creates such an oscillation, reminding the reader that s/he is holding a book. As a reader grows adept with the technology, turning pages and linking both take place at a secondary level of consciousness—in the same way that film cuts no longer require the literate viewer to consciously become aware of the transition in scene. Exposed to the ultimate seductiveness of a hypertextual docuverse which does not (supposedly) take itself seriously, the cyborg reader must take the text very seriously indeed. Whether in the currently elitist, masculinist culture of the Net or in some future vision of universal access and document linkage, the material reality of the Net will still reflect the greater economic and political reality—and in a total "docuverse" scenario, we can expect the informatics of domination—governmental and market-based—to permeate the hypertextual "space" to the same extent as and even more subtly than it does television.

Multiplicity and Responsibility

Will the kinetic, polyphonal structure of hypertext allow the nostalgia for unity to be mapped into its substance? More to the point, will the cyborg reader shaped by hypertextual practices resist the seductions of an ersatz coherence? Recent work on the psychology of narrative suggests s/he just might. The notion of a split self is, of course, fundamental to Western philosophy. The notion that the split might be between different subselves—in a sense, different *people*—has been around at least since the Freudian concepts of introjection and imagoes. Recent work, however, suggests that people are becoming more comfortable with the notion of being comprised of, not merely different aspects of the same person, but different people. The unitary notion of the self, in this schema, is not that of an ego, or dominant personality, but that of a *function*—a function of coordination and awareness. The difference between a "normal" person and a person with multiple personality disorder, then, is this coordinating function—the healthy person is comprised of a continuous polylogue, while the ill person suffers from a kind of repressive serial monology (Hermans and Kempen 120, and *passim*). These selves are both internalized from the "outside" social world of voices and narratives, both individual and collective, and synthesized "within." I'm placing these terms in quotes because the implications of the psychology of narrative, like those of hypertext, abolish the meaning of the distinction between public and private, social and individual: "There is no rigid boundary between self and not-self. On the contrary, the self/world boundary is highly permeable" (Hermans and Kempen 119).[16] Sherry Turkle and Allucquere Stone both examine the concept of identity in specific relationship to technoculture, concluding that netlife leads to an increasing sense of multiplicity. Turkle notes that the Internet has become "a significant social laboratory for experimenting with the constructions . . . of self that characterize postmodern life. . . . Are we watching the slow emergence of a new, more multiple style of thinking about the mind?" (180). Stone suggests that, "in contrast to the relentlessly monistic articulations of physical and virtual space that law and science favor [based on the identification of the unitary self with the material body], let us juxtapose the mode of the technosocial, of reinvention and encounter in a technological space viewed as itself a social and physical environment, as a kind of nature . . . [which] evokes unruly multiplicity as an integral part of social identity" (42).

While narrative psychology has been working toward a view of the self as multiple, feminist moral philosophers have been privileging narrative to move in the opposite direction—toward a notion of the self as unified and centered and an ethics that depends on care-respect for persons as subjects of I-Thou relationships. Margaret Urban Walker argues, "we don't and can't identify people's emotions, intentions and other mental states with momentary . . . phenomena. Instead we identify these features of people by attending to how their beliefs, feelings, modes of expression, circumstances and more, arranged in characteristic ways and often spread out in time, configure into a recognizable kind of story. Practically this means that [we are required to pay] acute attention to the minute and specific, to history and incident, in grasping cases in a morally adequate way" (167).

The fundamental question remains: how can a rhetorethics of hypertext be created which addresses both the "responsibility in the construction" of boundaries that Haraway calls for and the "pleasure" in their confusion and addresses the issues of identity and ethos that a responsible politics requires, which services both a multiplicity of selves and protects the distinctions between selves and others? And how can we engage a feminist ethics of care-respect if that requires the notion of a heavily contextualized encounter with a unified self which is identical with an identifiable subject position? In a hypertextual encounter with other voices, it is not possible or even desirable to read each utterance as part of an ongoing and highly centralized narrative of self. I would also argue that the notion of the central and centered self is disempowering in that it implies the imposition of a fairly static identity as a moral good.[17] However, although it is not always possible to "know" the other voices in a hypertext in the richly contextualized, long term fashion prescribed by the care-respect model, it is possible to know one's own selves in that way—that is, to narrate the selves in such a way as to acknowledge one's needs and to respond to the other voices in the hypertext—as a reader/writer—in a way that is consistent with one's own narratives and which maintains them in a caring manner. It is also ethically incumbent upon the reader/writer to make explicit those narratives as the meta- and context of any reading/writing. This will not make hypertext more inclusive, but it may make it less totalitarian and more humane. In short, the ethics of care, in the context of a communications technology which discourages the user from making judgments about texts based on an "ethos" which they can read into (or map onto) the text requires that one, insofar as it is possible, do that metatextual work oneself as part of "caring for" the other.[18] Self-knowledge and self-expression become not merely a right but a responsibility, because only when we know who we are can we understand that we cannot speak for or as others. Only then can we understand what is lost in the enforced mutenesses that allows some of us to be heard.

Notes

1. For examples, see Landow *Hypertext* (although in 1994 he does modify this position) and Bolter (7). For extended critiques of these claims, see Rosenberg and also Ess.

2. I am using the term *hypertext* all-inclusively here. First, let me define hypertext as the technology exists. Hypertext programs allow the writer to create "webbed" documents. The best example is the Web itself—a large hypertext. However, there are also smaller hypertexts which may be loaded onto the Web, or stored separately. In a text devoted to Shelley, the reader might, for example, begin on a screen that contains a paragraph from a novel by Shelley.

From there, the user could go to the next paragraph in Shelley, or to a screen containing biographical information on Shelley, or to information on the literary period of publication, or to a critique of the novel, or literally to any other text the author wishes to place on the Web. The reader can switch screens, or have several on view at once, or see an overview of what links (what other texts are connected) are available, or so forth. Additionally, with a multimedia package, it is possible to add sounds, graphics, scanned-in photos or videoclips. Theodore Holm Nelson has envisioned an all encompassing "docuverse" in which any and every text will be online and multiply linked, and the links will multiply exponentially, since every reader is potentially also an author—that is, readers can create new links, write their own text or enter someone else's and link that. As has been pointed out, e-mail lists and electronic bulletin boards function as a primitive hypertext now, forming a vast series of linked documents. (Hypertext fictions, as they exist now, have tended to be very author-controlled, and thus have yet to fully realize the possibilities inherent in the technology). Thus, when I speak of hypertext in this essay, I mean not only a specific hypertext like the In Memoriam Web, but the larger hypertextual universe of the Net and Web, and the forseeable docuversal future.

3. In more detail, here is the relevant part of the post: "I for one would be sorry if people kept their views to themselves or watched every word. Consider, also, some of the heuristic pleasure you would deprive us of: reading between the lines, the sense of some messages being exchanged behind other messages, the personality profiles that begin to emerge . . ." Clearly, this poster is strongly interested in issue of ethos—as a reader. As a writer, however, the poster refuses her/his reader those "pleasures" discussed above by refusing to sign—"no signature except the electronic address [which the poster probably cannot remove anyway], since I hope I speak for many" (June 26, 1994, [9:13:26] on VICTORIA@IUBVM.UCS.INDIANA.EDU).

4. See Bakhtin *Problems*. For a detailed discussion of the dia- and polylogism of the novel, see Bakhtin, "Discourse."

5. Compare to Marlow's comment in *Heart of Darkness*: "Now when I was a little chap I had a passion for maps. . . . At that time there were many blank spaces on the earth, and when I saw one that looked particularly inviting on a map (but they all look that) I would put my finger on it and say, When I grow up I will go there" (1763). The implications of the uses of landscape have been amply documented by a generation of critics since Baym, and the work done by theorists of colonialism is here of particular interest.

6. I am here making a supposition about Ulmer's motive in linking the following quote with others relating to spatial metaphors—i.e., I'm reading into Ulmer's link/gap.

7. Perhaps one example from Landow will serve as demonstration (*Hypertext* 148). The screen pictured is from a hypertext teaching database on English Literature. The screen shows that the user is reading Sara Suleri, and seeking further information. A graphic dominates the screen; it is a scanned-in photo of

an attractive South Asian woman—head only—in traditional costume, with a large nose ring. Clearly the graphic is meant to intrigue the program's users—the woman is young, beautiful, and exotic-looking, at least from a Western point of view. The title of this graphic—and of the wealth of information the user can access from this screen—is "South Asian Women OV [overview]."

I am working from an illustration in a printed book, and have not examined the database in question. But I would speculate that there is no equivalent screen which totalizes "North American Men" or even "North American White Men" in quite the same way. Depending on what one wanted to emphasize, it might be more appropriate to scan in either the farmer's face in "American Gothic" or a photo of Donald Trump. But if we did use either one, we would hardly worry about American college students mistaking such a representation as "true" or inclusive for the entire set of white American males. That, however, is not true of the "Other." The very fact that Southeast Asian women are "other" to most college-aged Americans demands some sort of representation of them, and simultaneously increases the likelihood that the representation will be accepted as definitive. My purpose here is not to criticize the database—a picture of a Southeast Asian woman in a Western business suit would be just as totalizing and inaccurate—but to point out that readers come with certain assumptions to the text which can at least be moderated by a clear sense of the writer's ethos—that is, it is easier to get "lost" in a sense of information as "fact" if one loses awareness of the specific authorial voice which situates itself in history and culture—in short, a subjectivity. In this scenario, it might be easier for a student to maintain awareness of a professor's subjectivity when s/he sees that fifty-five year old white male with a Texan accent in class than it is when information organized by that professor is simply presented on the screen in the form of decontextualized and recontextualized documents. In this instance, the dispersal of the author refers not to the author's authority, but to her/his responsibility—s/he can no longer be easily called to account.

8. I am using Schweickart and wa Thiong'o simply because they come to mind as particularly lucid and compelling discussions of the colonization of marginal subjectivity. However, there are many other theorists who have developed these same observations—the classic, of course, being Frantz Fanon's *Black Skin, White Masks*.

9. "Immasculate" is Schweickart's term for the process by which women have historically been taught to read as male or masculine subjects.

10. See Ong and also Fuentes and Ehrenreich. Women (and men) in "First World" countries also produce microelectronic components, often in the "homework" model, which often creates special problems in exploitation since homeworkers are isolated and more than usually economically dependent. It is important to note, however, that this issue is not specific to hypertext, but to the entire production of liberal humanist scholarship recently; e.g., this article was composed on a computer manufactured in developing nations and assembled in the U.S.

11. This combined author/reader has been graced with many neologisms, perhaps the most charming of which is "wreader," whose originator is unknown to me.

12. Diana Fuss argues "[W]ays of reading are historically specific and culturally variable, and reading positions are always constructed, assigned or mapped. . . . Readers, like texts, are constructed; they inhabit reading practices rather than create them *ex nihilo*."

13. See Iser; Fish.

14. It is astonishing how often Haraway is misread. William Covino, for example, has just recently read Haraway's cyborg as a "utopian vision" calling for a "giant self, a cosmological individual" (369, 368). Not only does this misread the original, but it takes no account of Haraway's subsequent commentary and refinement of the cyborg idea, which is "resolutely multiple" (hardly a "giant self"); as Haraway notes "the cyborg is from the start a polluted category. . . . It's an offspring of World War II nuclear culture, and there's no possibility of working out that position to imagine yourself in the Garden of Eden or returning to pre-Oedipal bliss. . . . Cyborg writing is resolutely committed to foregrounding the apparatus of its own authority . . . [without] eschewing authority" (Olson 4-5). Covino also makes the peculiar error of arguing that the cyborg's transgresssive properties are limited by the computer codes governing access to cyberspace: "The hyper-conventionality of the cyborg is perhaps too obvious to require an argument . . . governed as she is by a technological language that preceeded her emergence" (370). Covino seems to believe that computer language exists as Presence, preceeding the human beings who have created the language and programmed the software. (God in the machine?) Covino does make the crucial point, however, that Gingrich also wanted to see every subject "wired" and not toward the goal Haraway envisions. As he notes, the poor do not have access to cyberculture and this may mark a kind of transgression in itself—that *not* being wired may be a kind of resistance. The celebration of virtuality at the expense of materiality, of multiplicity in performance versus individual bodies, tends to hide the fact that the figure of the cyborg can be envisioned and used as a disciplinary construct. This is of course a very old science fiction theme.

15. Landow argues that the reliance on tropes of death and loss are endemic to print culture and are more specifically a critical reaction to the exhaustion of print: "Whereas terms like death, vanish, loss and expressions of depletion and impoverishment color critical theory, the vocabulary of freedom, energy and empowerment marks writings on hypertext . . . . Most poststructuralists write from within the twilight of a wished-for coming day; most writers of hypertext write of many of the same things from within the dawn" (*Hypertext* 87).

16. For a discussion of the philosophical discourse underlying the recent direction of narrative psychological research, see Kerby. I would suggest that this development in psychology reflects the general state of transition in a culture whose epistemology is being transformed, in part by evolving commu-

nications technology. Just as we impose the false and regressive trope of space on the Net and insist on coherence in a form which we celebrate for violating our expectations of unity, we become ready to accept the notion of multiple selves—a slippage of subject positions and the mingling of inner and outer, self and world which the cyborg represents—yet rely on the notion of an organizing function to keep those selves together, unified. As those boundaries become more permeable, they become very highly charged—we become obsessed with figuring out where they are and what they exclude precisely because they are so unstable and change so quickly. *We have no experience with not caring about meaning.* Hypertext's promised "freedom" may be freedom from (compulsory) interpretation. Perhaps this is why hypertextual theory comes back to the problem of closure and of coherence, why we read the text of the internet in search of ethos, and why scholarship in general has taken a renewed interest in the body in recent years—the body is the visible sign of the unity of the multiple subject positions that can make up one "person." Perhaps, as the cyborg reader develops, s/he will come to have no epistemological requirement for unity or coherence, little anxiety about personal boundaries, and will not cavil at the imposition of the ethos of any of a multitude of selves upon the text s/he evokes. In the meantime, however, we need to attempt to make the Net both materially horizontal and inclusive (which means resisting any rulings or laws which would reinforce informational elitism) and to avoid encoding an elite hypertextual ethos in a totalizing Edenic narrative.

17. I am here engaging Winnie Tomm's argument. Although I agree fundamentally with her premise that self exists in a tension between connectedness and separation in the context of interlocking circles of community and relatedness, I disagree with her emphasis on the centered self which is internally coherent over time. In a comment which might have been written about netting, but was not, Tomm avers "A theory of ethic must take into account the interconnecting circles of a person's existence. Recognizing self, home and community as interacting networks means acknowledging the interweaving strands of societal and personal rights and responsibilities. Justice and caring derive from the common source of the desire to express one's power. . . . It reflects the more abstract concern to protect the right of self expression in the face of conflicting expressions" (105).

18. Perhaps I will be accused here of a certain naivete in that the tradition of psychology gives us to understand that our urge to know ourselves is always subverted by our own defenses. However, that does not lessen our moral responsibility to act in accordance with our beliefs and values in so far as we are able to know them—here, "acting in accordance with" means also that we must articulate them—if nothing else to expose them to the scrutiny of others who may then choose to interpret our actions as contrary to our stated beliefs/intentions. Another kind of naivete is political—and certainly the call to an individual ethics may seem to elide political solutions. However, the Net does, at this time, by its nature preclude a rule-governed solution to its ethical

problems. And as Nel Noddings points out, although "our own ethicality is not entirely 'up to us'... we are fragile; we depend upon each other even for our own goodness.... [Yet] the duty to enhance the ethical ideal ... invokes a duty to promote skepticism and noninstitutional affiliation. In a deep sense, no institution or nation can be ethical.... Only the individual can be truly called to ethical behavior .... Everything depends, then, on the will to be good, to remain in caring relation to the other" (102).

Works Cited

Bakhtin, Mikhail. "Discourse in the Novel." *The Dialogic Imagination: Four Essays*. Ed. Michael Holquist. Trans. Caryl Emerson and Michael Holquist. Austin: U of Texas P, 1981. 259-422.

—. *Problems of Dostoevski's Poetics*. Trans. Caryl Emerson. Minneapolis: U of Minnesota P, 1984.

Baym, Nina. "Melodramas of Beset Manhood: How Theories of American Fiction Exclude Women Authors." *The New Feminist Criticism: Essays on Women, Literature and Theory*. Ed. Elaine Showalter. New York: Pantheon, 1985.

Belenky, Mary Field, et al. *Women's Ways of Knowing: The Development of Self, Voice, and Mind*. New York: Basic, 1986.

Bolter, Jay David. *Writing Space: The Computer, Hypertext, and the History of Writing*. Hillsdale, N.J.: Erlbaum, 1991.

Conrad, Joseph. *Heart of Darkness. Norton Anthology of British Literature* Vol. II, 6th ed, Ed. M.H. Abrams, et al. New York: Norton, 1993. 1759-1817.

Covino, William. "Grammars of Transgression: Golems, Cyborgs and Mutants." *Rhetoric Review* 14 (1996): 355-73.

Ess, Charles. "The Political Computer: Hypertext, Democracy and Habermas." *Hyper/Text/Theory*. Ed. George P. Landow. Baltimore: Johns Hopkins UP, 1994. 225-67.

Fanon, Frantz. *Black Skin, White Masks*. Trans. Charles Lam Markmann. New York: Grove, 1967.

Fish, Stanley. "Interpreting the Variorum." *Critical Inquiry* 2 (1976): 465-85.

Elizabeth Flynn. "Gender and Reading." *Gender and Reading: Essays, Texts, and Contexts*. Ed. Elizabeth A. Flynn and Patrocinio Schweickart. Baltimore: Johns Hopkins UP, 1986. 267-88.

Foucault, Michel. "What is an Author?" *Textual Strategies: Perspectives in Post-Structuralist Criticism*. Trans. and Ed. Josue Harari. Ithaca: Cornell UP, 1979. 141-60.

Fuentes, Annette and Barbara Ehrenreich. *Women in the Global Factory*. New York: Institute for New Communications; Boston: South End, 1983.

Fuss, Diana. *Essentially Speaking: Feminism, Nature and Difference*. New York: Routledge, 1989.

Gallagher, Catherine. *Nobody's Story: The Vanishing Acts of Women Writers in the Marketplace 1670-1820*. Berkeley: U of California P, 1994.

Haraway, Donna. "A Manifesto for Cyborgs." *Coming to Terms: Feminism, Theory, Politics*. Ed. Elizabeth Weed. New York: Routledge, 1989. 173-204.

Harpold, Terence. "The Contingencies of the Hypertext Link." *Writing on the Edge* 2 (1991): 126-38.

—. "Threnody: Psychoanalytic Digressions on the Subject of Hypertexts." *Hypermedia and Literary Studies*. Ed. George Landow and Paul Delaney. Cambridge, MA: MIT P, 1991. 171-84.

Hermans, Hubert J.M., and Harry J.G. Kempen. *The Dialogical Self: Meaning as Movement*. San Diego: Academic P, 1993.

Iser, Wolfgang. *The Act of Reading: A Theory of Aesthetic Response*. Baltimore: Johns Hopkins UP, 1978.

Johnson, Barbara. *The Critical Difference: Essays in the Contemporary Rhetoric of Reading*. Baltimore: Johns Hopkins UP, 1980.

Kerby, Anthony Paul. *Narrative and the Self*. Bloomington: Indiana UP, 1991.

Lakoff, Robin. *Language and Woman's Place*. New York: Octagon, 1975.

Landow, George P. *Hypertext: The Convergence of Contemporary Critical Theory and Technology*. Baltimore: Johns Hopkins UP, 1992.

—. "What's A Critic to Do?: Critical Theory in the Age of Hypertext." in *Hyper/Text/Theory*. Ed. George P. Landow. Baltimore: Johns Hopkins UP, 1994. 1-50.

Landow, George P., and Paul Delany. *Hypermedia and Literary Studies*. Cambridge, MA.: MIT P, 1991.

McDowell, Deborah. "New Directions for Black Feminist Criticism." *Black American Literature Forum* 14 (1980): 153-59.

Moulthrop, Stuart. "Polymers, Paranoia, and the Rhetoric of Hypertext." *Writing on the Edge* 2.2 (1991): 150-59.

Nelson, Theodore Holm. "Opening Hypertext: A Memoir." *Literacy Online: The Promise (and Peril) of Reading and Writing with Computers*. Ed. Myron C. Tuman. Pittsburgh: U of Pittsburgh P, 1992. 43-59.

Noddings, Nel. *Caring: A Feminine Approach to Ethics and Moral Education*. Los Angeles: U of California P, 1984.

Olson, Gary A. "Writing, Literacy and Technology: Toward a Cyborg Writing." *JAC: A Journal of Composition Theory* 16 (1996): 1-26.

Ong, Aihwa. *Spirits of Resistance and Capitalist Discipline: Factory Women in Malaysia*. Albany: State U of New York P, 1987.

Rosello, Mireille. "The Screener's Maps: Michel de Certeau's 'Wandersmanner' and Paul Auster's Hypertextual Detective." *Hyper/Text/Theory*. Ed. George P. Landow. Baltimore: Johns Hopkins UP, 1994. 121-58.

Rosenberg, Martin E. "Physics and Hypertext: Liberation and Complicity in Art and Pedagogy." in *Hyper/Text/Theory*. Ed. George P. Landow. Baltimore: Johns Hopkins University Press, 1994. 268-98.

Showalter, Elaine. *A Literature of Their Own: British Women Novelists from Bronte to Lessing*. Princeton: Princeton UP, 1977.

Schleiter, Mary Kay. "Using Computer Conferencing to Extend Class Discussion." *Information Technologies, Changing the Way We Learn*. University of Wisconsin, Parkside. 25 March 1994.

Schweickart, Patrocinio. "Reading Ourselves: Toward a feminist Theory of Reading." *Gender and Reading: Essays, Texts, and Contexts*. Eds. Elizabeth A. Flynn and Patrocinio Schweickart. Baltimore: Johns Hopkins UP, 1986. 31-62.

Stone, Allucquere Rosanne. *The War of Desire and Technology at the Close of the Mechanical Age*. Cambridge, MA: MIT P, 1995.

Tomm, Winnie. "Ethics and Self-Knowing: The Satisfaction of Desire." *Explorations in Feminist Ethics: Theory and Practice*. Eds. Eve Browning Cole and Susan Coultrap McQuin. Bloomington: Indiana UP, 1992. 101-10.

Trebilcot, Joyce. "Ethics of Method: Greasing the Machine and Telling Stories." *Feminist Ethics*. Ed. Claudia Card. Lawrence: UP of Kansas, 1991. 45-51.

Turkle, Sherry. *Life on the Screen: Identity in the Age of the Internet*. New York: Simon, 1995.

Ulmer, Gregory. "Grammatology (in the Stacks) of Hypermedia: A Simulation." (with discussion) in *Literacy Online: The Promise (and Peril) of Reading and Writing with Computers*. Ed. Myron C. Tuman. Pittsburgh: U of Pittsburgh P, 1992. 139-66.

wa Thiong'o, Ngugi. *Decolonising the Mind: the Politics of Language in African Culture*. London: J. Currey, 1986.

Walker, Margaret Urban. "Moral Understandings: Alternative 'Epistemology' for a Feminist Ethics." *Explorations in Feminist Ethics: Theory and Practice*. Ed. Eve Browning Cole and Susan Coultrap McQuin. Bloomington: Indiana UP, 1992. 165-75.

Part 4

Special Issues in Composition

Confronting the "Essential" Problem: Reconnecting Feminist Theory and Pedagogy

Joy S. Ritchie

In the current flowering of feminist writing, there is considerable debate about essentialism and constructivism. One consequence of this debate has been to divide feminist theorists and feminist teachers. On one side, feminist theorists assume that feminist pedagogy is "essentialist" because it often seems to be founded on an ahistorical, uncritical celebration of a fixed female position, a stance many theorists find reductive and dangerous. On the other side, feminist teachers often assume that to "do" theory, to explore the linguistic, social, and political construction of women as gendered subjects, is to participate in an esoteric activity (at best) and an activity tainted by reliance on male methodology and philosophy (at worst). Therefore, despite the fundamental feminist assertion that knowledge cannot be separated from the knower, many feminist academicians continue to operate within a binary perspective, placing intellect against emotion, separating reason from experience, and, ultimately, setting theory against practice. As a result, important connections between feminist theory and practice are masked, and we lose sight of our common purposes.

Furthermore, we lose sight of our students. Adrienne Rich observes that "it is easier, especially for academically trained white women, to get an intellectual/political 'fix' on the *idea* of racism than to identify with black female experience: to explore it emotionally as part of our own" ("Disloyal" 281). I believe this split among feminists occurs, in part, because it has also been easier for academically trained feminists to get a "fix" on abstract theories of gender construction than to explore the immediate implications of these theories for the lives of women students. While we have a profusion of feminist theoretical writing and a profusion of writing about feminist teaching and learning, we have little writing that seeks to connect the two or that demonstrates what might be the impact of feminist teaching and feminist theory on the lives of students in our composition and literature classes.

To begin exploring what these connections might be and how feminist teaching and theory might influence students' lives, I became a participant-observer in an undergraduate women's literature class taught by my colleague, Barbara DiBernard, a feminist teacher.[1] I was attempting to understand how students' experience in such a class might differ from their experience in other reading and writing classes, and, also, attempting to reconcile for myself some of the profound and troubling divisions I saw between the positions of feminist teachers and feminist theorists in academia.

Literary education has traditionally been justified by the claim that literature provides a mirror in which readers may examine the human experience and come to understand better their place within it. But women have been absent or invisible in that mirror. Thus, the attempt of women's literature classes has been to provide a new mirror filled with images of women and to help women arrive at a new definition of their human identity, one of presence rather than absence, of power rather than lack. In Barbara's class, I observed women taking part in literary study, in a process of reclaiming women's literature and history. But they were also examining social, political, and personal definitions of themselves as women. In short, they were exploring a central issue of current feminist theory—their own interpretation of gender construction in our culture.

The reality of the feminist classroom, as I observed and participated in it, demonstrates that the split between feminist theory and practice is artificial. In the women's literature class, the explicit agenda of feminist literary theory—to examine the symbolic and social-political structures that construct women as gendered subjects—also became the students' agenda. Although most students would shun the label "feminist" for themselves, the questions they explored in the women's literature class arose from the same basic question that academic feminists—theorists, critics, and teachers—have been exploring for two or three decades. And for these students, pursuing this problem was fraught with as much conflict as it is for feminist teachers and theorists. Carol voiced the feelings of a number of students: "I'm not sure how to absorb this way of thinking about women. I've never faced it before. I don't like all the anger and bitterness in this class. If this is what feminism is about, I'm not sure I want any part of it. It's really bothering me."

As I participated in the course, I was struck by the number of students who experienced conflicts as they read, wrote about, and discussed literature. The women in the course, aged nineteen to fifty, were frustrated and angry for a variety of reasons: at having their old myths challenged, at the contradictions that they began to see in their lives, at other women's denial and passivity, and at their own failures. But the tension that resulted in many class sessions was a version of the feminist community's longstanding debates.

The contradictions and questions that the students explored are inextricably connected to the central questions discussed by feminist theorists today. For both students and their feminist teachers, these questions arise from the problem Simone de Beauvoir articulated over forty years ago:

> If we . . . admit, provisionally, that women do exist, then we must face the question: what is a woman?
>
> . . . If I wish to define myself, I must first of all say: "I am a woman"; on this truth must be based all further discussion. A man never begins by presenting himself as an individual of a certain sex; it goes without saying that he is a man. (xvii)

The problem seems deceptively simple. But as the course progressed, the students became aware that asserting one's identity as a woman necessitates more than a joyous celebration of womanhood. Embedded within de Beauvoir's question are social, economic, political, linguistic, aesthetic, epistemological, and ethical questions. Students confronted the traditions that have positioned them as women and that they had consequently accepted as universal givens not to be questioned. The literature they read led them to acknowledge the immediate contradictions in their own political and social positions as women and to examine the historical consequences of these contradictions for their mothers and foremothers.

Initially, many students articulated a narrow, fixed "essentialist" female identity, but the dialogic nature of the class continually challenged this view by highlighting contradictory images of women. The perspectives of white, black, and Native American women, from the fifteenth century to the present, lesbian women, old and young, divorced and married women, childless women and women with children, poor women and privileged women—all these were articulated in the literature and, equally powerfully, in the voices of students themselves. Thus, the class became a rich source of multiple definitions of women that were continually posited, affirmed, examined, challenged, discarded, and rearticulated. The image of women that emerged in the class was not the singular, fixed, and universal image of the humanist mirror; instead, the course projected varied images in a multidimensional mirror, images that were not infinite duplications but each a variation, contradiction, or transformation of women's identity. As Amy's words suggest, the result was a changed vision of herself and the world, a vision so powerful that the old images were permanently transformed:

> I really had no idea of what to expect from this class. I just needed another class. I thought it would just be another English class, but when I first glanced at the required texts, I about gagged. Before this course I never really thought much about women, their history, their art, or even how my mother or grandma or I lived our lives. It was just not there. The class helped me take on a whole different way of looking at my family, my education, even my relationship with my boyfriend—the different points of view of a lot of people. These stories and poems and books have opened up a whole new way of seeing myself and the world. I won't be able to see it in the old way again.

The process that students experienced as they recognized and reexamined multiple perspectives on women's subjectivity suggests a crucial connection between theory and practice.

I would like to examine this process through the students' experience and view it in relation to the essentialism-constructivism debate in feminism. Using excerpts from students' journals and their comments in class discussions and interviews, I will trace their exploration of the contradictory and conflicting social-sexual identities that the class presented. I will examine their answers to the question "What is a woman?" and point to connections between questions that they wrestled with and fundamental issues that feminist theory examines. Finally, I'll argue that the power of this experience to change *what* students think and *how* they think presents us with insight for revisioning our discipline. The critical activity of examining and articulating women's positions as gendered subjects can serve as a model for education in composition and literature, an alternative to the one-dimensional critical processes that academia often promotes.

The Teacher-Midwife: Teaching from a Feminist Perspective

The first assigned reading was an article on feminist teaching that Barbara had written. Barbara believed that sharing her philosophy of teaching from the outset of the class was consistent with her desire to help them see "teaching as a political act." During the first class session, she talked about why the class was important to her:

> As professors, we may like to think we're off in some ivory tower, but someone is making a decision about what to teach and what to leave out,

> about how we get information. That is a political decision. I realize that my college education was characterized by silences. Women's voices were not a part of the literature I read, and many women, including myself, were silent because we were not comfortable with the combative, hierarchical nature of those classes.

Barbara wanted to create a different kind of atmosphere, allowing students access to women's writing, offering them the historical and social perspective that women's literature allows, and breaking down "the hierarchical views that denigrate the ways in which many women have expressed their experience" (DiBernard 3). She also wanted students to see beyond the view of human experience that mainstream Western European tradition depicts, to understand that our experience in that tradition is not universal. Women's literature, she said, gives us access to different experiences that encompass women from other social classes, age groups, races and ethnic backgrounds, sexual orientations, and ablebodiedness. She wanted students to reexamine their definitions of art by looking at poetry and novels, but also by thinking about women's letters, journals, and quilts as art forms. Furthermore, she wanted students to develop modes of reading and analyzing literature that would allow them to rely on their own experience and to consider multiple perspectives and methods of response. She believed that students who are not encouraged to take themselves seriously as intellectuals, to recognize their own capacity to solve problems, cannot be expected to take responsibility for bringing about change. She summarized her own role as that of teacher-midwife: "one who helps students give birth to their own ideas, to integrate the personal and the academic, and to empower themselves as readers and critics."

The class structure reflected this philosophy. Students wrote a reading-response journal for each week's assigned reading. Barbara explained that daily work is the kind of work women are most in touch with, and that doing daily work also "keeps us in touch with our own perceptions, reactions, and responses and allows us to journey back through the course to see ourselves, our former selves, because we will be different by the end of the semester." During almost every class, students did some sort of writing connected to the reading, and they worked in small groups to share ideas and questions and to bring them to the whole class. They also participated in activities in the university and the wider community and wrote papers on these activities. Barbara asked them to learn one another's names, to listen to one another, to support and encourage one another in their work, and to be patient and tolerant of others' ideas, something that was not always easy given the questions that students began struggling with. At the beginning of the semester, Barbara told me:

> I don't expect everyone to be comfortable. Some students will be upset by some of the texts. Some will be very angry, especially during the first few weeks. But I hope they'll hang on with enough trust to keep coming and reading and listening. I want them to learn information, but I want them to arrive at their own conclusions about literature and, more important, to become confident in themselves as learners and to think about their lives.

The Problem of Essence: What Is a Woman?

This question has set the agenda for feminist theory for twenty years, but it and a constellation of surrounding questions also lie at the heart of the students' experience in the class. Their responses to the question ranged from affirmation, recognition, and celebration to anger, contestation, and revision of their understanding of themselves as women. For feminist teachers and theorists, the pursuit of de Beauvoir's question has raised serious epistemological, philosophical, and political conflicts that parallel those of the women students. Before considering students' responses, I want to outline some of these theoretical questions in order to illuminate better the complexity of the conflicts that they faced.

De Beauvoir's question has pointed feminists toward an examination of the social, economic, and linguistic structures that give meaning to the biological sex differences that have traditionally defined women. As they attempt to analyze these questions, feminist theorists take philosophical perspectives that result in complicated and often indistinctly defined political and theoretical divisions. These divisions often fall under such labels as liberal, radical, cultural, socialist, Anglo-American, French, and poststructuralist feminism.[2] Each of these theoretical strands falls somewhere along a continuum on which gender is defined according to essentialist or constructivist paradigms. In an attempt to define essentialism, Linda Alcoff points out that women have always been seen as "essential"—easily defined, captured, always apprehendable as the object of male definition (258). Thus, as Alcoff notes, from the beginning of the women's movement, women have felt compelled to redefine their history, biology, psychology, literature, and epistemology as separate from the circumscribed definition that the masculine patriarchal tradition imposes. American feminists, in particular, have attempted to end the erasure and powerlessness that characterize women's place in the social order and to affirm women, selfhood, and community. In American academic institutions, women's studies courses have grown out of this tradition and, to the extent that such courses are perceived as subscribing to an essentialist position, they have become theoretically suspect. For as women articulate and celebrate what is intrinsically "female," they risk coming full circle to the very psycho-biological determinism—the "essentialism"—that has circumscribed women for so long. When women make a claim for a unique and powerful female identity, they are left once again in a traditional binary, oppositional position: male versus female, power versus lack.

Central to the problem of gender definition and the essentialist-constructivist issue is the problem of language itself. Working out of a psychoanalytic tradition, French feminists connect women's oppression to the symbolic forms in which they have been represented. Language, arising from the phallic-patriarchal order, has controlled the way that women's biological and social position is defined. Thus, in a sense, women have not had a language for articulating their identities apart from the language of patriarchy, a language that binds them into definitions of self that they cannot escape. Julia Kristeva points out that "as soon as the insurgent . . . speaks, it gets caught up in the discourses allowed by and submitted to the Law" ("From Ithaca" 511). Thus, the methodology and language that women use in the process of defining themselves are grounded in and tainted by the very structures that they are attempting to subvert ("Il n'y a pas" 134-35).

One theoretical solution to this dilemma, posited by radical feminists such as Mary Daly, is to create a new language, a new symbolic order separate from that offered by the male tradition. This new language, they suggest, is necessary to help women rediscover their true female essence—beneath the misdefinitions and perversions that male culture has perpetrated—and to develop a truly female culture. French feminists Hélène Cixous and Luce Irigaray are also linked to this essentialist position, proposing that the symbolic formations in which women have been fixed as "other" be fractured and destructured. Cixous proposes that female energy and imagination be celebrated, and Irigaray proposes that phallocentric categories be displaced through a continual reconnection of the female to the female body. While these positions are essentialist, they also arise from an awareness of the role that language and culture play in constructing women's identity; thus, they force an acknowledgement of "woman" as a political position. In this respect, Cixous and Irigaray are less aligned with essentialist theorists and more aligned with feminist theorists working from Marxist, psychoanalytic, and poststructuralist theories, theorists who hold that the "authentic self"—conceived by Western humanist tradition as existing below a veneer of ideology and cultural socialization—is merely a construct, part of the "apparatus" that the culture uses to maintain the individual in a "subjected" position, inscribed by ideology.

They argue that because human beings are constructed by the social discourse surrounding them, the concept of a special female essence is also a fiction, part of a binary system of discourse—male/female, culture/nature—to be dismantled and deconstructed. Thus, as Kristeva argues, if woman's position is a shifting social construction, then the only effective feminist position is one of negativity: "A woman cannot 'be'; it is something which does not even belong in the order of *being*. It follows that a feminist practice can only be negative, at odds with what already exists, so that we may say, 'That's not it' and 'that's still not it.'" ("Woman" 137). Kristeva rejects discussions of woman's identity and calls for discussions of "woman" as a position within language. She offers women the possibility of what Alcoff describes as "the 'free-play' of gender, of plurality and difference unhampered by predetermined gender identity" (270). But as many feminists argue, these positions do not offer women a clear direction for changing the political and social realities of their lives. The essentialist position leaves women trapped in a separate, idealistic, but ultimately powerless position as "other"; the constructivist position leaves women in an eternally fluid position of indeterminacy or in a position of negativity, constantly rejecting and deconstructing but also risking invisibility and the possibility for action and change.

This theoretical thicket might leave feminists paralyzed, but the very diversity of positions within feminism, what Paul Smith describes as the "internal heterogeneity of the feminist discourse" (138), points toward an understanding of women's identity that does not rely on binary positions of essentialism or constructivism. The strength of feminism is its ability to hold in tension an array of theoretical and practical perspectives and, thus, to arrive at a clearer understanding of the varied nature of women's positions.

While I do not intend to suggest that their positions are the same, Gayatri Spivak, Jane Gallop, and Teresa de Lauretis posit a "both/and" perspective that recognizes the complexity of women's identity. Such a perspective has allowed me to interpret more clearly the contradictory and conflict-filled experience of the students as they attempted to understand their position as women in our culture. For example, while Spivak opposes an "essential feminism," she argues that if we allow for the multiplicity of women's identities, we must acknowledge the role that women's experience of their bodies—and especially the subjugation of women's bodies by men—plays in shaping women's identities. Thus, she argues that women must "take the risk of essence" in order to increase the possibility of substantive resistance (150). In short, the claim of "essence" is a beginning point of contestation, but Spivak demands a continual process of historicization, even for those who posit an identity defined by the female body; any claim of women's identity must be analyzed in light of the multiple historical and social circumstances in which women live their lives.

Similarly, Gallop argues for multiple definitions, continually redefined:

> Both psychoanalysis and feminism can be seen as efforts to call into question a rigid identity that cramps and binds. But both also tend to want to produce a "new identity," one that will now be adequate and authentic. . . . I do not believe in some "new identity" which would be adequate and authentic. But I do not seek some sort of liberation from identity. That would lead only to another form of paralysis . . . of undifferentiation. Identity must be continually assumed and immediately called into question. (xii)

De Lauretis argues that women's subjectivity can best be defined through a continual analysis of the contextual conditions and contradictions inherent in social life. An understanding of subjectivity lies

> not in femininity as a privileged nearness to nature, the body, or the unconscious . . . not in female tradition simply understood as private, marginal, and yet intact . . . not finally in the chinks and cracks of masculinity, the fissures of male identity . . . but rather in that political, theoretical, self-analyzing practice by which the relations of the subject in social reality can be rearticulated from the historical experience of women. (*Alice* 186)

De Lauretis further describes a concept of women's identity that is neither fixed, powerless essence nor endlessly dissolving and invisible, but multiple and changing within a social, linguistic, and political context, and that has agency because of its reflective, self-analyzing power (*Feminist* 8-9). I believe this process can be seen clearly at work in the experience of students in the women's literature class.

Theoretical debates among academic feminists are complex and subtle (more complex and subtle, certainly, than I've presented them here). And because many feminists see them as peripheral to the goals of women's literature courses, they keep these political and theoretical conflicts in the professional closet, separate from their students and classrooms. Barbara's students were undergraduates, not feminist theorists or critics, yet the questions that emerged as they read and wrote about women's literature have a clear resonance with the problems that feminist theorists debate in professional meetings and publications.

Pursuing these questions, students engaged in a critical examination of the nature of language and its role in constituting women and their subjectivity; they considered aesthetic questions about the nature of art and literature; and they explored problems of racism and class, political power, and ethical responsibility. But they did not simply explore these questions on an abstract level; rather, they found themselves inevitably drawn into an examination of their own experience, the historical conditions surrounding their lives, and the dissonance inherent in them. These women began to recognize themselves as the outsider, as "other." Confronting contradictory views of themselves was painful and difficult for many, impossible for a few, and reaffirming for others. I want to avoid suggesting that all the women had the same response to the class or that every student went through a series of stages or transformations during the semester. Although they experienced the class in a variety of ways, it allowed them, some for the first time, to see the conflict between images of themselves as women that they confront daily (that some had accepted uncritically throughout their lives) and their actual experience as students, members of families, and people who participate in a network of social relationships. For some students, the class affirmed or clarified conflicts they had already recognized as women in our culture. The analysis of those contradictions, framed in a classroom taught according to feminist pedagogy, was the central feature in the students' experience. It demanded that they practice a new form of critical thinking and that they develop a new stance toward their own experience, toward other women, and, ultimately, toward knowledge and truth.

Denial and Resistance: Dethroning the Myth of Femininity

Adrienne Rich writes:

> A radical critique of literature, feminist in its impulse, would take the work first of all as a clue to how we live, how we have been living, how

> we have been led to imagine ourselves, how our language has trapped as well as liberated us, how the very act of naming has been till now a male prerogative, and how we can begin to see and name—and therefore live—afresh. ("When We Dead" 35)

From the first week, the class focused on the way women have been trapped by the myths and "names" that culture circumscribes them in, determining even the way women think about themselves. Students read the stories of Eve and Pandora and several contemporary women poets' revisions of these myths. Many students reacted with confusion and anger, demonstrating immediately the contradictions they experienced between the poets' views of women and the notion of femininity they had always accepted. Here are two students' comments:

> Bev: What's the big deal? So I'm a woman. This isn't sexism; it's just tradition or biology. Why are we making a big deal about women's differences from men? We're all human beings.
>
> Carol: Why do we have to look at the negative aspects of womanhood? I've always been treated fairly, gotten what I deserved. I can't say I've been discriminated against. Of course there were times when school officials would seem more interested in the football players or would select more guys than girls for academic teams, but it was just something to live with. That's just the way things are and have always been.

Like other women in the class, Bev and Carol held the view that "male" and "female" are fixed biological and social-psychological categories that resist examination. Paradoxically, they also believed that differences between male and female held few social or political consequences for people's lives. They resisted Barbara's attempts to point out that these distinctions promote a circumscribed and negative identity for women.

In general, the readings ignited intense discussion and evoked anger, resistance, and denial. For example, several students thought Stevie Smith's "How Cruel Is the Story of Eve," and other poems about Eve and Pandora, were "trashing men" and "putting down" traditional religious beliefs. Jennifer argued in class discussion, "That's not fair to the Bible. It's the authority of my life and I choose to believe what I believe and no one can change that." And Carol wrote in her journal about the danger and discomfort of talking about such ideas:

> I want to figure out why these women are so angry. Does it have any validity? Isn't there some possibility that women have been happy in some part of their lives, their history? If the object is to open our eyes to the oppression of women, then I'm not sure I want to be a part of it. Isn't it possible that men aren't always happy with their lives? They can't experience bearing a child—is that discrimination? I worry that I'll end up hating men.

Carol was not simply denying the identity that language and cultural myths had inscribed for her. She assumed a deterministic, essentialist position for women, believing that male and female roles are biological and should not be questioned. In this "common-sense" stance, Carol and others participated in the erasure of their own experience as they discounted the power of social structures to position them as females in society. They believed that their situations in academia and society were "inevitable," and they were uncomfortable with any contradiction of these beliefs.

Anger and Recognition: When We Dead Awaken

While some students denied that being a woman had consequences for them, others responded with recognition and anger. Amy wrote the following journal entry in response to these lines from Stevie Smith's poem about Eve: "He must make woman lower then / So he can be higher then."

> When I read those lines, my mind began to race. Time and time again, I come across events that seem to make women lower than men. When I first came to college I was enrolled in architecture, but now I am in civil engineering. Nonetheless, people (usually male, although some narrow-minded females tend to do the same) respond with much surprise. They cannot believe that a female, the sex which is less intelligent, is an engineering major. I am supposed to be submissive, a follower, basically a shadow of all males.

Recognizing her experience in these poems, Amy acknowledged that rigidly prescribed definitions of female subjectivity had affected her life. In contrast to Carol, Amy and other women recounted with anger the circumstances of their lives. Bonnie, a business major, spoke most vehemently: "Yes, this anger has validity. I'm thirty-eight years old, and I've seen sexism and discrimination in my own life, in my mother's life. I've seen it in the way I was raised, in my first marriage, and even still in my sons. We still send the boys out to play football and the girls to the kitchen."

To encourage the students to analyze their roles as women and to ground their reading in an examination of their own history and experience, Barbara asked them to do a response writing: "A number of you have pointed out that what we're talking about here is the powerful role language has in shaping our view of ourselves. Think about your own experience. Does language matter?" Students wrote their responses to Barbara's question and then shared them with other members of the class. For an hour and a half they poured out stories—of classes in which professors told them, "Don't worry about your grade; just stay home and have babies"; of art and history classes that ignored women's contributions to their culture; of myths that led them to feel embarrassed about their bodies and religious groups that would not allow women to participate fully. They spoke of the effects of language in families with grandparents who felt that women should be in the kitchen, about construction workers and fraternity men who yelled demeaning comments at them as they walked across campus, of films that left them embarrassed to be women.

Many feminist theorists have written about the powerful, even poisonous effects that the language of patriarchy has on women. Mary summarized its effect on her life in words that echo theirs: "I feel like all my life I have been brainwashed, like something was poisoning me without my knowing it, and it makes me angry." Bonnie also acknowledged her anger: "To change, you have to have it brought before your brain or you will stay with the status quo. The anger and bitterness are necessary." As Bonnie pointed out, anger allows women to begin to be truthful about their lives and provides momentum for change.

Carolyn Heilbrun says that women have often been dishonest in examining their lives, even in their autobiographies. She continues, "And, above all other prohibitions, what has been forbidden to women is anger, together with the open admission of the desire for power and control over one's life. . . . Nostalgia . . . is likely to be a mask for unrecognized anger" (13-15). Thus, the contradictions that some students resisted and glossed over with nostalgia or denial became a point of anger and recognition.

While some women found a beginning point for registering resistance against culturally prescribed identity, Carol and others refused to accept what they saw as a negative, critical view of gender relations. But at the same time, Carol was beginning to acknowledge the possibility of other perspectives. During the third week of class, she wrote in her journal:

> I'm getting extremely frustrated with this class because I'm realizing there is no right or wrong answer here. It's all opinions. That's why I like journalism, because you just deal with facts. But I suppose if I can organize my beliefs and formulate my own opinion about this whole "woman" issue, then I will have gained a great deal from this course. Right now, I'm not sure what I think, what my religion would think.

Although Carol was uncertain about the definition of women's experience she would accept, the class was providing her with a new way of thinking about women's identity. She also recognized an epistemology radically different from the dualistic one she experienced elsewhere in her academic life. In the first few class sessions, this course suggested to her that there were multiple perspectives to take into account in answering the question "What does it mean to be a woman?" Something in this process also suggested that she possessed the capacity to formulate answers, and she seemed almost willing to claim agency for herself.

Part of Carol's struggle is an echo, albeit a naive and paradoxical one, of the debate among feminists about defining women's subjectivity. She believed woman's position is "just the way things are," a natural part of the universal order. At the same time, she also resisted the view that women's history consists entirely of tragic oppression. She was moving toward a recognition of the contradiction in her position that female experience is "naturally" determined. In the literature and voices of women in class, she saw mounting evidence that women have been frustrated and angry in the roles prescribed for them by "the natural order." Paradoxically, Carol wanted to believe that women do possess agency and the responsibility to act in the world, that they are not simply the product of biology or of the "ideological apparatus" of culture, constructed as man's other.

Taking the Risk of Essence: Celebrating Women

Simone de Beauvoir writes,

> One is not born a woman; one becomes one. . . . The peculiarities that identify her as specifically a woman get their importance from the significance placed upon them. They can be surmounted . . . when they are regarded in new perspectives. (809)

It was toward these new perspectives that the readings pushed students in the next few weeks, particularly as we read *Daughters of Copper Woman*, Judy Grahn's *Common Woman* poems, and Alice Walker's "In Search of Our Mother's Gardens."

While Carol, Amy, and other students were articulating resistance, anger, and recognition in the face of contradictions between the image of woman they had come to accept and those the course was revealing, they needed to place women's identity in a new perspective in order to move beyond denial and anger to productive action. In *Daughters of Copper Woman*, Ann Cameron's version of stories told to her by northwest native American women, (a female mythology-history of a matrilineal culture), students experienced the affirmation that women are creative and powerful and can produce a culture that is strong and viable. Jennifer said, "For me it was like reading the Bible, in a women's form." Amy wrote, "I was envious of those women. They knew where they came from, who they were. Their roles as women were prepared for and celebrated. I wish I were part of a society of women who thought of their bodies and bodily functions as sacred and powerful." And Mary said:

> Suzi in *Copper Woman* reminded me of my years of drug and alcohol dependency, the insanity of my divorce, the splitting up of my children. In all of that I thought I was crazy. But I could relate to her courage. Women all over and through time have been walked on, subservient; they have learned to be strong, to endure, to survive. We are no less.

In her journal, Carol summarized the shift of the class mood: "The discussion was so much more positive. Up until now there has been a lot of bitterness and disagreement in class. This book made us all feel better about ourselves as women."

Discussion of *Copper Woman* allowed students to continue examining women's place in our culture, but it did so by holding up the mirror of an alternative woman's culture, of strong, proud, clever, wise, and enduring women. As Patrocinio Schweickart says, "As women have come to examine women's literature, not just the traditional male canon, a different reading task emerges for us and for our students. We no longer must occupy ourselves with . . . the negative hermeneutic of ideological unmasking" (51). That is, we can also engage in the task of recovering, exploring, and articulating literature that elaborates women's point of view and celebrates their strength, endurance, and wisdom. This more affirming task, Schweickart says, allows a woman "to read without condemning herself to the position of 'other'" (51).

The celebration of women continued as students read Walker's and Grahn's affirmations of artistry and richness in women's everyday lives. Amy wrote her own "Common Woman" poem, in which she celebrated herself and her capabilities. Many students wrote about art that they had never fully appreciated—their mothers', aunts', and grandmothers' artistry. Carol wrote: "My grandmother makes quilts, and she has a love for flowers and always keeps a roomful. I think my grandma's most creative outlet is through cooking. She makes the most wonderful Czech pastries and bread. I believe cooking can be an art form, and my grandma is the Renoir of cooking!"

In the academic community, women's literature and women's studies courses have gained a negative reputation for this sort of celebratory affirmation of women, although the purpose of such celebrations is to reverse the effects of centuries of erasure by restoring to women their history and literature and by allowing them to become participants rather than bystanders in history and culture. For some academicians, this celebration represents an uncritical, emotional, and anti-intellectual approach to literature and art. But, in some circumstances, it is equally criticized by feminist theorists because it asserts a coherent, biologically defined identity and because it fails to acknowledge the social and political contradictions in which women live.

Yet those who criticize this process have only seen it in isolation from the total intellectual and social dynamic of the course, a context that allowed for celebration and affirmation but also always demanded the reconsideration and decentering of women's identity. Having recognized themselves in the position of "other," defined and circumscribed by their culture, students needed to move away from the negative critique, to stand back from the "unmasking" of myths and language that they had first engaged in. Part of the process is to "take the risk of essence," as Spivak argues women must. The search for identity demands that woman's position as "other" be recognized. That recognition in itself takes women into an "essentialist" position. But that should be only a temporary point. The process of defining oneself as female doesn't stop with the assertion of essence. As Annette Kolodny says, the process is "female consciousness turning in upon itself attempting to grasp the deepest condition of its own unique and multiplicitous realities, in the hope, eventually, of altering the very forms through which the culture perceives, expresses, and knows itself" (159). The women's class provided an environment in which students could first take the risk of asserting an identity, a process necessary to self-definition, but it also provided that this assertion was never separated from an examination of the immediate social, historical, and political conditions in which one lays claim to a particular identity. Furthermore, it allowed the continual challenge and reexamination of those definitions and consideration of other perspectives.

Recognizing Contradictions: Anger Is Following Us Around

It was not possible to sustain affirmation and celebration for long. As students went on to read Margery Kempe's "On Female Celibacy," Anne Bradstreet's poems, and essays by Virginia Woolf and Adrienne Rich, they recognized that the contradictions inherent in these women's writing and in their own lives are always lurking in the corner at every celebration.

Reading Bradstreet, Woolf, and Kempe on the heels of *Daughters of Copper Woman* was difficult for some students because even though they tried to consider the conditions under which each author lived and wrote, some were angry and disappointed with the contradictions they saw. Kempe's mystical religious enthusiasm seemed to contradict any image of women resisting authoritarian and patriarchal institutions, despite her repudiation of the sexual responsibilities of marriage and her exhortations against Church fathers. In Bradstreet's writing, contradictory swings between self-effacement and self-assertion also confused them. The tensions in Woolf's writing and life—her patrician, intellectual background, her radical perspective on women and society, and her eventual suicide—didn't match some students' expectations that women writers should be unambiguous exemplars of stability and strength. In one contentious class discussion, several students said they felt that Bradstreet, Woolf, and even Kempe were weak and "waffling," caving into the established religious authority and abdicating to their husbands and social norms. "They were playing it 'safe,'" Betty said. "I think Kempe really was something of a freak," Karin said. "Why didn't they just rise up and do what they wanted to do?" Betty argued.

While Barbara attempted to help them recognize the contradictions they were experiencing, it was other students who spoke about the clear representation of the reality of women's lives that they found in Bradstreet and others. They recognized that women sometimes are able to resist and subvert social structures, but also sometimes negotiate or acquiesce in order to survive. Reading these writers, they began to view women's identity as a constant movement between shifting identities as the social context makes varying demands. But they also saw how women who become critically aware of conflicts refuse to live totally within the myth of a unified femininity. Woolf, Bradstreet, and Kempe located points at which they could resist and subvert the identities in which they had been circumscribed. Bonnie and Amy spoke about the double-bind women are often placed in and the multiple identities they often assume. Both women recognized that even in their own "liberated" circumstances with access to jobs and education, they often seemed ambivalent, made compromises, and felt alienated. Amy wrote in her journal:

> I feel I can tell you what's going on because it relates to what Woolf is saying about women writers and what Rich is saying about Woolf. Women are still only allowed to be a certain way. Like Woolf says, women cannot sound angry or write about their feelings. It made them bitter and angry and depressed, and I know what that's like. Last night my boyfriend said he was scared about our relationship because I had gotten an "A" on the calculus test and he hadn't. Chauvinistic! I could not believe that he could think that as a male he should automatically do better than me. I have had to deal with this all my life. What does this say about our society? It really makes me mad.

Bonnie spoke about "warping herself" to fit into male and female expectations: "Pretty soon you don't even know who you really are, because you've spent so much time sort of pulling yourself in here and then pushing yourself that way, tailoring yourself this way and that into something that's prim and proper." During class discussion, she said: "I can sympathize with Bradstreet. It isn't that easy. I feel uncomfortable when I'm the only woman out of fifty in accounting or management class. I wonder if I really ought to be there, if I'm capable of doing the work. I find myself keeping quiet a lot. I find it's not hard to be invisible." Mary added, "I have to fight this doubt all the time, wondering if I'm smart enough. I feel sometimes in classes like my ideas are way out on a limb. Sometimes I do risk saying something, but a lot of times I realize I'm playing the academic game, and for me that means playing it by men's rules."

These women understand the untenable position they are in. On one hand, they can submit to accepted ways of thinking and speaking, give themselves over to the symbol systems of the patriarchy. The alternative, to refuse to participate, forces them back once again to the margins of language and power. Bonnie and Amy pointed out the necessity of articulating women's experience in order to establish a point of resistance. Carol wrote in her journal that week: "I remember a line from *Copper Woman*: 'Who sees the other half of Self sees truth.' That applies to what we've been discussing in this class. We need to be able to see all sides of ourselves. Is it so bad to recognize who and what we are?"

Acknowledging Diversity: Speaking the Unspoken

In one of her most famous speeches, Sojourner Truth says,

> That man over there says that women need to be helped into carriages, and lifted over ditches, and to have the best place everywhere. Nobody ever helps me into carriages, or over mud-puddles, or gives me any best place! And ain't I a woman? (253)

If reading Bradstreet and Woolf evoked the contradictions in women's experience, the writing of black, lesbian, and native American writers and the presence of these women in class intensified the increasingly complex view of women's subjectivity. These women were loud reminders that to speak of a universal woman's experience is to erase the effects of racism, economic and social deprivation, and discrimination arising from differences in women's sexual orientation.

These students' voices, coupled with reading Toni Morrison, Leslie Silko, Gertrude Stein, Adrienne Rich, Audre Lorde, and Judy Grahn, brought the diversity of women's experience to the fore. Although I noted an increasing rapport and openness in speaking of their lives, I also noted continuing tensions as a few students enunciated diverse perspectives and values. I was also aware that some perspectives were not being articulated at all, though they were simmering in the background. Roberta told me in an interview:

> I was so disgusted the first few classes. I almost felt like dropping out. I had counted so much on finding a comfortable group here. But I couldn't say anything, because I realized my experience, my orientation, is so much different. I know it sounds arrogant, but I felt this class, with all these blind women in it, held nothing for me. I'm learning to deal with other people's realities even though they're in conflict with mine, without compromising myself or hiding the lesbian side of me. I struggle not to hide that side.

Although lesbian women, like Roberta, were a quiet presence in the class, their situations were tacitly evoked by the writing of lesbian writers. Students reacted less with disapproval or disgust than with a sense of strangeness and unfamiliarity. Amy wrote in her journal:

> Oh yuck! I'm sorry, but for the first time this semester, I didn't like what was assigned. Stein was so hard to read and understand. On the other hand, Richardson was very good. I was confused for a bit, but finally understood at the end. It really helped me to think about what it would be like to go through that.

Carol was more ambivalent:

> To be honest, I don't really know how to react to these pieces. I'm not sure I understand what's going on in Richardson's "Two Hanged Women." I am uncomfortable with this topic because I don't understand how lesbians feel. It is not for me to decide how people should run their lives or who should sleep in what bed. Although I try to be open-minded about homosexuality, I can't help but stand in disbelief. I am ignorant and I'm not completely sure I want to know. I have talked to a girl on my floor about it. Perhaps this is part of God's plan after all. I want to talk with my priest to find out more. This topic has really given me a chance to think, and this class is giving me a chance to evaluate my previous beliefs and is forcing me to see new perspectives. I like to be challenged to sort a moral question out.

Although students like Roberta may have felt that their experience had to be suppressed, from the beginning the class allowed women to challenge homogenizing pronouncements about women. In other circumstances the "blind women" that Roberta spoke about could have avoided challenges to their perspective, but this class, with its variety of social-sexual orientations, brought students face to face with alternate perspectives. By demonstrating that cherished myths about women do not hold, it challenged students like Amy and Carol to reexamine their values and assumptions about women's lives. As both of these students' journals show, the feminist classroom's focus on the lived experience of women fostered the exploration of differences in a tolerant and safe environment and, in doing so, added another set of images to the mirror in which women see themselves represented.

The most powerful challenge to the homogenizing impulse came from three black women in the class. Jennifer, Anna, and Karin reminded us over and over again that living as black women in a racist society had given them different experiences. Their responses to the writing of black women forced all of us to confront, in more than an intellectual way, what it means to be black in our culture. At the beginning of class discussion of Morrison's *The Bluest Eye*, several students posed the question "What is this Dick and Jane business doing in the story?" This discussion followed:

> Karin: "I grew up with that in school and on television. People of color are faced with those Brady Bunch, blond and blue-eyed images every day of our lives. Black people are just not there. But people think of that as the standard."
>
> Jennifer: "Yeah, if you're not light and bright, you're not right. That's what the blue eyes mean to Piccola."
>
> Karin: "Yes, but even if you're light, people want you to behave in a certain way. In high school when I didn't hang out with a lot of the black kids, white people said, 'What's wrong with you? You aren't like a black.' I can't win."

Several white students countered that at least black people had the Jeffersons and Bill Cosby on television, that racism was mostly a thing of the past since black people's lives had improved drastically in the past few years. Jennifer argued, "It's just a pacifier. It's a cover-up, a big white lie. No one wants to watch Bill Cosby because he's black." Another white student asked, "What *do* you want then?" Anna answered:

> I just want people to see me as a person. You can all say anything you want about how things have improved, but the fact still remains that none of you in this class would want to wake up tomorrow morning and be black, Bill Cosby or not. You would probably kill yourself. People right across there in the library will not take money from my hand because it is black.

Anna's words were more persuasive than any intellectual analysis of racism could have been. Carol wrote in her journal: "This was the first time in my life I experienced a black person's anger face to face. What Anna said stunned me. I guess, honestly, I found *The Bluest Eye* pretty horrifying, eye-opening. I never thought about the Dick and Jane mentality until now. A lot of people's lives don't fit that mold."

Confronting racism in this way allowed students to see the wider effects of oppression, to understand the anger they found baffling in some of the writers and the "negative" attitudes they saw in class. The experience was important for students like Amy and Carol, but it was also important for lesbian, black, and older women in the class as an affirmation of their experience and an opportunity to find some reconciliation with women from whom they felt separated.

The rejection of a universal "woman's" essence was vital because it contradicted the strong tendency to erase the experience of women of different race, class, and sexual orientation. But it was also important because it allowed women to speak about parts of their lives that had often been unrecognized and unspoken. In *The Cancer Journals*, Lorde says,

> I have come to believe over and over again that what is most important to me must be spoken, made verbal and shared, even at the risk of having it bruised or misunderstood. . . . In the cause of silence, each one of us draws the face of her own fear. . . . But . . . we fear the very visibility without which we also cannot truly live. (19-21)

The class allowed women to name the unspeakable and the unspoken: racism, lesbianism, sexism, physical and mental abuse, failures in their pasts, struggles with social-sexual relationships, having one's children taken away, or having lived with breast cancer. It also allowed them to hear the words of other women whose experiences were not their own, women they had often feared or rejected. But Lorde argues further that finding words to name and interpret one's experience is not enough. Transforming silence into language must lead to action.

Action and Responsibility: Ethics in Feminist Teaching

Though not the overt organizing themes of the course, personal responsibility and agency emerged as a crucial dimension of women's identity. The course began by reexamining the language, myths, and images that shape women's lives, but it did something many courses fail to do. As Judith Newton and Deborah Rosenfelt point out, most educational experience divorces the study of ideas, language, and literature from the study of personal, social, political, and economic conditions in which people live. Academic life often fosters the view that intellectual activity is a solitary undertaking without social origins and political implications.

Barbara, on the other hand, presented students with a model of intellectual life that integrated her own life as a reader-scholar with life in the university, surrounding community, and wider culture. She demonstrated how women can continually examine their own experience, monitor conditions in the world, make decisions about the implications of these conditions, and act in relation to them. On the first day of class, she remarked to the students that feminist theory enabled her to bring together all the parts of her life and work. At one point she said, "I would rather think that everything I do matters rather than that nothing matters. So I have to act accordingly, even if it is in seemingly small ways." Ethical considerations and the importance of individual decisions were also a prominent theme in the readings. For example, in her poem, "A Woman Is Talking to Death," Grahn writes of women's responsibility to one another, a theme also addressed in Susan Glaspell's play *Trifles*. Morrison, in *The Bluest Eye*, speaks about the responsibility members of a community have for the lives of its people. Lorde challenges, "Because I am woman, because I am black, because I am lesbian, because I am myself, a black woman warrior poet doing my work, come to ask you, are you doing yours?" (21)

Barbara tried to create opportunities for students to connect their lives to the readings and to connect both to action, to sensitize themselves to react to what goes on around them. She began every class with announcements of events on and off campus, and she required them to attend at least two outside activities and to write reports connecting them to the reading selections. Students' growing sensitivity to these events was apparent. They began writing about outside events in their journals or referring in class discussion to something they had seen or experienced. They increasingly applied ideas from class and the readings to their own situations.

The concept of responsibility and action that students took from this course was far from the aggressive militancy that Lorde urges women toward, and far from the vocal activism that many feminists would like to see in this "postfeminist" generation. Instead, it was a redefinition of responsibility, along the lines that Flynn and Schweickart point to. Traditionally, responsibility is linked to legal terms—accepting responsibility means not impinging on the rights of others and accepting the risk of liability that comes with authority. Flynn and Schweickart note that in female discourse "responsibility is more closely associated with responsiveness to the needs of others" (xx).

In class, students spoke and wrote most about their responsibility to support and encourage other women, to acknowledge their mothers' and grandmothers' accomplishments, and even to write about or speak out on issues that concerned them. One student said: "It bothers me a little, because now I've become so observant, so critical in a way. I can't let things go the way I used to—like even how waiters treat me differently from my boyfriend in a restaurant or how my dad talks about blacks, or when a professor uses textbooks that are sexist." The readings and the manner in which the course was taught clearly asserted that women are capable of critically interpreting the circumstances of their lives and that their actions do make a difference.

Critique and Transformation: Pushing at the Boundaries

In attempts to define human subjectivity, the problem of human agency is important, particularly in some versions of poststructuralist and Marxist theory. The question stated very simply is this: if human beings are constructed by the cultural and linguistic relationships, what, if anything, allows them to resist, to transform the conditions of their existence? Paul Smith says that many versions of the human subject leave us either with a deterministic definition of the individual as one who has neither agency nor autonomy or, at the other extreme, with a concept of the self that is constantly shifting, fading, and dissolving and, thus, that also has no possibility of claiming agency.

From its earliest tradition, feminist theory has assumed that although women are positioned and defined by a set of sexual and political ideologies, they nevertheless are not condemned to be pawns of these forces. Though poststructuralist feminists seem to imply a genderless "subject" in opposition to the biological "essential" subject of other feminists, theorists like de Lauretis point to a conception of the female subject that allows us to reconceive women's identity via the constant "engagement of a self or subject in social reality" and "political, theoretical, self-analyzing practice" (*Alice* 182, 186). She stresses the idea, reinterpreted from Lacan, that human beings are structured through language, through discursive practices, but not in a totalizing way, because language is not the only source of meaning and, also, because language itself allows the potential for resistance to discursive constructions. Language makes possible a continual reflective, critical analysis of unique histories and experiences. As in the class, this process gives people access to evidence of the nonunity, the discontinuous, in individual lives. Confronting what is contradictory and alienating in human experience allows women and men to resist definitions that society would impose. Seeing the cracks and fissures in such homogenizing definitions allows for the possibility of resisting, of reconsidering and reexamining our positions, and of claiming responsibility and action in the world.

Heilbrun urges women to return to such a critical process when she says that women must return to telling their own and other women's stories, not simply through the texts we read but also "in oral exchanges among women in groups hearing and talking to one another" (46). With de Lauretis, she concludes that women need to reclaim their life stories for these stories' potential to critique and revise women's lives (45). I believe Heilbrun is suggesting more than a return to naive consciousness-raising groups; she is asserting the importance of women's stories as an enactment of "women-ness," a dramatic portrayal through women's own life stories of the diversity and contradictions in which they live. This enactment holds within it the potential for historical, critical analysis and, thus, for action. It allows women to understand that the multiplicitous realities of their existence exceed all descriptions of essence.

Women's stories had such a dramatic power in the class, a power seen most tangibly in the students' writing. Amy's final essay described how themes in women's literature allowed her to "reestablish" her views in important areas of her life: her family, death, sexuality, physical appearance, and her conception of herself as a complicated person: "Of course I have a better understanding of women authors, but I also see growth in myself and more understanding of other people." Carol's final paper focused on a theme that she defined as "the power of women and the strength women give to other women." Her essay drew on the writing of Zora Neale Hurston, Audre Lorde, Susan Glaspell, Sarah Orne Jewett, and Ann Cameron to trace transformations in women's lives as they rejected traditional definitions and attempted to reinterpret their identities, gaining power not only for themselves but also for other women. As she traced this theme, she also reexamined her own intellectual process:

> Strength and power were in the characters and the writers, but they are also in the women in our class. I began to gain self-confidence because of the opportunity to listen to the views of women in class. The process was a slow one. At the beginning of the course I was frustrated and felt like I was being forced to think about things I didn't want to think about. It wasn't until later that I realized I could think any way I wanted so long as I wasn't hypocritical, blind, or unthinking. This new opinion came about as my previous beliefs were challenged and I was forced to reevaluate. For me, this may well be the greatest growing I did this semester. This ability to see reason in someone else's opinion is something I can and will carry with me for a long time to come.

Redefining Literary Education

This class provided all of us—students, teacher, and participant-observer—with multiple images of women's identity, a clear alternative to the false unity of the universal female essence and, also, to an endlessly dissolving, yet deterministic identity. It gave us images of ourselves as women committed to complexity, to responsibility, and to change. As a participant-observer, I came away with a sense of the inseparability of feminist theory and practice and of the importance of what, together, they offer as a model for education in both composition and literature.

Rich, Heilbrun, and others assert that feminist theory has potential for revolutionizing literary education, but this revisionary activity is highly suspect in the current debate about the nature of education in English. Some would consider Amy and Carol's experience and the "feminist teaching" that produced it as contributors to the "demise" of literary education today. Barbara Herrnstein Smith notes that Lynne Cheney's report, *Humanities in America*, not only decries the political and ideological turn that literature instruction has taken, but also argues for a return to an emphasis on the transmission of knowledge, information, and fact in place of the current emphasis on self-reflective processes. As Teresa Sullivan notes, women's studies and women's literature classes are especially suspect, both pedagogically and philosophically. Women's literature stands outside the boundaries of canonic texts, lacks the signs of methodological rigor, and appears to indulge in unrestrained ideological indoctrination and emotional, solipsistic examination of self. Still others, as Charles Paine acknowledges, assert that the relativism inherent in "radical pedagogies" leads students to a disabling nihilism. The experience of students in the class provides a much different view of the results of "radical" feminist pedagogy.

Feminist classrooms are not simply revisionary because they break with canonical content; they are also revisionary because they demand critical rather than solipsistic modes of thought and because they assert an ethical rather than a nihilistic stance. The women's literature course demonstrates that the diverse and multidimensional perspectives such a course makes available do not emerge simply from the literature students read or from the theoretical "correctness" of the class or its teacher; rather, they emerge from the dynamic of the entire course, from students' reading and interaction and the critical dialogue with lived experience that interaction makes possible.

This course engaged students in intellectual processes that offer much to the ongoing debate about the nature of education in English. According to de Lauretis, the process of "collective articulation of one's experience of sexuality and gender has produced, and continues to elaborate, a radically new mode of understanding the subject's relations to social-historical reality." Furthermore, de Lauretis points out, this process constitutes an "original critical instrument that women have developed . . . toward the analysis of social reality, and its critical revision" (*Alice* 186). Thus, the critical process that the students engaged in enabled them to develop and practice intellectual processes, to use "critical instruments" that can serve as models of processes that would benefit all students, if they are to live in a pluralistic society.

Revising the *content* of the English curriculum is not enough, then, and the reform needed in the English curriculum runs much deeper than a correct theoretical stance. It requires a methodology consistent with what theory has taught us about how human beings learn, a methodology that takes into account the diverse political and social realities of our lives as well as our students' lives, a methodology that encourages a critical practice that continually turns back on itself, continually monitors, challenges, and changes itself. In a recent essay, Arthur Schlesinger writes about the perils he sees in the rise of "absolutist" thinking in the United States, of the inability of our society to identify and value contradicting and multiple perspectives, and of our tendency to settle for reductive, monolithic representations of issues and ideas.

Feminism's "internally heterogeneous" perspectives offer a remedy to this habit of mind. But feminism will be handicapped if feminists maintain a division between theory and pedagogy. Contrary to the view of feminists like Nina Baym, who suggests that feminists must operate outside the theoretical questions, and contrary to the argument that feminist theory has only to do with the critical project of reading and analyzing texts and that pedagogy is peripheral, we cannot separate theory from practice. To do so endangers the effectiveness of feminism itself by stripping away the interrelationship between the personal, political, and theoretical and by perpetuating a hierarchical dichotomy. Such a separation subverts one of the most important contributions of feminism: the model of a discipline that constantly connects intellectual activity—the study of literature, language, and ideas—to the history and experience of people's lives. This interrelationship provides intellectual practice that allows students to see that we make our own knowledge rather than simply acquire "the facts," and that we do so in a reciprocal process of rethinking and reinterpreting the "word and the world," in Paulo Freire's phrase (35). A model of education that understands the reciprocal nature of theory and practice and constantly places students' experience at its center provides a check against narrowly ideologic forms of teaching that feminists and nonfeminists alike cannot indulge in. Many of our students make little connection between themselves and feminism of any sort, and they believe, further, that reading and writing are alien to their lives. The critical processes made available in the women's literature class—a class that allowed ideas to be held up to reexamination, to contradiction, and to the multiple stories of women's lives—hold at least some promise to counter the absolutist forms of thinking that prevail in our society and to allow more students to remake their view of the world.

Notes

1. This course, Introduction to Women's Literature, was taught during the fall semester, 1988. My study was one of several participant-observation studies that my colleagues and I have conducted in the Department of English at the University of Nebraska, in an effort to understand the contexts for student learning in academic cultures. I used standard participant-observation methodology in collecting data during the course: I participated in and took field-notes at every class session, read the assigned literature and did other assignments, and read students' weekly journals and their midterm and final essays. I also interviewed eight students and the teacher three times during the semester to gain their perceptions of the course.

2. These distinctions are more thoroughly outlined in Weedon.

Works Cited

Alcoff, Linda. "Cultural Feminism versus Post-Structuralism: The Identity Crisis in Feminist Theory." *Reconstructing the Academy*. Ed. E. Minnich et al. Chicago: U of Chicago P, 1988. 257-88.

Baym, Nina. "The Madwoman and Her Languages: Why I Don't Do Feminist Literary Theory." *Feminist Issues in Literary Scholarship*. Bloomington: Indiana UP, 1987. 45-61.

Cameron, Ann. *Daughters of Copper Woman*. N.p.: Press Gang, 1981.

Cixous, Hélène. "The Laugh of the Medusa." Marks and de Courtivron 245-64.

Daly, Mary. *Gyn/Ecology*. London: Women's P, 1979.

De Beauvoir, Simone. *The Second Sex*. New York: Random, 1952.

De Lauretis, Teresa. *Alice Doesn't: Feminism, Semiotics, Cinema*. Bloomington: Indiana UP, 1984.

—. *Feminist Studies/Critical Studies*. Bloomington: Indiana UP, 1986.

DiBernard, Barbara. "Feminist Teaching." *Women's Journal-Advocate* 6 (1987): 1-3.

Flynn, Elizabeth, and Patrocinio Schweickart. *Gender and Reading: Essays on Readers, Texts, and Contexts*. Baltimore: Johns Hopkins UP, 1986.

Freire, Paulo, and Donaldo Macedo. *Literacy: Reading the Word and the World*. South Hadley, MA: Bergin, 1987.

Gallop, Jane. *The Daughter's Seduction: Feminism and Psychoanalysis*. London: Macmillan, 1982.

Glaspell, Susan. *Trifles*. Gilbert and Gubar 1389-899.

Gilbert, Sandra M., and Susan Gubar. *The Norton Anthology of Literature by Women*. New York: Norton, 1985.

Grahn, Judy. "The Common Woman." *The Work of a Common Woman*. Trumansburg, NY: Crossing, 1978. 59-73.

——. "A Woman Is Talking to Death." *The Work of a Common Woman*. Trumansburg, NY: Crossing, 1978. 112-31.

Heilbrun, Carolyn. *Writing a Woman's Life*. New York: Norton, 1989.

Irigaray, Luce. "This Sex Which Is Not One." Marks and de Courtivron 99-106.

Kempe, Margery. "On Female Celibacy." Gilbert and Gubar 22-27.

Kolodny, Annette. "Dancing through the Minefield: Some Observations on Theory, Practice, and Politics of Feminist Literary Criticism." *The New Feminist Criticism*. Ed. Elaine Showalter. New York: Pantheon, 1985. 144-67.

Kristeva, Julia. "From Ithaca to New York." *Polylogue*. Paris: Seuil, 1977.

—. "Il n'y a pas de maître à langage." *Nouvelle Revue de Psychanalyse* 20 (1979): 119-40.

—. "Woman Can Never Be Defined." Marks and de Courtivron 137-41.

Lorde, Audre. *The Cancer Journals*. San Francisco: Spinsters/ Aunt Lute, 1980.

Marks, Elaine, and Isabelle de Courtivron. *New French Feminisms*. New York: Schocken, 1981.

Morrison, Toni. *The Bluest Eye*. Gilbert and Gubar 2068-184.

Newton, Judith, and Deborah Rosenfelt. *Feminist Criticism and Social Change.* New York: Methuen, 1985.

Paine, Charles. "Relativism, Radical Pedagogy, and the Ideology of Paralysis." *College English* 51 (1989): 557-70.

Rich, Adrienne. "Disloyal to Civilization: Feminism, Racism, Gynephobia." *On Lies, Secrets, and Silence, Selected Prose 1966-78.* New York: Norton, 1979. 275-310.

—. "When We Dead Awaken: Writing as Re-Vision." *On Lies, Secrets, and Silence, Selected Prose 1966-78.* New York: Norton, 1979. 33-49.

Richardson, H.H. "Two Hanged Women." Gilbert and Gubar 1210-214.

Schweickart, Patrocinio. "Reading Ourselves: Toward a Feminist Theory of Reading." Flynn and Schweickart 31-62.

Smith, Barbara Herrnstein. "Limelight: Reflections on a Public Year." *PMLA* 104 (1989): 285-93.

Smith, Paul. *Discerning the Subject.* Minneapolis: U of Minnesota P, 1988.

Smith, Stevie. "How Cruel Is the Story of Eve." Gilbert and Gubar 1684-686.

Spivak, Gayatri C. "French Feminism in an International Frame." *In Other Worlds: Essays in Cultural Politics.* New York: Routledge, 1987. 134-53.

Stein, Gertrude. "Ada." Gilbert and Gubar 1334-336.

Sullivan, Teresa, et al. "Valuing and Devaluing Women's Studies." *Academe* 75 (1989): 35-42.

Truth, Sojourner. "Ain't I a Woman?" Gilbert and Gubar 253-55.

Walker, Alice. "In Search of Our Mother's Gardens." Gilbert and Gubar 2374-382.

Weedon, Chris. *Feminist Practice and Poststructuralist Theory.* London: Basil Blackwell, 1987.

Woolf, Virginia. "From *A Room of One's Own.*" Gilbert and Gubar 1376-383.

Genders of Writing

David Bleich

Writing has become an important topic in academic circles. Much of the attention has come through the traditional subject of "composition" because of a sudden national cry ten or fifteen years ago that students were coming out of college "without knowing how to write." Other kinds of attention have come through literary theory, especially Jacques Derrida's concept of "grammatology"—the study of all forms of inscription, including speech—and the related critical idea of "intertextuality"—the interdependence of any one text on an indefinite number of other texts. Because of this attention, both the theories of composition and the ideas of what writing is are changing.

So far, however, this theoretical activity has not led to many changes in the teaching of writing in the university. By and large, all universities still assume that their role is to help students achieve fluency in standard English by providing intensive technical assistance. While there has been some recognition that the so-called ability to write is not a single definable thing, that writing in different disciplines requires different kinds of teaching techniques, and that faculty in different disciplines must participate in writing programs, virtually no one in any discipline contests the belief that we all ought to continue to teach "expository prose," the basic skill that underlies the ideal of academic discourse.

In this article, I will question this belief by suggesting that both expository prose and traditional academic discourse are constrained and distorted by ideological values that are carried along, invisibly, by the term "standard English," and that are kept in circulation, in large part, by false conceptions of gender. I will try to show that if we reject these values and conceptions, writing will seem a much different and richer subject, no longer rigidly tied to either expository prose or academic discourse, no longer subject to obsessive remediation, evaluation, and testing, a subject many more of us will want to include in the pursuit of our disciplinary interests.

Gender and Heterosexism

Most of us take for granted that the sex/gender system that governs our lives is a collective process of interaction between two genders, two kinds of people. There is neither more nor less than these two kinds: female and male. With this assumption, sexism is understood as the masculine domination of women, a situation that would be "corrected" if only the two genders were considered "equal." Rigorously applying eighteenth-century principles of political enlightenment, and perhaps changing the Declaration of Independence to read "All people are created equal" would eradicate sexism without changing the view that there are two and only two genders in the sex/gender system.

I think more than this is involved, however. Adrienne Rich writes, for example, "I believe large numbers of men could, in fact, undertake child care on a large scale without radically altering the balance of male power in a male-identified society." This statement is offered, in part, as a response to Dorothy Dinnersteins' and Nancy Chodorow's claims that mother-exclusive and mother-dominated child-rearing is one of the most identifiable causes of sexism. Although I don't think I agree with Rich (I do, though, agree with Dinnerstein and Chodorow), Rich is making the case that a key element in the ideology of sexism is "compulsory heterosexuality," a thesis which may sound strange and offensive to heterosexuals reading it for the first time. Rich implies that the ideology of compulsory heterosexuality precedes psychosocially, and perhaps historically, the practice that infants and children are to be cared for mainly by their mothers. She argues that the male sex drive and its enforcement by superior muscularity created compulsory heterosexuality, and it is from the continuing historical acceptance of the primacy of the male sex drive that sexism created mother-exclusive child-rearing and thereby defined narrow and unbalanced sexual categories into the present. As a result, heterosexuals do feel or think that their sexuality is natural and that homosexuality is unnatural, thus removing the question from ideological and political scrutiny. Heterosexuality is part of nature and is thereby exempt from cultural criticism.

Gerda Lerner's recent account of the creation of patriarchy seems to support the views of Chodorow and Dinnerstein, since she begins her historical account with what she considers a given: the human infant's complete dependency on the mother. She claims that mother-exclusive childrearing was *originally* biologically necessary but then became fixed culturally to everyone's detriment. She then uses this assumption to claim first that "sexual dominance underlies class and race dominance"

(209) and then that "the system of patriarchy can function only with the cooperation of women" (217), cooperation secured by a variety of coercive practices. She does not go back in history "further," so to speak, than the patriarchal family, but she does claim that other ideologies of domination like classism and racism derive from a primary sexism. Rich's claim about the primacy of the male sex drive, however, might well situate the origin of sexism actually before the establishment of the patriarchal family. Because Lerner's earliest historical evidence of the existence of sexism is the documented practice of the exchange of women among tribes and extended families, Rich's claim that the male sex drive is more primary is plausible. I, at least, asked myself in reading Lerner's book how she supposed the patriarchal family got into position to "exchange women" to begin with. Rich's view answers my question, even though I'm not so sure that there is such a thing as a "male sex drive" independent of or prior to culture and society.

However, even assuming that there is such a thing, this issue looks very much like a chicken and egg question, one that, for our purposes, need not, and perhaps cannot, be resolved with the establishment of some "proven" fact. I want only right now to entertain compulsory heterosexuality as a plausible and useful concept that will help provide a rationale for an enlightened concept of gender. In this connection, I would like to report on a recent event which makes Rich's view seem even more important. Last December, I asked my class of 150 first-year students to write an essay responding to the following question, the essay to be written in a lecture hall in about 40 minutes:

> Describe a conversation with someone either of your own or another sexual preference (lesbian, male homosexual, bisexual, asexual, heterosexual) on the issue of homosexuality. Give as many salient details as you can about this conversation, particularly how attitudes about homosexuality were *expressed.*

Perhaps as much as twenty percent of the class wrote essays that contained ideas like the following:

> Homosexuality is the only topic on which Mad Max and I have the same opinion. He says homosexuality is a menace to society and that the faggots should be stoned.

> We would joke about the homosexuals and make fun of their gay rights marches when we saw them in the paper. When the aids thing started we

> suggested shooting all of the queers or putting them on an island like lepers.
>
> I feel it [homosexuality] is an act of *sexual perversion* and they [gays] all should be shot, but I guess we don't have to waist the bullet; they are going to die of aids soon enough anyway.
>
> I remember one comment made about how all homosexuals should be put in one building and have the building blown up.

Each of these comments was given by a man, and perhaps twenty more men in this class thought it fitting and proper to advocate the murder of millions of people. Other men who did not advocate murder did endorse a variety of incidents of gay-bashing, such as ganging up on male homosexuals and beating them. No women in the class advocated either the murder of homosexuals or gay-bashing, but many women repeatedly said that homosexuality was "disgusting," swearing that they would never have a lesbian roommate. The strong homophobic feeling was present, therefore, in about sixty percent of this class.

In part, the behavior of the women is an example of what Lerner describes as the cooperation of women in the ideology of patriarchy; it is obvious from this sample anyway that the men are leading the way in a tone that may make heterosexual women feel that they had better agree. In a classroom in which all students thought that they could say and write what they really believed without penalty, we find this unabashed expression of fascism and genocidal wishes. Students who disagreed with one another about racism, sexism, and classism closed ranks on homophobia and let loose with this incredible outburst of sociopathic mob panic. Rich, of course, is much more aware than I that these sentiments exist on an almost universal scale, and in retrospect it seems clear to me that someone who wanted to explain such feelings would arrive at the conclusion that the ideology at work is compulsory heterosexuality, or as Rich also puts it, heterosexism. This is the belief not only that heterosexuality is compulsory but that the form of it forced on civilization by the hegemony of men is its only possible form.

I don't think that I nor anyone else can actually advocate some fixed taxonomy of gender. What I and many others do think, however, is that the flexibility and permeability of gender boundaries must be recognized and accepted by all. What has happened historically, I think, is that the fixed and hierarchical formation of gender arrangements in almost all known human civilizations has created values such as compulsory hierarchy and compulsory boundaries of thought. The evidence for this claim is not abstract. All authoritative social roles are held by men—in politics, medicine, law, religion, science, art, and, of course, the academy. It should come as no surprise that the style of thought developed by these men in the name of all people should correspond with the structure of social relations that sustains their social privileges. The young men in my class who advocate the murder of homosexuals feel that they are in the same class as those men who hold the "big guns" in our society, those men who believe without question what Joanna Russ observes in her story, "When it Changed": "When one culture has the big guns and the other has none, there is a certain predictability about the outcome" (2267). These young men learned long before enrolling in my class that holding the big guns is the key to their identity and security as social beings.

Writing: Genres and Genders

The genders of writing show significant correspondences to the genders that govern social relations. The usual term in the study of different forms of writing is, of course, *genre* and not *gender*; but I now use the term *gender* (as many others have already done) to emphasize the political ingredients in the idea of a "kind" of anything, in this case writing. In using this term I also want to include reference to Lerner's thought that sexual dominance underlies all other dominance—and to the related thought that gender categories probably are historically older and more influential than other categories, including race and class. Finally, I want to advance the idea that those kinds of writing produced by expository prose and academic discourse serve the traditional sex/gender system and inhibit what most of us accept to be the necessary and urgent task of reforming that system.

Ralph Cohen is now writing a study of literary history and theory in which the central focus is the concept of genre. One of his main aims is to revise this concept from its traditional use as the way to create literary taxonomies to a historically and socially informed concept. Cohen starts with his critique of Derrida's general term "writing" and Derrida's apparent advocacy of the meaninglessness of generic categories. "One does not write 'writing,'" Cohen observes, "one writes novels or plays or poems or letters, and the like." Any piece of writing comes to us in specific forms that are connected with other works in the same or similar forms and which use still other forms as "subgenres" in a variety of ways. Both the principal and marginal genres are rooted in social purposes and historical circumstances while they are in the process of helping to change these purposes and circumstances. In this way, a genre becomes an identifiable kind or species of language that cannot be understood in and of itself but as it exists in social and historical situations. Cohen's argument is not that writing must take one main form, but that it always appears in at least one form and is always made up of several other forms which, like the principal form, must be understood as being in the midst of social and historical change. Even though, for example, one could conceivably think of *Finnegan's Wake* as a dream tract, its present-time historical form is the novel, though this way of knowing this book may very well change into a dream tract or a joke, or whatever else one may see it as retrospectively.

Cohen's first principle is, therefore, that every work of literature is both a text and a kind of text and that the relationship between a text and how we identify it is historically and culturally determined. A second main point that Cohen makes is that genres themselves are always mixed or "combinatory." At each point in history, Cohen says, any one genre has been made up of a variety of others. Therefore, part of any genre's identity is its "manner of combination." Examples Cohen gives of genres whose manner of combination is more obviously part of their identity are the television spot, the miniseries, the prime-time soaps, women's journals, slave narratives. Here is part of Cohen's explanation of what he finally calls "mixed genres":

> Naming a text a "novel" or a "nonfictional novel," a "miniseries," or a "soap" identifies it and pins down what is unpinnable; in Derrida's terms, genre-naming fixes what is necessarily unfixable, encloses in boundaries that which crosses boundaries. Nevertheless if we think of people instead of maps, we know that border crossings are common practice in some countries (like our own) and that the reasons for such crossings are social and economic. Every time such a crossing occurs, it places the person in a dual relation—with his [or her] own and with a foreign country.... The point is that if texts cross borders or boundaries, they must have borders or boundaries to cross; they need group or class names to identify them. If all we have are textual crossings, we can make no distinctions between novels, nonfiction novels, and autobiographies that are also fictions and nonfictions. Genre naming or grouping is inevitably both necessary and loose. Critics may change the boundaries and the name. But they then continue with other strategies that, nevertheless, involve renaming and remapping.

What I want to emphasize here is Cohen's idea that genres—and I will add genders—are *both* necessary and loose. Traditional approaches to this question of genre have been of an either/or nature, and Derrida is traditional in this regard. Either there are boundaries or there aren't; for boundaries to be both necessary and loose challenges the axioms of hierarchy and noncontradiction and thus represents an unfamiliar use of academic discourse.

The key to the matter is Cohen's insistence on historical, social, and cultural practice, as opposed to abstract principles (writing), as being the point of reference for understanding literary kinds. This different social assumption changes his own academic discourse from being the sole authoritative determiner of cultural categories to being one participant among many in the task of understanding genres (and genders). Cohen continues:

> The purpose of naming a type of writing "feminist literary criticism" or "slave narratives" or "legal briefs" is to establish an identity that is socially and literarily related to other identities, to make a political assertion that is for one group and against another, to announce that a literary act cannot be dissevered from social action, to reject the belief that anonymity stimulates fairness.

Here Cohen establishes the principle that generic categories are necessarily political. In addition—and just as important, perhaps—he rejects the belief that "anonymity stimulates fairness." It is not hard to see how this silent axiom of our culture has kept varieties of gender and other political expression "in the closet." This axiom lies behind the false ideological commonplaces that "it doesn't matter what your race, gender, economic class, or national origin is." Letting students write out of the grading system—that is, out of the system of enforcement in schools—shows how much these categories, and many others, really do matter. Similarly, as Jesse Jackson pointed out in 1988 during his campaign for the presidential nomination, those Democrats who were making anonymous statements that he really couldn't win were cowards; in this case, I would add, anonymity attempts to hide, by appeal to some alleged objective fact, the political acceptance of racism. Not to give one's name and not to name is unfair because we know anyway that the categories and names are being assumed.

Finally, we have known for a long time that genders are themselves mixed, that there is actually a range of possible gender identities that exist in society, and that it makes a big difference to say that heterosexuality is a historically developed majority rather than a biologically compulsory category. In this instance in particular, the principle of "majority rules" turns out not to be a fair one, and the logical principle of the more "ruling" over the less does not serve the social principle of "justice for all."

Academic Discourse: An "Official" Gender

The teaching of expository prose and academic discourse itself may not even represent a majority value even though these two closely related genres (they are not the same, I think) appear in textbooks as the basis for "standard English." Richard Ohmann, in his classic essay, "Use Definite, Specific, Concrete Language," summarizes and examines this standard. His title is a composite of an instruction given by almost all composition handbooks. The instruction is a series of substrategies that add up to what Ohmann characterizes as a "preferred style" with an implied set of both language and social values. This style "focuses on a truncated present moment"; it "favors sensory news, from the surfaces of things"; it "obscures the social relations and the relations of people to nature that are embedded in all things"; it "foregrounds the writer's own perceptions," leading to an excessive involvement in oneself; and it urges the "denial of conflict" by picturing a world in which, for example, "the telephone has the same meaning for all classes of people" (396). In general, Ohmann continues, these handbooks

> push the student writer always toward the language that most nearly reproduces the immediate experience and away from the language that might be used to understand it, transform it, and relate it to everything else. The authors privilege a kind of revising and expanding that leaves the words themselves unexamined and untransformed. (396)

This is a standard not of language use in its full and complicated range of genres but of the writing skill of transmitting immediate information. Uses of language that give attitudes, opinions, generalizations, guesses, doubts, confusions, and similar commonplaces of socially interactive behavior are understood to be interferences to the basic need for "clear information." The affirmative purpose of this standard, Ohmann suggests, is to train people to use language as a kind of servant of large corporations, language that is neither interrogative nor challenging in any other way. The more negative purpose of this standard, Ohmann says, is to suppress the potential of language to encourage social involvement and activism; to discourage and discredit any gender of writing that does not fit into the hegemonic ideology.

Under the aegis of "standard English" given in expository prose and academic discourse, students are taught to separate language from themselves, their local interests, their groups and communities, and their own history of language use. The alternative to this strategy, Ohmann observes in *English in America*,

> would mean having students develop their writing skills in the process of discovering their political needs, and as an aid in achieving those needs. It would mean encouraging students to form alliances with one another based on real life interest, and letting the skills of writing grow through collective work. And of course some of these alliances would come into conflict, since different students are of different classes, races, and ages. In short, it would mean bringing politics—everyone's politics—into composition, rather than just the politics of the establishment, which are now implicit in the course and made to look like no-politics. (160)

Ohmann here points out that the actual politics of standard English is anonymous and thereby given out as objective or fair. But I don't think it requires us to accept any one political view to admit simply that what kinds or genders or genres of writing get taught in schools is related to *some* politics and that our task as teachers will be much better served by not suppressing the political forces that emerge in our writing any more than society is served by suppressing its variety of races and genders. As outrageous as it was to read all those essays I cited above, without having gotten those essays, I would have failed to engage the political realities of my students, and I would have failed to recognize just where I stand in relation to those students.

Janice Moulton's essay on the "adversary paradigm" in philosophical writing pertains to academic discourse in ways analogous to how Ohmann's essay pertains to expository prose. Moulton claims that the adversary paradigm has been a tacit principle of almost all philosophical writing. Under its aegis, philosophy

> is seen as an unimpassioned debate between *adversaries* who try to defend their own views against counterexamples and produce counterexamples to opposing views. The reasoning used to discover the claims, and the way the claims relate to other beliefs and systems of ideas are not considered relevant to philosophic reasoning if they are not deductive. (153)

In this description, Moulton contrasts the technique of the dyadic contest or competition through deduction with the technique of trying to interrelate whole belief systems and reasoning with one another. Notice how the insistence on deduction maintains a certain generic purity: in inquiring adversarily, each thinker is forced to assume the premises of the other, even if erroneous, and the argument must proceed point by point. A mutual evaluation of premises is not considered part of the process and can, very likely, yield no "winner" of a dispute. Without this evaluation, Moulton argues, proponents of certain views remain locked into their systems, and understanding is retarded or completely missed because the less deductive, less certain path of mutual evaluation—and perhaps the consequent combination of premises—is inadmissible.

The purpose in adversarial technique is extremely narrow: "to convince an opponent" (159). However, Moulton shows that because many others, in addition to opponents, may need to hear a point of view, other kinds of reasoning may be more suitable. Adversarial behaviors lack this social alertness and are virtually obsessed with the local task of merely prevailing in an argument. In this way, philosophy—and, I add, most academic discourse—loses its social bearings as it becomes ever-more deeply immersed in the characteristically socially masculine value of competing and winning according to strict rules. Basic questions, Moulton continues, such as "Why is this argument important?" are usually not considered pertinent in the argument itself: "one can consider not only whether Descartes' proofs of the existence of God are valid, but what good reasons there are for proving the existence of God" (161). It is considered unfair or beyond the "rules of the game" to raise the question of *why* Descartes wanted to offer his proofs to begin with, rather than simply going along with the premise that a proof is necessary. This unspoken rule about accepting one's opponents' premises makes it possible for one thinker holding more social authority to dominate a particular inquiry, and this is just what happens in the ordinary university classroom; the premises of the professor—as given, for example, in the reading lists, the kinds of writing required in a course, the style of classroom conduct, and the conception of what counts as a useful contribution—are not usually open to scrutiny and change. Lerner warns, in this connection, that a "thinking woman stays far longer than is useful within the boundaries or the question-setting defined by the 'great men'" (227).

Moulton makes another point about how academic discourse is restricted. She says that "experience may be a necessary element in certain reasoning processes" (162). Yet, most philosophical discussion, she observes, proceeds "as if experience plays no essential role in the philosophical positions one holds." Moulton is saying that in the discourse itself, reference is rarely made to actual human experience even though it is assumed that *some* aspects of *someone*'s lived experience renders the discourse rational to begin with. In philosophical discourse, the arguments usually proceed as if their reference to experience were either self-evident or unnecessary or both. Because winning the argument is the most important thing, particularizing one's points with clear reference to lived experience may reveal the argument's false generality, thus making it only partially valid and thereby losing the chance of winning. The obvious likelihood that two opposing arguments are both partially valid and thus complementary—a very productive result—is eschewed in favor of the unquestioned wish to establish some "winning," transcendental, or prevailing principle. This is also true in many other kinds of academic discourse, which is often marked by the citation of authoritative and published opinions but not the kind of experience that appears in conversation or other informal, "unofficial" sources.

Even if philosophers or historians or critics carefully reported their own experience, that would be a good start to establish a movement between experience and argument that would change academic discourse radically. (Shortly, I will give an example in literary criticism of what such a radical change might be like.) Academic discourse works in a tradition of deliberately *excluding* experience, of aiming to purify thought of both experience and feeling so that some ideal of pure truth, linked to the intellectual formulations of one or a few men, may somehow miraculously come to preside over everyone's common experience of living. This, too, is what Lerner is warning against in the historical role of so-called "great men."

Recognizing the Range of Genders

In *Research in the Teaching of English*, Stephen North reports on an interesting experiment. His aim is to give evidence that when a variety of kinds of writing and reading are used by students in an ungraded course in philosophy, a new "kind of individuality" emerges "that defies market surveys, political polls, and standardized test scores, and that bedevils an educational system designed to treat the class and not the student as its basic unit" (257). In his citation of many different styles of student writing, North argues for the necessity of taking all of it very seriously by using hermeneutic techniques normally applied to canonized texts in academic disciplines. In one case, for example, he sifts through many different kinds of statements to show, finally, how a student's religious beliefs enabled her to strike a certain consistent point of view, and to create her simultaneous awareness *both* of her own perspective as it developed in class and the philosophical issues presented to her by teachers and textbooks. Without claiming that the boundaries of his students' knowledge were permanently fixed, North shows that hermeneutic attention to the students' journals, to "their own experience as philosophers and thinkers, in and out of school," to the class discussions, to the syllabus, to the textbook, and to the influence of the instructors are all necessary ingredients for a responsible interpretation of a person's range of writing "genders" (233).

North further emphasizes the intersubjective character (255) of the literacy context he studied—the tendency of both writers and readers to assume a conversation with other members of the class—the instructors, the textbooks, or the other students. This assumption, permitted in part by the ungraded classroom, leads to usages not normally found in either expository prose or academic discourse. For example, there's the informal interrogative: "How come there is no Reese [the teacher] entry?" There's the generic use of the second person: Truth "is what you are aware of in your world, but it is not solipsism because your ego is the dichotomy of a world which is you and the objects which are not you" (253). (Notice how in this statement "you" becomes an enriched and philosophical category just following the informal uses.) And there's the use of colloquial black English to understand the teacher: "If what you put in the journal is insufficient he like, give you like give you different philosophers to—He ask you how you feel about them, y' know, you write your opinion on what you think, y' know, they mean to you" (244). Those who doubt that black English contributes to the cultivation of everyone's literacy can see in this citation its oral premises—the repeated y' know's—and how such premises exist in other forms in white English and in all people's writing and speech.

Although North does not discuss it explicitly in his essay, collaborative work is one of the classroom procedures that is also part of the approach to writing he describes. Because voices as well as texts are now included in what we mean by literacy, students can be urged, more and more, to write directly to one another. The underlying idea of engaging others directly is becoming essential to the teaching of language use. The interpersonal emphasis is helping to expand the actual written forms, and the context for writing is increasingly expected to be a living one—real people as opposed to hypothetical audiences. Insofar as writing and speaking are considered as one, new forms of writing can include a variety of combinations of styles both coming from traditional formal habits and those coming from the richness of everyday conversation, gossip, banter—forms which make it easier to include candid feelings, doubts, opinions, guesses, and other "subjunctive" moods.

The need to make the context of language use a living one is not limited to one discipline. Stiff formal, purely written writing is boring and inhibiting to everyone and every subject. But please note again the key ingredients for change: the inclusion of a variety of writing styles in the subject; the reduction or elimination of grading of various pieces of writing; the change in role of the teacher from an assumed authority to a reliable, participating respondent and guide; the regular oral and written engagement of all writers with other writers in the class; the pursuit of both individual language history as well as the set of social belongings and political interests brought to school by each person. In this last connection, I want to enlarge and change North's description of a "basic" unit in school. The "student" can no longer be understood as a single person; in fact, there is no longer any single basic unit. As we think more in terms of permeable boundaries, or categories that are both necessary and loose, no one item is necessarily basic, but each new class, each new course, establishes its own new categories.

In order to show finally that two or more mutually implicated but nevertheless flexible "genders" of writing are needed to mobilize each person's contribution to the language community, let me recount a development from one of my own classes. In my introductory graduate course in modern criticism, a folklore student, Ms. W, read Mary E. Wilkins Freeman's short story, "Old Woman Magoun." She wrote one commentary in a formal critical voice and another in an informal personal voice. I want to show that her criticism could not exist with only one of those voices, and that more than two genders of writing appear in her work.

Here, first, is a brief summary of the story. Old Woman Magoun, by holding out the promise of a good home-cooked meal, bribed the men in her town of Barry's Ford to finish building a bridge leading out of town. On the afternoon of the day that the men were about to finish work on the bridge, Old Woman Magoun sent her fourteen-year-old granddaughter and ward, Lily Barry, to the store for salt, something she was very reluctant to do because the store was a hangout for men. On the way to the store, Lily met Jim Willis, the handsome friend and possible cousin of Lily's estranged father, Nelson Barry, "the fairly dangerous degenerate of a good old family." Although Willis was "nicer than some," he was somewhat too interested in Lily. At the store, Lily meets her father, who gives her some candy. This event alarms Old Woman Magoun. After the dinner for the bridge-builders is over, Nelson Barry comes to Old Woman Magoun's home to inform her that he intends to take over custody of Lily. Magoun sees that Barry intends simply to give Lily to Jim Willis to pay off a gambling debt. On the way back from a futile attempt to have Lily adopted by a couple in another town, Greenham, Magoun does not stop Lily from eating deadly nightshade berries; she lets Lily die, promising her that she will go "to a beautiful place." After her death, life goes on in Barry's Ford as usual.

Here is some of Ms. W's critical commentary. Its voice and tone should seem familiar:

> On the surface it is the story of the building of a bridge in Barry's Ford, a community depicted as isolated, traditional, and stagnant, set apart from the world by both mountain and river. When one seemingly spiritually living creature in this community, an assertive Old Woman Magoun, shames the men into activity, the disruption in traditional stagnation signals a challenge to Nelson Barry who seemingly has the most to lose in authority from this innovation. The construction of the bridge, then, forms a frame for the first part of the story.... By separating herself from her granddaughter Lily in her preoccupation with the bridge, Old Woman Magoun thereby unknowingly sets out on a path which has only one recognized ending in view, as Freeman utilizes at this point the tale of Demeter and Persephone.
>
> Demeter, the Greco-Roman goddess of agriculture, had a single daughter by Zeus, the husband of Hera. That daughter, Persephone the "flower-faced maiden," was promised by Zeus, unbeknownst to either mother or daughter, to his brother Hades, ruler of the dead. While "playing apart from her mother," Persephone is lured by a deceptive display of flowers into Hades' clutches and is carried off. Her mother, grief-stricken, ravages the earth until she is returned to her. Demeter discovers, however, upon questioning the girl that she had innocently accepted "something edible, covertly, namely a sweet pomegranate seed, just one." Thus deceived Persephone "should not abide the rest of her days at the side of her mother," but must "redescend into the underworld," Hades' realm.

In this sample, so far, while both phases are recognizably academic discourse, only the second paragraph is expository prose. In the first paragraph, words like "stagnant" and "spiritually living creature" invoke values of criticism and represent the informed judgment of a responsive adult and a future academic. Statements like "forms a frame for the first part of the story" are part of conventional critical jargon, both inoffensive and useful in this context, I would say, but of a different type of authority from the earlier judgments I cited.

What Ms. W finally does with the expository narrative and the critical presentation of the story is to combine them toward a mixed genre; she develops a formal critical reading with reference to the myth. She notes that Lily is named for a flower, that Willis, like Hades, is related to the main villain, Lily's father, "who is 'looked up to . . . as to an evil deity'" in Barry's Ford. Ms. W also notes that at the time the story was written, people believed "that in past ages young, virgin women were sacrificed in propitiatory rites upon the completion of bridges. The assumption, on the part of these 'enlightened' scholars, that female blood and lives were appropriate complements to male labors would seem to tell us more about their own society than it would about that of hypothetical 'primitive' ancestors." Thus far, her combination of voices has given a straightforward mythological and/or folkloric reading of the story, which, of course, enlightened everyone in class, myself included. This reading then led Ms. W to the nub of her critical work, an interpretation of the story with special emphasis on the symbolism of the bridge:

> Built by men, the bridge is physically deceptive, its very structure, "a primitive structure built of logs in a slovenly fashion," shows its safety to be illusory. And as an opportunity of escape it is equally illusory, for the outside world, Greenham, is no different in essence than Barry's Ford. Mrs. Mason [the woman whom Magoun asked to adopt Lily] is denied Lily by her husband for the most arbitrary of reasons, despite her overwhelming need for a daughter. The bridge is a structure built by men, leading from a world of men, to a world of men. Attempting to use men's work, Magoun becomes a participant in men's work; Lily is first deceived by the men, believing "that man who walked to the store was nicer than some" and crossing with her grandmother is then deceived by her also, "those berries look good to eat, Grandma . . . they look real nice." Refusing to give Lily to the Barry's, Magoun instead gives her to the berries, a significant word play by the author signifying the basic equivalency of both actions.

With this reading, Ms. W brings her criticism into the contemporary scene. After using the myth to help solve the riddle of why a grandmother would sacrifice her own granddaughter, Ms. W then exposes the political situation which existed in classical times, in Freeman's time, and in our own time—the fact that a spiritually alive and assertive woman is forced into cooperation with the degenerate patriarchal villain, the best choice in her life being the murder by default of her own female kin—a theme, by the way, apparently revived recently by Toni Morrison in *Beloved.*

By traditional standards of critical discourse, there is nothing missing in this intelligent and courageous piece of work. You might wish to note what a good idea it is to completely ignore the grammatical errors in Ms. W's writing, the fragments, the run-ons, the misuses of apostrophe, as we are taken over by the sheer intelligence and conviction of the writing. But what we have no way of seeing in this piece of academic discourse is its rootedness in, as Moulton discusses, the actual experience of the writer. Ms. W, however, included this experience in her work, as well, and I would like to note the difference it shows in its "gender":

> Leafing back through the mental catalog of past experiences, I realized that I had in fact been there before. Years ago, in another country altogether. In fact, I had forgotten—purposefully—all about it. . . .
>
> I was hired by a family in a village in France called Malchamps. In terms of my personal experiences there I think it is appropriately named. . . . Transportation out of the village was obtained by hoofing it to the highway and hitchhiking from there. . . .
>
> It seemed ordinary enough. Big cheerful father, small invalid wife need household help to do housework, look after two very small children, ages one and two. When I saw the house it was very obvious that the wife needed help—it was frankly a filthy shambles. She was pregnant, and very ill, and the children were very healthy and extremely active. So I went to work for Daniel and Flory. . . .
>
> Flory was an Asian-Indian who spoke neither French nor English very well. She could not speak at all with her neighbors. . . . She seldom left the house because she was always so ill, this illness directly caused by being pregnant. . . . She has been continually pregnant since she had married Daniel. Curious. Daniel also had two children [from his first marriage] who lived next door with his parents. Curiouser.
>
> Like a complete idiot I never gave any of this appropriate thought until other things began to happen. Daniel began to become more and more attentive to me. He would be constantly requesting *petit baiser* but they seemed to constantly miss my cheeks and land square on my mouth. He always found occaisions [sic] to accidentally cop feels under the table. I began to dread Flory leaving the room because this seemed to signal for him a new opportunity to corner me and grab. But the worst was the night I went to bed at the same time as Flory. When Daniel came up he stopped in my room and insisted on his good night kiss, but oh no he didn't want to disturb me, just stay there in bed, I'll come in. . . .

Ms. W goes on to narrate how Flory knew about Daniel's behavior, his fondling of female guests at their wedding reception, and how she deceived her in order to keep her on to help. She reported how Flory "hated her life, she hated Daniel, she hated the village, but that she was trapped. I believe she hated me too because I *could* leave." Finally, Ms. W observes,

> I think that maybe I have been to "Barry's Ford" but had ample opportunity to leave. I know of someone who isn't leaving, however. I was aquainted [sic] with a large, sloppy degenerate who was very fond of his liquor and cigarettes—who seemed to be "nicer than some" when I first met him. And I was aquainted [sic] with the woman married to him, and was told how she felt. This places a bit of perspective on the type of choice Old Woman Magoun made, for me at any rate.

Historically, this experience preceded Ms. W's reading and interpretation of "Old Woman Magoun." In the essay, her account of the experience followed her critical discussion. Actually, however, there is no way to separate the two genders of writing. There is no way to separate misspellings, usages which directly integrate dialogue into the narrative without markers, and phrases like "hoofing it" and "cop feels" and "like a complete idiot," from thoughts such as "female blood and lives were appropriate complements to male labors." The same mind lives in both genders. The same person was a citizen of Malchamps, Barry's Ford, Fairmount (Ms. W's hometown in Indiana), Indiana University, the Folklore department, the English department, and my criticism course. Of course, neither expository prose nor academic discourse is essentially or intrinsically masculine. But the social isolation of these forms from other oral, colloquial, informal, and technically relaxed forms such as Ms. W's narrative of actual experience is maintained in the service of a masculine ideal of a pure discourse, like the private masculine language of Learned Latin described by Walter Ong, the language of abstraction uncontaminated by the loose ends and ragged edges of the mother tongues.

Mother tongues and any other tongues do not have no gender any more than expository prose as now taught has no politics. And they do not have *either* this *or* that gender. But as you can see from the various samples of writing I cited, including those in a more traditional idiom, even the most apparently homogeneous writing includes elements of other genres; any one piece or kind of writing turns out to include other kinds. Because of this fact, I think different genders of writing enjoy life in each subject matter, each discipline. To recognize this range of genders—why, *that's* the bridge out of Barry's Ford!

Works Cited

Chodorow, Nancy. *The Reproduction of Mothering: Psychoanalysis and the Sociology of Gender*. Berkeley: U of California P, 1978.

Cohen, Ralph. "The Autobiography of a Critical Problem." Midwest MLA Convention. Bloomington, IN, Nov. 1984.

Dinnerstein, Dorothy. *The Mermaid and the Minotaur: Sexual Arrangements and Human Malaise*. New York: Harper, 1987.

Freeman, Mary Eleanor Wilkins. *"Old Woman Magoun," "The Winning Lady" and Others*. n.p. Harper and Brothers, 1909.

Lerner, Gerda. *The Creation of Patriarchy*. New York: Oxford, 1987.

Morrison, Toni. *Beloved*. New York: Knopf, 1987.

Moulton, Janice. "A Paradigm of Philosophy: The Adversary Method." *Discovering Reality: Feminist Perspectives on Epistemology, Metaphysics, Methodology, and Philosophy of Science*. Ed. Sandra Harding and Merrill B. Hintikka. Dordrecht, Holland: D. Reidel, 1983. 149-64.

North, Stephen. "Writing in a Philosophy Class: Three Case Studies." *Research in the Teaching of English* 20 (1986): 225-62.

Ong, Walter J. *Orality and Literacy: The Technologizing of the Word*. London: Methuen, 1982.

Ohmann, Richard. *English in America: A Radical View of the Profession*. New York: Oxford UP, 1976.

—. "Use Definite, Specific, Concrete Language." *College English* 41 (1979): 390-97.

Russ, Joanna. "When it Changed." *The Norton Anthology of Literature by Women: The Tradition in English*. Ed. Sandra M. Gilbert and Susan Gubar. New York: Norton, 1985. 2262-269.

Beside Ourselves: Rhetoric and Representation in Postcolonial Feminist Writing

Susan C. Jarratt

The value of postcolonial theory for teachers of writing arises in part from its focus on the rhetorical situation of intellectual work applied to the question of difference. By pointing out that academic traditions of Western universities are built on several centuries of economic and cultural imperialism, this theory demands that scholars and teachers of literature and literacies ask rhetorical questions the answers to which had been for many years assumed: who speaks? on behalf of whom? who is listening? and how? It interrogates the assumption of any group identification and more specifically the relationship of the single "I" to a collective "we" (see Anderson, Mohanty, Roof and Wiegman[1]).

My aim in this essay is to address the problem of speaking for others by looking at how "others" speak. Employing the figures of metaphor and metonymy, I analyze the ways three postcolonial feminists open up the workings of representation—of the self, groups, and audiences—such that participants are no longer disposed in the classical rhetorical position, a single subject facing an audience, but rather, "beside themselves." This colloquial expression calls to mind situations of deep emotional turmoil—worry, anger, or maybe grief. Perhaps it means that, in times of intense emotional distress, one loses bodily or mental integrity and manufactures another version of oneself to express or absorb the pain. My appropriation of the expression bears some relation to its everyday use, in the sense that oppressed groups experience the pain of self-distancing or alienation (Fanon). As a rhetorician, though, I am interested in the way an experience of suffering is turned into a tool of language: an artful, rhetorical practice of self-multiplication used by speakers in response to their historical, rhetorical, and institutional circumstances. I am also interested in the way a painful image of self-division could be transformed into a hopeful vision of alliance. Tracing representational strategies of postcolonial feminist rhetoric might offer ways for composition teachers and students to imagine that scene—a difficult task in a culture that values individualism so highly. I hope this essay will contribute to that project in three ways: by analyzing changes in concepts of ethos and audience under the historical conditions of postcoloniality; by describing complex processes of writing the self; and, by attending to the ways teachers and students in U.S. universities "read" (about) formerly colonized people.

Figuring Structures of Relation

How can differences be imagined? In what forms of relation? Rhetoric is useful for addressing these questions because it gives names to figures which structure relations in language and in the material world. Any choice of a figure is a discursive act that also simultaneously configures a material relationship of power and difference. One of the ways postcolonial theory has heightened attention to the politics of representation is to point out that exercises of domination occur not only in the sphere of politics proper but also through cultural practices. They insist on the dual functions of rhetoric as both political and figurative representation.[2] Gayatri Chakravorty Spivak, in her now-canonical essay "Can the Subaltern Speak?" warns first-world intellectuals about the danger of obscuring their own acts of discursive imperialism in the process of facilely "representing" the interests of apparently silent subjects of oppression. She makes her point historically and philologically, using Marx's essay on the mid-nineteenth-century coup d'etat of Louis Bonaparte, who came to "represent" a peasant class politically through an exercise of executive power without their having any consciousness of themselves as a class—that is, without participating in an imaginative or political construction of themselves as a class (Marx 602, 608). The typical translation of two different German words (*Vertretung* and *Darstellung*) into a single English word, "representation," emblemizes for Spivak the danger of collapsing these two distinct processes: the first, a political or legal process of standing for members of a constituency group; the second a symbolic process of creating images of such groups ("Subaltern" 276; see also Landry and MacLean 198). She associates these two forms of representation with two kinds of rhetoric, persuasion and trope, graphically captured in the analogies of "proxy" and "portrait"—arguing that in her historical example of Louis Bonaparte the former assumes or enacts the latter: "The event of representation as [a political process] . . . behaves like an [imaging], taking its place in the gap between the formation of a (descriptive) class and the nonformation of a (transformative) class" ("Subaltern" 277). In other words, when someone uses power over others to represent them politically—to act for them—there is an unavoidable, concomitant symbolic process underway: the represented group is sketched, painted, described in a particular way through that process. And this description may or may not "represent" them in ways they themselves would endorse.

The reason Spivak writes "nonformation" is to emphasize that "identity" as a class does not take place naturally (at what she calls "ground level consciousness "), but rather must be constructed through acts of political agency and self-description ("Subaltern" 277-78). One cannot assume a class identity for the French peasants Louis Bonaparte forcibly represented in the absence of their own representations of themselves or of acts on their behalf as a class. The backlash against feminism in the U.S. (and other countries as well) offers a contemporary example of processes of "nonformation" and transformation. Many women on university campuses reject feminism—i.e., reject being identified as a politicized class, "women"—because they believe they haven't had a hand in constructing the symbolic representations of the class. In Women's Studies classes, female students actually read and discuss the works of feminists (as opposed to absorbing uncritically the grotesque caricatures offered on talk radio and other popular media). As they talk and write about the ways their self-identification fits with or differs from the representations they read, a process of class-formation/transformation takes place, creating a locally grounded understanding of the class "women" from which some will actually go forward to act out of that class consciousness (in campus activism, volunteer work, or career choices). Inevitably, their subsequent actions as "women" on behalf of other "women" will recreate the gap between political agency and self-description.[3]

Discovering the workings of these two forms of representation at any site, the interwoven operations of imaging—textual descriptions of otherness—and political representation—entailing identification of or with a group—is the work of teachers and students of language practices. Rhetoric mobilizes an interaction between representation (political) and re-presentation (cultural), possibly enabling the transformative practices Marx found missing in the nineteenth-century French peasants: i.e., driving the movement from descriptive to transformative class, or at least calling attention to where and by whom groups are described. It is my argument that some postcolonial feminists have been particularly useful in activating rhetoric in these two senses, and that an analysis of their work in these terms might advance the argument over identity politics, helping to delineate with more care and refinement the bases on which identities are constructed, claimed, and linked with others. This framework might serve the ethical aim of "recognizing the responsibility for linking" (Faigley 237).

My method in the body of the essay is to use rhetorical figures—metaphor and metonymy—to analyze the ways postcolonial feminist writing calls attention to these dual processes of representation: political and pictorial. In this analysis, I take metaphor as a figure of substitution: one thing or person standing in for another and, in the process, obscuring some particularities of what it represents.[4] A metaphoric style of representation occurs any time a speaker or writer functions as a spokesperson for a particular category of people—workers, women, voters in a particular constituency—the partiality of the single member standing in for the whole. Here is an example of a critic using this definition of metaphor to distinguish autobiography from *testimonio*:

> In rhetorical terms, whose political consequences may be evident, there is a fundamental difference here between the *metaphor* of autobiography and heroic narrative in general, which assumes an identity-by-substituting one (superior) signifier for another (I for we, leader for follower, Christ for the faithful), and metonymy, a lateral move of identification-through-relationship, which acknowledges the possible differences among "us" as components of a centerless whole. (Sommer 61)

Metonymy, on the other hand, as the passage above suggests, creates a chain of associations. It configures a relationship based on contiguity and context (Jakobson 79, 83, 90-91; Irigaray; Brady). The example of metonymy provided by Jakobson has an eerie resonance for postcolonial history. A hut may metonymically be associated with "thatched roof," "family of twelve," or "burnt by the army," each association creating a narrative or contextualized understanding of the word without displacing or blocking out the word itself. Applying metonymy to identity politics suggests that differences can be spoken of not in terms of exclusive categories but rather as places, descriptions, or narratives of relation. The writings of Gayatri Spivak and Trinh T. Minh-ha offer eloquent illustrations of what I see as a metonymic process of subject construction; each simultaneously makes visible the intellectual work of theorizing and gives voice to varieties of otherness, placing themselves not at the head of some silent group of followers but rather beside themselves. But in so doing, they unavoidably participate in a metaphoric process of representing "others," thus enacting a tension between these two modes. After analyzing rhetorics of linkage and spatial location in texts of the Spivak and Trinh, I will turn to a very different text. The 1983 *testimonio* of Rigoberta Menchú Tum,[5] a Quiché Indian peasant and peace activist, arose from the midst of the Guatemalan civil war, a situation calling forth different strategies of representation from those used by postcolonial feminist academics writing within the context of the U.S. academy.[6]

Immigrant Academics as Metonymic Subjects

My first two subjects are both professional "representers," engaged in literary criticism and cultural critique (Spivak); in documentary filmmaking, ethnography, and cultural theory (Trinh). These feminist theorists are hypersensitive to the constructed nature of the discourse of personal experience yet, nonetheless, acknowledge the need for the representation of others—to give others a vocal and visible presence. They both meet this need through the production of what Spivak terms "counter-sentences" by subjects of imperialism: alternatives to re-presentations—images of the "other"—produced from within dominant cultures. Such counter-sentences come into being through the strategic placement and voicing of narrative, but both Trinh and Spivak seek to avoid speaking for the other through displacement and indirection. Unlike the "Third World intellectuals" in metropolitan universities described by Ahmad who "materially represent the undifferentiated colonized Other. . . without much examining of their own presence in that institution" (92), Trinh and Spivak figure themselves with an awareness of their placement within systems of privilege and draw attention to the modes of production and consumption of their academic work.

I turn first to cultural critic, Gayatri Spivak, an upper-caste Indian, an economic immigrant from Calcutta who has studied and taught in English departments in U.S. universities since the early sixties. This biographical sentence introduces Spivak to those who don't know of her work but, by consolidating her into a unified, coherent subject, works against the grain of her own rhetoric. In the second half of the "Subaltern" essay, Spivak calls into question the desire of first world intellectuals for an authentic native voice when that desire is directed toward people like her.[7] Spivak is at pains to point out her difference from that Other. She complicates the illusion of a single "native voice" by delineating various positions among Indians under British occupation. Setting off a silent underclass from those in closer contact with their colonizers, Spivak uses as her prime example a colonial subject whose agency and voice had the least possibility of being heard—Indian widows who became victims of sati, sacrificial burning—to demonstrate how many of the historically colonized had in fact no legitimate platform from which to speak ("Subaltern" 297-308; see also Mani). Spivak argues that this situation is a problem not only for first-world intellectuals but for diasporic post-colonial academics as well in their own production of knowledge about their homelands. Her conclusion is that a postcolonial intellectual cannot speak for these unrepresented groups but only to them in an imagined conversation across class lines and historical distances ("Subaltern" 295). The emphasis here is on "imagined," for of course Spivak assumes no possibility of reaching the present-day remnants of this group through the rarefied discourses of Western academies.[8] Rather, she uses this formulation to displace the representative potential of her own voice, opening a space for others. "Speaking to" might be construed as a movement from the metaphoric to the metonymic. Instead of substituting one voice for another, the speaker adds another voice to the parallel strands of discourse, a voice without its own clear origin. Her writings stand along side other accounts and the person herself who continues to re-generate a speaking subject.

The ethical implications of Spivak's performance lie in its difference from, on the one hand, a rhetoric of substitution, and, on the other, from what Mohanty calls a "Western, postmodernist notion of agency and consciousness which often announces the splintering of the subject, and privileges multiplicity in the abstract" (37). Spivak's performance should be understood as an ethical practice of seeking to displace any fixed sense of knowledge of the "other" a Western listener might be tempted to grasp through an encounter with an elite, immigrant academic. When "card-carrying hegemonic" listeners listen for someone speaking as an Indian, a Third World woman speaking as a Third World woman, Spivak asserts, ignorance of a complex history is covered over with a fabricated homogeneity ("Alterity" 270). Within her chosen area of literary and cultural studies,[9] Spivak puts before a Western audience a multitude of postcolonial subjects—the Indian widow of 1829, the sixteen-year-old member of an Indian independence group who committed suicide in Calcutta in 1926, the women workers in today's Export Processing Zones—along with her own "selves."

Indeed, it seems that part of Spivak's strategy for multiplying others is achieved through the manufacture of more and more versions of herself. She has experienced an amazing degree of public scrutiny, and

I'm interested in examining how she has negotiated her self-constitution through that process. *The Post-Colonial Critic*, a series of interviews, collects and multiplies the many versions of this "highly commodified academic," as she ironically calls herself ("Word" 130). In an interview with Ellen Rooney, she acknowledges complaints that "Spivak talks too much about herself" ("Word" 130). Though this focus on the self might suggest the seduction of "representativeness," it might also be read as a continuing attempt to disperse the representative Indian in the U.S. academy.

Spivak is meticulous about her own processes of self-identification. Refusing several of the available options for self-representation—unmediated accounts of experience, the philosophical voice from nowhere, and the hollow echoes of the now-dead "author"—Spivak instead practices "deidentification . . . a claiming of an identity from a text that comes from somewhere else."[10] Resisting the Western academy's attempt to hear from her the voice of the native, she differentiates "talking about oneself "from a process of "graphing one's bio" such that it becomes representative of certain histories ("Word" 130). In this formulation, the text represents, not the self. This process of contexture and displacement begins when Spivak identifies herself with contingent and polemical labels—"woman," "literary critic," "Asian intellectual," "Non-Resident Indian." She then reveals the persistence of imperialist and sexist attitudes by recounting situations when one or another of those labels provoked conflict or effected marginalization in public forums. But instead of grounding these claims in authenticity, Spivak practices what she calls a reactive strategy, adopting different identities at different times to create a consciousness of the hazards of fixity and substitution. She seems to be saying, "If you take me to be a feminist, I'll show how I'm not the same as Western feminists. If you take me for an Indian, I'll explain elite immigrant privilege. If you define me as anti-institutional, I show you the disciplinarian." Spivak consistently cannot be found where she is sought. She signals the relatively minimal significance of color and former colonial status (those markers of difference through which she appears as the representative Indian) through references to her high caste status, the historical moment within which her immigration took place (the early '60s brain drain of Indians to the UK and U.S.), and the benefits accruing to her as the product of a British education from American academics' Anglophilia. In specifying the geographical, economic and class locations of her background and academic formation, she engages in the project Ahmad calls "periodizing": connecting academic practices with modes of production and larger historical movements, rather than assuming their distance from the material world (Ahmad 36).

In introductory passages contextualizing the essays in her latest book, *Outside in the Teaching Machine*, Spivak reflects on her positions in relation to other women (see especially 121-29, 141-46). Returning to early writing enables her to place positions side by side in a narrative sequence:

> When I wrote "French Feminism in an International Frame" my assigned subject-position was actually determined by my moment in the United States and dominated my apparent choice of a postcolonial position. . . . Now it seems to me that the radical element of the postcolonial bourgeoisie must most specifically learn to negotiate with the structure of enabling violence that produced her. (145)

Spivak now seeks to negotiate "white feminism" rather than simply resisting it; she seeks not "to neglect the postcolonial's particular generalization in the vaster common space of woman" (145). Throughout these passages she rearticulates the problematic of representation: "It is obvious that these positions [feminism, European Enlightenment, nationhood, etc.], logically defined, swirl in the inaccessible intimacy of the everyday, giving hue to being. To fix it in paint is to efface as much as to disclose" (144-45).

It is through a carefully crafted rhetoric that Spivak revises her early position.[11] Sometimes tortured, almost always tortuous, her prose seems at times almost to parody classical philosophical argument. Deeply engaged with the most traditional philosophical issues, Spivak's prose is full of "lurches": unconventional word use (e.g. "to operate" as a conceptual process), abrupt transitions, unexpected juxtaposition of subjects. Where most academic readers are accustomed to the Aristotelian format—state your case and prove it—Spivak seems to work laterally, moving from case to case, point to point, rarely offering examples.[12] Despite all her efforts, we see an operation of substitution emerging when Toril Moi suggests that Spivak's texts might be representative of "an enactment of the violent clash of discourses experienced by the subject in exile" (20). Though her writing at first seems radically different from the *écriture féminine* of French feminists, I find common elements: along with deep engagements with the canonical male texts of Western culture, there is "a courageous effort to explode linear sequentiality, a deliberate desire to enact the decentering of the subject and its discourses" (Moi 21). Simultaneous with the pretense of what Catherine Clément calls "democratic transmission" (Cixous and Clément)—i.e. the implicit agreement with a reader that she seeks to communicate—we find at times "a text where the connections are so elusive as to become private" (Moi 20). I've seen some of the same patterns in the writing of female students: a struggle under the burden of a masculine literary heritage, a movement from public communication into the realm of private codes, a break-down in the conventional structures of argument. I'm suggesting not that these textual features be celebrated as expressions of a gendered essence, nor praised as the curious idiosyncrasies of a brilliant thinker, but rather be read as symptoms—textual traces of a strained encounter with multiple forms of dominance. Within, then, Spivak's meticulous and principled renunciation of a representation of substitution, her highly artful theory and practice of metonymic association with others, I find an informing if painful case of writing difference.

Trinh T. Minh-ha claims writing without equivocation as the defining act for "third world women," a phrase she chooses despite its anachronistic assumption of a tri-partite division of world powers and the risk of homogenization. From the jacket of her first book *Woman, Native, Other: Writing Postcoloniality and Feminism*, we learn that she is a writer, filmmaker, composer, and academic. But, despite the fact that her text is full of first person pronouns both singular and plural, her one moment of specific self-definition is delayed until late in the book and displaced into third person: "From jagged transitions between the headless and bottomless storytelling, what is exposed in this text is the inscription and de-scription of a non-unitary female subject of color through her engagement, therefore also disengagement, with master discourses" (43). The self she creates in her text is figured by the broken mirror. It destroys a pure relation of "I to I" (23), but does not cease reflecting: "here reality is not reconstituted, it is put into pieces so as to allow another world to rebuild (keep on unbuilding and rebuilding) itself with its debris" (23). The subject is dispersed throughout her text, yet Trinh speaks at times with complete presence, easily adopting the role of "writing woman" (as opposed to "written woman") and using conventions of the "priest-god scheme" (her version of the critique of the author). Her discussion of commitment, responsibility, and guilt capture Trinh as a most consolidated subject: "In a sense, committed writers are the ones who write both to awaken to the consciousness of their guilt and to give their readers a guilty conscience. Bound to one another by an awareness of their guilt, writer and reader may thus assess their positions, engaging themselves wholly in their situations and carrying their weight into the weight of their communities, the weight of the world" (10-11). For those on the margin, Trinh suggests, constructing a "we" implies a responsibility for representation. While Spivak only goes to far as to speak of "unlearning privilege," Trinh foregrounds the ethical entailments of her representative status.

At other moments she delights in the multiplicity of voices in writing, dividing herself into subject and object through a play of pronouns: "writing . . . is an ongoing practice that is concerned not with inserting a 'me' into language, but with creating an opening where the 'me' disappears while 'I' endlessly come and go" (35). She then breaks the boundary of that "i": "Taking in any voice that goes through me, I/i will answer every time someone says: I. One woman within another, eternally" (37). Pronouns are powerful tools for Trinh, who doubles the "I" in capital and lower case, privileging the subject case (but multiple) "I" over the object "me." This mix of modes—metaphoric and metonymic—stymies attempts to categorize her and enacts her point that "Woman can only redefine while being defined by language" (44).

The visuals in her text—stills from her movies—illustrate her strategy of multiplication and a metonymic style of representation. Offering multiple images rather than a single image breaks apart a process of metaphoric substitution. That we see the "native woman" with a child and without, calls into question a Western stereotype of non-Western women as primarily reproducers of masses of "others." The subject smiles directly into the camera, presumably held by Trinh (or perhaps an associate), indicating her apparent ease and pleasure in the process of being represented by another "other," suggesting perhaps a collaboration in the process of representation (see Bal). That she is shown in various "sizes," with child and without, looking into the camera and looking off, suggests subjects in context, in motion—not able to be caught or reduced through a single process of substitution.

Trinh's most effective strategy for moving between metaphoric and metonymic subjectivities is her frequent use of a broad ironic tone. In the following passage, she sarcastically rejects the position of authenticity, mimicking (but at the same time using) a voice of unreflective autobiography: "I am so much that nothing can enter me or pass through me. I struggle, I resist, and I am filled with my own self. [Here the tone shifts.] The 'personal' may liberate as it may enslave" (35). On the same issue, she asks: "How do you inscribe difference without bursting into a series of euphoric narcissistic accounts of yourself and your own kind?" Trinh wants to find her way between "navel-gazing and navel-erasing" (28).

Trinh is sensitive to the current seductions of fashionable otherness in academic circles, devoting the better part of a chapter to what she terms the "special" third world woman issue. Parodying the title of a special issue of an academic journal, she points out how both the Western audience and the iconized postcolonial are complicit in dealing with otherness as a special issue: "Specialness as a soporific soothes, anaesthetizes my sense of justice; it is, to the wo/man of ambition, as effective a drug of psychological self-intoxication as alcohol is to the exiles of society" (88). The admonition is to be more sensitive to the systems of authorization, as well as the (very Western) myth of authenticity.

For Trinh, the relation to the collective is highly textualized but still there. Again we hear her mimicking one of the familiar voices of the American collective:

> A writing *for* the people, *by* the people, and *from* the people is, literally, a multipolar reflecting reflection that remains free from the conditions of subjectivity and objectivity and yet reveals them both. I write to show myself showing people who show me my own showing. I-You: not one, not two. (22)

I hear in this passage a bold refiguration of the "subject," involving the group in its formation and complicating visibility as it is theorized in classical Western systems of representation.

Trinh is more at ease than Spivak in making common cause across differences. She accepts the alliance of non-white U.S. minorities with citizens of the older non-aligned nations who made up the original "Third World" group. She finds more threat in the colonialist creed of Divide and Conquer than she does in the threat of obscuring differences when such pacts are made. The radical dispersion of self through writing coexists in this text with a voice of collective solidarity. This coexistence in the rhetorical scene is articulated metonymically: "The process of differentiation . . . continues, and speaking nearby or together with certainly differs from speaking for and about." (101). "Difference does not annul identity. It is beyond and alongside identity " (104).

What strikes me as most apt in the specifically *post*colonial rhetoric of these two feminists is the tension here between metonymic and metaphoric representation—between a poststructural dispersal of subjectivity and an ethical commitment to analyzing communication in terms of the material realities of speakers and listeners. Postcolonial feminists dare to commit theoretical inconsistency, deploying a pragmatic rhetoric that suits their multiple locations. The principled resistance to the temptation to speak for India, for Vietnam, for women is joined with the principled impulse to put the voice of the "other" in play in first-world academic discourse. When we hear Spivak's speaking to (rather than for or about) and Trinh's speaking alongside, we hear an attempt to move between the two poles in the double session of representation.

For both writers, the metonymic operation of speaking alongside is not divided sharply from a rhetoric of substitution; they co-exist, operating simultaneously. Practices of political representation cannot avoid the enactment of symbolic representation, the constant process of creating and recreating public images of difference. Actually appearing through symbolic representation entails access to public forums gained through (loosely defined) political processes. Both these writers are fully aware of their representational function: they do speak for the other. But they simultaneously recast images and frustrate any simple process of representation. As post-colonial subjects located in the metropolitan academic scene, both choose a complex construction of subjectivity in an ethical response to the exigencies of that placement.

These choices are consummately rhetorical, revealing a disruption of conventional assumptions about ethos and audience. Unlike the classical scenario, wherein the speaker constructs an ethos in relation to an audience—assuming it to be a group of which he was a member—the habitus of the postcolonial feminist is not shared by a Western academic audience.[13] The aim of this rhetoric is to open the distance between writer and audience rather than close it. Lunsford and Ede suggest a similar distancing in a recent self-critique of their earlier essay on audience, pointing out the "exclusionary tendencies of the rhetorical tradition" (174) in its assumption that the rhetor (and in their case, the student writer) would unproblematically seek to mold herself to the audience at hand. I believe these postcolonial feminist restructurings of ethos and audience might be helpful to teachers of writing and rhetoric. First, they illustrate through their elaboration of difference the power relations and assumptions about social similarity inherent in the classical model. Next, they might help us in developing strategies for our own speaking and writing that avoid reproducing unproblematically those older models, based on the assumption that speaker and audience will unquestionably share knowledge, goals, and habits. Finally, they might help us as we read student writing about the self to discover how students resist or refigure ethos and audience to characterize their own relations to the academy. I am not suggesting that students will consciously employ the complex tactics I have outlined in the writings of the two academic postcolonial feminists but rather that we might use Spivak's and Trinh's rhetorical gestures as guides for reading traces or symptoms of texts from students writing their own relations to institutional power. Imagining students capable of inscribing multiple selves could be an important reading posture for teachers concerned with subject construction in a postcolonial era.

I have proposed ways that the writings of Spivak and Trinh might contribute to rhetorical theory and to the reading practices of writing teachers.[14] The third subject of my analysis occupies a substantially different position in relation to composition studies in that (1) she was not a writer[15] and (2) her published account has appeared on reading lists for undergraduates across the country. As winner of the 1993 Nobel Peace Prize, Rigoberta Menchú Tum has gained international recognition as a spokesperson for her people. Given her chosen status as representative "other," her rhetorical task would appear to be quite different from that of the postcolonial immigrant intellectuals analyzed above.

A Revolutionary Subject

In the 1983 English translation of Guatemalan Indian Rigoberta Menchú Tum's *testimonio*, the construction of a subject appears in high relief from the opening lines:

> My name is Rigoberta Menchú. I am twenty three years old. This is my testimony. I didn't learn it from a book and I didn't learn it alone. I'd like to stress that it's not only *my* life, it's also the testimony of my people. It's hard for me to remember everything that's happened to me in my life since there have been many very bad times but, yes, moments of joy as well. The important thing is that what has happened to me has happened to many other people too: My story is the story of all poor Guatemalans. My personal experience is the reality of a whole people. (1)

There appears to be no hesitation here to claim representative status—no hedging about subject positions or the problem of speaking for others. Menchú Tum tells the story of Indian peasants deprived of land, freedom, and life by an oligarchic government using the army to suppress any attempts by the Indians to seek justice and stop exploitive land grabs and cruel labor practices.[16] Literary critics identify a distinctive articulation of the speaking subject as a feature of the genre, *testimonio*. John

Beverly's persuasive analysis places these accounts within the context of struggles for national autonomy: they are "novel or novella-length narratives told in the first person by a narrator who is also the real protagonist or witness of the events she or he recounts" (Literature 70). The claim of representation is at the center of these texts: "the situation of the narrator in *testimonio* must be representative (in both the mimetic and the legal-political senses) of a larger social class or group"; indeed, there is "an insistence on and affirmation of the authority of the subject" (Beverly, *Literature* 74, 76).

Neither the "deliverers," compilers, nor the critics of *testimonio*, however, are naive about the processes of textual construction involved in production of these accounts. Barbara Harlow, whose book *Resistance Literature* brings a number of these texts to the attention of Western readers, makes note of the ideological complexity of resistance organizations and national liberation movements (29). The involvement of a first-world intelligentsia in the collection of material complicates the question of authenticity further. Elizabeth Burgos-Debray, the compiler of Menchú Tum's *testimonio*, a Venezuelan social scientist living in Paris, documents the ways she constructed and adjusted the language in the oral account. In a recent visit to Miami University, Menchú Tum spoke about the caution she exercised in telling her story to Burgos-Debray. This caution involved presenting herself as a particular kind of subject, as well as withholding information about the Indian resistance fighters still at war in Guatemala at the time she was working for peace in Europe and Mexico.

Even though they acknowledge these mediations in the collection and production of *testimonios*, however, critics generally place more importance on the commonality of political goals between compiler and testifier. Beverly, for example, offers the examples of Margaret Randall, who assisted women in Cuba and Nicaragua through workshops in writing popular histories, and Nawal al-Saadawi, whose work with women in an Egyptian prison eventually led to testimonial novel *Woman at Point Zero*, as examples of politically committed *testimonio* compilers ("Margin" 15, n. 8; 17, n. 11; see also Harlow). These relationships are forged out of "mutuality in struggle against a common system of oppression "; the compiling of the testimony under these conditions is specifically not, Beverly argues, "a reenactment of the anthropological function of the colonial or subaltern 'native informant'" ("Margin" 21).

The *testimonio*, nonetheless, still offers interpretive challenges on the issue of representation, even if they aren't exactly the same as those created by the particular national, educational, and class circumstances of the immigrant academic feminists.[17] For both Spivak and Trinh, the denial of authenticity is a necessary position for the diasporic intellectual, one which forces the first-world academic to notice the difference between another academic and a suppressed history of colonization. For Menchú Tum, the claim to authority—to the truth of her lived experience—is central to her project. There still remains a question about how to interpret the representational force of the strongly asserted "I" in the *testimonio* and how to understand the relationship with the reader. Does this mode of representation constitute a rhetoric of substitution?

Interpreters of *testimonio* answer that question by changing the terms. In the material and historical circumstances of a revolutionary struggle, the idea of one speaker "blocking out" another, as though subjects were individual, strongly differentiated units, gives way to the exigencies of communicating as a collective. The elite intellectual postcolonial feminists, working within a Western discourse tradition, needed to take apart individual subjectivity from the inside; Menchú Tum, on the other hand, comes from a strongly communal Indian village culture with a completely different understanding of the relation of the self to the community. Despite the first-person of Menchú Tum's title, Lynda Marín notes that *testimonios* are marked by the "self-professed eschewal of the first person singular subject" in favor of a collective "we" (52).[18] Though these authors do specify their personal conditions, those details are less significant than the group struggle against state coercion. Their primary aim is getting out the reality of their collective experience to a metropolitan reading public, bringing to light experiences and events hidden in large measure from first world media. Doris Sommer, in an elegant reading of Rigoberta's continual reference to secrets about the community that cannot be revealed, claims that this strategy "defends us [first-world readers] from any illusions of complete or stable knowledge, and therefore from the desire to replace one apparently limited speaker for another more totalizing one" (57). Sommer goes on say that Menchú Tum "takes care not to substitute her community in a totalizing gesture. Instead, her singularity achieves its identity as an extension of the collective. The singular represents the plural, not because it replaces or subsumes the group, but because the speaker is a distinguishable part of the whole" (60-61). It is worth noting that Sommer's purpose in analyzing Menchú Tum is to distinguish the genre of *testimonio* from standard Western autobiography, a centuries-old locus for individuality: "Where autobiographies nurture an illusion of singularity [sic], assuming they can stand in for others, testimonies stand up among them" (61). John Beverly, similarly, attempts to redefine the terms through which subjectivity is expressed: "*testimonio* constitutes an affirmation of the individual self *in a collective mode*" ("Margin" 17). The oral delivery of *testimonio* and the political context of collective struggle combine to set aside figures of the "author" and "individual," and along with them, the problem of speaking for others as a gesture of substitution.

Looking at the *testimonio* from a rhetorical rather than a literary perspective actually makes it easier to imagine this shift. When we examined the postcolonial academic writers, the analysis was framed in terms of writing style. But for an orally produced text, the rhetorical category of ethos is more suitable. Sommer acknowledges the value of a shift to rhetoric: "while the autobiography strains to produce a personal and distinctive style as part of the individuation process, the testimonial strives to preserve or to renew an interpersonal rhetoric" (Sommer 65). The ethos/audience relation was redefined above for Asian postcolonial feminists to mark a difference and distance between rhetor and audience. In the case of Menchú Tum, *ethos* could signify the intense solidarity among members of the revolutionary group, as well as a powerfully rhetorical relationship to first-world readers.

Whereas the first two writers needed to disperse their subjectivity and representative-ness for Western readers, Menchú Tum, as a subject of a nation still in struggle, had a much stronger interest—indeed, a life-or-death need—to engage the audience. Written for a metropolitan public, the *testimonio* creates a bond with its readers, "involv[ing] their identification—by engaging their standards of ethics and justice in a speech-act situation that requires response" (Beverly, *Literature* 78). The rhetoric of reading *testimonio* is cast as a movement from identification to persuasion, or "complicity." Sommer uses that term to spell out the psychological dynamics of subject-formation and audience address in the public event of *testimonio:*

> When the narrator talks about herself to you, she implies both the existing relationship to other representative selves in the community, and potential relationships that extend her community through the text. She calls us in, interpellates us as readers who identify with the narrator's project and, by extension, with the political community to which she belongs. The appeal does not produce only admiration for the ego-ideal, of the type we might feel for an autobiographer who impresses us precisely with her difference from other women, nor the consequent yearning to be (like) her and so to deny her and our distinctiveness. Rather, the testimonial

> produces complicity. Even if the reader cannot identify with the writer enough to imagine taking her place, the map of possible identifications through the text spreads out laterally. (65)

In this lateral movement, the represented community, testifier, and readers are found beside themselves.

Reading Menchú Tum against the two Asian feminists enables us to see a reversal of the movement from descriptive to transformative class. We are to understand from Menchú Tum that the class she represents is solidly constituted, already engaged in political action. Her task is to create that group as a descriptive class—to bring the Mayan Indians of Central America into view for a U.S. and Western European public. Because the two poles in the double session of representation are so closely connected for her group, there is a strong justification for the representational strategy she uses. Her goal is exactly the opposite of Spivak's: not "deidentification" but identification. My goal in making this contrast is not to value one mode of representation over another. It is, rather, to develop more supple instruments for recognizing and responding to diverse subjects in the absence of stable criteria for doing so. It has become standard for feminists (and others) to complain of poststructuralist theory that it robs non-dominant groups of subjectivity before they've ever had a chance to have it. Gregory S. Jay raises a question about the terms of this dilemma: "it is not clear how the widely challenged classical schemas of representation can be replaced by a different representative system if there is no agreement about the 'unit' or basic element grounding the claim to representation [in the Enlightenment, the individual]" (15). Perhaps the rhetorical materials at use here might give us a way to describe subjectivities as something more multiple and diverse than "units," to discuss the question in terms less simply binary than presence or absence of a subject.

Pedagogy

The political reason we need something more complex than poststructural or postmodern critiques of the subject concerns the ways such arguments "travel." Criticisms of a representation of substitution—of "authentic voice" literature that makes claims to speak for others—from within non-dominant groups line up disturbingly with the derision of a right-wing dogmatist like Dinesh D'Souza, who uses the evidence of Rigoberta Menchú Tum's differences from the Indians she represents as an excuse to dismiss her as a "seemingly authentic Third World source" (72, emphasis added). That Menchú Tum was able to move from the position of silenced subaltern to vocal victim of oppression provides D'Souza the opportunity to dismiss the account of her experience, to hear her instead as a mouthpiece for "Marxist and feminist views," and to focus his critical energies on the travesty of her displacement of Western classics in the Stanford University canon.

The difference between John Beverly's reading of Menchú Tum as an organizer, organic intellectual, and "foreign agent" to the West—i.e., as specifically not "the subaltern"—and D'Souza's reading is that the former is doing a sympathetic reading of representational strategies; the latter rejects Menchú Tum's account in favor of silence: i.e., he disqualifies her representative status so as to silence her. D'Souza's response recalls a stance I've encountered in some students who find reports from the margins so disturbing that their very claim to be heard is called into question (see Lu). This reaction takes shape as the skepticism on the part of an autonomous knower toward any truth claim: the response of a Kantian subject who, in rejecting the authority of teacher and text, overcomes "tutelage," the barrier to ascendance into full personhood, a rejection made all the easier if that narrative in some way calls into question the status of that very subject. Is it possible to distinguish between a silencing skepticism and a nuanced reading of representation?

It is our responsibility as teachers to try to mark out that difference. Through our choices of texts and every word we say about them we inevitably represent others to our students. Choosing different reading strategies for different texts is an exercise of power, but then, Rigoberta Menchú Tum is not Louis Bonaparte and neither are "we": teachers of writing, language, and literature in U.S. universities. Every pedagogical moment is a complex fusion of re-presentation, exercises of executive power, and transformation of consciousness. If we enter into that process relying solely on what Linda Alcoff calls the "retreat" response—claiming to speak only from our own narrow positions—we not only blind ourselves to the multiple functions of pedagogical discourse, but also lose opportunities for political effectivity (17-19).

Many of us believe that we have remade the teaching scene so as to avoid careless abuses of power. But we can't control the processes of representation—of metaphorical substitution. As those in non-dominant positions well know, their voices are often heard as the voice of women, African-Americans, or lesbians despite disclaimers or qualifications. If, as teachers and scholars we retreated from the risk of representation, punctiliously refusing any occasion of speaking for others ourselves and vigilantly pointing out any instance of metaphoric substitution in others, we would avoid making a theoretical error. But, as Alcoff points out, "the desire to find an absolute means to avoid making errors comes perhaps not from a desire to advance collective goals but a desire for personal mastery, to establish a privileged discursive position wherein one cannot be undermined or challenged and thus is master of the situation" (22).

What is it we recognize? What parts of the whole do we "read"? What forms the links in the chains of association that lead us to act? Can we transform the modes of visibility through our teaching? Who is the "we" in these questions? By locating texts, including our own, in their different geopolitical contexts, teachers in U.S. universities can practice modes of writing and reading that allow us (students and teachers) to move collectively across the axes of metaphor/metonymy rather than speech/silence. And by enabling our students to write multiple versions of themselves informed by a knowledge of rhetoric in its political and figurative functions, we may give them access to their own experiences of conjunction and disjunction, of association and substitution. In doing this, we might more fully inhabit the meanings of the prefix to both figures, meta—which, in the poetic language of the Greek lexicon, places us "beside, alongside, among, in common with, with the help and favor of, in the midst of" others.[19]

Notes

1. In the Roof and Wiegman collection, see especially essays by Bow, Callaghan, and Sawhney.

2. See Mailloux for a related definition of rhetoric incorporating political effectivity and trope.

3. Mohanty offers a revealing critique of the ways some Western feminists have performed a similar operation on "third world women" by beginning their analyses with the descriptive category of "woman" (59). In the research she cites, universal groupings such as "women of Africa" become "homogeneous sociological grouping[s] characterized by common dependencies or powerlessness" (59). Mohanty explains the ways resistance activities of third world women—i.e., efforts toward representing themselves politically—are obscured by the assumption that they are "legal minors (read 'they-are-still-not-conscious-of-their-rights')" (72). Given Mohanty's endorsement of historical contextualization, it is odd that she ends her essay with the hope of moving beyond "the Marx who found it possible to say: They cannot represent themselves; they must be represented" (74)—a reference to Marx's "Eighteenth Brumaire" (see Marx 608). Marx is quite careful, in his analysis of the second

phase of the French Revolution (1848-1851), to distinguish between a group of peasants who have historically resisted the oppressions of the old order (609) and those who, because of their geographic isolation and other circumstances of their mode of production, are "incapable of enforcing their class interest in their own name" (608). It is the latter Louis Bonaparte claims to represent. The danger to which Mohanty and Spivak point is assuming in advance of such careful analysis that a subordinated group cannot speak for themselves.

4. This definition doesn't presume to be the only or best definition of "metaphor"; in fact, it is a specialized definition associated with one strand of twentieth-century rhetorical theory. An anonymous reader of an earlier version of this essay objected to my use of metaphor in this way, arguing that the figure works through analogy and comparison rather than substitution, the point of an analogy depending on both terms being present to the mind rather than one standing in for or blocking out another. This reader objected that my use of "metaphor" to suggest substitution would not be helpful to language teachers struggling to help students understand how figures work. These comments led me to think about (among other things) the way all figures depend on the resonance between tenor and vehicle, and the way all figures distort or misrepresent. I ultimately decided to stay with this figurative analysis, including the definitions given above, because of a body of work I've encountered using the term in a similar way. Barbara Johnson summarizes this work, locating its contemporary origins with Roman Jakobson's famous study of aphasia. Johnson traces Jakobson's formulation of the metaphor/metonymy distinction from a linguistic construct to its use in designating hierarchies of genre poetry based on a principle of equivalence (narrative, on selection) through French structuralist and poststructuralist theory (DeMan's association of metaphor with necessity and metonymy with chance) and finally to the political implications of separating similarity from contiguity (153-58). This trajectory follows metaphor from privileged trope to "the trope of privilege" (158). See also Laclau and Mouffe, Ryan, and Sommer. One could say that this use of "metaphor" is itself a metaphoric act—substituting one partial definition of the figure for a fuller, more varied one.

5. Originally titled *Me llamo Rigoberta Menchú. An Indian Woman in Guatemala*, before Menchú Tum married and changed her name.

6. My choice of three women as representative of postcolonial feminism performs the kind of metaphorical substitution I'm analyzing in the essay. I choose Spivak and Trinh because they revel in the act of writing, working over and through the problem of representation with a painful sensitivity I find appealing; Menchú Tum, because of the urgency of her situation. I choose them because I love to read them, each for different reasons. One of my purposes for writing this essay was to direct my responses away from a "conventional ethics of altruism" (Gunn 165) or an "uncritical hero-worship" (Sommer 69), and toward a "respect [that] is the condition of possibility for the kind of love that takes care not to simply appropriate its object" (Sommer 69).

7. Robert Con Davis and David S. Gross analyze Spivak's rhetoric in terms of *ethos*, raising some of the issues discussed below toward the end of pointing a direction for an ethical practice of cultural studies. They characterize Spivak's style in terms of "theatricality" and imagine the voice of the subaltern as produced by a kind of "ventriloquism" (69, 76).

8. In the analysis of Davis and Gross, the subaltern *ethos* does not refer to a particular group but rather to the impossibility of any discourse of the "other" available to the colonizer that has not been "defined by and related to the master discourse" (77).

9. Spivak differentiates her work from the "information retrieval" taking place in anthropology, political science, history, and sociology. She applies her critique of subaltern representation across these disciplinary boundaries, warning of potential for violence when historians et al. assume a consciousness of the subject under examination ("Subaltern" 295). Benita Parry takes issue with Spivak and others on this point, arguing that an over-scrupulous concern for such "violence" can have the effect of quelling efforts toward uncovering knowledge of colonized peoples and their resistant practices.

10. See Hennessy for a discussion of a related theory: Pecheux's concept of "dis-identification." Hennessy defines it as the practice of "*working on* the subject-form": "critique, enacted in the disruption and re-arrangement of the pre-constructed categories on which the formation of subjects depends" (96).

11. In a survey of work at the borders of feminism and rhetoric, Lisa Ede, Cheryl Glenn, and Andrea Lunsford discuss women's alternative styles and the challenge by feminists of color to white feminists on issues of representation (420-28).

12. See Ede, Glenn, and Lunsford for a discussion of feminist alternatives to classical rhetorical arrangement (414-20).

13. See Jarratt and Reynolds for a related version of classical *ethos* through postmodern feminist theory.

14. Although this discussion of Spivak and Trinh is focused more on theorizing than pedagogy, I have assigned portions of Trinh's book to upper-division undergraduates in classes cross-listed with Women's Studies and English. I know at least one colleague who has used her chapter "Grandma's Story" with first-year composition students, and another who has taught Spivak in undergraduate feminist theory courses.

15. I use the past tense to indicate that Menchú Tum's literacy has changed in the fifteen years since she provided the oral account that led to the publication of her *testimonio*. In 1982, she had been studying spoken Spanish for three years. In 1997, she reported being almost finished with a new book, which I assume she herself is writing in Spanish.

16. The postcolonialisty of Guatemala is multi-layered. As Menchú Tum explains in her book, the Spanish conquest of Central America left as part of its legacy a three-layered society, with the indigenous Indian groups at the bottom, *ladinos*—Spanish-speaking assimilated *mestisos*—in the middle, and upper-

class descendants of the Spanish conquerors at the top. Although Menchú Tum does not emphasize the intervention of the U.S. government in the struggle for power in Guatemala, the role of the CIA in supporting the military government (even to the point of abetting the murder of U.S. citizens) in its deadly campaign during the 1980s to take land from the Indians and force them to work in extremely exploitative conditions on plantations is finally beginning to be documented by mainstream media (Krauss; Weiner).

17. Susan Morgan makes this point eloquently in her recent book on Victorian women writers in Southeast Asia, arguing (through the title) that *Place Matters*. She points out major differences among Singapore, Thailand, and India in their histories of contact with the West, its economies, and its social structures, and shows how those differences matter in our interpretations of colonial and postcolonial literatures.

18. Other examples of *testimonio* include Domitilia Barrios, *Let Me Speak* (Bolivia, 1978); Eugenia Claribel Alegría, *They Won't Take Me Alive* (El Salvador, 1987); and Elvia Alvarado, *Don't Be Afraid, Gringo* (Honduras, 1987).

19. I am grateful to my writing group at Miami University—Alice Adams, Lori Merish, and Victoria Smith—and to Andrea Lunsford for help with this essay. I also appreciate the valuable comments of others who read or heard earlier drafts: John Beverly, Laura Mandell, Kelly Oliver, Alpana Knippling Sharma, Scott Shershow, and Lester Faigley and his graduate students at the University of Texas at Austin.

Works Cited

Ahmad, Aijaz. *In Theory: Classes, Nations, Literatures.* London: Verso, 1992.

Alcoff, Linda. "The Problem of Speaking for Others." *Cultural Critique.* (Winter 1991-92): 5-32.

Anderson, Benedict. *Imagined Communities: Reflections on the Origin and Spread of Nationalism.* London: Verso, 1983.

Bal, Mieke. "The Politics of Citation." *Diacritics* 21.1 (Spring 1991): 24-45.

Baumlin, James S., and Tita French Baumlin, eds. *Ethos: New Essays in Rhetorical and Critical Theory.* Dallas: Southerm Methodist UP, 1994.

Brady, Laura. "The Reproduction of Othering." Jarratt and Worsham 21-44.

Beverly, John. *Against Literature.* Minneapolis: U Minnesota P, 1993.

—. "The Margin at the Center: On *Testimonio* (Testimonial Narrative)." *Modern Fiction Studies* 35.1 (Spring 1989): 11-28.

Cixous, Hélène, and Catherine Clément. *The Newly Born Woman.* Trans. Betsy Wing. Minneapolis: U of Minnesota P, 1986.

Davis, Robert Con, and David S. Gross. "Gayatri Chakravorty Spivak and the Ethos of the Subaltern." Baumlin and Baumlin 65-89.

de Man, Paul. *Allegories of Reading.* New Haven: Yale UP, 1979.

D'Souza, Dinesh. *Illiberal Education: The Politics of Race and Sex on Campus.* New York: Vintage, 1991.

Ede, Lisa, Cheryl Glenn, and Andrea Lunsford. "Border Crossings: Intersections of Rhetoric and Feminism." *Rhetorica* 13.4 (Autumn 1995): 401-41.

Faigley, Lester. *Fragments of Rationality: Postmodernity and the Subject of Composition.* Pittsburgh: U Pittsburgh P, 1992.

Fanon, Frantz. *Black Skin, White Masks.* New York: Grove P, 1967.

Gunn, Janet Varner. "A Window of Opportunity: An Ethics of Reading Third World Autobiography." *College Literature* 19.3/20.1 (Oct. 1992/Feb. 1993): 162-69.

Harlow, Barbara. *Resistance Literature.* New York: Methuen, 1987.

Hennessy, Rosemary. *Materialist Feminism and the Politics of Discourse.* New York: Routledge, 1993.

Irigaray, Luce. *This Sex Which Is Not One.* Trans. Catherine Porter. Ithaca: Cornell UP, 1985.

Jakobson, Roman. "Two Aspects of Language and Two Types of Linguistic Disturbances." *Fundamentals of Language.* Ed. Roman Jakobson and Morris Halle. The Hague: Mouton, 1956.

Jarratt, Susan C., and Lynn Worsham, eds. *Feminism and Composition: In Other Words.* New York: MLA, 1998.

—., and Nedra Reynolds. "The Splitting Image: Contemporary Feminisms and the Ethics of Ethos." Baumlin and Baumlin 37-63.

Jay, Gregory S. "Knowledge, Power, and the Struggle for Representation." *College English* 56 (1994): 9-29.

Johnson, Barbara. "Metaphor, Metonymy, and Voice in *Their Eyes Were Watching God*." *The Future of Difference*. Baltimore: Johns Hopkins UP, 1987. 155-71.

Krauss, Clifford. "Guatemala's War: Ideology Is the Latest Excuse." *The New York Times*. 9 April 1995. E.5.

Laclau, Ernesto, and Chantal Mouffe. *Hegemony and Socialist Strategy: Toward a Radical Democratic Politics*. London: Verso, 1985.

Landry, Donna, and Gerald MacLean. *Materialist Feminisms*. Cambridge: Blackwell, 1993.

Lu, Min-Zahn. "Reading and Writing Difference: The Problematic of 'Experience.'" Jarratt and Worsham 239-51.

Lunsford, Andrea A., and Lisa Ede. "Representing Audience." *College Composition and Communication* 47 (1996): 167-79.

Mailloux, Steven. *Rhetorical Power*. Ithaca: Cornell UP, 1989.

Mani, Lata. "Cultural Theory, Colonial Texts: Reading Eyewitness Accounts of Widow Burning." *Cultural Studies*. Ed. Lawrence Grossberg, Cary Nelson, and Paula A. Treichler. New York: Routledge, 1992. 392-405.

Marín, Lynda. "Speaking Out Together: Testimonials of Latin American Women." *Latin American Perspectives* 18.3 (Summer 1991): 51-68.

Marx, Karl. "The Eighteenth Brumaire of Louis Bonaparte." *The Marx-Engels Reader*. 2nd ed. Ed. Robert C. Tucker. New York: Norton, 1978: 594-617.

Menchú, Rigoberta. *I, Rigoberta Menchú: An Indian Woman in Guatemala*. Ed. Elisabeth Burgos-Debray. Trans. Ann Wright. London: Verso, 1984.

Mohanty, Chandra Talpade. "Under Western Eyes: Feminist Scholarship and Colonial Discourses." *Third World Women and the Politics of Feminism*. Ed. Chandra Talpade Mohanty, Ann Russo, and Lourder Torres. Bloomington: Indiana UP, 1991. 51-80.

Moi, Toril. "Feminism, Postmodernism, and Style: Recent Feminist Criticism in the United States." *Cultural Critique* 9 (Spring 1988): 3-24.

Morgan, Susan. *Place Matters*. New Brunswick: Rutgers UP, 1996.

Parry, Benita. "Problems in Current Theories of Colonial Discourse." *Oxford Literary Review* 9.1-2 (1987): 27-58.

Roof, Judith, and Robyn Wiegman, eds. *Who Can Speak?: Authority and Critical Identity.* Urbana: U of Illinois P, 1995.

Ryan, Michael. *Politics and Culture: Working Hypotheses for a Revolutionary Society.* Baltimore: Johns Hopkins UP, 1989.

Sommer, Doris. "No Secrets: Rigoberta's Guarded Truth." *Women's Studies* 20 (1991): 51-72.

Spivak, Gayatri Chakravorty. "Can the Subaltern Speak?" *Marxism and the Interpretation of Culture.* Ed. Cary Nelson and Lawrence Grossberg. Urbana: U of Illinois P, 1988. 271-313.

—. "Feminism in Decolonization." *differences* 3.3 (Fall 1991): 139-70.

—. with Ellen Rooney. "In a Word: Interview." *differences* 1.2 (Summer 1989): 124-56.

—. *In Other Worlds: Essays in Cultural Politics.* New York: Routledge, 1988.

—. *Outside in the Teaching Machine.* New York: Routledge, 1993.

—. "The Political Economy of Women as Seen by a Literary Critic." *Coming to Terms: Feminism, Theory, Politics.* Ed. Elizabeth Weed. New York: Routledge, 1989. 218-29.

—. *The Post-Colonial Critic: Interviews, Strategies, Dialogues.* Ed. Sarah Harasym. New York: Routledge, 1990.

—. "Who Claims Alterity?" *Remaking History.* Ed. Barbara Kruger and Phil Mariani. Seattle: Bay P, 1989. 269-92.

Trinh T. Minh-ha. *Woman, Native, Other: Writing Postcoloniality and Feminism.* Bloomington, Indiana UP, 1989.

Weiner, Tim. "A Guatemala Officer and the C.I.A." *The New York Times.* 26 March 1997. 6

Defining Rhetoric—and Us: A Meditation on Burke's Definitions

Richard M. Coe

As others have before, Paul Hunter chided us at the 1989 convention of the Conference on College Composition and Communication for honoring North America's greatest rhetorician, Kenneth Burke, more than we use him. Though many composition textbooks make an honorific bow in Burke's direction by including a simplified version of his Pentad in their treatment of heuristics, few composition texts or courses are informed by Burke's insights into language and rhetoric. Especially in advanced composition, a Burkean approach has much to offer.

Though Burke gets upset every time I suggest this, many composition instructors have difficulty reading his work. If we understood Burke better, we could better devise approaches to composition that embodied his insights. In hope of engendering such understanding, I will here meditate on a text Burke presented at the 1989 CCCC Convention, about a half an hour after hearing Hunter's complaint.

Burke begins (and ends) with a definition of *humanity*. Not of *rhetoric*, *language*, *literature*, *culture*, or *discourse*, but of *humanness.* The first of the "five summarizing essays" in *Language as Symbolic Action* is "Definition of Man"—and it was a revised, expanded version of this definition that Burke presented at CCCC. Any comments on matters cultural, Burke asserts, must embody assumptions about the nature of the human beings who compose culture—and who compose themselves socially, rhetorically, in terms cultural (*Language* 2). One key to understanding Burke is understanding his conception of what makes us human.

If our purpose were merely to distinguish human beings from other beings, we might define people as animals that laugh, or as animals that use tools to make tools, or as erect, bipedal mammals with opposable thumbs, or in a variety of other ways. Though all these definitions can be derived from Burke's, he chooses none of them. Instead, he defines us like this:

Being bodies that learn language
thereby becoming wordlings
humans are

the symbol-making, symbol-using, symbol-misusing animal
inventor of the negative
separated from our natural condition
by instruments of our own making
goaded by the spirit of hierarchy
acquiring foreknowledge of death
and rotten with perfection

From the fullness of this definition, we could, in principle, derive the totality of Burke's insights into the species that uses language (though probably no one but Burke would in actuality).

Though Burke does cite the standard rule that a definition should have "just enough clauses [to define] and no more," his is not a standard definition. The rule usually means to use only as many distinctions (*differentia*) as necessary to distinguish what is being defined from the rest of the universe. But any one of Burke's clauses, even the last, which he calls a "wry codicil" (*Language* 16), suffices to distinguish us.

A definition, Burke asserts, "sums things up." Definition may well be what comes last in a writer's discovery process, "the last thing a writer hits upon," for it is hard to "sum up" what has not yet been observed or invented. In retrospect, however, it should logically be possible to derive the properties of whatever is being defined from the definition. And, indeed, Burke's definition is finally summed up in the word *wordling*. From the implications of this pun—human worldlings are wordlings, bodies that, of their nature, learn words (thus becoming more than mere bodies)—the rest follows.

The clauses of Burke's definition are not "just enough" to define; they are, rather, "just enough" to serve as chapter headings, titles for categories under which his observations of human beings can "be assembled, as though derived from." Burke's aim is "to get as essential a set of clauses as possible, and to meditate on each of them" (*Language* 3).

Symbolic

For Burke, everything essentially human derives from our being symbol-making animals. This derivation is logical, not biological or historical; it is a statement about the present, about the structure (*logos*) of human reality, not about first causes or origins. Our very perceptions—as well as our interpretations, attitudes, judgments, choices and the actions that follow—are all mediated by the symbols we make, use, abuse and are, in this sense, used by. We are, to be sure, not alone in our use of symbols. Burke himself notes that any animal, insofar as it learns from experience—one of his more famous examples is a trout that learns to distinguish bait from food (*Permanence* 5)—must generalize, and hence must come to perceive individual events as signifiers for categories of events. But our use of symbols is qualitatively beyond that of any other animal. We not only use language and other semiotic systems, we make them and are made by them. As Noam Chomsky emphasizes, human individuals are born with special abilities to learn language; and we are made human, interinanimated as social individuals, through our interaction with cultural semiotic systems that are essentially linguistic, semiotic, rhetorical.

As historical and social groups, we make language (and other semiotic systems). As individuals, we are to a significant degree, made by language—a fact that has important implications for composition as both a social and an individual process. The limited literature on feral children makes suggestively clear that human beings raised outside of human language and culture do not develop the ability to think abstractly (for example, if integrated in human society as adolescents, they can learn arithmetic, but not mathematics) and *perhaps consequently* never develop the human ability to love or act morally (at least not beyond the sense in which dogs can love and act morally). An erect, bipedal, mammal with opposable thumbs that cannot think abstractly or love or act morally may be biologically human; but it is precisely such abilities that really define our humanness. For Burke, these abilities all follow logically from our ability to abstract, which follows from our use of language. Taken together, these abilities make our behavior symbolic action, motives mediated by symbols, not mere motion (see, for example, Burke's "(Nonsymbolic) Motion/(Symbolic) Action").

Our errors, too, are mediated by our terms and other symbols. Indeed, our errors are often motivated by erroneous terms and tropes. We misuse our symbols not only immorally to gain advantage over others (as in machiavellian rhetoric), but also in self-abuse, blinding ourselves to our deepest fears, hopes and insights. Our naming (and misnaming) not only helps individuals evade personally (as per Freud), misnaming also keeps ordinary scientists from the sort of breakthrough insights that mark the great scientists (see Gould, for example).

Everything we do is mediated by our symbols. And it is we

(historically, socially, ecologically) who created these systems of symbols. They guide us to relevant insights but blind us to more radical insights. They conserve our traditions and lock us into those traditions. They help us evade what we wish not to see or understand. They function epistemically—and ideologically—to make us social as well as individual human beings.

Negativity

Language is the crux of our symbolicity. Human language is distinguished from various animal semiotics by the arbitrary relationship between signifier and signified. That is to say, among the various clauses used in defining language, the crucial one distinguishes semiotic systems where there is an analogy between signifier and signified from language where that relationship is arbitrary.

To use a currently popular metaphor, human semantics is primarily a left-brain function because of properties that follow logically from the use of arbitrary signifiers (but cf. Gardner 267 ff.). Another way to articulate the same distinction is to say that all animal communications are analog, but human semantics is digital. Analog systems can say "no" to what is present (can refuse what is offered), but only digital systems have the logical capacity to say "not" (as in "I am not writing now").

Thus, Burke's second clause is not a new defining feature; it is implicit in his first clause: it can be derived logically from the nature of the human symbolic, from our nature as "wordlings"; thus, it is technically redundant. Still, Burke is right to add this clause, for many crucial features of language, culture and humanness fall under the heading of "the power of negative thinking," which Burke calls "my positive negative."

Our culture—Burke's too—is in so many ways positive. We are for the most part logical positivists—even those of us (the vast majority) who don't know what the term means. We built our country by "thinking positively" to overcome obstacles to greatness. As inheritors of British empiricism (rather than French rationalism or German dialectics), we believe in the positive facts of practical realism and can grasp the virtues of negativity only with difficulty (often only with the aid of Asian spiritualism or Hegelian philosophy).

Burke thinks of the "positive negative" in terms of Greek drama, especially *Oedipus* and the *Oresteia*, juxtaposing Aristotle's *Poetics* with his *Rhetoric*. *Antigone* is Hegelian, he says. Pain is a "positive negative," as in catharsis—"a message, not an error," as when it tells us to remove our fingers from a hot stove (personal communication, 31 August 1989).

Part of what Burke has to offer is insight into the powers of negative thinking, which we lost (one time) when we accepted Plato's reactionary slanders against sophists and rhetoricians; which we lost another time when we reduced Aristotle's logic to his analytic logic (which includes the law against contradiction), thus deleting dialectic (which is founded on contradiction); and which we continue to lose because of our (anti-intellectual) mistrust of theory that cannot *immediately* demonstrate practical applications.

Having defined us in terms of our symbolic uses of language, Burke is absolutely right to define us next as "inventor of the negative." Linguistically, he is correct because what defines language, what separates human language from all other natural semiotic systems is its negative capacity. Other natural semiotic systems include a primitive, behavioristic *no*. A lion cub swatted across the head learns not to chew its mother's ears. After sufficient repetition of stern *no*'s, a puppy learns not to shit on the carpet (though it is the sternness, not the word, that embodies the primitive negative for the puppy). Even rats learn from psychologists' shocking negatives.

But the true propositional *negative* is uniquely linguistic. Only digital semiotic systems have true negatives, and the only natural digital semiotic systems on this planet are human languages. The logical negative allows human beings to conceive and communicate about what is not present. This means we can abstract and theorize—whatever else an abstract idea may be, it is not the concrete, positive reality it conceptually encompasses. This negative relationship—between positive reality and abstraction—is crucial to Burke's movement of mind.

Negativity also gives language its tenses, hence our ability to conceive and talk about what is *not* present because it is past or future. In a sense this is a form of abstraction, especially when, utopian, we speak of what does not, never has, and perhaps never will exist. Even to talk of the past is to negate the present (as various mystics have pointed out). Other animals are "just animals" in part because they lack this ability to communicate past and future. A dog, for example, can threaten—but only in the present perfect: its raised hackles and snarl say, "I *am going* to bite you" (because they are the beginning of the process that actualizes as biting); but a dog cannot communicate, "I *will* bite you next week."

In addition to abstraction and tense, the negative allows basic logical functions that animals are incapable of communicating: *if. . . , then . . .* and *either/or*. A dog can communicate desire ("I want to be fed") but not conditional action, not "If you don't feed me, I will bite you." Our ability to hypothesize about the future conceptually (instead of relying on trial and error) and our highly developed ability to conceive and make choices turn on these logical functions.

Without our ability to abstract, theorize, consider the distant past (historicize) and not-yet existent future (plan), to hypothesize and to weigh alternatives, we are not human. And all these cognitive abilities are part and parcel of our linguistic abilities.

Though he discusses this aspect of the negative, which he calls the "propositional negative," Burke emphasizes the "hortatory negative," the "Thou shalt *not*."[1] In the 1966 version of his definition, he added parenthetically that we are "moralized by the negative," for our morality turns on our ability to conceive abstract commandments. So again there is no real distinction: our nature as moral beings depends on our intellectual ability to abstract, which depends on the propositional negative we acquire with language. When people behave with extreme immorality—such as in Nazi extermination camps—we say they are inhumane, their actions inhuman. Upon moral imperatives, formally negative, we found our positive humanness.

Nature/Culture

Our experience is mediated by language, our actions moralized by the negative; thus we are removed from nature into culture. Indeed, "Thou shalt *not* commit incest" is the minimal definition of culture. As Anthony Wilden asserts, "In every human society there is a rule about kinship that has no parallel in nature, a rule so universally accepted that it is not even mentioned in the Ten Commandments: the prohibition of incest" (102). Though exact definitions of incest (that is, precisely which relatives are forbidden) vary considerably from one society to another, no society, no human culture exists without an incest taboo. "Like language," Wilden emphasizes, "kinship is a revolution rather than an invention" (102)—a revolution that separated us from nature, a revolution that created culture.

Incest is not literally an "unnatural act"; the prohibition of incest is a social, not natural law. The prohibition of incest is "a *spoken* rule hemmed about by social sanctions" (Wilden 102; emphasis added). Contrary to popular belief and royal hemophilia, moreover, a moderate amount of incest would more likely help than harm the gene pool; indeed, such mating is common among farm animals. Incest is socially, not biologically harmful.

Though it appears to be a rule about who not to marry, the incest taboo is more importantly a rule about who to marry. Naturally, one is likely to mate with those who are nearest, hence most available. If the incest rule redefines those nearest as unavailable, people "marry out." By marrying out of the nuclear family, out of the extended family, even out of the band or clan, people create links of kinship over geographical and ecological space. These links encourage trade and mutual aid among neighbors. They ease movement of people from one group to another. They also diminish the probability, hence decrease the quantity, of wars. As a positive mandate for exogamy, the incest prohibition engenders cooperation, encourages social and cultural development (Wilden 107).

The *genus* of Burke's definition, "animal," is both true and false. We are, biologically, animals; but we are defined, distinguished from other animals, by our use of symbols (instruments of our own making), especially language (the tool that is more than a tool), which allows us to develop culture, to think abstractly and morally about our experience past, present and future. Our culture separates us from nature, creates the nature/culture boundary. It frees us—but in the process alienates us (from our natural condition). Our condition becomes more social than natural, shaped by culture within only very broad biological and ecological parameters.

Culture in this sense *negates* nature, though *negates* must be understood dialectically, for nature is not destroyed by our transcendence, and we remain in nature as we go beyond it. *Beyond* is a key word for Burke, who talks about "beyonding" (in part to evade the technical philosophical term, *sublate*). Thus, separation does not mean we are not connected, just that a boundary has been drawn (hence the need for connection). The social is, in at least one crucial sense, natural, derived from nature, from the evolutionary process. We are "*bodies* that learn language/thereby becoming wordlings."

Since our connection-separation from nature is made by our symbolicity, Burke's third clause, too, is technically redundant—not a new defining feature but an additional heading for organizing our discussion of language, culture, and humanness. Indeed, the connection (between symbolicity, negative thinking, and the nature/culture boundary) is the insight. Not that we are social animals, separated from nature by our culture; but that this separation is a logical consequence of our languaging.

Order, Hierarchy, Levels

"Goaded by the spirit of hierarchy" is a rich metaphor, but it too is a logical consequence of our languaging, specifically of our language-based ability to abstract and sublate. For every abstraction is a sublation, which both conserves and transcends the concrete reality from which it is abstracted. As an abstraction, the term *love* in one sense is beyond the concrete experience of mother's love; yet, in another sense it encompasses that experience (note the well worn metaphor of drawing a circle around). So any abstraction "beyonds" (to use Burke's verb) experience, puts my experience in relation with yours (which can be titled with the same word), thus makes it not only mine. But that abstraction is also grounded in experience, in reality, in nature.

Among the most important hierarchies, for Burke, are ladders of abstraction, hierarchies of even more encompassing titles, of abstractions that point at what disparate events share. Thus, Samson's suicide in Milton's *Samson Agonistes* (see Burke's *Rhetoric* 3-19) is a unique and concrete event. But naming it "suicide" puts it in a circle with all other suicides (hence the need for the modifier, "Samson's"). And suicide is a form of death, so a larger circle is drawn, another level of abstraction established. And death is a form of transformation. And so on, up the ladder of abstraction, in principle *ad infinitum*.[2]

Samson's suicide does not, of course, cease to be Samson's suicide just because we have reconceived it. It is conserved as his unique suicide; we do not forget that when we rename it. But we do not understand Samson's suicide in its uniqueness until we understand it also as a transformation, as a transcendence which makes Samson's ur-sainthood. That is Milton's point; we do not understand Milton until we understand how Samson's suicide both is and is not a suicide—that is, how it both breaks and, more importantly, does not break the commandment against suicide, how it is both death (an ending) and transcendence (a beginning). Explicitly or implicitly, articulately or inarticulately, we must read Samson's act on at least these two levels before we understand it; if we read it only on the level of suicide, we do not understand Milton's play.

For Burke, such hierarchies are in the very nature of human understanding. This is why he added parenthetically in the 1966 version of the definition that being goaded by the spirit of hierarchy means being "moved by the sense of order." We are moved by the sense of order every time we expect a concrete event to conform to our abstract conception of that type of event, every time we expect a student to act like a student, a professional to act like a professional, a civil servant to serve civic purposes. When we use words, we title events; and when we title events we understand them not only in their concrete particularity but also in relation to the abstract concept that is signified by the title. This is a *both-*

and upon which Burke insists. It is also an important fact that belongs at the center of our teaching of diction.

Burke's insistence on thinking *both-and* rather than *either/or*, on thinking at once on several levels, is part of what makes him hard to read—at least for readers who were raised with the linear, analytic, either/or logic Aristotle articulated in his Law of [Non]Contradiction. So it is important to note that Aristotle said there were two types of logic, analytic and dialectic; but philosophers opted to formalize only analytic logic, thereby debasing both rhetoricians and dialecticians (Perelman 1-4).

On any one level, the Law of [Non]Contradiction holds: either/or is the correct procedure; *A* cannot be *not-A*. But as Bertrand Russell noted, certain paradoxes (some of which go back to Greek pre-Socratics and the sophists) can be resolved only by realizing what their apparently contradictory assertions mean on distinct levels. If *A* is Samson's suicide, then *A* (suicide) can also be *not-A* (transformation). This *A* and this *not-A* are not exclusive; rather, the *not-A* encompasses the *A*. Similarly, a horse can be both a horse and a symbol (of sexuality, for example, in a D.H. Lawrence short story).

Though we have no difficulty reading Lawrence on several levels (literal and symbolic), we who have been raised in a culture that stresses analytic logic are not very skillful when it comes to advanced thinking in terms of levels, hierarchical orderings. But one thing we can learn from Burke is how better to think about order, hierarchy, levels. Burke's value here is precisely that he negates one of the shortcomings of the dominant culture, teaches us another, fuller way to read reality.[3]

Rotten with Fore-Knowledge and Perfection

Burke explains that the clause "acquiring foreknowledge of death" was added from the perspective of his 90th birthday. In a sense, it too is redundant, for the ability to imagine our own deaths follows from the same propositional negative that allows us to abstract and to articulate the future tense. But Burke asserts that this clause

> reveals notable synergistic powers. Recall how zestfully Marx and Engels took to Henry Morgan's work on the development of the Greek clans. And recall Alban Winspear's *The Genesis of Plato's Thought*, which advises us that Plato was a member of the landed gentry, whose ancestors bequeathed them this particular acreage, and were honored by their descendants as tutelary deities. Death, immortality, and private ownership were thus all of the same parcel. (personal communication, 31 August 1989)

To say we are rotten with perfection not only evokes eternity and immortality, it is a particularly suggestive and powerful way to repeat that we are moved (motivated, goaded/go-ed/god-ed) by the sense of order, the spirit of hierarchy. For our abstractions become our ideals. At least in the abstract, we can conceive perfection, despite its being literally no-place (*u-topia*). Having conceived it, we strive for it, are moved toward it. Almost teleologically, the conception becomes the goad toward what is conceived. We conceive a potential and strive to actualize it.[4]

But this separates us from nature, from the here-and-now, makes us part of the fallen world, where things die and rot, leads us into all kinds of confusions and misapprehensions, this rotting within us, this dissatisfaction with what is, this humanness, our downfall and our wonder, our specialness, our potential to be more than what we are.

Rhetoric

For Burke defining humanness and defining rhetoric are hardly distinct tasks. What makes us human is our culture, which is founded in our unique form of symbolizing, our languaging, which is in its very nature rhetorical as it goads/gods us, moves/motivates us, makes us social, cultural (non-)animals, allows us to compose ourselves humanly. The study of language, culture, discourse, rhetoric, and humanity is one.

Burke's *Grammar of Motives*, *Rhetoric of Motives* and his unfinished *Symbolic of Motives* (studies toward which were collected in *Language as Symbolic Action*) were written because Burke had planned a book on human ethics, then decided he could not approach that subject except through a discussion of human motives, which for Burke necessarily meant a study of how our motives are mediated by our discourses. For Burke *Homo sapiens* is synonymous with *Homo rhetorica*; human wisdom is a discursive process.

Burke offers at least two types of definition for rhetoric. They are, of course, really two perspectives of one definition. One seems familiar: rhetoric as *addressed* (the traditional category of *audience*). Rhetoric is language used to have an effect on an audience, persuasive language. Thus, Burke begins by distinguishing *communication* from *expression* (etymologically, mere breathing out). But Burke, the dialectician, is never happy with the stasis of a dichotomous pair; his method is always to seek a third term. Consequently, the movement from *expression* to *communication* leads to *communion*, the state of identification with the community that is the logical outcome of persuasive communication. When an audience is convinced, they atone for their differences, stand atone with the rhetor and with each other—in their agreement on how Athens should respond to the Persian fleet or in their agreement on how writing abilities should be developed.

To stand together with others is to be *consubstantial* with them: *stance* = stand; hence *substance* = that upon which one's stance is based, grounded; *con* = with; hence *consubstantial* = to stand on the same ground with. Thus, Burke's definition of rhetoric as *identification*—the result of communally shared assumptions that allow us to work together, to cooperate, to identify even though we are not identical—is an implication of his definition of rhetoric as *addressed*.

Burke's most famous definition of rhetoric intertwines definitions of *language*, *symbolic*, *rhetoric*, and *humanness* to the point where all these terms define each other:

> For rhetoric as such . . . is rooted in an essential function of language itself, a function that is wholly realistic, and is continually born anew; it is the use of language as a symbolic means of inducing cooperation in beings that by nature respond to symbols. (*Rhetoric* 43)

In its final phrase, this definition of rhetoric is grounded in Burke's definition of humanity: our essence is not that we have a particular essence but that we respond to symbols, define our own variable essences through discourse, language, rhetoric, culture. We are not, as capitalist ideology would have it, naturally selfish and aggrandizing; nor are we, as anarchist ideology would have it, naturally cooperative and sharing; we are, rather, beings who continually define and redefine ourselves through the symbolic processes of language, discourse, rhetoric, culture.

Burke's is an operational definition; rhetoric is defined by what it does. The key phrase in this definition declares rhetoric "a symbolic means of inducing cooperation." In his important but difficult essay on the origins of language, Burke founds language in the need of our ancestors to cooperate in order to survive (*Language* 419-79). Language allowed our relatively slow, weak, vulnerable ancestors to coordinate hunting and gathering, childcare, and protection from predators. Theories about the origins of language are inevitably speculative, but Burke is less interested in his theory's historical truth than in its mythic validity as a representative anecdote which captures the functional essence of our languaging.

Burke emphasizes that the phrase "inducing cooperation" presumes that cooperation must be induced, that we are not genetically, instinctively cooperative, that at best we may be said to have an inborn capacity to cooperate (including a capacity to learn language, which facilitates cooperation). Thus, for Burke, cooperation arises from division. We must persuade, must induce cooperation, must socialize our children into our communities because we are individuals—"in-divide-you-alls," as one schizophrenic pronounced the word for R.D. Laing, a "joycing" Burke would appreciate.

We are, in various ways, divided, alienated—from nature, from each other, from other cultures, even from ourselves. As there are levels of division, so there are levels of rhetoric. In Burke's reading of Freud, we are divided within ourselves, contain a parliament of voices which must be harmonized into an identity, an individual who acts in the world with some consistency (which we call the individual's personality or character). Socially, on various overlapping levels, we are divided from other people. And by our nature separated from nature, we must talk ourselves into patterns of action that embody ecologically valid strategies for survival—for if a culture talks itself into ecologically invalid strategies, its people fail to survive and that is the end of the culture; its discourse, its symbols disappear with the people who spoke them. (In the same sense that, biologically, all organisms, including people, can be interpreted as DNA's way of evolving and reproducing itself, so, rhetorically, people can be interpreted as cultures' ways of evolving and reproducing themselves.)

This dialectic of division and cooperation, individual and social, underlies Burke's definition of rhetoric—and us. When we convince an audience (or a subculture or a whole society) to share a perspective, we create at-one-ness, togetherness, the basis of cooperation in action. Shared attitudes lead to cooperative actions, for attitudes are leanings, "incipient actions." In the nature of the rhetorical situation, however, we inevitably divide those we persuade from those who remain unpersuaded. When we socialize our children to share the broad values of our culture, we divide them from other children socialized in other cultures. When we teach students to adopt the discourse of a professional community, we divide them from other communities; then rhetoric is needed to bridge those divisions, to enable cooperation between people of distinct cultures.

If rhetoric is language used persuasively, then argumentation is the tip of the iceberg. How language brings a community to share assumptions and perspectives is a much larger and more important rhetorical question. And one of Burke's major contributions to rhetoric, a contribution that virtually creates the New Rhetoric, is his broadening the subject of rhetoric by emphasizing the submerged seven-eighths of the iceberg.

Rhetoric becomes primarily the process whereby a community comes to share a symbolic discourse—or whereby a communally shared discourse creates consubstantiality, subliminally persuades individuals to identify with the community, even to sacrifice their lives for their country and flag (and what it stands for). Or to refuse to listen to, understand or publish nonstandard discourse. How do human individuals, with their "unique" perceptions, come to agree so often and so profoundly? Consider how much two people must agree upon in order to argue about whether a base runner was out at second base. Consider what leads millions of individuals to choose to wear their skirts at mid-thigh in 1927, at mid-shin in 1933, to wear their hair long and natural in 1969, clipped and greased into purple parody in 1989. These are all unique individuals with free will; surely the remarkable levels of agreement and conformity need more explanation than occasional differences.

In revising his definition of human beings, Burke has added to it. The second part (or verse) now reads,

From within or
from out of
the vast expanses of the
infinite wordless universe
we wordy human bodies have carved
many overlapping universes of discourse
which add up to a
pluriverse of discourses
local dialects of dialectic

Thus, rhetoric, as a study of how wordlings word, becomes also a study of discourse communities and how they commune.

For Burke, the discourse of any community, in addition to whatever else it may do, represents strategies for encompassing situations: "These strategies size up the situations, name their structure and outstanding ingredients, and name them in a way that contains an attitude toward them" (*Philosophy* 3). The situations are real; a discourse is "an adjustment to a particular cluster of conditions" (*Counter-Statement* 107). Like Nietzsche or Derrida, Burke often uses a nihilistic perspective to work ideas, but Burke is no nihilist. A discourse must represent strategies that work, at least to such an extent that the community survives. The discourse must also work socially, must be persuasive and rhetorical, must produce consubstantial identification, must bring people into community—or it will be like a manuscript that no one but its author wants to read (or publish).

The third part of Burke's expanded definition, not yet fully formed (or versed) is about how wordlings are constituted. Burke has long been fascinated by constitution, the process of how we constitute ourselves. At the far end of his life (and his definition) he is looking at how we constitute ourselves both by masterpieces of verbal process—he cites both the U.S Constitution and the "Communist Manifesto"—and by what he calls technological constitution, nowadays "fittingly defining itself by a mode of Artificial Intelligence."

I could continue—and I intend to elsewhere. But the point here is not to sum Burke up (or down—summaries really are down, reductive), just to provide a basis for reading Burke and for grounding our teaching of composition in some understanding of his critical insights into beings constituted as rhetorical animals.

Notes

1. See "A Dramatic View of the Origins of Language" (*Language* 419-79). Commenting on a draft of this article, Burke said, "I feel uneasy [about the discussion of analog/digital] without reference to Gestalt psychology, computers, etc." See, therefore, my "Dracula" (236-40) and Burke's comment thereon. Burke also referred me to *The Harper Dictionary of Modern Thought*, specifically to "synergy": "This concept reflects the classical opinion that 'the whole is greater that the sum of its parts.'... Synergy is formally studied as a property of systems by cybernetics. . . . More generally still, the term is applied to the generation of unplanned social benefits among people who consciously cooperate in the pursuit of their own interests and goals."

2. For an important distinction between abstraction and generalization, see my *Grammar* 22-25, 79-82, and works cited therein.

3. Though this may seem difficult, it is pragmatically powerful; I have tried to suggest some implications for composition in the section on "negative invention" in the second chapter of my textbook. Also see Elbow, Part IV, "Contraries and Inquiry."

4. See the Utopian U heuristic in Shor 155-80.

Works Cited

Burke, Kenneth. "A Comment on 'It Takes Capital to Defeat Dracula." *College English* 49 (1987): 221-22.

—. *Counter-Statement*. 1931. Berkeley: U of California P, 1968

—. *A Grammar of Motives*. 1945. Berkeley: U of California P, 1969.

—. *Language as Symbolic Action: Essays on Life, Literature, and Method.* Berkeley: U of California P, 1966.

—. "(Nonsymbolic) Motion/(Symbolic) Action." *Critical Inquiry* 4 (1978): 809-38.

—. *Permanence and Change: An Anatomy of Purpose.* 2nd ed. Indianapolis: Bobbs-Merrill, 1965.

—. *The Philosophy of Literary Form: Studies in Symbolic Action.* 1941. New York: Vintage, 1957.

—. *A Rhetoric of Motives.* 1950. Berkeley: U of California P, 1969.

Coe, Richard M. "It Takes Capital to Defeat Dracula." *College English* 48 (1986): 231-42.

—. *Process, Form, and Substance: A Rhetoric for Advanced Writers*, 2nd. ed. Englewood Cliffs, NJ: Prentice, 1990.

—. *Toward a Grammar of Passages.* Carbondale: Southern Illinois UP, 1988.

Elbow, Peter. *Embracing Contraries.* New York: Oxford, 1986.

Gardner, Howard. *The Mind's New Science: A History of Cognitive Revolution.* Rev. ed. New York: Basic, 1987.

Gould, Stephen Jay. "For Want of a Metaphor." *The Flamingo's Smile: Reflections in Natural History.* New York: Norton, 1987. 139-51.

Hunter, Paul. "Freire and Burke: A Pedagogy for the Non-Traditional Student." CCCC Convention. Seattle. 17 Mar. 1989.

Perelman, Chaim. *The Realm of Rhetoric.* Tr. William Kluback. Notre Dame, IN: U of Notre Dame P, 1982.

Russell, Bertrand. "Mathematical Logic as Based on the Theory of Types." *American Journal of Mathematics* 30 (1908): 222-62.

Shor, Ira. *Critical Teaching and Everyday Life.* Boston: South End, 1980.

Wilden, Anthony. *The Rules Are No Game.* London, Routledge, 1987.

Winspear, Alban D. *The Genesis of Plato's Thought.* New York: Russell, 1940.

Defining Advanced Composition: Contributions from the History of Rhetoric[1]

William A. Covino

> But that use of wit and knowledge is to be allowed, which laboureth to make doubtful things certain, and not those which labour to make certain things doubtful.
>
> So then that knowledge is worthiest which is charged with least multiplicity.
>
> Francis Bacon, *Advancement of Learning*

Francis Bacon ushers in the Enlightenment when in 1605 he equates *advanced* knowledge with uniformity and universal principles, with certainty, with the schematization of diverse phenomena under the rubric of "simple Forms or differences of things, which are few in number" (2.7: 96). Later in the seventeenth century, the Royal Society of London for Improving Natural Knowledge would reaffirm the importance of reducing and containing the diversity of the world, reinforcing the prevailing belief that intellectual maturity coincides with order, perspicuity, and closure, and calling for a reform of language that would "reject all amplifications, digressions, and swellings of style, [and] return back to the primitive purity, and shortness, when men delivered so many *things*, in an almost equal number of *words*" (Sprat 113). In general, these and other influential post-Cartesians associate less advanced intellection with "kalendars of doubts" not yet "thoroughly sifted and brought to resolution" (Bacon 2.7: 103), and they associate advanced intellection with statements of manifest unity and coherence expressed in precisely controlled language.

This post-Cartesian conception of advanced knowledge remains dominant today and informs our definitions of advanced composition. An advanced composition course often differs from a beginning course in that the former emphasizes reading, research, and topics of greater breadth, difficulty, and complexity, and it demands greater rigor in managing and reducing the complex; advanced students, that is, must demonstrate mastery of closure and conventions, from the arrangement of a formal argument to the small particulars of MLA style and documentation. In departments outside English, advanced composition is often the label for upper-division practice in a schematic professional or academic genre; the advanced composition course for business majors, for example, might be an internship in report writing. And sometimes, advanced composition courses merely emphasize theme-writing of the sort required by graduate competency tests or graduate-school hurdles like the LSAT, drilling students in the prototypical Introduction + Examples + Conclusion formula.[2] In short, the products of advanced writers are expected to be more "finished" and "polished" than those of beginners. Thus, advanced composition pedagogy seems to mirror Bacon's notion that intellectual maturity is connected to consistency, coherence, unity, certainty, and resolution. I intend to propose a definition of advanced composition that calls into question these virtues of closure, a definition which can be drawn from the works of rhetoricians since Antiquity. For example, Plato, Aristotle, and Cicero distinguish "advanced" from "beginning" rhetors by associating the former with tolerance for ambiguity and intolerance for formulaic discourse and its precepts. All three rhetoricians identify their worst students with obedient mastery of stock forms and formulae, and the very form of their own rhetorical theories—wandering prose that frustrates students who want their rhetoric quick and easy—questions the virtue of single-mindedness. However, these rhetoricians' conceptions of advanced rhetoric have been largely ignored, and the history of rhetoric has presented these thinkers as advocates rather than opponents of homogenized, rule-managed writing.[3] Looking to Plato's *Phaedrus*, Aristotle's *Rhetoric*, and Cicero's *De Oratore*, we can define advanced composition as *the open intellectual play of multiple perspectives*, a definition later reaffirmed by Montaigne, Vico, and De Quincey, who follow in the tradition of the Ancients by emphasizing discursive license and continuing to define advanced composition as endless wondering.

Classical Perspectives on Advanced Composition

Plato's *Phaedrus* and Cicero's *De Oratore* both posit the mature rhetor as a lover of dialogue and persistent questioning who demonstrates inconclusiveness and uncertainty. In both works, this mature rhetor is counterpoised with the students who want clear instructions and prefer summary to speculation. The Phaedrus of Plato's dialogue, for instance, craves unambiguous advice about discourse. He is confused by Socrates' two speeches (critiques of Lysias's speech on love) that extend and complicate the nature of both love and rhetoric:

> **Socrates**: Would you like, then, to take that speech of Lysias you have with you and the ones I delivered and examine them for points which illustrate what we may call art and the lack of it?
> **Phaedrus**: Oh yes, that would be splendid! For what we are saying now is too abstract. We need some workable examples.
> **Socrates**: And by some special stroke of good fortune it looks as though the two speeches offer an illustration of how a man who knows the truth may play with words and lead his audience astray. It's the local divinities, Phaedrus, that I judge to be the cause of this; or perhaps the Muses' prophets, singing overhead, may have breathed their inspiration into us; for I, at any rate, have no gift of speech.
> **Phaedrus**: All right, as you please. Just tell me what you mean! (262)

As Socrates continues to discuss the speeches on love, the responses of Phaedrus portray a student less interested in thinking things over than in merely assenting, whether he understands or not: "Yes"; "Of course"; "We certainly do"; "That's the way it is"; "Why, of course" (262-63). Phaedrus feigns complete understanding at every turn, revealing his strong desire for packaged knowledge and his impatience with being "led astray" from quick understanding by the intellectual play of Socrates, who knows that truth is broad and complex and can only be pursued through continual, irresolute dialogue. Further, Phaedrus is all too eager to admire the "outstanding quality" of Lysias's completeness: "Of all the points of the subject worthy to be enumerated, [Lysias] has neglected not one." But Socrates defines complete understanding as a worthy but impossible goal, approachable only through successive definition and division, in discourse that is always changing and that is "exactly attuned to every changing mood of the complicated soul." Truth is not reducible to summary; the investigation of truth is foreclosed by thinking, speaking, and writing that convert complexity and ambiguity to doctrine, that "lay down laws in written form." Writing that does not exploit the persistent curiosity (so striking in Socrates and so absent in Phaedrus) which defines philosophy "is a disgrace to the writer" (277).

Cicero echoes this theme in *De Oratore*, a dialogue that identifies intellectual accomplishment with the "knowledge of a vast number of things" refracted through a number of perspectives (1.5: 10). The mature orators Crassus and Antonius fill hours and days speculating on "the perfect orator," thereby demonstrating that this topic cannot be reduced to a system of precepts, and exasperating the students who are listening. By constructing his most inclusive work on rhetoric and eloquence as a dialogic drama of viewpoints, Cicero associates the accomplished rhetor—himself—with incessant, inconclusive discourse; and he dissociates himself from the younger Cicero who had written the formulaic *De Inventione* (1.2: 7), and from Sulpicius and Cotta, students who, like Plato's Phaedrus, want teachers to offer schematic advice amenable to efficient obedience.

Early in the dialogue, following Crassus's initial argument that the perfect orator must constantly pursue wide-ranging knowledge ("the reason and nature of every thing and of all sciences"), Antonius begins to respond that such a philosophical life is impractical: life is too short to occupy oneself with study, reflection, *and* action (1.18: 26). However, Antonius counters Crassus by demonstrating the breadth of his own intellect and experience and the power of his memory, thereby joining Crassus as one disinclined to take the efficient way to a conclusion. For five excursive pages, Antonius reconstructs a past excursion to Athens, where he talked with "most learned men" who themselves recalled earlier generations of philosophers, reaching back to the origination of rhetoric with Corax and Tisias (1.18-21: 26-31). Thus, Antonius responds to Crassus in a dialogue recollecting another dialogue containing still further recollections of still other dialogues. Antonius's response is finally inconclusive and circular, ending where it had begun, with tribute to Crassus as the perfect orator.

The student Sulpicius protests that Crassus and Antonius should so "insensibly glide into a discourse of this kind" and asks to be taught "something worthy to be remembered . . . fully and exactly" (1.21: 30-31). When Crassus responds by further insisting that the accomplished rhetor must continually pursue unlimited knowledge, he is met with silence. Asked later to speak on the principles of style, Crassus digresses to a survey of Greek philosophy only to be met with another student demand for stock information, "the ordinary knowledge of common affairs" (3.36: 234). Through such conflicts between teachers and students, Cicero repeatedly associates "beginners" with a reductive view of rhetoric as an absolute system of set forms founded on "ordinary knowledge," and he associates "advanced" rhetors with a playful refusal to ossify thought and language.

A response to Plato and a source book for Cicero, Aristotle's *Rhetoric* does not exploit dialogue as a genre but does make dialectical thinking a requirement for the rhetor who claims more than perceptive knowledge of the art. In his conclusion to the *Rhetoric*—"I have done; you all have heard; you have the facts; give your judgment" (1420)—Aristotle suggests with a "textbook" peroration that rhetoric and judgment are simple matters of fact, adopting the very technique that orators find useful for closing debate and calling for an absolute verdict. Clearly, the attitude toward language and knowledge mimicked in this peroration is the same one we have seen in Phaedrus, Sulpicius, and Cotta, but it is an attitude that Aristotle refutes through the meandering irresolution that defines rhetoric in the *Rhetoric*. Aristotle's peroration leaves the dull novice with the comfortable illusion of closure and invites the more alert and curious to reconsider equating mastery with final pronouncements. The *Rhetoric* identifies rhetoric with inquiry: the function of rhetoric is "not so much to persuade, as to find out in each case the existing means of persuasion" (1355b). Sustained questioning—that habit of mind that contends with Aristotle's neat peroration—defines the style and substance of rhetoric:

> The question whether a thing has or has not happened must be considered from the following points of view. . . . If a man was able and wished to do a thing, he has done it; for all men do a thing, when they are able and resolve to do it, for nothing hinders them. Further, if a man wished to do it and there was no external obstacle; if he was able to do it and was in a state of anger; if he was able and desired to do it; for men as a rule, whenever they can, do those things which they long for, the vicious owing to want of self-control, the virtuous because they desire what is good. (1392b)

For Aristotle, we can do no better than to require that students persist in raising questions and practice "knowing" as inquiry. With a commentary that itself resists system and closure—full of always irresolute and incomplete lists of perspectives—Aristotle dissociates the aim, or "end," of rhetoric from final judgments.

Assaults on the Classical Perspective

Despite the Ancients' warning mockery of eager decisiveness in their students, that quality receives continued emphasis in the formulary rhetoric and pedagogy that extend from the Hellenistic revisions of Aristotle's *Rhetoric* through the schools of imperial Rome and the medieval Church.[4] And the preference for language that maintains *established* knowledge gains popularity from the late Renaissance onward with the aggressive containment of philosophy and science. Peter

Ramus's *Dialectic* (1546) is one of his influential assaults against broad and complex classical explications of rhetoric and logic. In response to a philosophical rhetoric whose "method" exploits the instability of knowledge, Ramus defines method in simple, absolute terms: "method is . . . the arrangement of various things brought down from universal and general principles to the underlying singular parts, by which arrangement the whole matter can be more easily taught and comprehended" (Murphy 17).

In *The Advancement of Learning* (1605), Bacon refuses the strictly binary schemata that inform Ramus's construction of knowledge, but he echoes the call for an organized, methodized learning of truths that can be weighed, measured, and subordinated to universal and mechanical laws. Bacon associates immature learning with entertaining multiple truths: "Children at the first will call every woman mother, but afterward they come to distinguish according to truth, so experience, if it be in childhood, will call every philosophy mother, but when it cometh to ripeness, it will discern the true mother" (2.8:104). Similarly, in *Discourse on Method* (1637), Descartes associates intellectual growth with the ability to reach uncontestable conclusions.

Ramus, Bacon, and Descartes are founders of a powerful epistemology, adopted by the French Academy and the British Royal Society and leading to the association of ambiguity in thought and language with children and primitives. Hugh Blair supports this view in his tremendously popular *Lectures on Rhetoric and Belles-Lettres* (1783):

> The Progress of Language . . . resembles the progress of age in man. The imagination is most vigorous and predominant in youth; with advancing years, the imagination cools, and the understanding ripens. Thus Language, proceeding from sterility to copiousness, hath, at the same time, proceeded from vivacity to accuracy; from fire and enthusiasm, to coolness and precision [and to] simple style, plain arrangement. Language is become, in modern times, more correct, indeed, and accurate. (1.6.124)

Sustaining a "Renegade" Tradition

While classical emphases on open discourse as the sign of intellectual maturity still go unrecognized as civilization "advances," the equation of closure with ignorance has been pressed on by thinkers whose influence on education is, unfortunately, negligible. Following Ramus and preceding Bacon, Michel de Montaigne in *Essays* (composed and revised from 1572 through 1588, and first translated into English in 1603) continues the classical parody of the Phaedruses among us, who associate intellectual progress with patterned language:

> They keep us four or five years learning to understand words and stitch them into sentences; as many more, to mold them into a great body, extending into four or five parts; and another five, at least, learning how to mix and interweave them briefly in some subtle way. (1.26: 124-25)

Writing here in "Of the Education of Children," Montaigne identifies the typical student of advanced composition as the master of a formula, as one whose education culminates in the facile rearrangement of standard rhetorical parts. Montaigne's own "development" culminates in insistent uncertainty, reiterated throughout his final essay, "Of Experience": "the inference that we try to draw from the resemblance of events is uncertain, because they are always dissimilar: there is no quality so universal in this aspect of things as diversity and variety" (3.13: 815). Diversity of experiences and ideas makes all assertions uncertain and fragile; further, positing any inference as more advanced or correct insists that language accommodates certainty. For Montaigne, language mocks certainty:

> I ask what is "nature," "pleasure," "circle," "substitution." The question is one of words, and is answered in the same way. "A stone is a body." But if you pressed on: "And what is a body?"—"Substance."—"And what is substance?" and so on, you would finally drive the respondent to the end of his lexicon. We exchange one word for another word, often more unknown. . . . To satisfy one doubt, they give me three; it is the Hydra's head. (818-19)

Rejecting the language of disciplined judgments as fraudulent, Montaigne allies the strongest intellect with the endless generation of new perspectives:

> It is only personal weakness that makes us content with what others or we ourselves have found out in this hunt for knowledge. An abler man will not rest content with it. . . . It is a sign of contraction of the mind when it is content, or of weariness. A spirited mind never stops within itself; it is always aspiring and going beyond its strength; it has impulses beyond its powers of achievement. . . . It is an irregular, perpetual motion, without model and without aim. Its inventions excite, pursue, and produce one another. (817-18)

Celebrating generative, variegated, unsystematic writing, Montaigne offers an implicit rebuttal of Ramus and rejects in advance Bacon's valorization of coherent knowledge.

At the beginning of the eighteenth century, Giambattista Vico begins a direct and explicit critique of Descartes. As Professor of Rhetoric at the University of Naples, Vico delivers a speech, *On the Study Methods of Our Time* (1708), in which he cautions against the prevalence of Cartesian analytics, whose mastery he associates with adolescents whose narrow minds keep them from mature, copious discourse. Emphasizing the importance of topical invention (14), Vico proposes that students immersed in "the totality of sciences and arts" and aware that "probabilities are many" can contribute vitality to an intellectual community. Like the Ancients' students that he describes, Vico's ideal students would not practice the insolent ignorance or obedient silence typical of those controlled by formulate knowledge:

> They would not feel the impulse to step rashly into discussions while they are still in the process of learning; nor would they, with pedestrian slavishness, refuse to accept any viewpoint unless it has been sanctioned by a teacher. . . .
>
> A five-year period of silence was enjoined upon all of Pythagoras' students. After that time, they were allowed to maintain what they had learned, but had to ground their reasons only upon the authority of their master. "He said it," was their motto. The chief duty of a student of philosophy was to listen. (19-20)

Identifying Descartes with Pythagorean learning and himself with the topical imagination exploited by Aristotle, Vico proposes that the conflict between ambitious ignorance and the art of wondering is not new, and he yearns for teachers and students who define intellectual progress as an ever-widening sense of complexity, aware that "nature and life are full of incertitude" (15).

By the early nineteenth century, when advanced education in rhetoric was identified with the "perspicuity and precision" stressed continually in Blair's *Lectures*, Thomas De Quincey eulogizes the "renegade" tradition I have surveyed here:

> The rhetorician's art in its glory and power has silently faded away before the stern tendencies of the age; and, if, by any peculiarity of taste or strong determination of the intellect, a rhetorician *en grande costume* were again to appear amongst us, it is certain that he would have no better welcome than a stare of surprise as a posturemaker or balancer, not more elevated in the general estimate, but far less amusing, than the acrobat, or funambulist, or equestrian gymnast. No; the age of Rhetoric, like that of Chivalry, has passed among forgotten things. (97)

De Quincey's own prose demonstrates the "inversions, evolutions, and harlequin changes" that define the lost art of rhetoric as he admits the futility of making or finding those rhetors whom Plato, Aristotle, Cicero, Montaigne, and Vico would call masters of the art—rhetors for whom composition is "progress and motion, everlasting motion" (129). De Quincey looks into the nineteenth century of industry and science—and beyond, to the reign of bureaucracy and technology today—when he concludes that the "urgency of public business" makes virtues of efficiency and conviction and insists that "where conviction begins, the field of rhetoric ends" (82).

Dialogic Writing in Advanced Composition

The theorists I have discussed posit advanced thinking and writing as the opposites of ready conviction, and they challenge those of us who teach advanced composition to reconsider what our subject is and how it might be taught. Notably, each identifies close-mindedness in students and teachers with closed rhetorical forms, and each would replace the mechanical recitation of divisions and subdivisions with prose that moves through variegated substance. Further, the writing of each suggests that dialogue—understood as an interplay of voices and perspectives taking place in the mind of a single narrator (as with Aristotle, Montaigne, Vico, De Quincey) or among several characters (as with Plato and Cicero)—creates the dynamic rhetoric of open discourse; dialogic writing necessarily evades the consistency, coherence, and blindness of an insistent "thesis."

Teaching advanced composition may mean introducing "new" genres that require and enfranchise dialogic writing; the most obvious of these genres is the dialogue itself. Perhaps we need to encourage our advanced students to engage in their own dialogic writing. For example, the following is a dialogue assignment that encourages students to keep an issue alive; the definition of advanced composition that I have followed through the history of rhetoric is implicit in the topic and constraints for this assignment. Writing is identified with the "unexplored, unsettled, ambiguous, or confusing," so that our student writers—following Plato—practice writing as *engaged ignorance*. However, maintaining that ignorance means *research*; only by "piling up" (Montaigne's term) substantial and inconsistent propositions can students continue to think and defer its opposite—thoughtlessness. The students' research must be comprehensive rather than "focused"—their minds filled with a drama of voices.

In line with the letter and the spirit of the historical texts I have surveyed, this assignment insists upon *substance* while discouraging a particular *stance*. Further, with its emphasis on planned discourse, it encourages license without vagueness; thus, students are warned against words which "tumble out under the blindest accidents of the moment" (De Quincey 142). Following Aristotle and Cicero, they must know all sides of an issue. Following Vico, they must create a *sensus communis*, or common sense, by enlarging the lexicon of viewpoints that comprise human history and decisions. Following De Quincey, they must set aside conviction to practice rhetoric.

The Dialogue
Topic: An unexplored, unsettled, ambiguous, or confusing element of a subject that matters.

Characters
(1) Three experts on your topic, each with a different viewpoint. These are *real* experts, with significant reputations and published work (which you have reviewed).

(2) Two curious, critical, undecided students with a substantial interest in the topic.

Constraints
(1) No one makes stupid or uncharacteristic statements.

(2) No one wins; that is, no one view finally seems more intelligent, persuasive, or undeceive than the others.

(3) Each character speaks at least three times, for at least half a page at each turn.

(4) The experts occasionally quote or paraphrase themselves or each other; each character is familiar with the others' published work.

(5) No one delivers "throwaway" lines or transitions, such as "How true, tell me more."
(6) Each character's words are planned and crafted. This is thoughtful deliberate writing, neither spontaneous nor casual, as if the characters had revised and edited their spoken words for publication (see, for instance, the occasional dialogues that have appeared in the "Forum" section of recent issues of *Harper's*).

Notes

1. I present some of the points in this essay more extensively in *The Art of Wondering*, without a focus on advanced composition.

2. In the California State University system, for example, upper-division writing proficiency is required for graduation and has been measured by either a timed theme-writing test or in courses in formulaic composition. In either case, advanced writing proficiency is identified with efficient, regimented thinking.

3. Knoblauch and Brannon present the classical tradition as many commentators throughout the centuries have portrayed it: as a collection of narrow, long-irrelevant rules and procedures. (See especially Chapter 2.)

4. The pseudo-Ciceronian *Ad Herennium*, which identifies composition and oratory with strict arrangement, was the prototypical rhetoric throughout the Middle Ages.

Works Cited

Aristotle. *The Rhetoric of Aristotle*. Trans. Lane Cooper. Englewood Cliffs, NJ: Prentice, 1932.

Bacon, Francis. *The Advancement of Learning*. Ed. G.W. Kitchin. Totowa, NJ: Rowman, 1973.

Blair, Hugh. *Lectures on Rhetoric and Belles-Lettres*. Ed. Harold F. Harding. Carbondale: Southern Illinois UP, 1965. 2 vols.

Cicero. *De Oratore (On Oratory and Orators)*. Trans. J.S. Watson. Carbondale: Southern Illinois UP, 1970.

Covino, William A. *The Art of Wondering: A Revisionist Return to the History of Rhetoric*. Portsmouth, NH: Moynton, 1988.

De Quincey, Thomas. *Selected Essays on Rhetoric*. Ed. Frederick Burwick. Carbondale: Southern Illinois UP, 1967.

Descartes, René. *Discourse on Method*. Trans. Paul J. Olscamp. Indianapolis: Bobbs, 1965.

Knoblauch, C.H., and Lil Brannon. *Rhetorical Traditions and the Teaching of Writing*. Upper Montclair, NJ: Boynton, 1984.

Montaigne, Michel de. *The Complete Essays of Montaigne*.

Afterword
The Legacy of James L. Kinneavy

Phillip Sipiora

In the First Century A.D., Quintilian wrote a monumental twelve-volume tract, *Institutio Oratoria*, which attempted to articulate the best possible education for the son of his friend, Marcus Victorius. The study of rhetoric was an integral component of Quintilian's concept of a classical education, and he defines the ideal rhetor as "a good man speaking well": *vir bonus dicendi peritus*. Quintilian could easily have been speaking of James L. Kinneavy, a scholar, teacher, humanist, and beloved figure to hundreds of colleagues and students across the country. Kinneavy lived his life in the richness of the tradition Quintilian sought to define in his enduring treatise. It might be said that no other twentieth-century rhetorician, or scholar of any other discipline, is more deserving to be recognized as Quintilian's ideal than this kind, humble man of letters. As he approached his ninth decade, James L. Kinneavy continued to lecture, write, and remain actively involved in the profession he so loved.

The essays in *The Kinneavy Papers* represent the kind of vigorous, seminal thinking and writing that so characterized James Kinneavy's life. The heart and soul of Kinneavy's professional life was the active promotion of theoretical and applied scholarship, not only his own and that of his students (as well as senior colleagues who often sought his counsel), but also of those in the profession whom he did not know, particularly those in the early, formative stages of their careers.

For nearly fifty years, Kinneavy traveled around the country speaking at academic conferences and holding seminars and workshops, all the time emphasizing the message that rhetoric and composition are, indeed, respectable intellectual activities. He taught graduate courses in rhetoric at the University of Pennsylvania, Pennsylvania State University, and other institutions. He consulted with nearly one hundred other colleges and universities across the country. Dozens of Kinneavy's former students hold positions at colleges and universities across the country, and many of them are writing program administrators. He was among the first in the nation to propose a graduate degree in rhetoric and composition within an English department (at the University of Texas). There is no question that Kinneavy's influence looms large in diverse ways. In 1983, the University of Texas honored Kinneavy for his distinguished career as a scholar and teacher by naming him the Blumberg Centennial Professor of English. In 1992 and 1995, respectively, two independent *Festschriften* were published in his honor.

Since the 1971 publication of his major theoretical treatise, *A Theory of Discourse*, Kinneavy has generally been recognized as one of America's major rhetorical theorists. In *Theory* Kinneavy systematically investigates the historical and theoretical bases of what he calls the aims of discourse (referential, persuasive, literary, and expressive) through extensive analyses of discourse that include a wide ranging discussion of practical applications and implications. Kinneavy's revival of dialectic as exploration has, arguably, been partly responsible for the recent "respectability" of the study of rhetoric and composition. Yet, Kinneavy's major contribution to contemporary discourse is the historical case *Theory* builds for the importance of rhetoric throughout Western history, specifically through his rearticulation of aims of discourse as a reassertion of the liberal arts tradition. This continuing reassessment was the lifeblood of so much of Kinneavy's work over the past two decades. Indeed, Kinneavy devoted considerable intellectual energy too bringing together rhetorical history, theory, and *praxis* in a pragmatic synthesis that would reestablish rhetoric as the natural center of the liberal arts curriculum.

Kinneavy's influence is by no means limited to *A Theory of Discourse*. In 1987 he published *Greek Rhetorical Origins of the Christian Concept of Faith*, an historical examination of the influence of Greek rhetoric, principally *pistis*, on the New Testament concept of faith. The treatise has been well received in theological studies and continues to draw scholarly attention to the theoretical relationships between the secular and the sectarian. Kinneavy's historical essays on situational context and timing, "Kairos: A Neglected Concept in Classical Rhetoric" and "Kairos in Aristotle's Rhetoric," have generated significant scholarship and have laid the groundwork for a collection of historical and contemporary examinations and applications of this seminal concept in classical and contemporary rhetoric (Sipiora and Baumlin, *Rhetoric and Kairos*.) To my knowledge, James Kinneavy is one of a handful of scholars who has criticized, in writing, his own work. In "Theory, Theories, or Lack of Theory" (*Composition Chronicle* 4 [May, 1992]: 5-

6), Kinneavy critiqued *A Theory of Discourse*—a rare and refreshing gesture in today's scholarly world.

Moreover, Kinneavy's skill as a rhetorician has been more than theoretical. Throughout his life, he practiced the art of rhetoric. He gained national recognition at the University of Texas in 1974 when he became involved in a controversy over the right of the faculty to have a voice in the selection of a new president. Kinneavy had been elected by the general faculty to a committee that was to recommend, from hundreds of applicants, a short list of seven candidates. The Regents had agreed to make their selection from this list. However, they eventually selected someone who was not on that list. A general faculty meeting was called, and more than one thousand professors attended, which was more than half the university's faculty. Kinneavy was nominated to chair the meeting. He characterized the speech he made on that occasion as the most important speech of his life. He became the spokesperson of the general faculty and was interviewed by major newspapers, magazines, and television networks. The Regents hired their candidate, and the faculty protested by refusing to meet for six months. Yet, Kinneavy's unsuccessful efforts to give the faculty a voice in choosing the president gained him their lasting respect. According to Robert Jeffrey, former Dean of the College of Communication, "Jim Kinneavy handled himself graciously and objectively, without personal animosity, basing his arguments on academic integrity and freedom."

Kinneavy was no stranger to national politics, and he supported the professionalization of writing teachers at every level by advocating adequate pay, equal access to tenure and promotion, and fair grievance procedures. For many years, he supported rights for marginalized faculty, usually called adjuncts or lecturers, and his voice was eventually heard in the most powerful organization in English studies: the Modern Language Association. For the past few years, the MLA has established official recommendations for the fair treatment of temporary faculty, who most often turn out to be those teaching lower-division writing courses. These changes were the direct result of Kinneavy's indefatigable efforts in working for social justice.

In the 1990s Kinneavy turned to writing about a subject he had engaged professionally since 1941: ethics. In 1999 he co-edited a collection of essays, *Ethical Issues in College Writing*, which includes essays from leading scholars on various perspectives of ethics and their relevance to the contemporary writing scene. Kinneavy's essay in this volume, "Ethics and Rhetoric: Forging a Moral Language for the English

Classroom," investigates the relationship of ethics to the English classroom. This essay is a synoptic version of his book-length work on the formation of a common moral code that might be accepted by both religious and non-religious individuals and could be taught in the public school system. Such a moral code, according to Kinneavy, must necessarily be undogmatic (insofar as this is possible), without the restrictive and debilitating influences of inherited sectarian dogma. Kinneavy continued to work on this book, *A Moral Code for Use in Public Schools and Colleges*, until his untimely death on August 10, 1999, following a brief illness.

It is no exaggeration to say that Jim Kinneavy devoted a significant part of his life to helping others. Each year he would carefully read the essay that had won the ***JAC*** award he had established. Often, he would asking probing questions of the author after the award ceremony. Indeed, he took this award very seriously, and he never failed to present the award to the winning writer at each year's CCCC meeting. Jim Kinneavy was always there for his friends, family, and strangers; this memory of selfless living and unconditional love is his professional and personal living legacy. He will be dearly missed by his family, friends, and colleagues across the country and across the seas, and by those students who never knew him personally but who were touched by his brilliance and humanity in his writings and lectures. The legacy of James L. Kinneavy will live on in the essays of this volume.

Index